Macintosh Pascal

COMPUTERS AND MATH SERIES

MARVIN MARCUS, EDITOR
University of California at Santa Barbara

Lowell A. Carmony and Robert L. Holliday
Macintosh Pascal

Lowell A. Carmony, Robert J. McGlinn, Ann Miller Millman, and
Jerry P. Becker
Problem Solving in Apple Pascal

Marvin Marcus
Discrete Mathematics:
  A Computational Approach Using BASIC

S. Gill Williamson
Combinatorics for Computer Science

Macintosh Pascal

Lowell A. Carmony
Lake Forest College

Robert L. Holliday
Lake Forest College

COMPUTER SCIENCE PRESS

Computer Science Press, Inc.
11 Taft Court
Rockville, Maryland 20850

2 3 4   88 87 86 85

Library of Congress Cataloging in Publication Data

Carmony, Lowell A., 1943–
   Macintosh Pascal.

   Includes index.
   1. Macintosh (Computer) 2. PASCAL (Computer program language) I.
Holliday, Robert. II. Title.
QA76.8.M3C37 1985   001.64   84-19901
ISBN 0-88175-081-6

Schläft ein Lied in allen Dingen
Schlummert träumend fort und fort,
Und die Welt hebt an zu zingen
Triffst du nur das Zauberwort.

Joseph von Eichendorff

PREFACE

Pascal is a landmark language providing the reader with an elegant vehicle for studying important concepts of computer science. The Macintosh is a landmark computer providing the reader with a degree of user-friendliness and pedagogical features unparalleled in any other machine. We are excited and delighted to present the reader with this self-study guide to *Macintosh Pascal*.

This book is designed for the beginner to Pascal as well as a reference to the reader who already knows some Pascal. The book begins at an elementary level and contains all the information needed by the novice to get started. New constructs are carefully developed with ample examples. The reader who works through the material presented here and writes the programs suggested in the exercises will have gained a thorough understanding of Pascal.

This text contains a careful explanation of the Macintosh Pascal operating system as well as Pascal so that the reader has, in one place, all the material needed. Learning Pascal and at the same time learning to guide a program through the computer can be frustrating if you must flip back and forth between a Pascal text and various computer manuals. In this book we guide the beginner step by step through the language and the operating system.

Macintosh Pascal is an extension of standard Pascal. We have made every effort to indicate which features belong to standard Pascal and which are extensions so that the reader can transfer the knowledge obtained here to other Pascal systems. In particular, we have included detailed discussions of random access files (because they are useful) and graphics (because they are stunning). The main nonstandard feature that we have included in the core is the string type. This decision was made to keep the presentation as simple as possible. In our experience beginners are not ready for the subtleties of arrays of characters, especially if they have never heard of arrays! We do, however, eventually tell the truth about strings, introduce the character type, introduce records, and show the reader how to live in a Pascal without strings. We also include the built-in random number generator early in the text because it provides the opportunity for very nice exercises. Hence, although this is a text meant to be used with the Macintosh, it strives to present a balanced approach to Pascal so that the successful reader will have no trouble in moving to a Pascal on another machine.

This is a book that emphasizes **structured programming**. The method of structured programming is taught through an extensive number of problems solved in the text. Functions and procedures are introduced early and used throughout the remainder of the book. Since problem solving and sound programming skills are only learned by the reader actually solving problems and writing programs, we urge the reader to write programs for as many of the exercises as possible. Fortunately, the computer checks programs carefully and gives the reader feedback about the programs presented to it. For our part, we have tried to provide interesting and challenging exercises that we hope you will enjoy as have our many students over the years.

Another convenience for the reader is that a disk is available to accompany the book. This disk not only contains the sample programs from the book so that the reader can run or modify them, but it also contains text files for some of the exercises, as well as buggy programs. We have saved some of our students' best errors and provide them to hone your debugging skills. There is much to learn in the debugging of programs. Indeed, you can't call yourself a programmer until you can debug your programs. (Information on ordering this special disk is provided at the end of the book.)

Finally, the Macintosh's features entitle it to its own Pascal text. We do not want to give away the exciting story that follows, but we believe that the interpreted nature of Macintosh Pascal, together with the 'windows' into the mind of the computer, will revolutionize and humanize the study of Pascal. May your journey be as exciting as ours was.

About this book

Appropriately enough, this book was typeset on a Macintosh. The text was created with MacWrite using 12 point Geneva font. The pages were then reduced to fit a standard 6 by 9 inch format. Each chapter had to be divided into many pieces due to the limitations of the 128K Macintosh and early versions of MacWrite. The pieces were then cut and pasted together on a 512K Mac or on a Lisa running MacWorks and then printed on an ImageWriter printer. We are deeply grateful to Paul Collete and Jim Fiester of Lake Shore Computers in Lake Forest for letting us use their "Fat Mac" and to our colleague Jim Fryxell for making his Lisa available to us. So much effort was given to the task that rumors spread on campus that Bob was spending many hours in his office with Lisa while Lowell was in his office with Mac.

The program listings were produced from Macintosh Pascal and pasted into the text. Since all of the programs have been tested, this serves to ensure that no devastating typos have crept into the listings. In addition, all of the exercises have been solved to ensure that they are reasonable and can be done with the techniques at hand at the time they are given.

Acknowledgments

Our work in producing this book was made easier by the considerate help of a number of people. We extend our appreciation to Don Enns, Larry Jacober, and Bonnie Koven who worked through the material and provided suggestions for preparing the final manuscript. Special thanks go to Joe Hofmeister and George Pryjma who read the final manuscript and offered many valuable suggestions. Also thanks to Steve Lipton who first brought Koch's snowflake to our attention and suggested recursive graphics (Chapter 15) on the Macintosh. Permission to quote material from *GAMES* magazine is greatly appreciated. We gratefully acknowledge McGraw-Hill, Inc. for permission to quote from *The Devil's DP Dictionary,* by Stan Kelly-Bootle (copyright (c) 1981 by McGraw-Hill, Inc.). Finally, we are also deeply indebted to the dedicated staff of Lake Forest Computer Camp who so graciously filled in for us during the summer of 1984 so that we could complete the first draft of these materials.

Lowell A. Carmony
Robert L. Holliday

CONTENTS

Chapter 1

Introduction

COMPUTER SCIENCE – A study akin to numerology
and astrology but lacking the precision of the
former and the success of the latter.
Devil's DP Dictionary

The invention of the computer has caused a revolution in today's society. One need not look very far to find seminars on "computer literacy" or "computer awareness," summer camps for children (and adults) on "computer programming," special sections in nearly every bookstore for computer related magazines and books, and segments on television news shows about the latest developments in computer technology. If a TV news reporter asks a group of youngsters why they are so interested in computers, one of the responses would likely be: "Understanding computers will be *necessary* for success in tomorrow's society."

While the preceding statement might not be true for everyone, the point is that the amount of attention given to computers is unlike the attention focused on any other human invention. Microwave ovens, washers and dryers, and video recorders have "revolutionized" modern life, but we seldom see a "washer/dryer" section in a bookstore or a videocassette recorder camp.

The revolution brought about by the computer is best called an "information-processing revolution." The magnitude of this revolution can be appreciated when it is likened in importance with such events as the discovery of fire, the invention of the wheel, the invention of the printing press, or the industrial revolution. Only the future will tell whether such comparisons are justified, but there is little doubt that computers will continue to have a major impact on the quality and style of life we experience. Whether these impacts are positive or negative is an important question, but is not one for us to address directly here. Instead,

1

we will be concerned with learning enough about the computer so that we can make it do what we want.

Why has the computer become the focus of such attention? There are several reasons. For a long time, science fiction authors have endowed computers with all-powerful, humanlike qualities. Although there are no thinking, reasoning HAL computers as in "2001--A Space Odyssey," many people think of computers in this way. On a more practical level, computers have proved their worth in many diverse areas: information storage and retrieval, scientific research, education, and recreation. It is this "general purpose" nature that we believe contributes most to the universal appeal of computers. That is the reason this book is about programming--so that we can learn to take advantage of the general-purpose capabilities of the computer.

We mention one last reason why computers have become so prevalent --affordability. Unlike nearly every other phenomenon, as computer technology has increased, the cost of this technology has decreased. The amount of computing power that is found on many executives' desks today is hundreds of times less expensive and tens of times more powerful than the computers of just 30 years ago. It has been said that if the automobile industry worked like the computer industry, then everyone would be driving a Rolls Royce that costs $3.95, never needs any maintenance, and gets 250 miles to the gallon.

The technological developments associated with the computer age have been truly remarkable. There have been certain events that have shaped much of what has followed--the switch from tubes to transistors, the integrated circuit, the "personal" computer.

The introduction of the Macintosh by the Apple Computer Corporation on January 24, 1984, is another important event in the evolution of a computer society. Far from being just another computer on an already crowded market, the Macintosh represents a real step forward in personal computer technology. The potential of this machine to create opportunities for innovative techniques is tremendous. In particular, programming on a Macintosh is unlike programming on any predecessor machine. The Macintosh, because of its raw speed and power, offers the personal computer owner features and conveniences heretofore unavailable. Thus, it is both exciting and worthwhile to investigate programming in Pascal on the Macintosh, and the rest of this book will be devoted to that task.

Before we begin the actual material on programming, we must first learn a little about the Macintosh itself. This we do in Chapter 2. For now, we will take a brief look at the history of computing. We think it is important to see the development of the computer in its historical perspective. Moreover, this will provide a good opportunity to introduce some of the terminology of computer science. One does not have to read very many advertisements to get the impression that the computer field is loaded with buzzwords and technical jargon. This can be very discouraging to the beginner. We emphasize that one need not be technically inclined to deal with computers, just as one need not be mechanically inclined to drive an automobile. However, because of the widespread use of the buzzwords, it becomes necessary to include many of them in any discussion on computers.

A Historical Sketch of Computing

Man has been computing for thousands of years. The earliest form of computing was simple counting--for example, a shepherd counting his sheep to make sure all of them returned from grazing. Man has used tools to assist him with computing for thousands of years also. The early shepherd likely used pebbles to help count sheep. A very common counting device that is as much as 4000 years old is the abacus. This device consists of beads and rods and was used by Chinese merchants to handle business transactions. It is still used by millions of people throughout Asia today to perform routine numerical calculations.

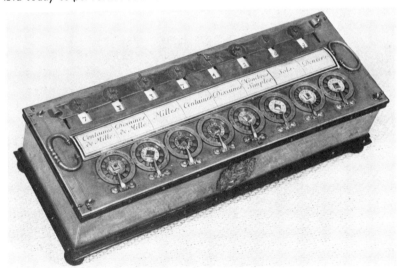

Figure 1.1 The Pascaline
(Courtesy of International Business Machines Corporation)

In the mid-1600's, a French philosopher and mathematician named Blaise Pascal developed a mechanical adding/subtracting machine, the Pascaline. Pascal's father worked for the "French IRS" and was continuously adding long columns of numbers by hand. The young Pascal believed that this was the sort of work appropriate for a machine, so he constructed one using gear-driven counter wheels. Although other such machines had been tried previously, Pascal's was one of the first such machines to be reliable. Because of this contribution to computing, the programming language that we will study in this book is named after Blaise Pascal.

Before we turn to other more general computers, we mention two other names associated with calculating machines. In 1671, Gottfried Leibniz, who along with Isaac Newton developed calculus, invented the first calculator that could multiply and divide as well as add and subtract. His machine also worked on a gear-driven principle, and in fact, this principle was used in nearly all mechanical calculators up through the 1950's. Of course, calculators are now electronic, but the staying power of Leibniz's idea is a feat seldom repeated today. In 1884, William Burroughs developed the first commercially successful adding machine. Today, the Burroughs name remains at the front of the computer industry.

Figure 1.2 Jacquard's Loom

The advent of more general computers, i.e., tools that can do more than just numerical calculations, is often traced to an unexpected place-- the looms of France and Emil Jacquard. As Jacquard watched the weavers constantly resetting the looms for the various patterns, he came upon the idea of using punched cards to record the loom settings and in 1801 designed a loom that could read these punched card "instructions."

In the late 1800's, Herman Hollerith used Jacquard's idea to develop a punched card system to handle the 1890 United States census. While the 1880 census took nearly 10 years to count by hand, Hollerith counted the 62.5 million people of 1890 in just over a year. The punched card was also the way early programmers often communicated their instructions to computers, and, in fact, was widely used, particularly in learning environments, through the mid-1970's.

Figure 1.3 Hollerith's Tabulating Machine
(Courtesy of International Business Machines Corporation)

While the Jacquard/Hollerith punched-card idea is familiar to many people, a more fundamental, but less well-known, development occurred in the 1830's. In 1833, Englishman Charles Babbage conceived the first general-purpose computer, that is, a computer that could do more than just numerical calculations. Babbage's computer had the capability of accepting different sets of instructions to carry out different tasks. Babbage was truly a man ahead of his time. Because there were no transistorized circuits in his day, Babbage's computer, called the

Analytical Engine, would have been driven by steam and been the size of a football field. Unfortunately, the technology of the 1830's was not advanced enough for Babbage to build a working model of his Analytical Engine. Babbage did build some calculating machines, called Difference Engines, but because of the steam technology, they turned out to be too slow and unreliable. These setbacks caused years of struggling to receive funding from the British government for his Analytical Engine project, and he eventually gave up his work and died a bitter man. Interestingly enough, when some of the 1950's pioneers of the first electronic computers became aware of Babbage's work, they were amazed at the similarity of Babbage's design of the Analytical Engine and the actual design of the early computers. Many people feel today that if anyone deserves the title "Father of the Computer," it is indeed Charles Babbage.

In 1842, Ada Augusta, the Countess of Lovelace and the daughter of the poet, Lord Byron, read, carefully analyzed, and refined Babbage's theoretical work. Not only was she convinced that Babbage's ideas were sound, she actually wrote sets of instructions that the Analytical Engine could conceivably carry out. Thus, Ada Augusta was the first computer programmer and it is in her honor that the latest Department of Defense language is named. This language, Ada, is considered by many to be the "language of the future," or at least the language of the 80's and 90's.

The Ada programming language is the result of a United States Department of Defense international design competition that lasted from 1975 to 1979 and involved those individuals who were considered to be the best language designers in the world. It is worth mentioning that all four finalist languages in the competition (including Ada) are considered to be derivatives or "descendants" of Pascal. That is, the overall design of Pascal was in some sense a starting point for these new languages. So a good way to learn Ada for the future, admittedly a difficult language to master, would be to learn Pascal now.

Let us now investigate the "modern" history of computing. The impetus for the birth of computer science was World War II. Both the United States and Great Britain were expending tremendous efforts to build computers to assist in the war effort. The first general-purpose computer was the MARK I, built at Harvard in 1944 under the guidance of Howard Aiken. This computer used electromagnetic relays and was very slow, requiring six seconds to perform a multiplication.

In 1946, the ENIAC, Electronic Numerical Integrator And Calculator, was developed at the University of Pennsylvania. This was the first electronic digital computer. It used vacuum tubes to store information (similar to the tubes found in older radios and television sets). The entire memory of the computer could store only twenty 10-digit numbers. Twelve vacuum tubes were needed to store each digit. The ENIAC could perform about 300 multiplication operations per second, weighed 60,000 pounds, occupied 1600 square feet of floor space, and required a roomful of air conditioners to offset the heat of the vacuum tubes.

During this time period there were several other machines developed, with equally strange sounding names. One that deserves special mention is the EDVAC, Electron Discrete Variable Automatic Computer, developed in 1952. One of the individuals working on the EDVAC project was John Von Neumann. While Von Neumann made numerous important contributions to the field of computer science, we mention two that first appeared with EDVAC.

The first of these was the concept of a **stored program**. Without becoming too technical, the major components of a computer system include the input/output device, memory, and the processor/controller. The input/output device is necessary so that people can communicate with the computer. The memory store is where information (for example, numbers) is kept during processing. The processor/controller is that part of the computer that reads the instructions of a computer program, determines what is to be done, and does it. It is in the manner in which the processor/controller finds the instructions that Von Neumann had his impact. With early computers, each time a new program was to be executed, the actual circuits had to be set, either by rewiring or by positioning a number of switches. Von Neumann felt that the set of instructions should be loaded into the memory store, just like the data on which the instructions were to operate. It would then be up to the processor/controller to distinguish between instructions and data. Although this makes the processor/controller more complex, it greatly facilitates the entering and running of new programs. Thus, the flexibility of the general-purpose computer can be realized. Because of his idea, the modern-day computers are often referred to as Von Neumann machines and the general layout of a computer is called Von Neumann architecture.

Von Neumann's second contribution to EDVAC was in the way computers do arithmetic. In general, computers operate based on the presence or absence of electrical current. The presence is usually indicated by a 1 and absence by a 0. Thus, inside a computer, all one really finds are strings of 0's and 1's. Humans, of course, use more than just 0's and 1's to communicate. When communicating numerically, we use the digits 0 through 9 and operate in the base 10 or decimal system. Although this is very natural for us, this is not the natural way for computers to do things. So Von Neumann proposed that computers do their arithmetic in base 2, or the **binary** system. This idea made the inner workings of computers much more efficient, and today all computers operate using a binary system.

We take this opportunity to mention some terminology. The numerals that we humans use are called digits. The 0's and 1's of a computer are called **b**inary digits, which you may have seen abbreviated as "bits." So a **bit** in a computer is simply a 0 or a 1. The memory of a computer is filled with thousands of bits. Dealing with information bit by bit is very slow and tedious, so bits are generally grouped together. A group of 8 bits is called a **byte**. A byte is a convenient grouping because it is used to store one character of alphabetic information. A computer's memory is usually given by the number of bytes of information that it can store. 1024 bytes are called one **K** (for kilobyte). Think of a K as approximately equalling 1000. So a computer with a memory of 64K can store approximately 64,000 characters of information.

Some computers move information around in memory one byte at a time. Such machines are called 8-bit machines. The typical personal computer of the late 70's and early 80's was an 8-bit computer. There exist 16-bit, 32-bit, and 64-bit machines. In general, the more bits a computer can handle at a time, the faster the computer operates. The number of bits handled at a time is often referred to as the **word** size.

Computers of the Modern Era

In the 1960's, the vacuum tube was replaced by the transistor. Computers using tubes are often called first generation computers, while those employing transistors are second generation computers. What the bulky vacuum tube could do, the tiny transistor could accomplish at a much smaller cost. Because the transistor does not give off nearly as much heat, its reliability is also much greater than that of the vacuum tube. In the late 1960's, the integrated circuit, a cluster of very tiny transistors packed onto a chip of silicon, was introduced. In 1970, scientists were able to pack about 3000 transistors on a single chip of silicon about the size of a baby's fingernail. In 1975, the figure rose to 8000, in 1980 to 70,000, and the predictions for 1985 are for 400,000. Packing thousands of transistors onto a chip is known as LSI (Large Scale Integration) technology, and computers using this technology are known as third generation computers. VLSI (V for Very) technology, like the 1980 and 1985 figures above, constitutes fourth generation computers.

From a cost standpoint, one dollar bought 300 transistors in 1970, while one dollar in 1980 bought 5000 transistors. These statistics should make it clear to the reader why the computer industry can offer more for less as long as such progress continues. How much more? Well, how does the Macintosh compare with the ENIAC? It is 50 times faster, at least 1000 times more reliable, 1/30,000 of the volume, 1/100,000 the cost, and consumes the power of a light bulb instead of a jet plane.

In the past year, the Japan Information Processing Development Center proposed a plan to develop an advanced computer by the year 1990. Following this announcement, the race began to see who will build the first fifth generation computer. Such computers are expected to make use of advances in the field of **artificial intelligence**, that area of computer science concerned with computers that can perform functions normally associated with human behavior, e.g., learning and improving.

Terminology

We now give a survey of some computer terms. With the mastery of these terms comes the ability to read sales pitches for various computer-related products. The order of the terms is not alphabetical, but rather designed for ease of discussion.

Computer--a device (usually electronic) that is capable of storing and retrieving data and of executing logical or mathematical operations without human intervention. With the previous historical sketch, we hope this definition is understandable. Because many people tend to be frightened by computers (because of their seemingly mystical capabilities), we recommend that the reader keep in mind the following alternate definition (given with the companion definition of a human being):

A computer is a fast, accurate **moron.**
A human being is a slow, error-prone genius.

Note the the computer, moron that it is, has some good qualities that most people lack, namely speed (we're talking speed of light here, so don't be offended) and accuracy. But with all of its wonderful qualities, computers do not possess one bit of intelligence. That is where the human comes in. Although most of us possess less intelligence than we would really like, there is never any reason to be intimidated by a computer.

Memory--this is the area where the computer stores information. This information can of course be recalled, or **fetched,** any time it is needed.

Think of memory as consisting of rows of cells, or mailboxes, each with its own address. There are several adjectives that pertain to memory that should be discussed.

RAM (random access memory)--this is the memory that is available to the user of the computer. For our purposes, this is where the programs that we write are stored.

ROM (read only memory)--these are memory cells in the computer that contain information necessary for the operation of the computer itself. When information is fetched from a memory location, we are "reading" from that location. When information is placed into a memory location, we are "writing" to that location. So random access memory is read/write memory, i.e., we can change the contents of RAM if we wish. ROM, on the other hand, has special information in it that the programmer can access but cannot change. Thus, it has the designation "read only."

Volatile--this refers to the memory inside the computer and is also called internal memory. Volatile memory loses its contents when the power source is disconnected. So, a program stored in the computer's internal memory is lost if the computer is turned off, if there is a power failure, or if there is a blown fuse.

Nonvolatile--this refers to external sources of memory, for example, floppy disks, hard disks, magnetic tape, and punched cards. This memory retains its contents indefinitely, short of natural disasters like fires, floods, and spilled coffee. Any program that is used repeatedly is stored on an external source, usually a disk, and is simply loaded into the computer's memory when needed. The loading of information from a disk into a computer is performed by a mechanical device called a **disk drive**. The Macintosh has a built-in disk drive. Most earlier computers used a separate, external disk drive.

Hardware--any component of a computer system that you can touch. The keyboard, which is the standard input device for most computers, the monitor (TV screen, sometimes called a CRT for "cathode ray tube," the method by which the information is relayed to the screen), the chips inside the computer, the disks, and disk drives are all hardware components.

Software--computer programs. Without instructions, the computer hardware just sits there. Computers contain some built-in software, called the **operating system**, that allows the computer to function properly. When you purchase a commercially developed program, such as an accounting program, an inventory control program, or a word processing program, you are paying for the software, that is, the instructions that allow the computer to behave as an accountant, an inventory controller, or a word processor. In this book, we are going to learn how to develop our own software. Writing good software is not easy. The following ironic definition of software is often given: Software is the *hard* part of a computer system. We mention that the suffix "ware" is one that has certainly made its impact on computer jargon. In fact, with the *diskware* that accompanies this *bookware,* we hope we have provided you with excellent *courseware* for learning Pascal.

Documentation--the comments or explanatory remarks that accompany software. Documentation comes in two types--internal and external. Internal documentation consists of comments included with a computer program. External documentation is like an automobile's owner's manual and should be provided on any software project that is sold commercially or that is of a complex nature.

Printer--an output device that provides a paper copy (hard copy) of a computer program or its execution. Printers are divided into several categories. Dot matrix and letter quality are two of the most common kinds. Dot matrix printers draw the characters by using tiny dots (the same way the monitor displays characters on the screen). Letter quality printers strike a ribbon with some type of wheel that contains the raised imprint of the characters. Printer technology, like all computer technology, is changing rapidly. Laser printers, capable of printing dozens of pages per minute, soon will be available even for personal computers.

We next give some terminology specific to the Macintosh.

Mouse--this is the small box that we roll around on the desktop. The mouse lets us move a pointer on the screen without using the keyboard.

Menu--this is the list of options presented to us on the Macintosh screen. We use the mouse to "point" to the option that we want.

Click--pushing (and releasing) the button on the mouse. We do this to activate the option we have chosen. Occasionally, we will **double click** the mouse, as explained in the next chapter.

Drag--moving the mouse while the button remains depressed. The need for dragging is also explained in the next chapter.

A Few More Remarks about the Macintosh

Without becoming too technical, we would like to make some general observations about the Macintosh. Certainly the attention paid to the Macintosh, which is reflected in the number of books about it within weeks after its introduction, seems to imply that there is something special about it. We agree. The Macintosh is based on the Motorola 68000 microprocessor chip. The significance to the user is that the Macintosh is a 32-bit machine. The speed and power of a 32-bit machine, which was once only found in large, mainframe computers occupying a room and costing in the hundreds of thousands of dollars, is now available at the personal computer level. The Macintosh screen is of extremely high resolution. The images on the screen are drawn using tiny dots called **pixels**. The Macintosh screen has 512- by 342-pixel resolution, nearly twice the resolution of previous personal computers. With the increased resolution, the graphic images drawn on the Macintosh screen are extremely clear. This allows the Macintosh to be **icon** (picture or symbol) oriented. That is, menu choices can be displayed using pictures instead of jargon. This, along with the mouse technology, contributes to the overall "user-friendliness" of the system. By this we mean that the Macintosh is easy for the computer novice to use, since recognizing pictures, moving the mouse, and clicking a button are skills not generally associated with computer whizzes. Although earlier computers could have used the mouse technology with the high-resolution screen, it is the 32-bit power of the Macintosh that makes it all possible. With the standard 8-bit power of most personal computers, the user would have soon tired of waiting for the computer to draw all the nice pictures. So the 32-bit architecture is clearly an important step in the evolution of personal computers.

A second important feature appearing for the first time in a popular computer is the use of the Sony 3 1/2-inch disk. The personal computer standard has been the 5 1/4-inch floppy disk. In addition to being able to fit nicely into a shirt pocket, the important advantages of the smaller disk are its reliability (the disk is completely enclosed in a durable casing with a tiny trap door that is opened once the disk is completely inside the computer), its ability to store more information (400K bytes on a single side), and its lower cost (when the density of storage and durability of the disk are considered). Many people feel that the 3 1/2-inch Sony disk technology is better suited for personal computers of the future and that the Macintosh will move the industry in that direction.

The original Macintosh machines were built with 128K bytes of RAM and 64K bytes of ROM. The Macintosh is now available with 512K bytes of

RAM, allowing the Macintosh to run most programs with ease. The machine itself is nicely packaged in a small box (less than 10 by 10 by 14 inches), contains an uncluttered, professional, detachable keyboard, and with the keyboard and mouse weighs 22.7 pounds.

Although we marvel at the engineering feats of the Macintosh design team, this book is about programming a computer. This is the area of computer science where the Macintosh excites us the most. Because of the speed of the machine and the flexibility of the display screen, the Macintosh provides more assistance and as nice a programming environment as any we have seen on any size computer. The amiable relationship between machine and programmer will be made apparent in the subsequent chapters of this book.

Programming a Computer

Since this book is really about programming, it is appropriate that we close this first chapter with some remarks about programming. The first and most important remark is that this book is really about *problem solving*. Beginners often lose sight of this fact, and it is for this reason that programming often becomes a difficult activity. Programmers must first be problem solvers. That is because a program is nothing more than a careful, specific sequence of instructions for the computer to carry out to solve a problem. The computer executes the instructions, but it is the programmer who must write the instructions in the first place. Many beginners spend far too much time learning all the technical aspects of a programming language and far too little time sharpening their problem solving skills. Such people never get much of a chance to use their programming knowledge because they get stuck at step 1--what to do after the problem is posed to them. Throughout this book, whenever a new feature of Pascal is introduced, think about how it can be used. Analyze the examples to see these features in action. Most importantly, be able to generalize the circumstances where various features are appropriate.

The preceding paragraph used the word Pascal. Pascal was developed by Niklaus Wirth of Switzerland in 1969. Wirth intended Pascal to be an educational language, so he kept the design small. Pascal will be the vehicle by which we learn this problem-solving process called programming. Earlier in this chapter we saw that the computer is a binary machine, storing everything as either a 0 or a 1. If we wanted to (we don't, take our word for it), we could communicate to the computer in its native language, its **machine language**, by using strings of 0's and 1's. Such a language is called a **low-level language**. This is in fact the way the earliest programmers worked with computers. Not only was this process extremely tedious, it was also unnecessarily complicated, making programming a very specialized activity. The advent of **high-level languages** in the 1950's has proved to be as important a factor in making programming a common activity as has the technological progress outlined in this chapter, which made the computer affordable. High-level languages make computers understandable. High-level languages are closer to English than they are to machine languages. People who have had no training at all in programming are sometimes able to look at high-level programs and figure out what they do.

If we are to write programs in a high-level language and if the computer can only "understand" its native machine language, there must be something that performs a translation process between the programmer and the computer. This translation process is in fact performed by another computer program, called a **compiler** or an **interpreter**, depending on how it carries out its translation. We simply point out that compilers tend to perform much faster than interpreters, but interpreters, like the one used for Macintosh Pascal, generally provide a much friendlier environment for programming, particularly at the beginning level. The writing of a language translator is an extremely complicated task requiring several thousand person-years of work. A translator is an example of a **systems program**.

For historical reasons, we list three very important high-level languages.

FORTRAN--Like most early languages, the name is an acronym, where the letters of the name stand for words. FORTRAN stands for FORmula TRANslator. FORTRAN was developed around 1957 and is a scientific language, meaning it was designed to do numerical calculations. FORTRAN was used extensively in scientific programming in the 1950's and 1960's, most notably in the space program, and is still in wide use today.

COBOL--COmmon Business Oriented Language, released in 1959. COBOL was developed at the request of the United States Department of Defense. It is truly the language of the business world and is probably the most widely used language in the world today.

BASIC--Beginner's All-purpose Symbolic Instruction Code. BASIC has been the language of the microcomputer. By this we mean that a BASIC interpreter is built in to the ROM by the manufacturer of nearly every personal computer. It is an easy language to learn and has succeeded in introducing millions to computer programming. We point out that the Macintosh does not include a built-in version of BASIC, another radical step for a personal computer to take. This can be viewed as a positive step, though, because independent software vendors will be encouraged to develop versions of BASIC to be sold to Macintosh users. In general, with personal computers, versions of BASIC implemented by independent software houses are usually "enhanced" and better than the built-in versions. The BASIC that is being developed for the Macintosh will make use of the computer's power and will provide a unique and powerful BASIC programming environment.

A common buzzword in computer programming these days is **structured**. Programs should be structured and languages should be structured. None of the above three languages is generally considered to be a modern, structured language. Pascal, on the other hand, is usually classified as a structured language. This classification alone is enough to prompt some people to say that we should learn to program in Pascal. Unfortunately, these people stop right there, without ever bothering to define what this buzzword means. We agree that structured programming is important and that Pascal is a modern structured language as opposed to FORTRAN, COBOL, and BASIC. So that we can support our contention that Pascal is an excellent language for students serious about learning to program, we will explain what structured programming means to us.

Often a program is a piece of work written by one group of people to be read by another group of people. A well-written composition is more than just a bunch of paragraphs thrown together. Likewise, a computer program is more than just a bunch of instructions thrown together. Each needs to be held together by some overall structure. It is this structure that is the primary focus of most beginning writing courses, although some time is spent discussing grammar, spelling, punctuation, and sentence construction. Similarly, in a beginning programming course, a certain amount of time must be spent learning the atomic constructs of a programming language so that these may be combined to form complete programs. We must also learn how to manipulate a computer if we want to see the results of our programs. But like the writing course, the bulk of the emphasis should be on the ability to solve a problem and convey that solution in a complete, well-structured program.

Some synonyms of structured programming are **top-down programming** and **modular programming**. To us, all of these terms mean the following: When presented with a problem to solve, don't try to solve it all at once. Don't start worrying about the intricate details.

Instead, break the problem up into major components and focus on each of these components in turn. Apply this same technique to each of these components until you have broken the problem down into subproblems that are easy to solve. Solve the subproblems and then combine these solutions into one overall solution for the original problem. While this strategy is worthwhile in almost any type of environment, it is especially appropriate in the programming environment. When dealing person-to-person, we can sometimes be a bit sketchy in our instructions, allowing the recipient to use his or her own intelligence to figure out our intent. But because the computer is a moron, extremely detailed instructions must be given so that there is absolutely no doubt about what is to be done. Most major software projects are so complex that one soon becomes lost in a forest of details if the problem is not first cut down to size.

Now we know what a structured program is. What makes a language structured? If we attack a problem as above, we should be able to write the solutions to the subproblems as their own separate programs, called modules. A language is structured if it provides the programmer with the features necessary to carry out this modular approach easily and to link these modules together conveniently into a complete program. It is our hope that the readers who work through the chapters in this book will possess the ability to write structured programs and provide their own arguments that Pascal is indeed a structured language.

It is not unusual for the beginning programmer to make the following statement: "There's something wrong with this computer." Such a statement usually follows a frustrating session where the computer won't follow even the simplest of instructions. There is even a chance that the statement might actually be true. Silicon chips do go bad either by misuse or on their own (every hundred years or so). Disks do get damaged through misuse or normal wear-and-tear. Because of their tremendous complexity, compilers and interpreters actually get written and marketed with mistakes in them. This happens more often than it should, but it is the price we pay to avoid writing in machine language. Nonetheless, there is probably a 99.9% chance that the beginner's statement above is false. The statement should read: "There's something wrong with the instructions I gave to the computer." If you take this approach and start analyzing your instructions, you may overcome your problem much more quickly. All too often, our human pride causes us to insist that the first statement is true and we continually give the same instructions to the computer with the same undesired results. Not only is the computer a moron, it is also infinitely patient. Thus, it is so stupid that it can't help us find and correct our mistakes and it doesn't mind when we keep asking it to do the same thing over and over.

The level of precision required in programming is typically much higher than has ever been required of the programmer in any other activity. For this reason, be suspicious and critical of the instructions you give to the computer. It is only through a critical look that you can convince yourself that your programs are correct. Never expect the computer to make any kind of distinction between what you type and what you mean. Make sure that you type *exactly* what you mean. Computer languages are often criticized for being overly picky, with every punctuation mark having a significant impact. This is just the nature of computers and we must learn to accept some things. But to show the importance of punctuation in natural languages, consider the following prize-winning paragraph from the May, 1984 issue of **GAMES** Magazine:

> "My wife. I think I'll keep her. In a spaceship, orbiting the globe until the end of time, I could never find another woman on earth like her. If I wanted to, I could go on and on about her face and figure. I'm reminded of Henry Kissinger when the subject of her intelligence comes up. I often think of the time the neighbors' Chihuahua gave birth to brain-damaged pups. My wife, my gracious Clara, was willing to sit up nights with the pups. In an effort to learn to speak more effectively, Clara began taking a night class at the local college. She's learning how to become a human relations counselor. Sam Wilkins, from the school, told me Clara is at the head of her class. When it comes to 'stupidity' -- golly, the word's not even in her vocabulary."

Note what happens when this paragraph is *only* repunctuated--none of the words is changed.

> "My wife. I think I'll keep her in a spaceship, orbiting the globe until the end of time. I could never find another woman on earth like her, if I wanted to. I could go on and on. About her face and figure -- I'm reminded of Henry Kissinger. When the subject of her intelligence comes up, I often think of the time the neighbors' Chihuahua gave birth to brain-damaged pups. My wife -- my gracious! Clara was willing to sit up nights with the pups in an effort to learn to speak. More effectively, Clara began taking a night class at the local college. She's learning how to become a human. Relations counselor Sam Wilkins, from the

school, told me Clara is at the head of her class when it comes to stupidity. 'Golly' -- the word's not even in her vocabulary."

The above paragraphs were submitted to **GAMES** by Joyce Rogers in response to a contest (**GAMES**, Jan, 1984) asking readers to create double messages by changing punctuation. The magazine closed the challenge with the following information:

"All entries will be considered. If they are clever, however, they will be eliminated. If sufficiently stupid, any entry stands a good chance of winning."

Of course, the intended message was:

"All entries will be considered if they are clever. However, they will be eliminated if sufficiently stupid. Any entry stands a good chance of winning."

The reader will get an opportunity to repunctuate some other passages in the exercises at the end of this chapter.

Summary

Although the concept of the present-day computer has been around since Babbage's Analytical Engine of the 1830's, it is the technological advances of integrated circuitry that have brought computers into the home, into the reach of the average person. Along with the technological advances have come advances in software design, most notably high-level languages, which have placed the power of computers into the hands of the average person. Because of these phenomena, the computer will have an impact on society like few other human inventions. Most people will benefit from computers and, in the near future, everyone will be a computer user. But to really understand how a computer works and to actually harness and control the power of the computer, one needs to learn programming. While programming comes naturally for some people, it proves to be quite a challenge for many others due to the cold logic of the computer and the precision required of the programmer. The environment provided by the user-friendliness of the Macintosh computer coupled with the features found in a small, modern, structured language like Pascal can help make the beginning programmer's experience an enjoyable one instead of a frustrating one.

Exercises

These first four exercises are designed to show the logic required of computer programmers.

1.1 A boy is sent to a stream with a 5-quart jug and a 3-quart jug and is asked to bring back 4 quarts of water. How can he do it? Can you come up with two different ways of obtaining 4 quarts of water?

1.2 A jeweler has in his possession 8 gold coins and a two-pan balance. One of the coins is counterfeit and is lighter than the authentic coins. How can the jeweler, with just two weighings, determine which coin is the counterfeit coin?

1.3 Consider a very strange universe where there are only two types of people--Computer Programmers, who always tell the truth except on Mondays, Tuesdays, and Wednesdays, when they always lie, and Computer Salesmen, who always tell the truth except on Thursdays, Fridays, and Saturdays, when they always lie. (We are being generous to the salesman, at least according to the following old joke: How can you tell when a computer salesman is lying to you? Answer: When his lips are moving.)

a.   You meet two people one day and they make the following statements:

First person: I'm a computer salesman.
Second person: I'm a computer programmer.

What day is it and which person is which?

b.   Later, that same month, you come across the same two people. Your digital wristwatch is broken so you don't know what day of the week it is.   However, the two acquaintances help you with the following statements:

Programmer: I lied yesterday.
Salesman: I lied yesterday, too.

What day of the week was it?

1.4 A word processor is a device that assists in the writing of documents. Word processors have a variety of commands that can be used to correct mistakes. Suppose you own a very limited word processor that has only one correcting command, namely a change command of the following format:

CHANGE*first word*second word*

The CHANGE command will find all occurrences of the word listed between the first two asterisks and change each occurrence to the word listed between the last two asterisks. You are typing an important document and notice the following paragraph:

> "Morris is the dog on commercials who doesn't like to eat his food. Sylvester is a dog on cartoons. "**Old Yeller**" is a movie about a cat that makes almost everyone cry. Probably the most famous cat is Lassie. I wonder if a dog really does have nine lives. Elvis Presley sang a song about a hound cat."

Obviously, you have been careless and completely mixed up the uses of the words "cat" and "dog". How could you use the CHANGE command (maybe more than once) to make the paragraph read normally? (Note: This isn't as easy as it first seems.)

The remaining exercises in this chapter are courtesy of **GAMES** Magazine. Exercises 5 and 6 are from the May, 1984, issue and were submitted by Ellen Jackson and Bob Schnitzer respectively. Exercise 7 appeared in the January, 1984, issue. You are to repunctuate each of the passages to give a passage with a completely different meaning.

1.5 Dear President Reagan,
         I would like to compliment you. I can't stop thinking that you are one of the best Presidents we have had. So many leaders go ahead and propose policies and then botch the job. We expect it. From you, in years to come, I know we will get better results.

1.6 Car for sale. A classic! Lemon yellow coupe. Exterior is completely rust-proof. Can be delivered upon request. No engine runs better. If the sun is out, you can remove the roof for the feel of wind in your hair. Go ahead and kick the tires. As soon as they see it your neighbors will hassle you for a ride. Call 222-4401.

1.7 Dear John,

I want a man who knows what love is all about. You are generous, kind, thoughtful. People who are not like you admit to being useless and inferior, John. You have ruined me for other men. I yearn for you. I have no feelings whatsoever when we're apart. I can be forever happy. Will you let me be yours?

Gloria

Chapter 2

The Operating System

In this chapter we are going to enter, debug, and run our first Pascal program on the Macintosh. For the beginner, there are two hurdles to overcome: One is to learn a little Pascal and the second is to learn to "steer" a program through the computer. That is, once we have a program we must learn how to enter it into the computer, how to edit the program, how to run it, how to get a printed listing, and finally, how to save our program. These housekeeping tasks are performed by the operating system. On many computers, the operating system is another foreign language that stands between the user and the computer. Fortunately, the Macintosh permits us to communicate our wishes by pointing, clicking, and dragging. Nonetheless, the full operating system is powerful and will require some study. This chapter introduces those features of the operating system that the beginner needs. Further information about advanced features of the operating system is given in Chapter 6.

A First Program

The listing on the next page shows a complete program called Simple. More will be said about the structure of Pascal programs in the chapters to come, so there is no need to worry about understanding the program now. In fact, you can probably guess what Simple will do. The first line names the program and the **var** section declares that "Name" will be a **string** variable, i.e., that Name will be able to hold a string of up to 30 characters. The executable portion of the program begins and ends reasonably enough with 'begin' and 'end.' (Note the period.) The 'Writeln' statements write lines on the screen for us and the 'Readln' stops and allows the user to enter some value from the keyboard. Thus, Simple is very simple and is not a very useful task to give to a computer. Our objective here, however, is to place only one hurdle at a time before you. In this chapter we will accept the simple program Simple and use it to illustrate how we "mouse" a program through the Macintosh.

```
program Simple;
var
  Name : string;
begin
  Writeln('My name is Macintosh.');
  Writeln('What is your name?');
  Readln(Name);
  Writeln('Good to meet you, ', Name)
end.
```

Listing 2.1

Loading Pascal into the Macintosh

If you have used the Macintosh with other software applications, then you can quickly scan this section. Find your disk labelled Macintosh Pascal. Turn on the Macintosh by flipping the switch on the left rear. You can locate the switch by feeling for the smooth spot on the left side of the cabinet. Hold the disk as shown below and insert it into the Macintosh.

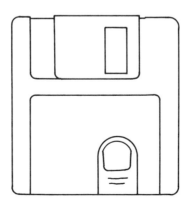

Figure 2.1

Note that the front, right corner is clipped off. Push the disk all the way in until it snaps into place. After about twenty seconds, your screen should appear like figure 2.2 or perhaps figure 2.5. If your screen is different, you are not starting with a fresh copy of the Pascal disk. Ask your instructor to help you prepare your disk for our discussion, or read through this section and begin with the instructions on closing files. Your screen may appear darker than ours. We have modified the appearance of the Macintosh "desktop" to sharpen the contrast for our figures.

Suppose your screen appears as in figure 2.2. Move the mouse and watch the arrow move on the screen. Move the mouse so that the arrow is over the words at the upper left. Push and hold the mouse button with the arrow over one of the words and a "window blind" will roll down revealing a menu of options. Figure 2.3 shows the file menu and its list of selections. Hold the mouse button down and move the mouse down until the **Open** selection is highlighted as shown in figure 2.4. Note that the selection that is being pointed to is shown in inverse on the screen. Release the mouse button and you have commanded the system to open the Pascal disk. The result should be similar to figure 2.5. Don't worry if you have slightly different objects on your screen. For practice, pull down the file menu again and select **Close** as in figure 2.6. This returns you to figure 2.2. Practice the loop through figures 2.2 to 2.6 several more times to get the feel of using the mouse to give commands to the computer.

Starting from figure 2.2, move the mouse over to the trashcan and "click the trashcan." Clicking an object simply means pushing the mouse button with the arrow over the object. The trashcan should now be highlighted as in figure 2.7. The item that you have selected by clicking will always appear highlighted on the screen. You should be able to move back and forth between figures 2.2 and 2.7 by alternately clicking the trashcan and the Pascal disk in the upper right hand corner. Starting from figure 2.7, again choose **Open** from the file menu. This time you should obtain the screen shown in figure 2.8. That is, **Open** will always open the currently selected object. In this case we used **Open** to command the computer to open the trashcan. Since we are assuming that your disk is a "clean" one, we suppose that the trashcan is empty as indicated by there being 0 items in the Trash. Please choose **Close** from the file menu and then click on the disk to select it and return to figure 2.2.

Open and Close Shortcuts

Since **Open** and **Close** are such common commands, both have shortcuts that you will probably prefer to use. Starting as in figure 2.2,

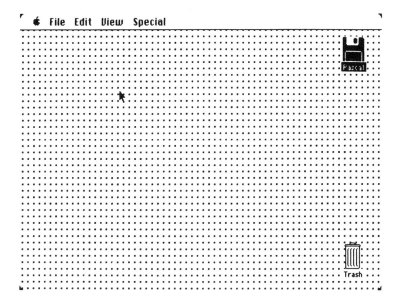

Figure 2.2

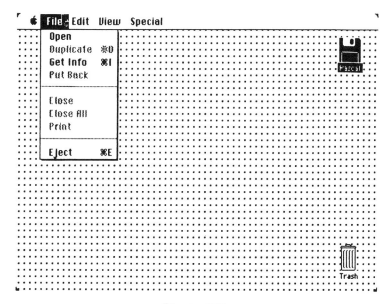

Figure 2.3

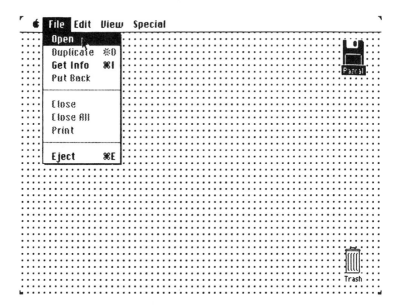

Figure 2.4

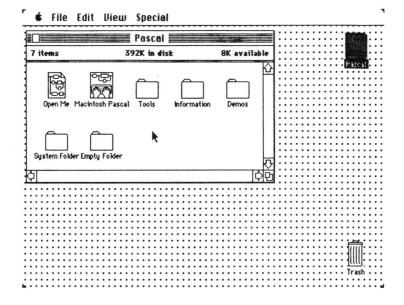

Figure 2.5

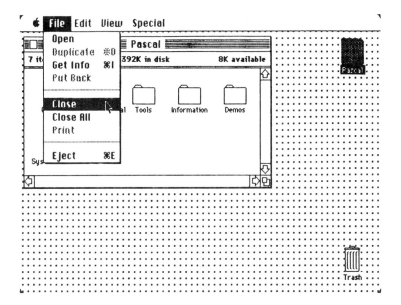

Figure 2.6

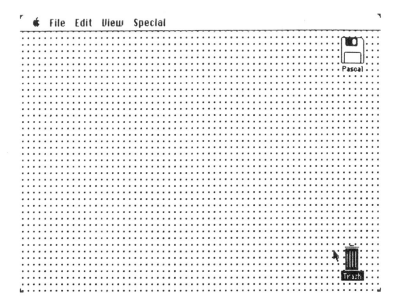

Figure 2.7

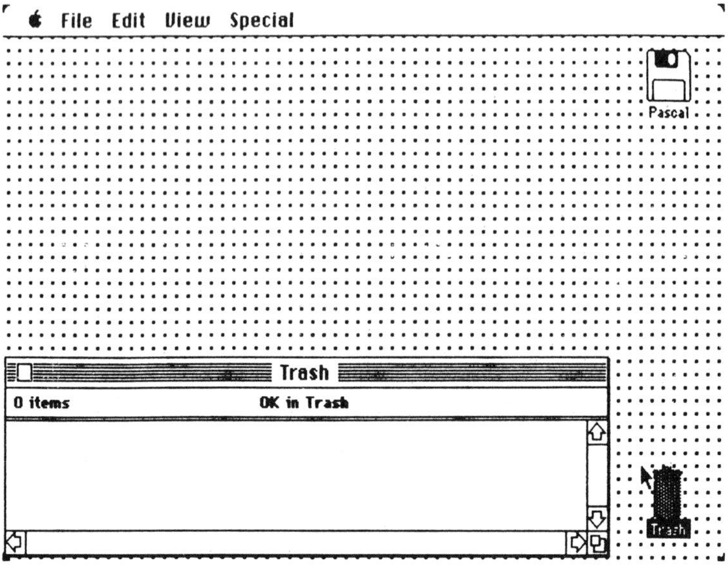

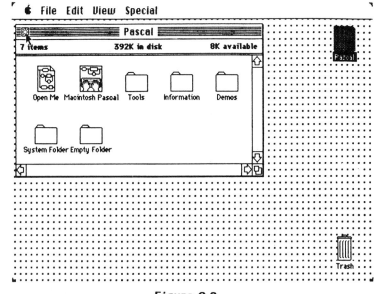

Figure 2.8

Figure 2.9

double click the disk icon. "Double clicking" is performed by depressing the mouse button twice in succession. Clicking once selects an object. Clicking twice selects and opens that object. Hence, your screen should again appear as in figure 2.5, i.e., the Pascal disk should now be open. It takes a little practice to get the correct timing on a double click. If nothing happens or if the disk icon jumps a little, then try it again. A double click should be two distinct, consecutive clicks. You'll quickly get the hang of it.

Each window has a small box near its upper left corner. Figure 2.9 shows the mouse pointing to this box on the Pascal disk window. This is the 'close box' and is the shortcut that closes the window. Click the close box and return, once again, to figure 2.2.

Practice using double clicks to open things and the close box to close things. Note that more than one window can be open at once. See if you can get your screen to look like figure 2.10. Then close the Trash to get it out of the way.

Opening Macintosh Pascal

Now we are finally ready to open Macintosh Pascal. You may either select the Macintosh disk icon by clicking it, and then choosing **Open** from the file menu, or you may double click the Macintosh Pascal icon. The icon is shown in figure 2.11. Note that even if an object is already selected, you may open it by double clicking it. After the disk whirls for a few seconds, your screen should appear as in figure 2.12. You have now loaded Macintosh Pascal!

Your screen, like figure 2.12, should show three windows, labeled "Untitled," "Text," and "Drawing." The text in the "Untitled" window is shown in inverse video (white letters on a black background). The reason for this is explained later. For now click anywhere in the "Untitled" window to make the text return to normal video (black letters on a white background). Note that the "Untitled" window is the only window that has a close box and is the only window with 6 grey bars across the top of it. These bars indicate that this is the **active** window. As we shall see, commands usually apply only to the currently active window. To activate another window, simply click anywhere inside it. Figure 2.13 shows the "Text" window as the active window.

Each window has a different purpose in Macintosh Pascal. The "Untitled" window is where you will see the listing of your program. The name will change from "Untitled" to whatever name you choose for your program when you save your program (as we shall learn to do later). The

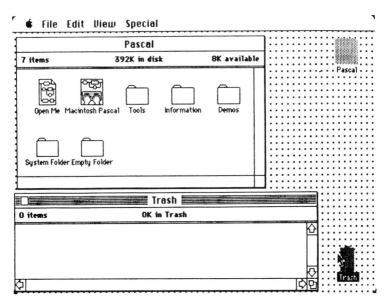

Figure 2.10

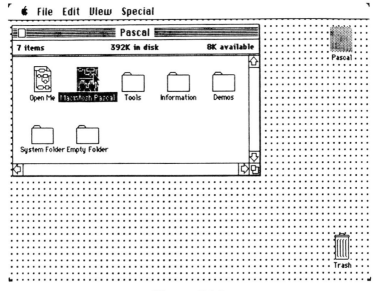

Figure 2.11

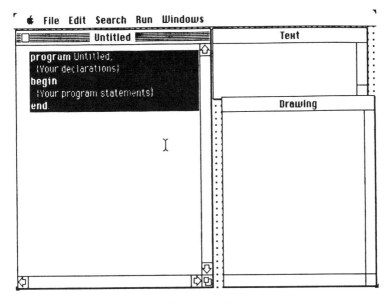

Figure 2.12

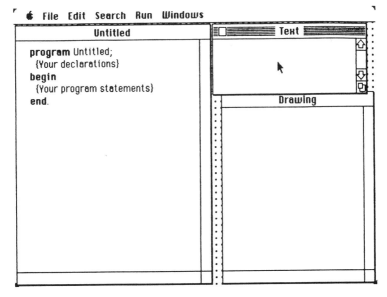

Figure 2.13

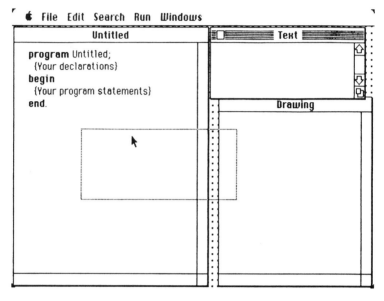

Figure 2.14

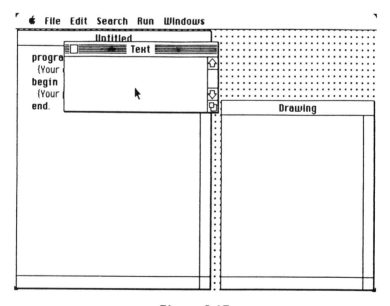

Figure 2.15

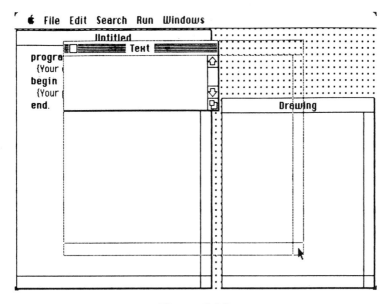

Figure 2.16

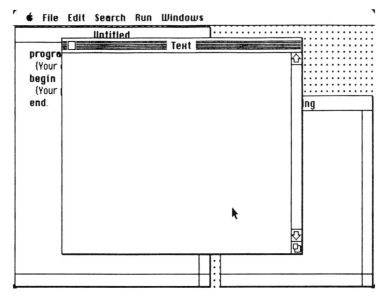

Figure 2.17

"Text" window is where the normal output from your program will appear. The "Drawing" window is where graphics produced by your program will appear. Thus, Macintosh Pascal permits you to view the listing of your program while that program executes, creating both textual and graphical output.

Moving and Adjusting Windows

The text window in figure 2.13 seems a bit small to hold all the output from our sample program Simple. Fortunately, we may move the window around on the screen as well as adjust its size. We accomplish these feats simply by clicking and dragging the mouse.

Beginning with the "Text" window active, as in figure 2.13, move the mouse into the grey bars at the head of the window and drag the window to some other position on the screen. Dragging is accomplished by moving the mouse while holding the mouse button down. An outline of the text window will move with the mouse. See figure 2.14. When you release the mouse, the text window will jump to this position. Practice dragging the text window around the screen and end up with it positioned approximately as shown in figure 2.15. Note that the text window is still the active window, and that the active window has some small boxes in its lower right hand corner. These are the stretch and shrink boxes for changing the size of a window. Position the mouse on these boxes and drag the mouse down and to the right as shown in figure 2.16. This time when you release the mouse the text window will grow to fill the new area as shown in figure 2.17.

Now, the text window appears large enough for the output, but most of the program window is covered. By clicking anywhere in the "Untitled" window, you make it the active window and bring it to the top of the desk as shown in figure 2.18. By repeatedly clicking anywhere in the text and program windows you should be able to flip back and forth between figures 2.17 and 2.18. To make the program window wider, let's drag the stretch and shrink box of the program window to the right as shown in figures 2.19 and 2.20.

As an exercise in window management, make the text window active again, reduce its width a little and then drag the entire window into the upper right hand corner of the screen. Your screen should appear as in figures 2.21 or 2.22 depending on which window is currently active.

Figures 2.21 and 2.22 illustrate a handy arrangement of the program and text windows. When the program executes (our first programs will have no graphics and, hence, not use the drawing window), we will use the

situation depicted in figure 2.21. In this case, the output of the program
is on top, but the program window is clearly visible too. During creation
of our program, we will use the situation depicted in figure 2.22. In this
case, even fairly long program lines are visible on the screen.

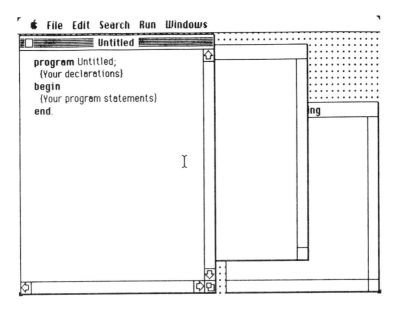

Figure 2.18

Creating and Editing a Program

Finally, we are almost ready to enter our program, Simple, into the
Macintosh. Since we humans are error prone, the system provides ways for
us to correct our errors easily. In this chapter we shall not introduce the
full power of the Macintosh system. Rather, we shall only introduce
enough for you to easily enter and run simple programs. As your
familiarity with the system grows and the size of your Pascal programs
increases, we will introduce the full features of the system. For those too
impatient to wait, the complete options of the system are collected in
Chapter 6.

We begin with editing since the program window currently contains
the program outline shown in listing 2.2.

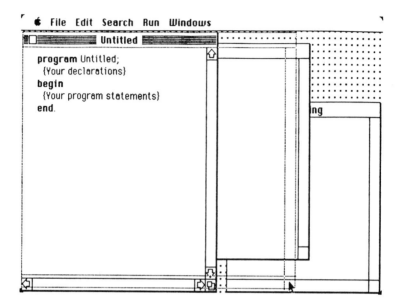

Figure 2.19

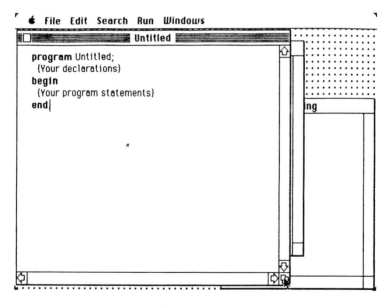

Figure 2.20

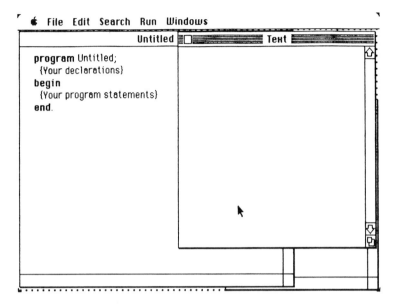

Figure 2.21

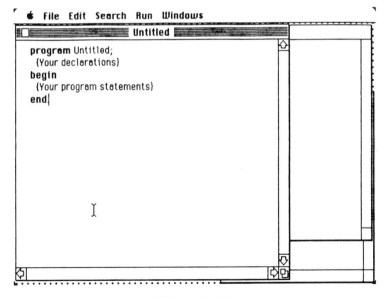

Figure 2.22

```
program Untitled;
 (Your declarations)
begin
 (Your program statements)
end.
```
Listing 2.2

Remember to click anywhere in the program window if your text is still shown in inverse video (black letters on a white background). Our objective is to replace this program with our program, Simple, whose listing is repeated in listing 2.3.

```
program Simple;
 var
  Name : string;
begin
 Writeln('My name is Macintosh.');
 Writeln('What is your name?');
 Readln(Name);
 Writeln('Good to meet you, ', Name)
end.
```
Listing 2.3

The first change we note is that the name "Untitled" (after the word **program**) needs to be changed to "Simple". To do this, move the mouse until it is over the word "Untitled." Note that when the mouse is inside a window where text is expected the arrow changes into an "insertion marker" (⌶). Position this marker at either end of the word "Untitled" and drag the mouse to the other end of the word. Upon releasing the mouse the word should be highlighted as in figure 2.23. (To save space, figures will only show the pertinent parts of the screen instead of the entire screen.)

By clicking at any other position in the window, the highlighting will disappear. Try highlighting the word "Untitled" several times, from the front as well as from the rear. Notice that if you drag the mouse up or down as you drag it across the word, the line above or below is also highlighted. No harm is done by this and if you haven't released the mouse yet, you can recover by returning the mouse to the given line. If the mouse has been released and incorrect material is highlighted, then you can click anywhere on the screen and start again.

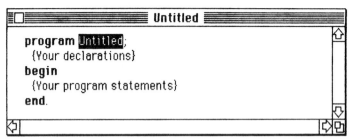

Figure 2.23

Since highlighting a word is a common occurrence in Macintosh Pascal, there is a short cut for this also.   Beginning with the word "Untitled" not selected or highlighted, move the mouse anywhere into the word and double click the mouse.   Double clicking a word selects that word and accomplishes the same as dragging the mouse from one end of the word to the other. A further shortcut is triple clicking. If you triple click anywhere on a line, then that entire line is selected.   Practice a couple of triple clicks. You will probably want to remember these short cuts, but you will also need to drag the mouse when you want to select only a portion of a word, or a portion of a line.

Assuming the word "Untitled" is selected as in figure 2.23, we replace "Untitled" by "Simple" by typing "Simple". If you watch carefully, as soon as you type the "S", the entire word "Untitled" disappears and is replaced by an "S". The cursor is represented by a vertical bar, "|", and characters are inserted, as typed, to the right of the cursor. Your program window should now appear as in figure 2.24.

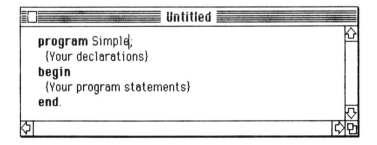

Figure 2.24

That is, to replace one word with another, we simply select the word to be changed and retype the correction. The same idea is used to make small corrections or insertions to the text. For example, move the mouse and drag it over the "i" in "Simple." Remember, if you don't do it correctly the first time, don't panic. Simply click somewhere else in the program window and try again. Your window should appear as in figure 2.25.

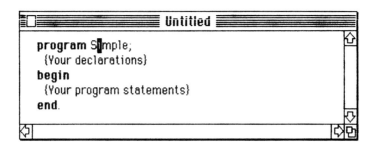

Figure 2.25

Now type an "a" and presto, program "Simple" has become program "Sample" with the cursor flashing between the "a" and the "m." By typing the backspace key, we can erase the "a" and retype the "i" to restore the name "Simple." That is, another way to make corrections is to use the mouse to place the cursor after the text to be changed, then backspace over the text and then type the new material.

As an exercise, use this method to change "program" to "procedure" and then back to "program" again. Insertions are just as easy. Position the cursor after "Simple" and then type "ton" to change the program name to "Simpleton." Deleting text is also easy. To delete "ton" from "Simpleton," you may either position the cursor behind the "ton" and then backspace three times, or you may highlight "ton" by dragging the mouse across it and then type the backspace once. Obviously, the latter method is more useful for making large deletions. To illustrate, let us delete the phrase "{Your variable declarations}" from the program. To do so, position the cursor behind the phrase and drag the mouse to the left and up a little bit. The window should appear as in figure 2.26.

By dragging the mouse across a line you highlight that line. By dragging the mouse up or down you highlight or select entire lines. Now hit the backspace key and your program should appear as in figure 2.27.

Remember, if you accidently select the wrong phrase, just click somewhere else in the window and try again.

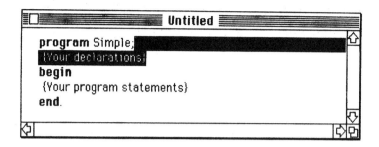

Figure 2.26

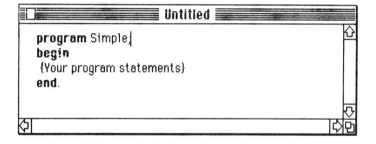

Figure 2.27

Let's try it again, this time deleting the phrase "{Your program statements}". However, this time select only the given line by dragging the mouse from the left brace to the right brace, and then hit the backspace key. See figures 2.28 and 2.29. Notice that this time the deletion left a blank line in the text with the cursor flashing on this line. This is the subtle difference between figures 2.26 and 2.28: In figure 2.26 we selected and subsequently deleted the line return as well as the given line. Note that in the current case, if we want to, we can eliminate the blank line by typing a few backspaces.

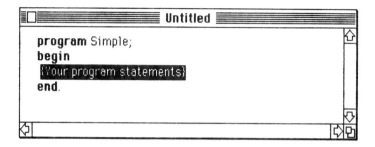

Figure 2.28

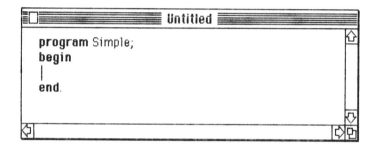

Figure 2.29

Now it is time to finally enter our simple first program. Position the cursor after the first line and type in the declaration for the variable "Name". That is, type "var" followed by the Return key, and then type "Name: string[30];". You do not need to worry about indenting the lines as shown in the listings or about the boldface type of certain words. Simply type the lines. When you type the semicolon at the end of the line, the line will jump to its proper indentation and the system will take care of boldfacing. Then position the cursor after the "**begin**" and enter the four given lines. Please type them carefully, noting the punctuation with special care. That is, don't forget the parentheses, use single quotation marks, and place a semicolon after every line except the last. If you make any typographical errors, correct them with backspacing or by mouse as explained above. Figure 2.30 shows the program in progress. Note that the last "Writeln" statement has not yet jumped to its proper indentation and that there is something wrong in the **var** section of the program. Whenever you see text in the program window in outline form, you can be sure you have committed some Pascal syntax error. In this case, we accidentally left the "a" out of "var". To fix the problem, we place the cursor between the "v" and the "r" and type the "a" followed by the **Enter** key. The purpose of the Enter key is to ask the system to do a new syntax check of the given line. If it finds no errors in the line, then it indents and formats the line to the proper specifications. Figure 2.31 shows the complete program. Make sure that your program is exactly like ours! Note that we have capitalized our variable, "Name," as well as the first letter of each statement. This is simply a matter of preference, but we believe that it makes programs more readable.

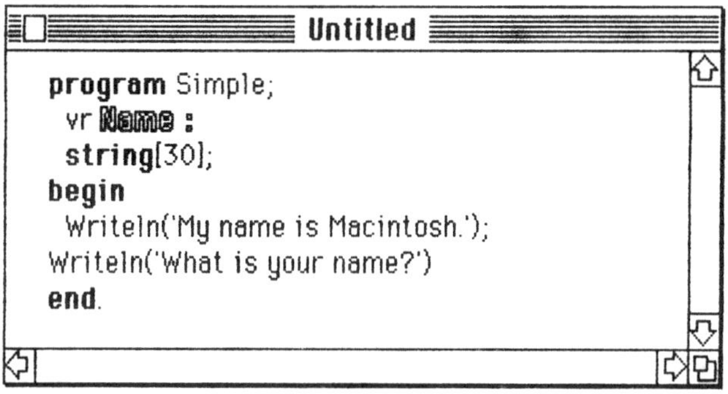

```
program Simple;
  vr Name :
  string[30];
begin
  Writeln('My name is Macintosh.');
  Writeln('What is your name?')
end.
```

Figure 2.30

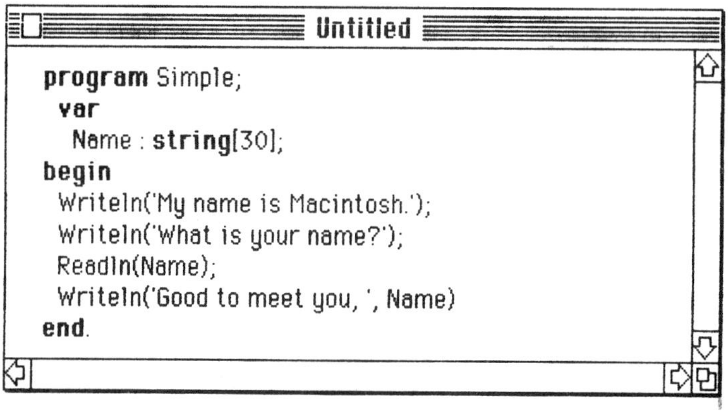

```
program Simple;
  var
    Name : string[30];
begin
  Writeln('My name is Macintosh.');
  Writeln('What is your name?');
  Readln(Name);
  Writeln('Good to meet you, ', Name)
end.
```

Figure 2.31

Recall that when text is highlighted, it can be deleted by typing the backspace key. If you refer again to figure 2.12, you see that the entire program shell appears highlighted when you boot (startup) Macintosh Pascal. By typing a backspace, you can delete the entire shell and begin with a blank program window. This is a matter of preference, but some find it easier to type in the entire program rather than edit the shell.

Saving Programs and Initializing Disks

Even before we run our program, let's save it to the disk. Once it is saved to the disk we will be able to recall it at will. (See the section on loading programs from disk.) Right now our program is vulnerable. Should the power fail, our valuable program would be lost and we would have to type it in again. This is because the program is currently only stored in the volatile memory of the computer. This memory fails when the power is turned off. However, saving the program to disk creates a version stored electromagnetically (much like music is stored on tapes), which will not be disturbed when the power is disconnected. Another reason to save our program before we run it is that novice programmers have been known to write such confusing instructions that they "hang" the computer. That is, the computer seems to go out for lunch and never comes back. The computer will not respond to any command, either from keyboard or mouse. The only way to proceed is to reset the computer (see the section below on the reset button) and start over. If your program hasn't been saved, you will need to retype it.

When programs become longer, a word to the wise is always save your new version every fifteen minutes or so. That way you never lose more than fifteen minutes worth of work. Every campus or office has horror stories about people who failed to heed this advice and lost hours of work.

To save our program, we pull down the **File** menu and choose the **Save As** option as shown in figure 2.32. This presents us with a dialog box similar to the one shown in figure 2.33.

At this point, there are several possibilities. If you have two drives, then, by clicking on **Drive**, you make the other disk the active disk. The name of the disk to which the save will be made is shown above the **Eject** box. (If you have only one drive, the **Drive** option will not appear in your dialog box.) Here, we will assume that you have one disk drive and want to save your programs on another diskette, rather than the Pascal system diskette that is now in the machine. If you wish to save your program temporarily on the system diskette, proceed to the discussion concerning figure 2.37.

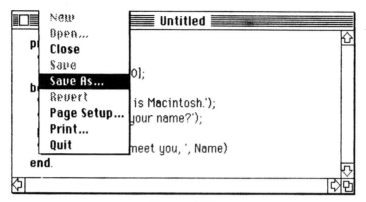

Figure 2.32

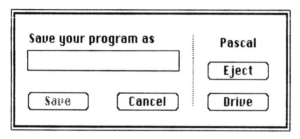

Figure 2.33

To switch diskettes, point to the **Eject** box and click. In a few seconds the Macintosh Pascal diskette will be ejected. Insert the diskette that you would like to save your programs on. If your diskette has never been used before you will see a dialog box as in figure 2.34. If your diskette has already been initialized, meet us at the discussion concerning figure 2.37.

Respond to figure 2.34 by clicking inside the **Initialize** box. The disk will whirl for a couple of minutes as the sytem prepares the diskette for use. You can think of initialization as the "drawing" of boundaries on the disk so that the system will later be able to store and retrieve information from the disk.

At the completion of the process you should see the dialog box shown in figure 2.35. Type the name that you would like this disk to have. In figure 2.36 we have given the disk the name "Programs". After naming your disk, click the **OK** box as shown in figure 2.36.

Figure 2.34

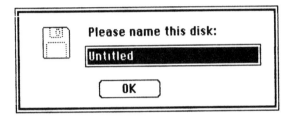

Figure 2.35

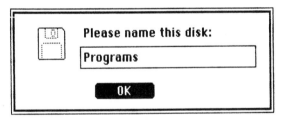

Figure 2.36

Your dialog box should now appear much as in figure 2.37 (which is also like figure 2.33). The name of the diskette, or a portion of it, will be displayed above the **Eject** box. Of course, if you have two drives, the **Drive** option will also be available.

The **Cancel** box is there in case you suddenly remember one more change that you need to make to your program before you save it. **Cancel** will take you back to the program window where you can make your change, then start the save process again. Notice that the **Save** option in figure 2.37 is grey rather than black. This indicates that **Save** is not currently one of your possible options. How, says the system, can I save your program before you give me a name for it? Hence, take the keyboard in hand and enter some name for this program. Notice as you type that the **Save** option becomes active by turning black instead of grey. As shown in figure 2.38, we have entered the name "Simple" for this program.

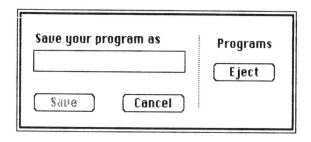

Figure 2.37

Figure 2.38

For your own sanity, we suggest that you name your programs on disk with the same names used in the **program** statement of the program listing. We will follow this advice in this text so that if you look at a listing you will know how to find the program on the sample disk that is available for this book and vice-versa. Note that the system does not care what name you give to the program. You may call this program "Complex" if you feel that way about it. Whatever name you've chosen, click on the **Save** box and your program will be saved to disk. With a one drive system, you will also be prompted to reinsert the Macintosh Pascal disk into the machine. Finally, your screen should clear of dialog boxes and look like figure 2.39. Note that now the "Untitled" line has been replaced by "Simple."

```
program Simple;
  var
    Name : string[30];
begin
  Writeln('My name is Macintosh.');
  Writeln('What is your name?');
  Readln(Name);
  Writeln('Good to meet you, ', Name)
end.
```

Figure 2.39

While we are on the subject of saving programs, let's pretend that we have made some changes to our program and want to save the new version of "Simple." To do so, we pull down the file menu and choose **Save as** again. This time we get the dialog box of figure 2.40. That is, now the system knows that our program has been saved as "Simple." If we wish we can change this name to "Simpler" or whatever.

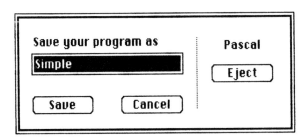

Figure 2.40

If we change the name then the disk will keep both versions of our program. We may at some time want to keep various versions of a program, but keeping each version of a program under a different name will quickly fill up your disk. Hence, we will usually save the program under the same name. Don't forget to eject the disk or click **Drive** if you want to save your program on another disk. On a one drive system, after inserting our disk Programs, the dialog box should appear as in figure 2.41.

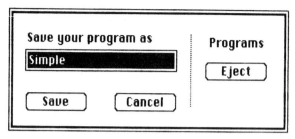

Figure 2.41

Now click **Save**. Since there is already a version of "Simple" on this diskette, the system seeks confirmation before destroying the first version and replacing it with the second version. This dialog box is shown in figure 2.42.

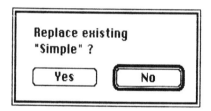

Figure 2.42

Note that the **No** box of figure 2.42 is much more prominent than the **Yes** box. The reason for this is that if you are lost and not sure of what you are doing, the **No** box is the safe box to choose. The **Yes** box will destroy the current version of your program and could replace it with junk if you didn't know what you were doing. We know what we are doing, so we choose **Yes** by clicking it. This saves our new version of "Simple" and returns control to figure 2.39, after asking us to reinsert the Macintosh Pascal disk.

Running and Simple Debugging of Programs

Finally it's time to run our marvelous program. First, we need to bring the "Text" window to the top. We accomplish this, of course, by clicking anywhere in the portion of the "Text" window that sticks out from behind the program window. Your screen should now look much like figure

2.43, except that your program and text windows are probably larger than ours. To save space in our figures, we have reduced both windows as much as possible and are showing only the top portion of the screen.

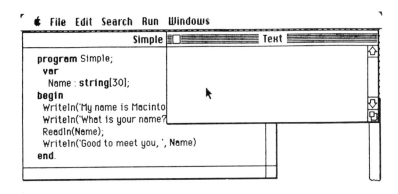

Figure 2.43

If you forget to bring the text window to the top, your program may well run, but you may not see any of the output. No real harm is done, but you will have to click the text window to the top.

To run the program, hold down the **Run** menu and select the **Go** option as shown in figure 2.44.

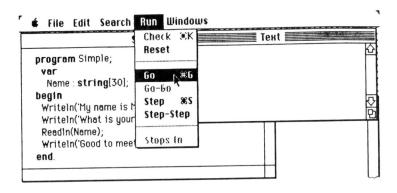

Figure 2.44

If you haven't made any typing mistakes, your text window should begin to show output from the program. Respond to the question and then push the Return key. If your program has an error in it, you will see an error message box at the top of the screen (as in figure 2.47). If you get an error message, click in the message box (after studying it), then click in the program window, make any necessary corrections, and try again. Below we introduce some intentional errors so that you will see how the system responds to them. Assuming that you have no errors, your final output should appear somewhat as in figure 2.45.

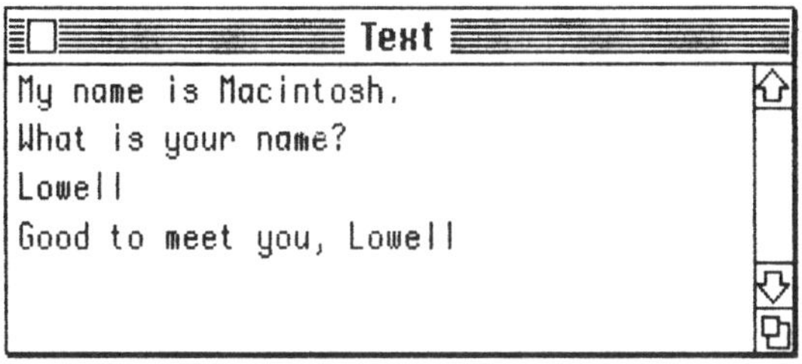

```
┌─────────────────── Text ───────────────────┐
│ My name is Macintosh.                     ⇧ │
│ What is your name?                          │
│ Lowell                                      │
│ Good to meet you, Lowell                    │
│                                           ⇩ │
│                                           ⊡ │
└─────────────────────────────────────────────┘
```

Figure 2.45

As an exercise in debugging, let's place some errors in our program and see how the system responds. If you were not successful in getting your program to run, then keep reading. We hope this section will help you find and eliminate those "bugs" in your program.

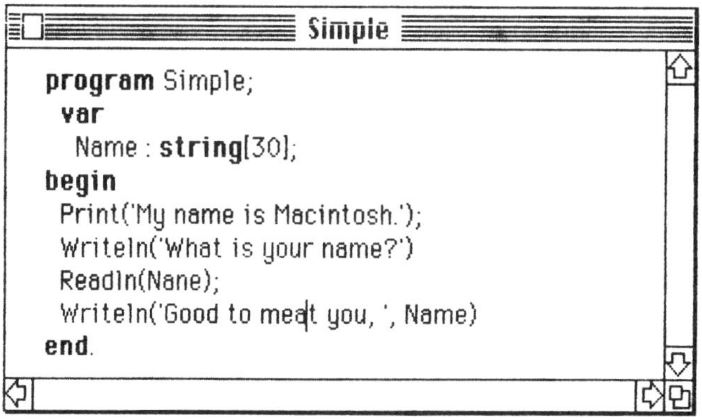

```
┌─────────────────── Simple ──────────────────┐
│ program Simple;                           ⇧ │
│   var                                       │
│     Name : string[30];                      │
│   begin                                     │
│     Print('My name is Macintosh.');         │
│     Writeln('What is your name?')           │
│     Readln(Nane);                           │
│     Writeln('Good to meat you, ', Name)     │
│   end.                                    ⇩ │
│ ◁ ▭                                      ▷⊡ │
└─────────────────────────────────────────────┘
```

Figure 2.46

Let's agree to try the following errors in the program: In the first Writeln statement, we will accidentally write "Print" for "Writeln". In the second Writeln, we will forget the semicolon. In the Readln statement, we will spell "Name" as "Nane" and in the final statement, we will spell "meet" as "meat". To make these changes, first click in the program window to make it the active window, then use the mouse to move the cursor as necessary to make the required changes. Make sure your program appears as in figure 2.46

This time, let's not save this new version of the program, since, as we know, it really isn't an improvement. Hence, pull down the **Run** menu and **Go**. Your screen should appear as in figure 2.47. The "thumbs down" symbol appears by the first line after the **begin,** and the error message **"The name "Print" has not been defined yet"** appears near the top of the screen.

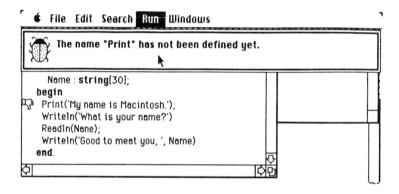

Figure 2.47

Learn to interpret error messages with a proper amount of scorn. What the computer is trying to say is that it doesn't know how to "Print." With a little practice you will learn to understand error messages. You may get plenty of practice on your own, but we also have included some buggy programs on the sample disk accompanying this book so that you can practice the important skill of debugging programs. In this case, the location of the "thumbs down" symbol and the message should be enough to jog our memory that in Pascal we use "Writeln" instead of "Print." To continue, click anywhere in the error box and the error message will disappear. Then use the mouse to move the cursor to the offending line and change the "Print" back to a "Writeln". As you enter the word Writeln, the "thumbs down" symbol should disappear from the line.

Pull down the **Run** menu and try **Go** again. This time you should get a small surprise. The "thumbs down" symbol is on the third line, not the second line, even though we know that the error is the missing semicolon on the second line. The error message, as shown in figure 2.48, however, indicates that the problem is with the previous line.

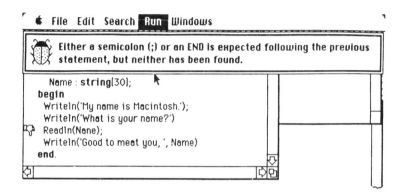

Figure 2.48

As we shall learn in the next chapter, the semicolon is used in Pascal to separate statements. Since we forgot the semicolon, a very common error for beginners, the computer thinks statements two and three are one statement. Thus, from this simple example an important moral should be learned. The "thumbs down" symbol does not always point to the line with the error on it. Learn to recognize this error message and keep in mind that a missing semicolon on the line above is a common cause of it.

To proceed, click in the error message and then insert the semicolon after line 2. Try **Run** and **Go** again. This time you should get the error message shown in figure 2.49.

As we shall also soon learn, in Pascal, every variable that is used in our program must be declared in the **var** section of the program. This time due to a typing error, we have a variable "Nane" that is not delcared in the **var** section. Of course, the problem is that "Name" was intended, but a typo gave us "Nane". Remember that the computer is a moron and treat its messages appropriately. The computer is saying that "Nane" is not defined and seems to want us to declare it. That would make the error go away, but it wouldn't make the program work properly since then there would be no connection between the variable "Name" as used in line four and the variable "Nane" as used in line three.

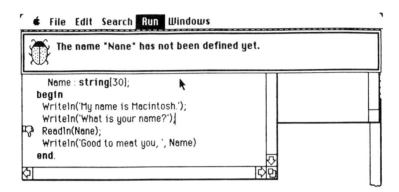

Figure 2.49

To proceed, click in the error message and then change "Nane" back to "Name". Try **Run** and **Go** again. If you've been following along with us, your program should run with no error messages, but you won't see anything because we forgot to bring the text window to the foreground. The best thing to do in this case is to choose **Pause** by clicking it with the mouse. The **Pause** option only appears during the execution of a program. Since your program was interrupted while waiting at the "Readln" for you to enter your name, you should get the message shown in figure 2.50.

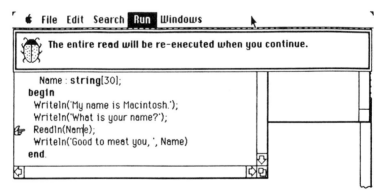

Figure 2.50

To continue, click in the message box and then click in the text window. You should now see the first part of the ouput as shown in figure 2.51.

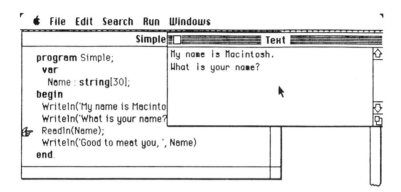

Figure 2.51

The hand is pointing at the "Readln" simply to indicate that it is the statement on which the execution was interrupted. At this point, there are two ways to proceed. If you choose **Go** from the **Run** menu, the program will resume execution from the "Readln" where it was previously interrupted. If you first choose **Reset** and then choose **Go** from the **Run** menu, then the hand will disappear, the text window will be cleared, and the program will execute from the beginning. That is, **Reset** resets the system so that the **Go** is a fresh start from the top rather than a continue from the current position. The other options from the **Run** menu will be explained later.

     We hope you were not too startled by the fact that the computer generated no error message regarding the misuse of the word "meat". As you have probably guessed, the computer prints anything that you put between single quotes. As long as you don't violate the syntax of the language, the computer doesn't care what kind of garbage it produces. However, your failure to spell one of Macintosh Pascal's keywords (like **program, begin,** or **writeln**) or failure to spell one of your own variables (like "Nane") will cause you a bit of grief. Your failure to spell even "McIntosh" correctly will go unnoticed as long as it is between single quotes.

Closing Windows and Files

Within the Pascal system, the "close box" is used to hide a window. To see this, click in the program window to make it the active window and then click in the small close box in the upper left corner of the window. The text window should become the active window and your screen should appear as in figure 2.52.

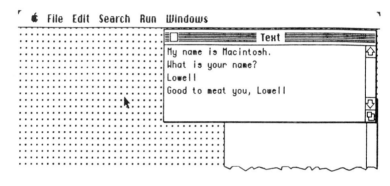

Figure 2.52

How, you ask, do we get the program window back? Pull down the **Window** menu as in figure 2.53.

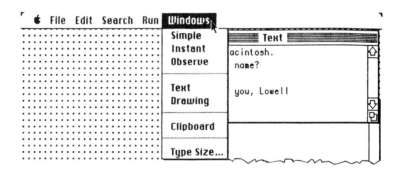

Figure 2.53

The first option is **Simple** (or **Untitled** or whatever your program has been saved as) and by selecting this option the program window is restored to the screen and made the active window. Notice that two of the other options are **Text** and **Drawing**, which likewise can be used to recover the text and drawing windows. **Instant** and **Observe** are two very powerful new windows that will be introduced later (after you learn some Pascal), while the **Clipboard** is a window where we can store things temporarily. **Type size** allows you to choose any of three different type sizes for the windows. Play with any of these options. Use the menu to restore windows; use the close boxes to hide windows. Eventually, restore at least the program window and make it the active window so that your screen appears as in figure 2.54.

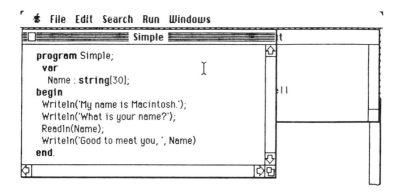

Figure 2.54

To leave the program "Simple" and go on to better things, we must pull down the file menu and choose the **Close** option as shown in figure 2.55.

Since we have made some changes to our program since we saved it, the system presents the helpful message shown in figure 2.56. That is, if the system simply closed the file as we had asked, any changes we have made would be lost. Here it is giving us a chance to save the latest version of our program. As shown by the shading, the expected response is **Save**. However, in our case, the current version is not an improvement (it has the misspelling "meat" in it), so we choose the **Discard** option. **Cancel** would, of course, cancel the command to close the file and return us to figure 2.54.

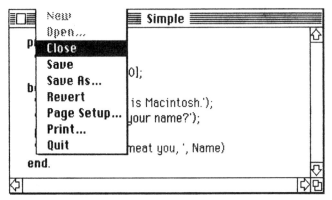

Figure 2.55

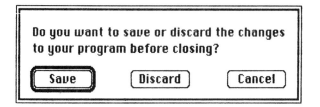

Figure 2.56

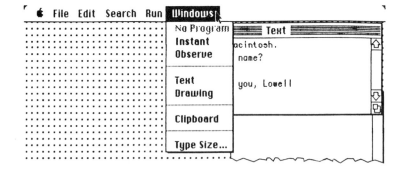

Figure 2.57

After choosing **Discard** or **Save,** the disk will hum for a few seconds and then the program window will disappear as above. The difference between the close box and the close option from the file menu is that the close box only hides the window while the close option from the file menu effectively removes the given program from the computer's memory (but not from the disk). To see that "Simple" can not be quickly recovered, try the **Window** menu. In grey, there is **No Program** available. See figure 2.57.

Loading Programs from Disk

We have now eliminated our old program "Simple." How do we continue? By pulling down the **File** menu we see there are three choices as shown in figure 2.58.

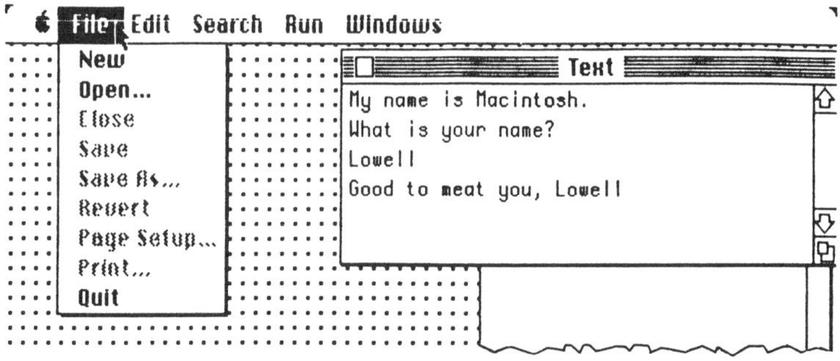

Figure 2.58

We may choose **New, Open...,** or **Quit. Quit** is our choice if we want to quit the Macintosh Pascal system. **New** is our choice if we would like to create our own new program. **Open...** is our choice if we would like to open or load one of the programs from the disk. For the present let's choose **Open** with the intent of loading the program "Buggy" from the disk accompanying this book. (If you do not have the disk, you can load one of the sample programs from the Macintosh Pascal disk.) After you select **Open...,** you should see a dialog box such as shown in figure 2.59. Don't worry if the names listed in the little window are not exactly the same. These are the sample Pascal programs provided on the Pascal diskette. By clicking the up and down arrows, you can make the window scroll up and

down so that you can see the other choices. Since we want to load a
program from another diskette, click on the eject window to eject the
Pascal diskette. Then insert the sample diskette that accompanies the
book. You should have a dialog box much like figure 2.60. Of course, if you
have two drives, you do not need to **Eject** the Pascal disk. Simply click on
Drive to see the programs on the other disk.

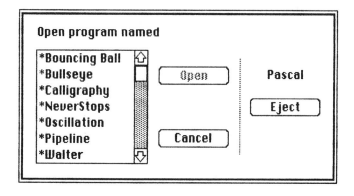

Figure 2.59

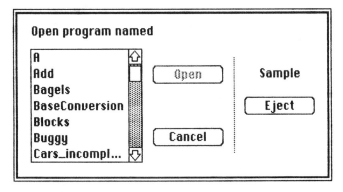

Figure 2.60

Note that the programs on the Sample diskette are listed alphabetically .
By scrolling up and down with the up and down arrows, you can see the
names of the programs on the Sample disk. For now, scroll back towards
the top and select "Buggy" by clicking on it as shown in figure 2.61.

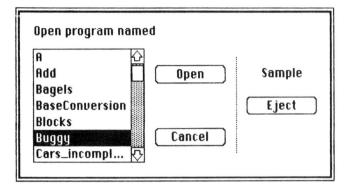

Figure 2.61

Now choose **Open** by clicking it and you will be asked to reinsert the Pascal system diskette. Then you will find yourself with "Buggy" loaded into the computer as shown in figure 2.62.

```
≣□≣≣≣≣≣≣≣≣≣≣≣≣≣ Buggy ≣≣≣≣≣≣≣≣≣≣≣≣≣≣
  program Buggy;
   var
     First : string;
  begin
    Writeln('What is your first name?');
    Readln(Fist);
    Writeln('Remember, ', First, ', we computers -');
    Writeln('even Macintoshes - are fast, accurate morons');
    Writeln('but you, while slow and errror prone,')
    Wirteln('are clearly a genius!')
  end.
```

Figure 2.62

The method just described for loading a program presupposes that Macintosh Pascal is already loaded into the computer. If you would like to begin a session by loading a particular program, then the following alternate method for loading a program may be useful. If the program you wish to load is on the Macintosh Pascal disk, then you simply need double click that program's icon to load it and Macintosh Pascal into the system. If the program you wish to load is on another disk, then proceed as follows. For simplicity we assume the program we wish to load is named "Buggy" and that it is on the disk named SAMPLE. Turn on the Macintosh and insert the Macintosh Pascal disk. Then eject (from the **File** menu) the Macintosh Pascal disk and insert SAMPLE. Open SAMPLE, if necessary, by double clicking its disk icon. Open the folder CH 2 by double clicking it and finally open "Buggy" by double clicking it. Follow instructions and reinsert Macintosh Pascal and the SAMPLE disk as requested by the computer.

Printing a Listing of a Program

You will probably want to keep listings of all your programs for quick reference. Sending a listing of the program in the program window to the printer is very simple. Simply pull down the **File** window and select **Print...** as shown in figure 2.63.

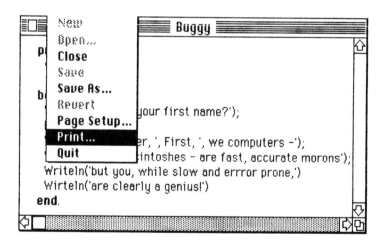

Figure 2.63

You will then see the dialog box shown in figure 2.64, which allows you to make various selections about the printing. For example, you may choose from three print qualities. The better the quality, the slower the printing. You may also choose to print all of the document or certain pages of the document, as well as choosing how many copies to print. You indicate whether you are using continuous fanfold computer paper or single, cut sheet paper. If you select **Cut Sheet**, then the printer will stop after each page and let you insert another page. Finally, select **OK** to begin the printing. After a brief pause and a message about saving the copy to disk, your program should be printed.

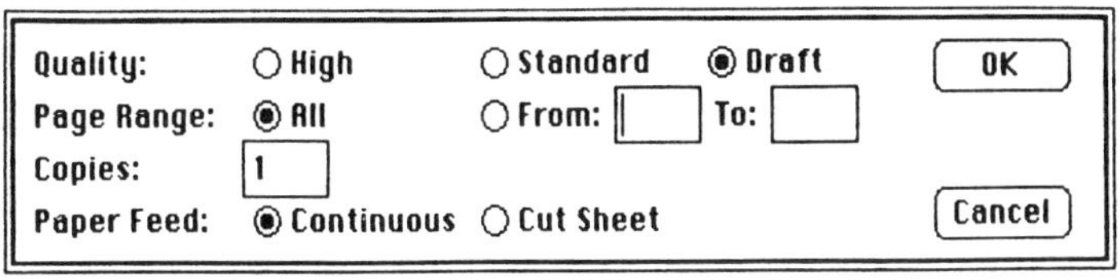

```
┌─────────────────────────────────────────────────────────────────────┐
│  Quality:      ○ High      ○ Standard   ● Draft       ┌──────────┐    │
│                                                       │    OK    │    │
│  Page Range:   ● All       ○ From: ‖    ‖ To: ‖    ‖  └──────────┘    │
│  Copies:       ┌─┐                                                    │
│                │1│                                                    │
│                └─┘                                    ┌──────────┐    │
│  Paper Feed:   ● Continuous  ○ Cut Sheet              │  Cancel  │    │
│                                                       └──────────┘    │
└─────────────────────────────────────────────────────────────────────┘
```

Figure 2.64

If you are using an ImageWriter printer, both the green "power" and "select" lights on the printer must be on, the red "paper error" light must not be on, and the cable between printer and computer must be properly attached. After the program in the program window is printed, your screen should return to figure 2.62.

In the next chapter, when you begin to write Pascal programs, we will show you how to get the program to send its output to the printer. For now, the following trick should suffice. After a program has executed, and the "Text" window is active, you may print the "Text" window by simultaneously pressing the **Shift, Fan,** and **4** keys. Make sure that the Caps Lock key is not down. (The **Fan** key contains the symbol ⌘ and is to the immediate left of the space bar.) This will print only the portion of the active window that is visible on the screen, not necessarily the complete output of the program. Nevertheless, this trick should work for now to provide you with hard copy of a program's output. We mention in passing that **Shift, Fan,** and **4** will print the active window while **Shift, Caps Lock, Fan,** and **4** will dump the entire screen to the printer.

Quitting Macintosh Pascal

The debugging of "Buggy" is left as an exercise. Here we demonstrate the method of exiting from Macintosh Pascal. Pull down the **File** menu and choose **Close**. Save any changes, if you've made any, to "Buggy" before closing the file. Now pull down the **File** menu and choose the **Quit** option. This should return you to figure 2.5, which is repeated here as figure 2.65. You may close the disk or leave it as it is. In any case, the final step is to choose **Eject** from the **File** menu as shown in figure 2.66.

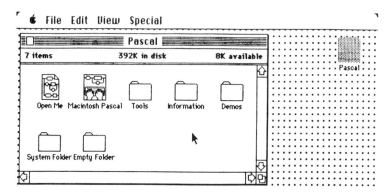

Figure 2.65

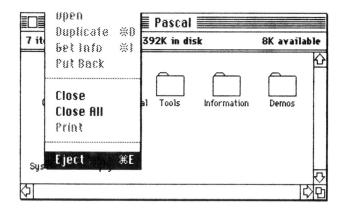

Figure 2.66

This will cause the system to eject the Pascal diskette. You may then power off the Macintosh and the printer.

Renaming Programs and Disks

You may at some time wish to change the name of one of your programs or even of your disk. The nice feature of the Macintosh is that the editing skills you have already learned apply to this new situation. Figure 2.67 shows the contents of our disk, Programs. Suppose we want to change the name of the program "Simple." As figure 2.67 shows, we have used the mouse to highlight "impl" in "Simple." Simply by typing backspace or any other character, we can edit the name of the program just like we would edit any other text on the Macintosh. Likewise, one can even edit the name of the disk by using these same procedures on the text below the disk icon.

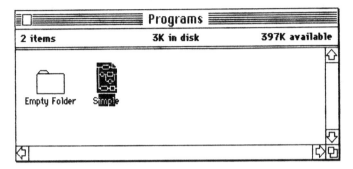

Figure 2.67

The Reset Switch

Your Macintosh is shipped with a reset switch that is not installed. If your reset switch has not been installed, we suggest that you have your dealer help you put it on. To find out whether your Macintosh has its reset switch in place, look on the left side of the computer. If your Macintosh has the switch, it will be near the back, lower corner of the left side. The purpose of the switch is to reset the computer should you bring it to its knees. A commercial program should be so well "idiot" proofed that the user cannot crash the system. On the other hand, a not-completely debugged student program may occasionally "hang" the system. If you ever lose your mouse, or the computer will not respond to any key, hit the reset switch to reboot the system and continue.

Final Words of Encouragement

We hope this introduction to the Macintosh operating system has been successful for you. You should work through the examples in the text with your Macintosh until you feel reasonably comfortable about the system. The entire system has not been presented in this chapter, but the subset of the system that we have discussed should be enough for the beginner to use to create, debug, run, save, and load simple programs. Later, we shall introduce cutting and pasting for quick editing of programs and we shall introduce powerful debugging aids. First, however, you need to learn some Pascal, and that is the subject of the next chapter (indeed, of most of the rest of this book).

As a final caution, consider the following situation. The user wants to save the program "Simple," which as you can see from figure 2.68 has run properly. But as you can also see, the **Save As** option of the **File** menu is not active. The system is not allowing the user to save the program. See if you can discern the problem before you read on.

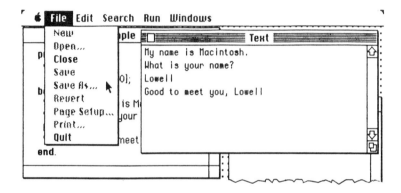

Figure 2.68

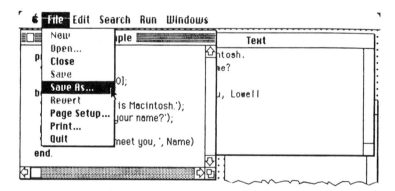

Figure 2.69

The problem is that commands usually apply only to the active window. In figure 2.68, the text window is the active window. The system doesn't save text windows, so **Save As** is not one of the possible commands that can currently be given. Remember this example! If the command that you want to give is not available, then that command does not currently apply.

The problem may well be that you need to make the program window active before the command makes sense. That is the problem, of course, in the given situation. If the user clicks anywhere in the program window, then **Save As** makes sense as shown in figure 2.69.

Exercises

2.1 Enter, debug, and run the following program Squares. Note, Squares is a correct program, so you will not need to debug it unless you add your own errors.

```
program Squares;
var
  Number, Square : Integer;
begin
  Writeln('Please enter a small whole number.');
  Readln(Number);
  Square := Number * Number;
  Writeln('The square of your number is ', Square)
end.
```

2.2 Make some intentional errors to your program Squares to see how the system reacts. In particular, omit the declaration of the variable "Square" in the **var** section, and change the ":=" of the third line after the **begin** to an "=" by itself. This last error is another common one for beginning programmers. Hence, it is a good idea to get used to the error message that it generates.

2.3 Load the program "Buggy" from the Sample disk into the computer (i.e., Open Buggy) and correct the errors in "Buggy" so that it runs and produces correct output.

Chapter 3

Beginning Pascal

> PROGRAM – A sequence of detectable and
> undetectable errors aimed at coaxing
> some form of response from the system.
> **Devil's DP Dictionary**

In this chapter, we will learn how to write computer programs in Pascal. A program is nothing more than a set of instructions that the computer carries out (or executes). Programs can in general be executed without human intervention, and it is this property that makes computers so useful and so much more powerful than calculators, which can of course do many of the things that a computer can do. For example, averaging three bowling scores is a simple task on a calculator. We enter the three scores, adding each one to the previous total and then divide by three. But a secretary of a bowling league might find this process a little tedious after handling dozens of bowlers. Since the process of averaging is the same regardless of the scores involved, it would be nice if we could "teach" our calculator how to average three numbers. Then, whenever we needed to prepare a league statistics sheet, we could provide the numbers to the calculator but we wouldn't have to keep repeating the add and divide instructions. This is essentially what computers (and some programmable calculators) can do.

To "teach" the computer how to do something, all we need to do is figure out for ourselves how this something is to be accomplished, and then communicate this to the machine in a language that it understands. Interestingly enough, while it is the second job that most people consider computer programming, it is the first task which is the most important. So we state here for emphasis a fundamental truth of programming: **The computer cannot solve any problem that the programmer, in principle, cannot solve first.**

Throughout this book, we will try to introduce methods whereby both of the above tasks can be learned. While Macintosh Pascal will be our vehicle for communicating with the Macintosh, we will use what are considered to be sound, general programming techniques that can be applied to nearly any other situation.

A Pascal Program

Because computers are unable to think and interpret the way humans do, when we communicate with them, we have to be very precise about how we say things and we must learn to obey exactly the rules of the language we are using. Pascal is no exception. This precise way of expressing a program is known as the **syntax** of the language, i.e., how programs are physically constructed, or even more specifically, what strings of letters, numbers, and punctuation marks constitute a legal Pascal program. We begin by looking at the overall structure of a Pascal program.

```
program Example;
begin
  Writeln('Here is a complete Pascal program.');
  Writeln('Even though I am just learning, I think');
  Writeln('I can figure out what it does.')
end.
```

Listing 3.1

Listing 3.1 is an example of a complete, but very simple Pascal program. There is a **heading**, which consists of the word **program** followed by the name of the program. The name is selected by the programmer, should start with a letter and then be followed by letters or numbers, and can be pretty much whatever we want except for some **reserved** words (or **keywords**), which mean special things in Pascal (like **begin, end, program**). A list of Macintosh Pascal reserved words is found in the Macintosh Pascal Reference Manual. The manual also indicates that "(Input, Output)" is required in the heading immediately after the program name. However, like many versions of Pascal, the inclusion of (Input, Output) is, in fact, optional. Note that the program name is followed by a semicolon.

Following the heading is the **body** of the program. The body begins with the keyword **begin** and ends with the keyword **end**. The keyword **end** may occur several times in a Pascal program, but there is always an **end** to mark the end of the program and this end must be followed by a period. In fact, this is the only time that **end.** should occur in a program.

Between the **begin** and **end.** of the body come the statements of the program. These statements are the instructions that the computer is supposed to carry out. The next several chapters of this book will introduce you to the kinds of statements that you can use in a Pascal program. There aren't that many, so it really doesn't take that long to master the Pascal syntax. This is the easy part of programming. There also aren't that many keywords to worry about. Most of the keywords do what they should, e.g., **begin** marks the start of something, **end** marks the end.

The first Pascal statement we will consider is the Writeln statement. Writeln is an example of an output statement and causes something to be written or printed to the Macintosh screen. It is Pascal's way of allowing us to get information out of a computer. In a Writeln, if we place something in parentheses between single quotes, the computer will print exactly what it sees. To emphasize how precise we need to be in programming languages, we point out that using regular quotation marks, "like this," instead of single quotation marks, 'like this,' will cause a syntax error, as will forgetting either parenthesis.

Every language has an output statement, but different languages may say things differently. So instead of Writeln, you might have to say Print or Put, but the effect is the same. Many beginners to programming ask why things have to be different. The answer is that different languages were designed by different people and there is no reason to expect that computer language designers as a group should be able to get along and agree on things any better than any other group of people. There are several brands of microwave ovens on the market, and their "keyboards" look very different, with ENTER keys and START keys and COOK keys that perform the same function. And as Steve Martin once pointed out in a comedy routine, "Those French have a different word for everything!" Actually, because computer languages are small and more uniform than most other forms of communication, the differences among them are easily overcome once we become programmers. Good Pascal programmers can learn BASIC in a few hours and FORTRAN in a few days. So the moral of the story is: **Learn the concepts. Mastering the language will then follow.**

If we expect programming languages to be logically designed, it is certainly fair to wonder a little bit about the choice of "Writeln" for writing something. What's wrong with Write? The answer to that is nothing. In fact, Write is the other type of output statement in Pascal. If all of this is supposed to be logical, why a Writeln *and* a Write? Remember that a program is generally run without human intervention. Many times, the output of a computer program is an extensive written report and the most important thing about the appearance of the report is its layout on the paper--for example, maybe in five columns across the page. Since programs are run without human intervention, we don't have anyone to throw the typewriter carriage for us to get to the next line. The computer has to know when to advance the output to the next line. But the computer doesn't know unless we tell it. That is what the 'ln' after the word Write does. It is simply a signal to the computer to move to a new line *after* it has written the Writeln message. Thus, the program in listing 3.1 should print out the quoted message on three lines while the program in listing 3.2 will print its message on two lines.

```
program Example_2;
begin
  Write('Now I see the difference between "write "');
  Writeln(' and "writeln"');
  Writeln('and will never confuse the two.')
end.
```

Listing 3.2

Figures 3.1 and 3.2 below show the output from the programs in listings 3.1 and 3.2 respectively.

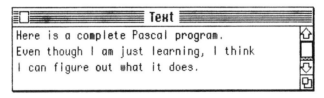

Figure 3.1

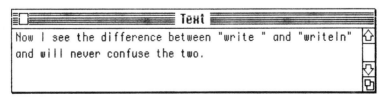

Figure 3.2

We point out that figures 3.3 and 3.4 also show output from the above two sample programs.

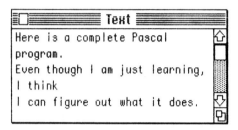

Figure 3.3

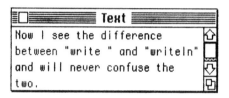

Figure 3.4

The reason for the differences in the figures is simply that the text window in the latter two figures is too narrow to hold a normal line of output. So the Macintosh will start a new line when it runs out of room. However, note that instructions conveyed by Write (don't move to a new line after printing) and Writeln (do move to a new line after printing) are still carried out. In the future we will assume that the text window is wide enough to allow for a normal line of output in our discussions. We also mention that if the text window is accidentally left too small, after the program has executed, the window can be stretched to a more normal size and the output will be automatically adjusted.

We, of course, will not discuss every aspect of Pascal in such agonizing detail. As we become more comfortable with the Macintosh and with Pascal, a few remarks will usually suffice. But there are two points to the above discussion:

1. Pascal (for the most part) is a well-designed language and there is usually a good reason for why things are done the way they are.

2. Even in these simple examples, you should be able to see that the "power" of these sample programs (i.e., when to start printing on a new line) is derived from the programmer *telling* the computer what to do and not vice versa.

We make one final comment about the syntax of the above examples. The body of a Pascal program consists of a sequence of statements. To *separate* one statement from the next, Pascal uses the semicolon. Notice that the last statement in each program does not have a semicolon after it. That is because the semicolon does *not terminate* statements (like the period does in English), but is used *between* statements. Although this seems like nitpicking, probably the most common syntax error made by beginning programmers is an error involving a semicolon. More will be said about this later when we deal with compound statements. For now, our programs will consist of a sequence of simple statements. Place a semicolon after each one except the last one.

Variables and Memory Locations

In this section we introduce the concept of a variable. This concept is the most important one for a beginning programmer to understand completely. Edsgar Dijkstra, a most important voice in the computer science community, said, "Once a programmer learns the concept of a variable, he has learned the quintessence of programming." We strongly concur with this sentiment, and in fact believe that it also applies to female programmers as well. Once you learn exactly how variables behave, you should have no trouble grasping the more complex features of programming.

We begin with the analogy of a simple calculator. Many hand-held calculators have a special button, usually called M or MEM or STORE, for storing a particular value. This is useful in the following type of situation:

Compute (123 + 456 + 789) / (987 + 654 + 321).

Note that we really have to compute several additions before we can even begin to think about performing the division. If we had a primitive calculator (with no Memory key), we might want to have a pencil and piece of paper nearby to help perform this calculation. We first add 987, 654, and 321, obtaining 1962. Then we clear the calculator, add 123, 456, and 789 to obtain 1368. So all we do is divide 1368 by, uh, let's see, what was the result of that first calculation? I forgot, so I'll do it again. That's right, 1962. So I divide 1962 into, uh, now I forgot the result of the other calculation. With a pencil and paper, we could at least write down the 1962, then when we do our second set of additions, we simply look at the paper to find our divisor. But how much simpler this becomes if our calculator has a Memory key. We do the first calculation and *store* the answer using the M key. The calculator will remember this result for us. For the time being, the M key can help us get this result back. That is, we can imagine that M equals 1962. Now after we add 123, 456, and 789, we simply instruct the calculator to divide this sum by M. No pencil, no paper, no repeating any calculation. Our memory is not so good, so we use the calculator's memory.

If you followed the above example, you should appreciate how convenient it is that the calculator had a memory, even though maybe it could only remember one number for us. In fact, it doesn't take us very long to wish our calculator could remember two numbers for us. Consider the computation

(321*987 - 123*789) / (123 + 456 + 789).

If we had two memory keys, M1 and M2, we could add 123, 456, and 789 and store the result in M1. Then, we multiply 123 by 789 and store that result in M2. Finally, we multiply 321 by 987, subtract M2, and then divide that result by M1.

Of course, it is not long before our greed begins to show, and we think that the more memory locations we have, the more things we could do. Well, from a memory standpoint, computers are essentially like calculators. But computers have thousands and thousands (some even millions) of memory locations that we can use. In fact, when you hear people, mostly computer salespeople, talking about K's, as in 64K-machine, they are telling you how many RAM memory locations you have to work with. The Macintosh has at least 128K of RAM, so that should be enough to take care of us for awhile. All we have to do is learn how to use these memory locations. This is where variables come in.

Imagine a very large keyboard with keys M1, M2, M3, ... , M100, ... , M128000. Without the concept of variables, this is what we might be stuck with to handle the approximately 128,000 memory locations in the Macintosh. Like a calculator, the computer would keep track of the names of the locations for us. Not only would the keyboard be rather awkward, but we might also have a hard time remembering whether we put the calculation that we did five minutes ago in M3478 or in M3487. The power of variables is that the computer allows us to call the memory locations anything we want! In other words, **a variable is just a name for a memory location**. While this may seem like a small breakthrough, it is precisely this idea that makes programming so accessible. Now, when we want to save a piece of information, we think up a name for where this information should be stored. Then when we want this information back, all we have to do is remember the name. The important point here is that *we, the programmers,* are allowed to select the name. So if we are computing how much money we spent last month on recreation, we could store our subtotals in memory locations called Movies, Restaurants, and Skiing instead of locations like M1, M2, and M3.

Variables in Pascal

In Pascal, variable names must start with a letter and then be followed by letters, numbers, or underscores. The underscore in variable names serves the purpose of a blank space, which is not allowed to appear in variable names. So First Name is an illegal variable, but First_Name is legal. Again, we must avoid using the reserved words of the language. Beyond that restriction, and an occasional restriction on how long a variable can be (for example, no longer than 255 characters on the Macintosh), our choices for variable names are unlimited. Because of this freedom of choice, we state a very important principle for good programming. This principle is one of the easiest to obey and yet one of the most abused: **Use descriptive variable names!** While this may seem like an unimportant rule for some of our early, short programs, this principle is indispensable in dealing with long complex programs over a long period of time. Computer programs are documents that are meant to be read by other people. So although the computer doesn't care whether we use variable names like M1, M2, and M3 or Principle, Interest, and Payment, the human reader (maybe even a grader) will be most appreciative of the latter choices.

The Assignment Statement

With a calculator, we store a value in memory by pushing the Memory key. In a programming language, we give values to variables by using an assignment statement. The syntax of the assignment statement in Pascal is:

<variable> := <expression>

where the left hand side is a legal variable name and the right hand side is some expression resulting in a value. For the time being, think of <expression> as being any arithmetic expression. The Macintosh Pascal Reference Manual contains the complete set of syntax rules for Pascal. These rules prescribe precisely how syntactically legal Pascal statements and programs are formed.

While the syntax can be described quite precisely, the **semantics**, that is, the meaning, of most Pascal constructs is expressed in English. The assignment statement has the following semantics: The <expression> is evaluated and the resulting value is assigned to the memory location with the name <variable>. Let us consider some examples. Suppose that Result is the name of a variable that can be assigned integer values. Then Result := 7 would assign the value 7 to Result while Result := 2*(3+2) would assign the value 10 to Result, since in Pascal (and most other languages), * is the multiplication symbol. If Result is currently equal to 10, then Result := Result + 2 would assign the value 12 to Result. Finally, if Number were another variable currently equal to 6 and if Result were currently equal to 12, then Result := 3*Result - 2*Number would assign the value 24 to Result.

It is important to realize that the assignment operator in Pascal is ":=" and not just the equal sign. Think of this as one symbol and do not put a space between the colon and the equal sign. The assignment statement simply assigns a value to a variable; it does *not* make any assertion about equality. Many other languages use the equal sign alone as the assignment operator, resulting in the following kind of assignment statement:

Result = Result + 1

This is often read "Result equals Result plus 1." Of course, Result does *not* equal Result plus 1. Result equals Result. Instead you should read an assignment operator as "becomes" or "is assigned." So in Pascal, read

Result := Result + 1

as "Result is assigned the value Result plus 1." All an assignment statement ever does is give a new value to the variable on the left hand side of the assignment operator.

Variable Types

In the above examples, we assumed that Result and Number were variables that held integer values, that is, whole numbers. Such variables are said to be of **type** integer. There are other types available to the Macintosh Pascal programmer. We will mention two of them now. In later chapters we will examine other types and eventually we will see how a programmer can define new types.

The other types we consider now are the real type and the string type. Real variables, like integers, also hold numeric values, but these values do not have to be whole numbers. Computers generally have two ways of expressing real numbers. The first way is using standard decimal notation, e.g., 2.5, 3.14159, 1.414, and so on. The other way is called **scientific notation** (or E notation). This method is used to handle very large numbers (the number of inches to the sun) or very small numbers (the weight, in pounds, of a politician's brain). Rather than writing a number that requires many digits, scientific notation allows us to specify how many digits to the right or left the decimal point should be moved to give us the actual number.

Examples: The speed of light is 186,000 miles per second, or 5,865,700,000,000 miles per year. In scientific notation, these numbers are written as 1.86E5 miles per second, or 5.8657E12 miles per year, where E5 means "move the decimal point 5 places to the right" and E12 means "move the decimal point 12 places to the right."

The mass of an electron is 0.00000000000000000000000000911 grams. This is much easier to write as 9.11E-28, where E-28 means "move the decimal point 28 places to the left."

A few general comments are in order. Because computers can only represent a finite number of objects, there is a limit to how many numbers can be represented on a computer. The limitations concerning real numbers are discussed briefly in Chapter 8. Integer variables on the Macintosh are limited to values from -32767 to +32767. While this range may be different for other computers, all versions of Pascal have a built-in constant, called **Maxint**, which represents the largest possible integer value. So on the Macintosh, Maxint is an integer constant that equals 32767.

When writing numbers on a computer, *do not* use commas. Commas serve a purpose in Pascal, but it is not to make numbers easier to read. Also, when using scientific notation, it is standard practice to express the number between 1 and 10 and then indicate the number of places to move the decimal point. However, this is not required. So we could also say that the mass of an electron is 91.1E-29 or 0.911E-27 grams. Furthermore, not all real numbers must have a decimal point. 1E34 is an example of a real number with no decimal point. But all real numbers with decimal points must have at least one digit on each side of the decimal point. Thus, .5 and 3. are examples of illegal real numbers. These number should be written as 0.5 and 3.0 respectively.

Because modern computers deal as much with character information as with numbers, it is also convenient to have variables that hold alphabetic information as opposed to numeric information. The string type is the simplest example of this. (Although Standard Pascal does not have a string type, most versions of Pascal provide one. In Chapter 10, we will see how we could get by without a string type, but throughout this book, we will use the string type freely.) A string value in Pascal is nothing more than a sequence of characters. When we explicitly write the values of strings in programs, we enclose them in single quotes. For example, the following two Pascal segments have the same output (assuming Str is a variable of type **string**):

Writeln('This is an example of a character string.');

Str := 'This is an example of a character string.';
Writeln(Str);

Each of the above segments will cause the quoted sentence to be printed. Note that the object of an output statement can be a variable name. In this case, the *value* of the variable is printed. In general, the object of a write statement can be a variable, a constant (i.e., a number constant like 7 or a string constant like 'Seven'), an expression (for now think of an arithmetic computation), or any sequence of these separated by commas (now we see a use for the comma in Pascal). The program segment in listing 3.3 illustrates various output statements, where we suppose Num1, Num2, and Num3 are integer variables while Str1 and Str2 are string variables.

The statements in listing 3.3 will produce the output shown in figure 3.5. Observe that the numbers from the first output statement are printed right justified in columns of width 8. Notice how 'Writeln;' by itself is used to force a blank line to appear in the output. Finally, make sure you see how the blanks are placed between the words "sentence" and "Strings" in the last line.

```
Num1 := 1;
Num2 := 2;
Num3 := 3;
Str1 := 'Strings can be used to label output.';
Str2 := 'If you want to insert spaces, do it between quotes';
Writeln(7, Num1, Num2 + Num3);
Writeln(Str1);
Writeln(Str2);
Writeln('Str1 is the sentence:', Str1);
Writeln;
Writeln('Str1 is the sentence:  ', Str1)
```

Listing 3.3

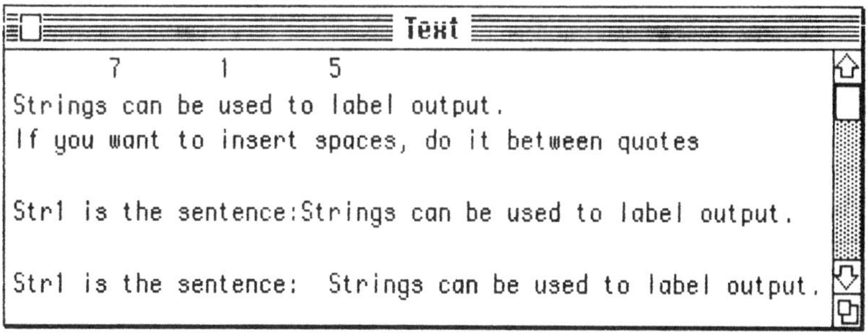

Figure 3.5

To see that you really understand variables and output statements, do you know what the output of the following segment is?

```
Num := 5;
Writeln(5);
Writeln(Num);
Writeln('Num')
```

The answer is:

```
        5
        5
Num
```

Note the different manner in which the system "formats" strings and integers. Soon we will learn to format these to our own specifications. If you do not understand exactly how the above three lines of output were produced, you should go back and reread the preceding discussion.

The var Section

Now that we know about variables and types, it is time to add to our Pascal programs. Pascal is a **strongly typed** language. To the beginning programmer, this means several things:

1. Each variable must have a single type throughout the program.
2. The values that are assigned to variables must be compatible in type. For example, an integer variable cannot be assigned the real value 2.54.
3. The programmer must explicitly declare at the beginning of each program the names of the variables that will be used and their types.

The explicit declaration of variables comes after the program heading and before the program body. The declaration section begins with the reserved word **var**. Following this come all the variable declarations. A variable declaration consists of a list of variable names (separated by commas), followed by a colon and the name of the type (either integer, real, or string for now). The variables can be declared in any order. It is important that every variable that is used in the program be declared and that no variable be declared more than once. A semicolon follows every declaration, including the last one.

Suppose we are writing a program called Printing with integer variables Num1, Num2, and Num3, real variables Score1 and Score2, and string variables Word1 and Word2. Then each of the **var** sections shown in listings 3.4 and 3.5 shows a proper way to declare these variables. That is, there can be more than one integer, real, or string declaration, and these can be in any order.

```
var
   Num1, Num2 : Integer;
   Score1, Score2 : Real;
   Word1, Word2 : string;
   Num3 : Integer;
```

Listing 3.4

```
var
   Num3 : Integer;
   Word1 : string;
   Score2 : Real;
   Score1 : Real;
   Num2 : Integer;
   Word2 : string;
   Num1 : Integer;
```

Listing 3.5

When string variables are declared as above, the Macintosh will reserve space for 255 characters. If we don't need that much space, we can specify how much we need by placing a number in square brackets after the word **string**. For example, Word1 : **string**[20]; would reserve space for a string of length 20. We will study strings in detail in Chapter 14.

While strong typing places a responsibility on the programmer to inform the computer what variables will be used, any inconvenience the programmer experiences is offset by the capability of the Pascal system to detect spelling errors in the names of variables. For example, BASIC is not a strongly typed language. Comment on the output of the following BASIC program (which uses only BASIC assignment and output statements):

```
10  LET N1 = 7
20  LET N2 = 3
30  LET N3 = 8*N2 - 3*N1
40  PRINT N3
```

This program produces the output:

24

Do you agree with the output? If this were a thousand-line program with hundreds of computations, would you agree with the output? If the value for N1 were 0.03768 and the value for N2 were 34.78654, how would you know to be suspicious of the output? If you were suspicious, would you perform all the calculations by hand? If so, why write a program in the first place? Actually, the intended output is 3 so you were right to disagree. The program above has an error in that N1 ("N ONE") is given a value in line 10, but in the calculation in line 30 we accidentally use Nl ("N

LOWER CASE L"). Languages like BASIC, which are not strongly typed, usually assign a value of 0 to Nl and proceed merrily on their way. While this may seem like a contrived situation, this error actually occurs fairly often, particularly with programmers who learned to type several years ago. Earlier typewriters did not have a 1 key and in fact it was proper to use the lower case L to represent a 1. In general, any spelling error that you make with variable names in BASIC is undetected and erroneous results are sure to follow.

The same mistake in Macintosh Pascal would produce the following message:

The name "Nl" has not been defined yet.

So instead of a program that runs, produces erroneous output, and lets us hunt for the error, we get a message from the system that allows us the chance to correct our program and obtain reliable results.

The fact that some languages automatically assign a value of zero to numeric variables (and blank spaces to string variables) is worthy of comment because such a policy can lead to some sloppy programming habits. Standard Pascal requires the programmer to explicitly **initialize** variables in the program before using them. Many beginners believe this means setting all variables equal to zero. This is not the case unless a zero is the desired initial value. Initialization of variables simply means the following: The first time a variable is used in a program, it should appear *only* on the left hand side of an assignment statement or as the object of a **Read** or a **Readln** statement (see Chapter 4). If you follow the above practice, no matter which language you use for programming, you are taking matters into your own hands and making sure that variables have the desired initial values and not values assigned automatically by the system (or worse, "leftover" values from previous calculations). Some versions of Pascal (unfortunately, Macintosh Pascal automatically initializes numeric variables to zero) will report an error if you forget to assign an initial value to a variable. While such actions may seem like a bother to some programmers, this is just a case of the system trying to protect us from ourselves.

A feature of Macintosh Pascal that is seldom found in other versions of Pascal is the automatic formatting of programs. That is, the system is very helpful in making Pascal programs appear neatly on the page. Macintosh Pascal automatically boldfaces reserved words for us, places each statement on its own line, and provides a standard indentation scheme to make programs more readable. (Although it is not technically a reserved word, Macintosh Pascal also boldfaces the word "string".) We may insert spaces at will as long as we don't insert spaces into variable names or in the middle of the assignment symbol. The system will adjust our typing to a standardized format with regard to spacing. Additionally, we mention that the Macintosh interpreter doesn't really care whether we type in upper case, lower case, or a mixture of the two. To see the helpfulness of the Macintosh system, try to type in the following example program, which averages three exam scores, just as you see it here:

```
program sloppy;
var x1,x2,x3
:real;x4:real;begin
x1:=67.5;x2:=57.8;x3
:=78.2;x4:=(x1+x2+x3)/3;
writeln(x4) end.
```

While the above program is legal in standard Pascal, note in listing 3.6 the nice appearance provided by the Macintosh system.

If this program is in fact a program to average three quiz scores, the choice of variable names is poor. Even the helpful Macintosh system can't provide any assistance with this problem. It is entirely up to the programmer to choose meaningful variable names. We prefer the version in listing 3.7.

```
program sloppy;
 var
   x1, x2, x3 : real;
   x4 : real;
 begin
   x1 := 67.5;
   x2 := 57.8;
   x3 := 78.2;
   x4 := (x1 + x2 + x3) / 3;
   writeln(x4)
 end.
```

Listing 3.6

```
program Neat;
 var
   Quiz1, Quiz2, Quiz3 : real;
   Average : real;
begin
 Quiz1 := 67.5;
 Quiz2 := 57.8;
 Quiz3 := 78.2;
 Average := (Quiz1 + Quiz2 + Quiz3) / 3;
 Writeln(Average)
end.
```

Listing 3.7

Arranging Output

In an earlier example, we saw that when we printed the three integer values 7, 1, and 5, each appeared right justified in a column of width eight. The width of eight is just the standard way of printing numbers in Macintosh Pascal and unless we ask for something different, this is what we will get. However, it is very easy to ask for output in some format other than the standard format, and this is an important step in making the results of computer programs easily readable.

Special formatting instructions are placed in output statements, i.e., in either Write or Writeln statements, and are specified immediately after the values that we want to format. For example, suppose we wanted the values 7, 1, and 5 to be printed in columns of width six. Then the following statement would accomplish this:

Writeln(7:6,1:6,5:6)

With integer values, simply follow the value to be printed with a colon and then the width of the printing field. If the number of digits to be printed is less than the field width, then the value is right justified. That is, blanks are inserted to the left of the value so that the total number of characters (blanks and digits) equals the field width. Of course, formatting instructions can also follow variables and expressions as well as constants. So if Num is an integer variable with current value 4926, then the following statements

```
Writeln(Num:4);
Writeln(Num:6);
Writeln(Num)
```

will produce the following output:

```
4926
  4926
    4926
```

If real numbers are formatted like integers, that is, with a specified field width, then they will be printed in scientific notation. We have found that scientific notation numbers are not right justified, but rather, are printed in the following strange format:

A blank is printed. Then (W-4) characters are printed, where W is the width specified. Finally, three trailing blanks are printed.

If we want real numbers to appear in decimal notation, we specify two values:

1. A total field width, that includes the decimal point
2. The number of digits to the right of the decimal point.

For example, suppose Pi is a real variable with value 3.1415926. Then these statements

```
Writeln(Pi);
Writeln(Pi:15);
Writeln(Pi:10);
Writeln(Pi:7:5);
Writeln(Pi:8:3)
```

will produce the following output:

```
 3.1e+0
 3.141593e+0
 3.1e+0
3.14159
   3.142
```

Note the three leading blanks in the last line and also note how the Macintosh rounded the value of Pi in each case to the given specifications. We will discuss the rounding of numbers later in the chapter.

We make one final remark concerning formatting of numbers. If you ask for a field width that is smaller than the actual width of the number to be printed, the system will still print all of the number. That is, if you ask for a five-digit number to be printed in a field of width four, the entire number will be printed, but the rest of your formatting on that line may be inconsistent. Of course, the inconsistency of formatting is preferable to getting only four digits of a 5-digit number.

Simple Arithmetic

Just like inexpensive calculators, we expect more powerful computers to be able to perform numeric calculations. In fact we have included such calculations in some of the previous examples. Because of the different types of numbers that Pascal allows, we need to be specific about some of the arithmetic operators. We first consider real numbers.

The standard operations of addition, subtraction, multiplication and division are denoted by +, -, *, and / respectively. For those readers who are familiar with an exponentiation operator (raising a number to a power), we remark that Standard Pascal has no built-in exponentiation. We shall see later that Macintosh Pascal provides a version of exponentiation, and we will also learn how to construct one ourselves. As in standard mathematical practice, there is a **precedence** of operations. Therefore, * and / have precedence over + and -. That means that multiplications and divisions are performed *before* additions and subtractions. If we want to change this order, we must group quantities in parentheses. Since * and / have equal precedence, those operations are performed left-to-right unless altered by parentheses. The same holds true for + and -. For example,

    3+4*5 is 23
    (3+4)*5 is 35
    12/6-4/2 is 2-2 or 0
    12/(6-4)/2 is 12/2/2, which is 6/2 or 3
    12/((6-4)/2) is 12/(2/2), which is 12/1 or 12

There are no restrictions on calculating with real numbers, except of course *do not* try to divide by 0. Someone new to computers should realize that the machine will occasionally introduce errors into calculations. There is a good explanation as to why this happens. There is an infinite number of real numbers, but even the largest computers can still represent only a finite number of these. Therefore, the computer has to approximate many numbers. Consider, for example, the number 1/3. Although the computer doesn't really use a decimal representation, we may think of 1/3 as being stored in the computer's memory as a decimal number. From elementary mathematics, we should know that 1/3 is *exactly* equal to .3333333..... where we have an *infinite* number of three's. However, the computer can approximate only 1/3 to a certain finite number of terms. Although this may be a very close approximation, there is still a slight error. As programs get more complex and thousands and thousands of computations are performed, these errors sometimes get magnified and results may become worthless. Although this is a real problem, especially to numerical analysts, we won't have to worry much about this while we are learning to program.

Now we turn to integers. The arithmetic operations are sometimes called **binary** operations because they take two inputs (for example, the numbers to be added) to produce an output (the sum). In a strongly typed language like Pascal, the binary arithmetic operations produce an output that is of the same type as the inputs. Note that this causes no problem with addition, subtraction, and multiplication; and, in fact, the same three symbols, +, -, and *, are used also with integers. But when we divide the integer 5 by the integer 2, what is the quotient? Another way of phrasing the question is, "How many times will 2 go into 5?" If we insist on an integer answer, then the only logical answer is 2.

When performing integer division, the / is replaced with **div** and the quotient is computed as above. In other words, we disregard any remainder in the division. So 10 **div** 3 is 3, 10 **div** 4 is 2, and 10 **div** 5 is 2. Note that this can cause some unusual results. Observe that in dealing with integers, the order of division and multiplication can be significant, since (14*6) **div** 4 is 84 **div** 4 or 21, while 14 * (6 **div** 4) is 14 * 1 or 14.

The rules for integer division involving negative numbers are demonstrated with the following examples:

   7 **div** (-3) is -2.
   -7 **div** 3 is -2.
   -7 **div** (-3) is 2.

Note that when the second operand is negative, then we must use parentheses. So we are allowed to write X * (-3) or -3 * x, but not X * -3. The reason again is the order of precedence of the arithmetic operators.

Although it appears that we lose something (namely the remainder) when we perform integer division, there is a way to retrieve the remainder when dealing with positive integers--the **mod** operation. This operation is a standard mathematical operation, and A **mod** B is defined to equal the remainder upon dividing A by B. So 17 **mod** 5 is 2. In Macintosh Pascal, A is allowed to be negative. B must always be positive. Even if A is negative, the result is always nonnegative and we no longer obtain the remainder. In fact, the result is equal to the remainder *plus* B. So -17 **mod** 5 is 3.

Conversion between Integers and Reals

For beginning programmers, there is often a great deal of confusion about how the two numeric types can be mixed. Technically, there shouldn't be any mixing if Pascal is truly a strongly typed language. But for convenience, there are a few times when types can be mixed. It seems proper to consider the set of integers as a subset of the set of real numbers. That is, an integer can be viewed as a real number whose fractional part just happens to be zero. However, it doesn't really make any sense to try and consider a real number, like 3.14159, as an integer. With this in mind, it should be easy to remember the following basic rules:

1. Integer values can be used where reals are expected, but not vice versa.
2. In performing a computation, real values and integer values can be mixed as long as the overall result is supposed to be real. However, when mixing, do not try to apply **div** or **mod** to real numbers.

To see why we might want to mix integers and reals, consider converting a Fahrenheit temperature to a Celsius temperature. The formula for doing this is Cels = 5/9 * (Fahr - 32). So if we start with a Fahrenheit temperature of 66, its Celsius equivalent will not be a whole number, but rather a decimal number. Suppose we wanted to compute the area of circle with a radius of 2 inches. Then we need to multiply PI (which is approximately equal to 3.14159) by 4 (the square of the radius). Again, we start with an integer, but expect a real result.

Now we give some examples that demonstrate the above rules. Because there is no context for the following statements other than to demonstrate the type mixing rules, we will temporarily allow ourselves to use short, nondescriptive variable names (since there is nothing to describe). So suppose I, J, and K are integer variables and A, B, and C are real variables. Then each of the next seven statements is legal:

```
I := 1;
J := 2;
K := 3;
A := 1;
B := 2.0;
C := I;
A := (A*I+(J mod K)/B)
```

Each of the following three statements is illegal:

```
I := 2.0;
J := B;
K := (A*I+(J mod K)/B)
```

What we have seen so far is that the computer will automatically convert integers to reals. There is no automatic conversion in the other direction, but sometimes we want to convert reals to integers. In this situation, we have to do the conversion explicitly. We do this with either of two built-in functions. The first of these is Round, and as its name implies, it rounds a real number to the nearest integer. So Round(3.4) is 3 and Round(3.7) is 4. Macintosh Pascal rounds 3.5 up to 4 and -3.5 down to -4. In general, Macintosh Pascal rounds the "halfway" numbers "away from zero," (that is, to the number of greater absolute magnitude). Other versions of Pascal might always round the "halfway" numbers "toward zero." Be sure to check this on other versions of Pascal.

The second operation is Trunc, which always chops off the fractional part of a real number (i.e., Trunc chops toward zero). So Trunc(3.7) is 3, Trunc(3.0) is 3, and Trunc(-3.7) is -3. Thus, if I and J are integer variables and X is a real variable, then the following two statements are legal:

```
I := Round(X);
J := Trunc(X)
```

We close this section by pointing out that there is more to the numeric types than we have explained in this chapter. We are just trying to get started, so we don't want to get lost in a forest of details. We will see in Chapter 8 that there are really different varieties of integers and reals. We will learn about the Macintosh's limits on how big or small numbers can be, and how precise the Macintosh is when dealing with the various kinds of numbers.

Commenting Programs

One of the most important jobs a programmer has is to make computer programs readable. This is not a difficult thing to do and we believe it is largely a matter of cultivating good programming habits. For example, one of the most important things that beginning programmers should learn is the value of choosing good variable names. Another good habit that has already been mentioned is producing clear output. This can be accomplished with ample labelling (using string constants to tell what results mean) and using the formatting capabilities of Pascal. Just as important, and often neglected, is the use of **comments** in programs. Comments are ignored by the computer--they are exclusively for humans. Comments in Pascal are enclosed in braces, { and }, and can occur at the end of any program line, or as a line by themselves. All programs should contain a heading comment stating such information as the author, date, and purpose of the program. For beginning programs, this may be all that is necessary. But as programs get longer and more complex, comments can also explain what is really going on in complicated parts of the program. We feel that it is extremely beneficial to get in the habit of using comments in every program.

In case the reader feels we are being overdramatic concerning readability, we quote some findings reported by Elshoff and Marcotty in the August, 1982 issue of "**Communications of the ACM**" (Association for Computing Machinery). Much of the information came from a survey of programmers for General Motors.

"About 75 percent of all programmers' time in a commercial data processing installation is spent on program modification."

"...it was found that most programs were poorly written. They were very large, extremely difficult to read, and more complex than necessary."

"A readable program always seems to exhibit a common set of properties. The program is well commented....Variable names are mnemonic."

"Comments can be the most important contribution that a programmer makes."

A Complete Example

Since all we currently have at our disposal are the assignment statement and the output statement, we conclude this introductory chapter with a couple of examples that require only these constructs. The first example is a series of three attempts to solve a simple problem. All three attempts do solve the given problem, but not all three are of equal quality. We hope the reader can recognize the better efforts and from them learn to write better programs. Also, the third solution introduces the important concept of a **constant**. We will make some remarks about constants after the example. The final example of the chapter is a bit more complicated and again demonstrates that it is the programmer, not the computer, who must solve the problem.

Example: Write a program to print out the area and circumference of a circle whose radius is 6.72 inches. Recall that the area of a circle is given by the formula Pi*R*R and the circumference of a circle is 2*Pi*R, where Pi is approximately equal to 3.14159.

Solution A: The first solution to this problem is found in listing 3.8 and produces the output of figure 3.6.

```
program A;
begin
  Writeln(2 * 3.14159 * 6.72 : 12 : 6, 3.14159 * 6.72 * 6.72 : 12 : 6)
end.
```

Listing 3.8

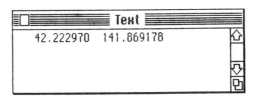

Figure 3.6

Solution B, Circle, is given in listing 3.9. Its output is found in figure 3.7.

```
program Circle;
var
  R, Pi, X, Y : Real;
begin
  R := 6.72;
  X := 3.14159 * R * R;
  Y := 2 * 3.14159 * R;
  Writeln('The area of a circle whose radius is 6.72 inches');
  Writeln('is ', X : 6 : 2, ' square inches, while');
  Writeln('the circumference is ', Y : 6 : 2, ' inches.')
end.
```

Listing 3.9

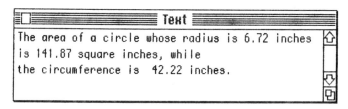

Figure 3.7

Solution C, Circle_2, to this example is found in listing 3.10. Its output is the same as that from Solution B.

Discussion: Although solution A produces the correct answers, one needs to look at the program to see what the answers mean. And even then, it may not be easy for someone other than the author to decipher things. In particular, someone who knows very little about the mathematical formulas for a circle would likely be lost. Another comment worth making is that output statements are for printing and assignment statements are for computing. Try to keep computations within output statements to a minimum.

The program Circle produces good, clear output, but the program itself is not particularly nice to read. Again, someone who is unfamiliar with circle formulas can't really tell what is being computed without looking at the output statements. Clearly, better names could have been chosen than the all too popular X and Y.

```
program Circle_2;

(This program computes the area and circumference of a circle.)
(It also demonstrates the use of CONSTANTS. Constants look like)
(variables, but are not allowed to change value during the program.)

  const
    Pi = 3.14159;
    R = 6.72;

  var
    Area, Circum : Real;

begin
  Area := Pi * R * R;
  Circum := 2 * Pi * R;
  Writeln('The area of a circle whose radius is ', R : 4 : 2, ' inches');
  Writeln('is ', Area : 6 : 2, ' square inches, while');
  Writeln('the circumference is ', Circum : 6 : 2, ' inches.')
end.
```

Listing 3.10

The program Circle_2 is a well-written program that produces clear output. The use of constants is something new, so we discuss them now. As stated in the program's comment, constants look like variables, but are not allowed to change in the program. Notice that constants are **defined** in a constant section, which precedes the **var** section and begins with the reserved word **const**. We point out two significant differences between constant definitions and variable declarations. First, there is no mention of a type in a constant definition. This is because the type is implicit in the value that we give the constant. For example, the constants Pi and R are both real because we have given them real values. Secondly, the constant definitions use the equal symbol and *not* the assignment operator. This is because the constant name is really *equal* to the indicated value all through the program.

There are two general advantages to using constants. First, constants provide some security against a programmer accidentally changing a value that should not be changed, since Pascal systems will not allow constants to change value. This can be very important in long, involved programs. Secondly, constants can help us rid our programs of "magic numbers." These are numbers that occur throughout a program, but often the quantities they represent are not readily apparent. For example, instead of cluttering up a program with lots of 3.14159's, we should use Pi instead. Moreover, we can save ourselves some work if we have to use a better approximation for Pi, like 3.14159265, in a later version of the program. We can simply change the constant definition for Pi without having to change any of the other statements in the program.

The careful reader might object to our use of the variable R as a meaningful variable. In fact, one-letter variable names are usually poor choices. However, in this case, such a choice may well be justified because anyone who is familiar with the circle formulas would probably recite them using R's ("Pie are squared!"). Of course, any other one-letter variable would be a poor choice, and we would certainly not argue against the choice of Rad or Radius as a variable name.

Finally, note that although both solutions B and C produce the same output, the first Writeln statement in program Circle_2 is more flexible because it doesn't contain the magic number 6.72. To compute the area and circumference for a different circle, program Circle would need to have its first Writeln statement altered, as well as the R assignment statement. Circle_2, on the other hand, would only need to have the R constant definition changed. Computer programs should be as flexible as possible so that modifications to them can be kept to a minimum. Since variable names and constant names add to that flexibility, use them.

We conclude this chapter with a more complex example.

Example. Sonny Tan has just completed another trip from the windy city of Chicago to the sunny beaches of Miami, a distance of 1397 miles. As an almost law-abiding citizen, Sonny averaged a driving speed of 57 miles per hour. While lying on the sand soaking up the sun, Sonny decided to experiment with his new digital wristwatch/stopwatch. After timing everything in sight, Sonny began timing the blinking of his eyes. He noticed that he blinks about 17 times each minute and even determined that each blink lasts about 0.12 seconds. With all of this information, determine how long it took Sonny to drive from Chicago to Miami, how many times he blinked during his trip, and how many miles he drove with his eyes closed.

The solution to this problem is given in listing 3.11. The output from this program is shown in figure 3.8.

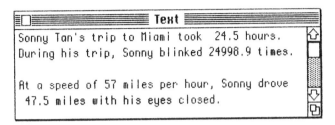

Figure 3.8

Note the built-in flexibility of the program. If we change a quantity like the duration of each blink, the number of blinks per minute, or the driving speed or distance, we need only modify a single line of the program. Although we used constant names for several quantities, we did not use a name for converting times from one unit to another. In this case, the "60" is not really a magic number. Most people would know what purpose the 60 is serving, particularly in the context of the statements, and it would make the program unnecessarily wordy to introduce a constant like "MinutesPerHour" that is set equal to 60.

We point out that we printed the apostrophe (single quote), by entering it *twice* in the Writeln statement. That is, we used the following Writeln statement in our program:

Writeln('Sonny Tan''s trip to Miami took ',Hours:5:2);

There are *two* single quotes between the n and the s above and not one double quote. If we had used a double quote, the computer would have printed a double quote. If we had used just one single quote, the Macintosh would have interpreted this as the matching, closing quote for the first quote before the word Sonny. Thus, to print out an apostrophe, always enter it twice.

Finally, note that it is the programmer who *solves* the problem. If we don't know which conversions to perform when, the Macintosh will not be of much help to us. Computers do not solve problems. People do.

```pascal
program Sonny;
(This program uses the assignment statement and the write statement)
(to determine how far Sonny Tan drove with his eyes closed on his trip)
(from Chicago to Florida. We are given the distance of the trip, his)
(driving speed and the frequency and duration of his blinks.)
  const
    Distance = 1397;  (miles)
    Speed = 57;  (m.p.h.)
    Frequency = 17;  (blinks per second)
    Duration = 0.12;  (seconds)
  var
    Hours, Minutes : Real;
    Blinks : Real;
    Miles, Miles_Blind : Real;
    Hours_Eyes_Closed : Real;
    Minutes_Eyes_Closed : Real;
    Seconds_Eyes_Closed : Real;
begin
  (Determine how long the trip took in minutes.)
  Hours := Distance / Speed;
  Minutes := Hours * 60;

  (Now determine the total number of blinks.)
  Blinks := Minutes * Frequency;

  (Next, find out length of time Sonny's eyes were closed.)
  Seconds_Eyes_Closed := Blinks * Duration;
  Minutes_Eyes_Closed := Seconds_Eyes_Closed / 60;
  Hours_Eyes_Closed := Minutes_Eyes_Closed / 60;

  (Compute distance travelled with eyes closed.)
  Miles_Blind := Hours_Eyes_Closed * Speed;

  (Finally, output the results of the program.)
  Writeln('Sonny Tan''s trip to Miami took ', Hours : 5 : 1, ' hours. ');
  Writeln('During his trip, Sonny blinked ', Blinks : 5 : 1, ' times.');
  Writeln;
  Writeln('At a speed of ', Speed : 2, ' miles per hour, Sonny drove');
  Writeln(Miles_Blind : 5 : 1, ' miles with his eyes closed.')
end.
```

Listing 3.11

Exercises

3.1. What is the output of the following Pascal program? In particular, how many lines of output are there and what is on each line?

```
program Rhyme;
begin
  Writeln('Mary had a little lamb');
  Write('Little lamb');
  Writeln('Little lamb');
  Write('Mary had a little lamb');
  Writeln('Its fleece was white');
  Write('As snow.')
end.
```

Write well-commented, readable, and correct Pascal programs to solve the following problems:

3.2. Suppose Sonny Tan was in a much bigger hurry than in the example problem and averaged 85 m.p.h. instead of 57 m.p.h. Modify the program "Sonny" to determine in this case how far he drove with his eyes closed. Guess whether the distance will increase, decrease or stay the same. Explain any relationship you notice between this answer and the answer from the example in the text.

3.3. Write a program to convert a temperature of 75 degrees Fahrenheit to Celsius. Convert a temperature of 17 degrees Celsius to Fahrenheit. The conversion formulas are as follows:
$F = 9/5*C+32$
$C = 5/9*(F-32)$

3.4. The amount of beer brewed in the United States in 1975 was 4,894,000,000 gallons. If all this beer were placed in 12-ounce cans and if all of these cans were stacked one on top of the other, how high would the stack be in inches? How high in feet? How high in miles? How many times would the stack reach the moon? The following conversion factors will be helpful:

1 gallon = 128 ounces	1 mile = 5280 feet
1 beer can = 4.75 inches	1 moon trip = 239,000 miles

Note: You should use reals for all variables in problem 4 because the numbers will become too large for integers. We will discuss such problems in Chapter 8.

Problems 5 through 9 were taken from the article "Second Guessing," by Monny Sklov and Bob Spitzer, which appeared in the September, 1983 issue of **GAMES** Magazine. The article was a quiz to see how well people could quickly judge the proper unit of time (i.e., seconds, minutes, hours, days, weeks, months, years, decades, centuries) that a task would take. Take the quiz yourself on the following problems. Check the answers below and then write Pascal programs that compute the time for each task in the correct unit. Again, you should use real variables because of the large quantities involved.

3.5. Suppose you can swim 3.8 miles per hour with flippers on. How long would it take you to swim around the world at the equator? (Assume a distance of 25,000 miles.)

3.6. Suppose you can write an average person's name in 6 seconds. How long would it take you to write all the names of the people living in New York City (approximately 7 million people)?

3.7. A cement company has just built a sidewalk from your front door to the sun (93 million miles away). After you've put on your hiking boots, how long will it take you to walk to the sun (assuming a hiking speed of 3 miles per hour)?

3.8. Every day for 18 years your father takes one foot of 8mm film of you in action. On your 18th birthday, your father shows you the film in its entirety. How long will the film last? (It takes approximately 3.18 seconds for 1 foot of film to pass through the projector.)

3.9. You own a square mile of land. If one-tenth inch of rain falls on your land and you catch all the water before it hits the ground, how long will it take you to drink all the water, assuming a drinking rate of 3 gallons of water per day? There are 231 cubic inches in one gallon.

(Answers: The proper units of time for problems 3.5 through 3.9 are: months, years, centuries, hours, and centuries respectively.)

Chapter 4

Interactive Input and Text Files

> **PROMPT** – **A delayed message from the system demanding an immediate response from the user.**
> **Devil's DP Dictionary**

One of the features of a computer that has caused some of its greatest impact is that people can use and execute complex programs without having the slightest idea of how the programs are put together or what makes them work. From the business people who use spreadsheet programs like VisiCalc to the secretaries using word processing programs to the airline ticket agents who book seats on an airplane, thousands of computer users have little idea about how things work. Of course, someone must eventually know what is going on. This is the programmer's job. But from the previous discussion, it becomes apparent that another job of the programmer is to write programs that are used easily by others. One very fundamental way to do this is through **interactive input**, which is the primary emphasis of the first part of this chapter.

All of the programs in the previous chapter ran from start to finish without any interruptions by the user. This is sometimes a good thing because we may not want to be around while a long program is executing. We want to be able to start the program and walk away. Such behavior was especially common in the early days of computers when programmers presented a deck of punched cards (the program and the data) to a computer operator. The computer operator would then read the cards into the computer at the proper time and the computer would execute the program. If the program generated some output, the operator would return the printout to the programmer. Such a system is referred to as a **batch** system since the programs are run in batches.

With the advent of terminals, programmers began "writing" programs on a screen instead of using a keypunch, and programmers had the capability of executing their programs from their own terminals. Under this environment, it became feasible for programs to request additional information while they were running. This type of environment is called an **interactive** environment because there is a continuous interaction between the programmer and the computer. This interaction can make programs extremely flexible and it is this flexibility that makes programs easy for the nonprogrammer to use. The Macintosh is, of course, such an interactive computer.

For example, consider the situation of the airline ticket agent. There is usually a computer terminal hooked into an extremely complicated reservation program. When you approach the agent, the program is already executing. But in this case, the program halts several times to obtain information, such as your name, destination, date of travel, etc. It is precisely this interaction that allows you the flexibility to book a seat on any flight on any day with any agent at the counter. And, of course, the agent probably has no idea of how the program works, but can respond to such questions as "destination?", "first class?", "non-smoking?". We are not ready to write airline reservations programs, but we will see how to add these interactive features to our simple Pascal programs.

Exercise 3.3 had you write a program to convert 75 degrees Celsius to Fahrenheit. Now suppose we wanted to convert a different temperature, like 29 degrees. If you have a solution to exercise 3.3 available, this new problem is easy. Simply change the "75" to "29" and run the program again. Although this is easy, notice that this simple task requires us to know how to list the program (i.e., look at it on the screen), to be familiar enough with Pascal to realize which statement needs to be changed, and to be familiar with the editing mechanisms of the computer to generate a new program. Finally, we need to know how to run the program. Of all these tasks, running the program is the simplest. Wouldn't it be nice if, when the program is run, we would be asked to enter from the keyboard the temperature we wanted to convert? Then we would only need one program to handle any Celsius temperature. This is precisely how the **Read** and **Readln** statements work in Pascal.

Read and Readln

In Chapter 3, we learned how to assign values to variables using the assignment statement. Of course, when we use the assignment statement, we have to know the values ahead of time because these values are typed into the program while we are creating it. In many cases, as the above example indicates, we need more flexibility. We may not always know when the program is written what values we will be working with.

To give us the flexibility we need, Pascal contains two statements that provide a facility for interactive input. These statements are:

Read (List of variables)
Readln(List of variables)

We will explain how these statements execute and then detail the differences between the two.

In essence, the Read and Readln statements behave like assignment statements in that they assign values to variables. The variables that receive the values are those in the list after the word Read (or Readln). The values themselves are entered through the keyboard. We will give several examples, and again we take this opportunity to mention that since there is no context for the variable names in these examples, we will use one-letter variables.

Example: Suppose A, B, and C are integer variables, and we execute the statement:

Readln (A,B,C);

If the person at the keyboard types in

2 4 6

and then presses the Return key, A would contain the value 2, B the value 4, and C the value 6.

As with assignment statements, Pascal requires that types be compatible. If the data entered from the keyboard were 2 4.2 6, many versions of Pascal would report a type incompatibility error for trying to assign the real value 4.2 to the integer variable B. The Macintosh Pascal system behaves differently. Any illegal character produces a "beep," is *not* printed, and *terminates* the current number being input. So in the above situation, the decimal point would terminate the second input, the 2 would be considered the third input, and the space between the 2 and the 6 would terminate the third input. So with Macintosh Pascal, the above mistake assigns 2 to A, 4 to B, and 2 to C, even though the screen appears like this:

2 42 6

If you notice a typing error before an input value has been terminated, you can use the backspace key to correct the error. However, once you have terminated an input value (with a comma, a space, or an illegal character), that value cannot be changed. The system, in fact, does not even allow you to backspace to the error. So, the first lesson to be learned from all of this is that you should be very careful when entering input from the keyboard. With the Macintosh's convenient **Pause** feature, we can easily start all over. This wouldn't be bad in a short program. But if we make a mistake on the 99th piece of data in a program that reads in 100 pieces of data, starting over would prove undesirable. We will find a way around this kind of problem later in the chapter.

When the Macintosh reaches a Read statement in a program, it automatically pauses until it receives through the keyboard all the values that it is expecting. It also puts in the **Text** window a flashing cursor (I), referred to in the Macintosh documentation as an "insertion pointer." In the above example, if only two values, say 2 and 4, were entered, the computer would wait and wait and wait (forever if necessary) until a third value for C is entered. Once all expected values have been entered, the execution of the program proceeds normally.

One might ask what happens if we type in too many values. With the Read statement, as soon as the Macintosh gets the values that it is expecting, it resumes execution. Any extra value that is entered will be assigned to the next variable appearing in the next Read statement.

Example: Consider the following segment:

    Read(A,B);
    Writeln(A,B);
    Read(C);
    Writeln(C)

When this segment is run, the Macintosh pauses at the first Read statement and waits for two values. Suppose you type

    45 67 89 (Return).

As soon as the computer obtains the 45 and the 67, the Read statement is complete and the first Writeln statement is executed. So before you can even type the 89, the values of A and B are read and printed, and the computer begins waiting for a value for C. The Macintosh is so fast that

the 89 that you typed is typed *after* all of the above activity takes place.
So the computer is already waiting on a value for C when you type the 89,
and, hence, the 89 is assigned to C and printed. Thus, the screen appears
like this:

```
45 67   45    67
89    89
```

On other versions of Pascal, the input of 89 might be lost (or ignored)
because the first Read statement is not executed until the Return key is
pressed. In this situation, the Writeln(A,B) would then be performed and
the computer would wait for a third input. Always check other versions of
Pascal for their behavior in this situation.

Now it is time to explain the difference between Read and Readln.
Although the difference is similar to the difference between Write and
Writeln, the input statements tend to cause more confusion among
beginning programmers. Stated simply, Read statements will take their
data values as a continuous stream of values, with no regard to how many
lines they are on. On the other hand, once a Readln statement has obtained
all of its values, any data values for the next input statement (whether a
Read or a Readln) must begin on a new line. As a consequence, input for a
Readln statement must always be terminated by a Return key. This is not
the case for the Read statement, and that is why the output from the
previous example occurs on the same line as the input. The following
examples illustrate the difference between Read and Readln. In all cases,
we assume that X, Y, and Z are integer variables.

Examples: The statements

```
Readln(X,Y);
Readln(Z)
```

with keyboard input 2 4 6 (Return) would assign 2 to X and 4 to Y. The
computer would continue waiting for a third data value because after the
first Readln statement is completed, the next input statement needs data
from a new line. Thus, the 6 is lost.

```
Readln(X);
Readln(Y);
Readln(Z);
```

with the keyboard input

    2 4
    6 8
    10 12

would assign 2 to X, 6 to Y, and 10 to Z.

As a final example, suppose the Readln(Y) statement above were changed
to Read(Y) and that we tried to type in the same input. In this case, the 2
would be assigned to X, the 6 to Y, and the 8 to Z. The values 10 and 12
would then be used with the next input statement. If there were no
subsequent Read or Readln statements, the system would "beep" at us and
would not even allow the typing of the 10 and 12.

When reading strings, always use Readln (instead of Read) and try to
read strings by themselves. That is, do not try to read in the data line

    Mickey Mouse, 50

by using the statement

    Readln(Name, Age)

According to the manual, when reading a string, Macintosh Pascal reads
until the end of the line. So in the above example, if Name were declared
large enough to hold all the characters read, then Name would have the
value 'Mickey Mouse, 50' and the Macintosh would wait for a value of Age
to be entered. If Name were not declared large enough, then you get the
following error message:

A STRING value is too long for its intended use.

In neither case is 'Mickey Mouse' assigned to Name and 50 to Age.
    Several things can go wrong when using interactive input. Sometimes
it is difficult to tell whether the computer is busy doing computations or
is instead waiting on the person at the keyboard to enter some data. Also,
as programs get more complex, there might be several items of data that
need to be entered. How does the airline agent know whether the computer
wants a name, a destination, a date, or a seating class? To avoid type

compatibility errors and to make sure that the right values get assigned to the right variables, it is important for the person at the keyboard to know what is expected. Thus, we arrive at the fundamental rule for interactive input:

Always precede interactive Read or Readln statements with a prompt message to the screen explaining what type of information is expected.

The purpose of the message is to tell the *user, not the programmer,* how to interact with the running program. For example, if we want to convert someone's height from inches to meters, the following sequence would be appropriate:

    Writeln('Enter your height in inches.');
    Readln(Height)

Note the importance of the phrase "in inches" to coax the proper response. Moreover, if a program might be executed by a total beginner, the following sequence might be better:

    Writeln('Enter your height in inches.');
    Writeln('Then press the "Return" key.');
    Readln(Height)

The point here is that the programmer will likely not be around when the program is executed and so should think of as many problems and plan for as many contingencies as possible. Programs with interactive input statements should be written in such a way that the person at the keyboard has no question as to what information is being requested.

We now consider an extended example. Let us figure monthly car payments for the purchase of a new car. The information we need includes the customer's name, model, and price of car being purchased, down payment, trade-in value, number of months in the payment plan, and the interest rate. Although this is not a terribly complex problem, it is a bit more involved than our previous examples. So we will take this opportunity to demonstrate that we should plan some sort of strategy before diving in to the actual writing of the program, or coding, as it is called by professionals. We mention here one of "Murphy's Laws" of computer programming: The sooner you start coding, the longer the project will take.

This is an ideal setting for the use of interactive input. The information about the automobile will vary from customer to customer, and the interest rate will vary according to the economy. So all of this information should be input from the keyboard at the time the program is run. Once we have obtained the information that we need, we then compute the monthly payment. There are many formulas for computing payments involving interest charges. We will not go through the mathematical derivation of a formula, but will simply use one. The point here is that it is not necessary to "reinvent the wheel" each time a program is written. When other tools are available, use them. The use of this mathematical formula is no different than our use of the formula F = 9/5*C + 32 to convert a Celsius temperature to Fahrenheit. The payment formula is just more complicated. Actually, the formula for computing the payment is simple:

Monthly Payment
   = Monthly Interest Rate * Amount Financed * Compounding Factor

where the Monthly Interest Rate is just the Annual Interest Rate divided by 12, and the Amount Financed is the purchase price of the car minus the combined value of any down payment and trade-in. The complex formula involves computing the Compounding Factor. It is:

$$\text{Compounding Factor} = \frac{(1 + \text{Monthly Interest Rate})^{\text{Number of Months}}}{(1 + \text{Monthly Interest Rate})^{\text{Number of Months}} - 1}$$

We should first notice that the above formula involves raising a number to a power, that is, multiplying a number by itself a certain number of times. For example, 3^4, read "three to the fourth power," means 3*3*3*3. The 3 is called the **base**, the 4 is called the **exponent**, and the process is called **exponentiation**. As we mentioned in Chapter 3, Standard Pascal has no built-in exponentiation operator. However, because there are many numeric tools that we would like to use that are not provided in Standard Pascal, the authors of Macintosh Pascal have provided a **library** of such tools. The official name of the library is The Standard Apple Numeric Environment Library. This name is fortunately shortened to SANE for use in Pascal programs. We will discuss the SANE Library in more detail in Chapter 7. A list of SANE Library resources is found in the Macintosh Pascal Reference Manual. There are in fact several libraries available to the Pascal programmer. The other one that we will consider in detail in

Chapter 12 allows us to make use of the Macintosh's graphics capabilities. For now, we will just learn enough to be able to use the SANE exponentiation operator.

First, we must inform the Macintosh system that we wish to make use of the library. We do this with a **uses** clause, which comes after the program heading and before the **var** section. A **uses** clause consists of the word **uses** followed by the name of the library, so in this example we will say **uses** SANE;. There are several exponential operators in SANE. The one that we want to use is called Xpwrl (for "X to power I"). To use this operation, we simply list in parentheses after Xpwrl the values that we want to use for X and for I, that is, the base and the exponent. To raise Pi to the fifth power, we would write Xpwrl(Pi, 5). This particular exponentiation operator requires the exponent to be an integer.

Now that we know essentially what information we are going to need and what we should do with the information, let us write a **pseudo-code** version of the program. This is an important step in the programming process, particularly in longer, more involved programs. Pseudo-code is an "English version" of a program. Without using the syntax of a particular programming language, we will write down, in precise order, the steps that we need to follow to solve our problem. Once this is accomplished, we then only need to translate our pseudo-code into corresponding Pascal statements. Pseudo-code for this example follows:

Car Payment Program
Enter the customer's name, make, and model of the car.
Enter the purchase price of the car.
Enter the down payment amount, if any.
Enter the trade-in value, if any.
Enter the length of the payment plan, in months.
Enter the current annual interest rate.
Compute the monthly interest rate (annual rate divided by 12).
Compute the compounding factor (use magical formula).
Compute the monthly payment.
Print out a summary stating the Customer's name, Model, price, trade-in, down payment, monthly payment, and the number of months financed.

In this simple case, the translation from pseudo-code to Pascal is straightforward. The program is shown in listing 4.1 with a portion of a sample execution in figure 4.1. Note how the use of descriptive variable names adds to the readability of the program.

```
program Car_Payment;
 uses
  Sane;
{This program computes the Monthly payment on the automobile of}
{your dreams.  This program uses true amortization formulas;}
{See text for an explanation.  Be aware of the fact that}
{many auto dealers use "mirrors" to compute Monthly payments!}
 var
  Name, Model : string[25];
  Sticker_Price, Trade_In, Down_Payment : Real;
  Ann_Interest, Mo_Interest : Real;
  Amt_Financed : Real;
  Compounding, Numerator, Denominator : Real;
  Months : Integer;
  Mo_Payment : Real;
begin
{First obtain input from the user.}
 Writeln('Please enter customer''s name');
 Readln(Name);
 Writeln('Enter the make and model of the new car.');
 Readln(Model);
 Writeln('Enter the sticker price of the car.');
 Writeln('Do not enter commas or the "$" in the price.');
 Readln(Sticker_Price);
 Writeln('Enter the Amt of the down payment.');
 Readln(Down_Payment);
 Writeln('Enter the trade in value - enter 0 for no trade in.');
 Readln(Trade_In);
 Writeln('Enter the number of months payments are to be made.');
 Readln(Months);
 Writeln('Enter the current Ann interest rate, ');
 Writeln('expressed as a decimal, i. e. 10.5% is 0.105.');
 Readln(Ann_Interest);

{Now compute, using magic formula of text, the monthly payment.}
 Mo_Interest := Ann_Interest / 12;
 Numerator := Xpwrl((1 + Mo_Interest), Months);
 Denominator := Numerator - 1.0;
 Compounding := Numerator / Denominator;
 Amt_Financed := Sticker_Price - Down_Payment - Trade_In;
 Mo_Payment := Mo_Interest * Amt_Financed * Compounding;
```

(Continued)

(Now we print a summary for the user.)
  Writeln(Chr(12)); (Clear Screen)
  Writeln('Summary prepared exclusively for: ', Name);
  Writeln;
  Writeln('You will be delighted with your new ', Model, '.');
  Writeln('While its sticker price is a hefty $', Sticker_Price : 8 : 2, ',');
  Writeln('with your trade in of $', Trade_In : 8 : 2);
  Writeln('and your down payment of $', Down_Payment : 8 : 2, ',');
  Writeln('your payment, at ', Ann_Interest * 100 : 5 : 2, '% annual interest,');
  Writeln('will only be $', Mo_Payment : 8 : 2);
  Writeln('each month for only the next ', Months : 2, ' months.')
end.

Listing 4.1

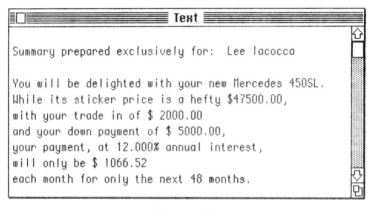

Figure 4.1

Note that after the input is recorded and before the output is printed, we "clear the screen" with a 'Writeln(Chr(12))' command. We will explain such statements in more detail in Chapter 8.

Although this program is fairly simple, it can rightfully be considered a powerful program because of its great flexibility. Lee Iacocca can easily determine the monthly payment for the car of his dreams under a multitude of circumstances without understanding how this program works. It is interactive input that allows such great flexibility.

Redirecting Input and Output

An alternative to interactive input is to prepare and save data to disk before a program is run. Of course, the program can no longer be interactive, but if there is a large amount of data, and that data is fixed, then a disk file can be handy. With interactive input you must enter all of the data each time you run a program. Since you may make several runs before you completely debug the program, interactive input, while providing great flexibility, can become very tedious. Also, we have seen that if you type the wrong data in an interactive program, you may have to start all over. By saving the data once to a **text file** on disk, execution becomes faster, more automatic, more reliable, and easier for the user.

A data file on disk also provides an easy way for us--or your instructor--to provide data for programming exercises. The disk available for this book contains many such data files that are referenced throughout the exercises.

Our intent at this point is only to show you how to read data from such files. Chapter 11 presents file processing in a much more general setting. We should mention in passing, however, that text files such as we are discussing here may be created with MacWrite, the Apple Macintosh word processor. It is beyond the scope of this book to discuss MacWrite, but suffice it to say that MacWrite is very similar to the Macintosh Pascal editing system and, hence, MacWrite is very easy to learn. Our only technical word of caution is that you must save text files (that are to be used in Pascal programs) in MacWrite with the **Text Only** option rather than the **Entire Document** option. Small text files can also be created using the Text Editor in the Tool folder on the Macintosh Pascal disk.

As an example of the use of a text file, let us suppose a two line text file, SalesData, has been created for a salesperson. Suppose line one of that file contains the salesperson's name and line two contains sales amounts for that salesperson for each day of the week (Monday--Friday). For example, the file might contain

Blaise Pascal
53.27 48.64 22.38 79.46 58.38

Let us write a program that will read the file SalesData and total the sales for the given salesperson. Admittedly, this is not a very useful program, but in the next chapter we will learn how to modify the program so that it will process the weekly sales for 100 or 1000 salespersons. If you learn the simple skill of reading from text files, then, when combined with the methods to be learned in the next chapter, you will be able to write powerful programs.

To redirect input so that it comes from a data file, SalesData, rather than from the keyboard, we only need add two statements to our program.

These are

    Close(Input);
    Reset(Input, 'SalesData');

While Close and Reset are discussed in more detail in a later chapter, their
effect can quickly be described as follows: Close(Input) breaks the
connection between input to the Macintosh and the keyboard. Reset(Input,
'SalesData') establishes that input will come from the external file
SalesData. The adjective external refers to the fact that the information
in the file does not reside in the Macintosh's memory, but rather outside
the Macintosh, on a disk. Of course, the name SalesData is arbitrary and
you can use the name of any text file. As with variable names in programs,
it is good practice to give meaningful names to text files as well. Don't
forget the single quotes around the filename in the Reset statement. Also
don't forget to close input before you try to reset it. If you forget, you
will get a **file in use** error message.
    After input has been redirected to come from a disk file rather than
the keyboard, every Read or Readln in your program will get values from
the file rather than the keyboard. This means that the programmer must
know the structure of the data file. That is, the programmer must know
that SalesData consists of a name followed by five real numbers on the
next line. Note that the programmer does not need to know the name or the
actual values involved. Whenever, in an exercise, we ask you to read
such-and-such data file, we will always explicitly give you the structure
of that file. This is your starting point for the analysis of the given
problem.
    Listing 4.2 shows the program Sales that reads the file SalesData and
totals the sales figures, and figure 4.2 shows the execution of the
program. This program assumes that the file SalesData resides on the
Macintosh Pascal disk. If it is not there you will get a **"File does not
exist"** error message. To place a copy of SalesData on the Pascal disk see
the brief section on Copying Files at the end of this chapter.
    If you have two drives, then SalesData can reside on drive 2, but you
will have to modify the program so that the system can find it there. In
Macintosh Pascal, you may specify a **volume** name. The volume name is
simply the diskette name. For example, if SalesData is on the diskette
Sample, then

    Reset(Input, 'Sample:SalesData')

instructs the system to redirect the input so that it comes from the file SalesData on the diskette Sample. Warning: Do *not* type any blanks between the colon and SalesData. These blanks are significant and the system will look for a nonexistent file name with blanks in it.

```
program Sales;
(This program reads data from the textfile 'SalesData')
(and totals sales figures for a given salesperson.)

var
  Name : string;
  Mon, Tues, Wed, Thurs, Fri : Real;
  Total : Real;

begin
  Close(Input);                      (Redirect Input to be from)
  Reset(Input, 'SalesData');   (the textfile 'SalesData'.)
  Readln(Name);
  Readln(Mon, Tues, Wed, Thurs, Fri);
  Total := Mon + Tues + Wed + Thurs + Fri;
  Writeln('The weekly total for ', Name, ' is $', Total : 8 : 2)
end.
```

Listing 4.2

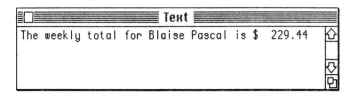

Figure 4.2

Note that the Readlns of program Sales have no prompts before them. Is this a violation of our earlier Programming Practice of always preceding Read's with Write's? No. *Interactive* input from the keyboard should *always* be prompted so that the human will know what to do. But it is silly and unnecessary to prompt a computer that is reading data from a text file. The moronic computer will not understand the prompts; rather, it is the responsibility of the programmer to understand the structure of the data and sequence the Reads and Readlns so that the computer finds appropriate values for each input statement it executes.

If we can redirect input so that it comes from a file, we should also be able to do the same with output. In this chapter, we only take up redirecting output so that it is sent to a printer. Again, Chapter 11 discusses the general case of reading and writing files; here we learn how to get the execution of a program to print on paper (for your scrapbook or your instructor).

The following two statements will redirect output to the printer:

Close(Output);
Rewrite(Output, 'Printer:');

Note the single quotes in the Rewrite statement around the word printer and note the colon at the end of the word printer. The purpose of these statements is to break the connection between output and the Macintosh screen and then to re-establish the printer as the output device. Note also that we use "Reset" with input devices and "Rewrite" with output devices.

The program Hard_Copy, on the disk that accompanies this book, is a modification of the program Car_ Payment. Hard_Copy produces a "hard" (paper) copy of its output for the customer to take home and study.

Hard_Copy and Car_Payment differ only in that Hard_Copy includes the two statements "Close(Output);" and "Rewrite(Output, 'Printer:');". What is worthy of discussion is the placement of these statements within the program Hard_Copy. They are *not* at the top of the program, but rather are located just above the section that produces the output. The reason for this is that we want the first section of the program to be interactive. We want to print prompt messages on the screen and have the user interactively enter information about the new car purchase. Since we do not want the prompt messages sent to the printer, we must not redirect the output too early.

Another point to ponder, especially with output to a printer, is the following good programming habit: **Always "echo" the input into the output**. In the current example, this means we should send to the printer all the information about the purchase, that is, the model, price, down payment, etc., as well as the monthly payment. The final monthly payment, while important, is not very useful if we don't know or can't remember what it is the monthly payment for!

Consider the very simple program, Not_So_Good, in listing 4.3, which prompts the user for a number and reports the square root of that number (using the built-in, Standard Pascal square root function Sqrt).

```
program Not_So_Good;
  var
   Number : Integer;
begin
  Writeln('Please enter a positive integer');
  Readln(Number);
  Close(Output);
  Rewrite(Output, 'Printer:');
  Writeln('The square root of your number is ', Sqrt(Number) : 6 : 3)
end.
```
Listing 4.3

The output of Not_So_Good is sent to the printer and is shown below:

The square root of your number is 18.628

Much better is the output of program Better:

The square root of 347 is 18.628

The program Better, which you are asked to write in the exercises, is better simply because it observes the above programming practice of echoing our input, 347, back to us.

You may occasionally need to restore Input so that after reading a text file, you can again enter data from the keyboard. The statement

Close(Input);

is sufficient to redirect input to come from the keyboard. Likewise,

Close(Output);

restores output to the screen.

Copying Files from One Disk to Another

If a program reads from a text file, that text file must be available when the program executes. That is easy if you have two drives. Simply put Macintosh Pascal in drive 1, your data disk in drive 2, and modify the reset statement to

Reset(Input, 'Sample:SalesData');

which initiates the reading of SalesData from the diskette whose name is Sample.

However, if you have only one drive, then it will be necessary to copy the text file onto the Macintosh Pascal disk. To do this, start with the Macintosh Pascal disk (**Quit** Macintosh Pascal if already in use) so that your screen appears as in figure 4.3.

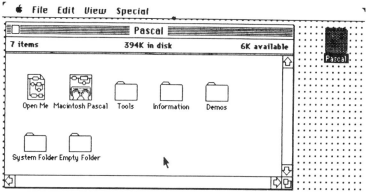

Figure 4.3

Then choose **Eject** from the **File** menu and insert the disk that holds the text file. Arrange the windows of the disks to occupy opposite halves of the screen, and then drag the file from one disk to the other. Figure 4.4 shows the window for the Pascal disk on the left and the window for Sample on the right. Further, the CH4 folder of Sample is open and SalesData is being dragged from Sample to the Pascal disk. We point out that this method is general and can be used to copy programs, as well as text files, from disk to disk. Note that the original file is not removed, so after the copying process, you have the file on both disks.

You will not be able to copy many files to your Macintosh Pascal disk before it becomes completely full. To make more room on your Macintosh Pascal disk, used the above method to copy such files as Open Me, Tools, Information, and Demos to another disk. Then remove these files from the Pascal disk by dragging them to the trash can.

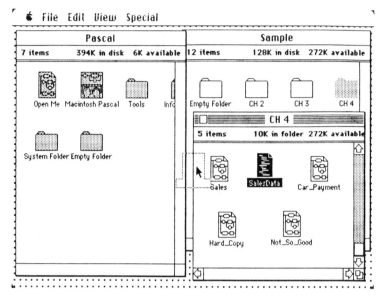

Figure 4.4

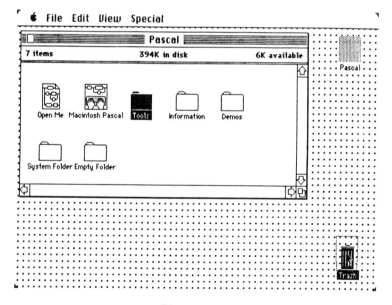

Figure 4.5

Figure 4.5 shows Open Me on the way to the trash can. To put a file in the Trash, be sure to place the pointer of the mouse over the trash can. Also, be sure to choose the **Empty Trash** option from the **Special** menu to actually delete the files that you have placed in the trash can.

Exercises

4.1 Write a program that interactively requests three real numbers from the keyboard and prints out the average of the numbers.

4.2 Write a program that interactively requests a person's height in feet and inches and converts the height to centimeters. One foot equals 30.48 centimeters.

4.3 Write a program that interactively requests a mileage figure before the last fill-up, a mileage figure before the current fill-up, and an amount (in gallons) of gasoline purchased. Then print out the miles per gallon obtained on the last tankful of gas.

4.4 Write an interactive program for Pepi Roni's Pizza Parlor that fills pizza orders as follows: Request both the customer's name and phone number. Then obtain the number of small, medium, and large pizzas requested by the customer. Prices are $5.80, $7.20, and $8.60 respectively for small, medium, and large pizzas. Then add a 6% sales tax and print out a total bill that is clearly labeled with the customer's name, phone number, and a breakdown of the pizzas purchased. (Note that since the phone number is not really an arithmetic quantitiy and since it contains a hyphen, it should be read as a string.)

4.5 Write a program to read the information in the text file SalesData and print out the average daily sales for the salesperson involved. (You should pretend that you don't know what data is in the file. All you know is the structure of the file. In other words, if your program has the name Blaise Pascal in it, you have missed the point.)

4.6 Write the program Better, which sends its output, shown at the end of this chapter, to the printer.

4.7 Three friends are starting a software company. They have agreed to name the business **X, Y, and Z Software** where X, Y, and Z are to be replaced by their actual names. They want you to write a program that will output all six possible orderings of their names so they can determine which ordering sounds best. Read the three names from the three-line text file Friends.

4.8   Modify the Car_Payment program to print out the total amount financed and the total interest charged over the life of the loan.

4.9 Modify the program Sales so that it reads from the file SalesData and sends its output to the printer.

4.10 Write a program for Ferty Lizer's Lawn and Garden Shoppe. The user will enter the width and depth of the lawn in feet. The program will compute the area of the lawn, subtract 2,500 square feet for an average house and driveway, and then tell the user how many bags of fertilizer are needed to fertilize the lawn. One bag of fertilizer covers 5000 square feet. Since Ferty wants to sell products, if the customer needs 3.2 bags, the computer should indicate that 4 bags are needed. See if you can devise a Trunc or Round trick to "round" 3.2 "up to" 4.

4.11 The program SalesTax (on the disk Sample) contains several bugs. Debug it. The program should compute the total amount due on a given purchase assuming a 6% sales tax.

Chapter 5

Fundamental Control Structures

> **LOOP – The repetition of a certain sequence of program steps while a set of unforseen circumstances prevails.**
> **Devil's DP Dictionary**

It is in this chapter that the real power of the computer is finally introduced. The programs that we have written in previous chapters have not been worthy of an expensive computer. Each program has asked the computer to perform some fairly trivial computations and output its results. The form of each program has been nearly the same: Execution begins at the first statement and continues directly to the bottom of the program. Each statement is executed exactly once. Hence, it has been more bother than it was worth to write a program to solve one of our problems! Now, all of that changes. We will learn in this chapter how to alter the flow of control so that programs can make decisions and choose between executing one group of statements or another group of statements. We will also see how the computer can perform a series of statements over and over, without getting caught in an infinite loop. These fundamental control structures allow us to write short, powerful programs that produce interesting output. The material of this chapter is key to the understanding of Pascal. No program in the remainder of the book fails to contain one of the features learned here. Time spent studying and understanding these concepts will pay the student hefty dividends.

In the previous paragraph we stated that the computer is able to make decisions. This sometimes makes people nervous. They think that making decisions implies intelligence, and therefore moronic computers should not be capable of such acts. We simply point out that many mechanical devices make simple decisions. My toaster decides when my toast is burned and then presents it to me. My smoke alarm decides that when my

119

toaster has completed its task, the fire department should be called! My clock radio decides when I have finally gotten back to sleep and keeps reminding me every 5 minutes that I have dozed off again. My car speaks to me when it decides that I don't have enough gas to reach the next station. Therefore, it should really be no surprise that the computer can make simple decisions. It is the blinding speed of the computer that allows it to make what seem like complex decisions. For example, landing a space shuttle, as complex as it seems, can be broken down into simple, discrete steps where each decision is as simple as deciding if the toast is burned. We repeat our caveat from Chapter 3:

You won't get the computer to solve any problem that you cannot, in principle, solve yourself.

Computers can land space shuttles only because the mathematics and physics involved in such procedures is well understood. We will not consider examples of such complexity in this chapter. But always begin by trying to understand the problem and then proceed to divide and conquer the problem until eventually it is in pieces small enough to give to the computer.

Boolean Variables

Before we can actually discuss the main content of this chapter, we must take care of a couple of preliminaries. The first of these is the notion of a **logical** or **Boolean** variable. The term 'Boolean' is taken in honor of George Boole (1815--1864), a British logician who discovered many of the fundamental laws of logic. Boolean variables are among the simplest of concepts in Pascal as they are variables that may only take on one of the two values True or False. In this regard, True and False should be regarded as constants known by the system, just as 0 and 3.14159 are numeric constants of the system. Do not misquote us as saying that "Pascal knows the meaning of truth." It is simply that Pascal has decided upon some internal representation for True and False and will allow us to use these terms as an aid in writing programs. Also, as we shall see, Pascal already knows some fundamental logical operations (**and**, **or**, and **not**, for example) and these can be used to greatly simplify the expression of our algorithms.

A Boolean variable, then, is simply a variable whose only possible values are True and False. We declare Boolean variables just like integers, reals, and **strings**:

var
    Count : Integer;
    Rate : Real;
    Maybe : Boolean;
    Name : **string**;
    Done : Boolean;

The point of this example is that variables can be declared in any order. Of course, Count is now allowed to take any integer value. Likewise, Maybe can take any Boolean value, i.e., Maybe can be True or False. Boolean variables can also be used in assignment statements:

    Done := False;
or
    Maybe := True;

or even the more interesting example:

    Done := (Count > 10);

Here, "Count > 10" is an expression, but it is a *Boolean* expression, not an arithmetic expression, i.e., it evaluates to True or False. That is, if the current value of Count is greater than ten, then Done is assigned the value True, while otherwise Done is assigned the value False. We shall soon see how such Boolean expressions are used to alter the flow of control within a program.

Simple Boolean expressions can be created from the following **relational operators**:

Algebraic Symbol	Pascal Symbol	English Meaning
<	<	less than
>	>	greater than
=	=	equals
≤	<=	less than or equals
≥	>=	greater than or equals
≠	<>	not equals

Here are some more examples of simple Boolean expressions. Note that these are expressions like "2+3" is an expression. They are *not* complete Pascal statements. Also, of course, the value of each expression, True or False, depends upon the current value of the variables in the expression:

Rate <> 0.135
Name = 'Mickey Mouse'
Sum <= 100.0

Boolean expressions can be combined into compound expressions using the logical operators of **not**, **and**, and **or**. While not as familiar as the arithmetic operations such as + and *, the logical operations are surely as simple to understand. The conjunction operator is **and**. We use it when we wish to make two assertions and assert that both are, in fact, true. That last sentence is a conjunction, for example. In Pascal the keyword **and** stands between the two expressions that you wish to conjoin. Of course, the value of a conjunction is True only if both parts are True. Otherwise, the conjunction is False. Thus,

(Count < 10) **and** (Name = 'Mickey Mouse')

is True if and only if Count contains some value smaller than 10 and Name contains exactly the value 'Mickey Mouse'.

The disjunction of two expressions is formed by using the **or** operator. Reasonably enough, a disjunction is True if either or both of the expressions are True. The disjunction is False only if both parts are False. For example,

(Rate > 1.12) **or** (Sum <> 50.0)

is True if Rate exceeds 1.12 or if Sum has any value other than 50.0.

Finally, the negation of an expression is formed by applying the **not** operator. This gives the expression exactly the opposite truth value. So,

Not (Count <= 25)

is True if and only if Count exceeds 25. The results of these operators are often summarized in so-called truth tables:

And	true	false		Or	true	false		Not	true	false
true	true	false		true	true	true			false	true
false	false	false		false	true	false				

The reader should check that these are consistent with our interpretations above. For example, the conjunction is True only if both conjuncts are

True. Often the beginner tries to memorize tables such as these. That is the wrong approach. If one really understands the discussion that precedes these tables, then there is nothing to memorize. Once they have been understood they are so simple that one cannot forget them!

One very important word of caution when forming complex Boolean expressions is the following: Always use parentheses around the operands of the expressions unless they are simple Boolean variables. That is, we must write

(Count = 10) **and** (Rate > 1.0)

rather than

Count = 10 **and** Rate > 1.0

As additional examples,

Maybe **or** Done

and

Maybe **or** (Name = 'Donald Duck')

are both okay. The reason for the parentheses is the order in which the relational and logical operators are applied. In Chapter 3, we discussed the order of precedence of the arithmetic operations. Here is the order of precedence of the arithmetic, relational, and logical operations:

Highest Precedence:	**not**
Second Precedence:	*, /, **div**, **mod**, **and**
Third Precedence:	+, -, **or**
Lowest Precedence:	=, <>, <, >, <=, >=

This means that in the absence of parentheses, **not** will be applied first, then the "multiplying" operators, then the "adding" operators, and then finally the "relational" operators. Within any level, evaluations will be from the left. Thus,

X + Y * Z

means

X + (Y * Z)

since the * operator has higher precedence than the + operator. Likewise,

    X + Y - Z
means
    (X + Y) - Z

since the operators are of equal precedence, and, hence, evaluation proceeds from the left.

To return to our logical example, we see that

    Count = 10 **and** Rate > 1.0

is evaluated as

    (Count = (10 **and** Rate)) > 1.0

which is, unfortunately, nonsense. Remember, parentheses are needed to force the meaning we want:

    (Count = 10) **and** (Rate > 1.0)

Rather than memorize all the technical details of precedence, we suggest you remember that the "multiplicative" operators (*, /, **div**, and **mod**) have higher precedence than the "additive" operators (+ and -), but otherwise simply use parentheses to guarantee your expression has the meaning you desire. For example, even though

    This **and** That **or** Whatever
and
    ((This **and** That) **or** (Whatever))
and
    (This **and** That) **or** Whatever

all have the same meaning, the last expression is the clearest. Don't use every parenthesis possible; don't omit every parenthesis possible. Strive for clarity.

Compound Statements

We need one more syntactical ingredient before we begin the main event. A compound statement is simply a mechanism whereby we can combine many statements into one statement. Its format is

```
begin
   Statement;
   Statement;
   . . .
   . . .
   . . .
   Statement;
   Statement
end;
```

where each 'Statement' is replaced by any legal Pascal statement. Note that since semicolons are used to separate Pascal statements, no semicolon is needed after the last statement *before* the **end**. We have shown a semicolon *after* the **end**, but this semicolon is only needed if there is another Pascal statement following the compound statement. We should point out that placing a semicolon after the last statement before the **end** does not give an error--it is simply unnecessary. In this book we will not include extra semicolons, except that in segments that are not complete programs we will place a semicolon after the last statement shown because we expect other statements (not shown) to follow our segment.

A common error that beginners make is to write

Statement-1 **and** Statement-2

when they want the computer to do Statement-1 and then do Statement-2. The intent may be clear to the programmer, but Pascal does not understand such nonsense. The operator **and** is only allowed to stand between two Boolean expressions, that is, **and** is only allowed as a logical operator. To combine the two statements into one, the programmer needs the compound statement:

```
begin
   Statement-1;
   Statement-2
end;
```

The **begin** and **end** should be thought of as big grouping symbols. In this regard they are like the **begin** and **end**. that delimit the actual executable portion of the program. Note that the **end** in the compound statement does not include a period. The necessity for the compound statement and for Boolean variables will now be made clear.

The Conditional Statement

The conditional statement is used to decide, based upon the value of some Boolean expression, which of several courses of action the computer should take. The conditional in Pascal takes on two forms, the first of which is known as the "If ... Then." Its format is:

> **if** Boolean expression **then**
>   Statement;
> Next_Statement

When this statement is executed the computer evaluates the given Boolean expression. If the expression is False, then the action of the **if** is complete and execution continues with the next statement. On the other hand, if the given Boolean expression is True, then the statement following the **then** is executed and then control passes to the next statement. It is important to realize that in either case the flow of the program continues with the next statement. If the condition happens to be True, then an extra step is added; otherwise, it is skipped. The flow diagram of figure 5.1 may help to make this situation clearer.

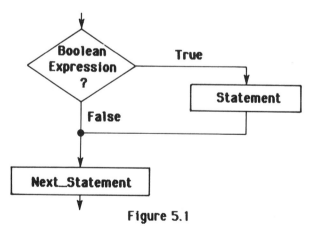

Figure 5.1

If the Boolean expression is True, then program control flows to the right and then on to the next statement. On the other hand, if the expression is False, then flow "falls through" directly to the next statement.

For example, suppose we would like to print the value of the variable Count only if Count is a multiple of 100 (Count = 100, 200, 300, etc.). This we could do with

    if Count **mod** 100 = 0 **then**
      Writeln('The value of Count is ', Count);

Of course, the statement following the **then** may be, as you have probably guessed, a compound statement. Suppose that each time Count is a multiple of 100 we would like to print Count and assign to the variable Century the value of Count divided by 100. To do so, we could write

    if Count **mod** 100 = 0 **then**
    begin
      Century := Count **div** 100;
      Writeln('The value of Count is ', Count)
    end;

Any time you want to perform more than one action in the **then** clause, remember that you need to use the compound statement to bind all of your actions together into one statement. What happens if you forget? Suppose you type

    if Count **mod** 100 = 0 **then**
      Century := Count **div** 100;
      Writeln('The value of Count is ', Count); {Logical error!}

The system finds no syntax error and your program runs but it does not execute as you expect. You find that the value of Count is printed every time, whether Count is a multiple of 100 or not. This helps us see how the computer interprets the above segment. Since there is no **begin**, the **then** clause has only one statement in it. Thus, if Count is a multiple of 100, then the assignment is performed and execution continues with the Writeln statement (which is what we wanted). However, if Count is not a multiple of 100, then the assignment is skipped and control proceeds with the next statement, which is the Writeln. Thus, the flow of control is as shown in figure 5.2a rather than what we had intended in figure 5.2b.

Actually, Macintosh Pascal makes it easy for you to spot this error. As soon as you type another line, or choose **Go**, the indentation is automatically changed to

if Count **mod** 100 = 0 **then**
  Century := Count **div** 100;
  Writeln('The value of Count is ', Count) (Logical Error)

That is, Macintosh Pascal ignores the indentation (if any) that you used to enter the program and formats the program as it understands it. In this case, the Writeln is not part of the **if** and this is clear since the Writeln is not indented under the **if**. Very few systems provide such helpful debugging aids. Learn to read your program listings carefully. The computer can't read your mind and decide whether you want the Writeln as a part of the **if** of not, but Macintosh Pascal helps you see that in the present case, it is *not* part of the **if**.

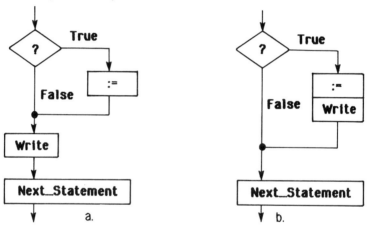

Figure 5.2

For completeness, we provide the following example of *poor* programming technique.

if Count **mod** 100 = 0 **then**
  begin
    Writeln('The value of Count is ', Count) (Poor style.)
  end;

The problem, of course, is that no **begin/end** block is needed here. When you only have one statement in the **then** clause, there is no need to make it a compound statement. The **begin/end** pair is overused in Pascal as it is.

Try not to use extra pairs that are not needed. They only make your program more difficult to read.

The other form of the conditional in Pascal is very handy for choosing between two alternative courses of action. Its format is:

if Boolean expression **then**
Statement
else
Statement;

When execution reaches this **if...then...else** statement, the given Boolean expression is tested. If True, the **then** clause is executed and control skips the **else** clause and proceeds to the next statement. However, if the given expression evaluates to False, then the **else** clause is executed and then execution continues with the next statement. Thus, the flow diagram for this situation is as shown in figure 5.3. Of course, either the **then** or the **else** clause can be compound as we shall see in the examples below.

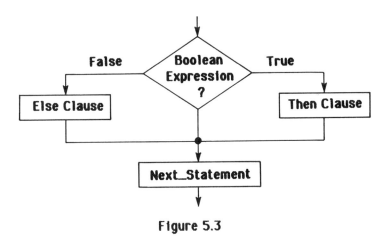

Figure 5.3

The easiest Pascal error to make is to insert a semicolon after the statement in the **then** clause:

if Boolean expression **then**
Statement;   (This is a syntax error!)
else
Statement;   (This ';' is needed if another statement follows.)

The semicolon before the **else** ends the **if**. The system is then not able to attach the **else** to the **if**, and it complains immediately to you by outlining the **else** as shown in figure 5.4 *Never* put a semicolon before an **else**.

```
if (Num mod 2 = 0) then
  Writeln('Even');
else
  Writeln('Odd');
```

Figure 5.4

Let us begin our examples with the standard case of regular pay versus overtime pay. Let us suppose that the variables Rate and Hours already have values. We are to write a segment that computes the appropriate value of the variable Pay. Naturally, if the value of Hours is 40 or less, we use the simple formula

```
Pay := Rate * Hours;
```

If the employee has worked more than 40 hours, we must compute time-and-a-half for the overtime hours. So we use the formulas

```
Regular := Rate * 40.0;
Overtime := 1.5 * Rate * (Hours - 40.0);
Pay := Regular + Overtime;
```

All of these except perhaps the middle one should be clear. The middle one computes the Overtime pay by multiplying the overtime rate (1.5 * Rate) times the number of hours that were overtime (Hours - 40.0). In Pascal our segment becomes

```
if Hours <= 40.0 then        (Regular Case)
  Pay := Rate * Hours
else                         (Overtime Case)
  begin
    Regular := Rate * 40.0;
    Overtime := 1.5 * Rate * (Hours - 40.0);
    Pay := Regular + Overtime
  end;
Writeln('The pay is $', Pay:6:2);
```

You should trace the above segment to see that if Rate has the value 5.00 and Hours is 30, then the output is:

The pay is $150.00

while if Rate is 5.00 and Hours is 50, then the output is:

The pay is $275.00

This example also points out that the **else** clause may be compound while the **then** clause is simple. In this case, it would be possible to make both clauses simple by combining the overtime formulas into one long formula:

```
if Hours <= 40.0 then        (Regular Case)
  Pay := Rate * Hours
else                         (Overtime Case)
  Pay := (Rate * 40.0) + 1.5 * Rate * (Hours - 40.0);
Writeln('The pay is $', Pay:6:2);
```

The advantage of this method is that the program is shorter and therefore a little clearer. The disadvantage of this method is that the overtime formula is a little complex and hence the **else** clause is perhaps less clear. In other words, it is a trade-off and a personal decision as to which method is better. Remember to strive to make your programs as clear as possible. Sometimes too many variables will muddle the situation, while too few variables are sure to make the program very hard to read. In this situation, either of the above is acceptable, but watch for this trade-off as you write your own programs. Here is definitely a poorer version of this same segment. Can you spot the problem before we tell you?

```
if Hours <= 40.0 then
  begin                      (Regular Case)
    Pay := Rate * Hours;
    Writeln('The pay is $', Pay:6:2)
  end
else                         (Poor style)
  begin                      (Overtime Case)
    Pay := (Rate * 40.0) + 1.5 * Rate * (Hours - 40.0);
    Writeln('The pay is $', Pay:6:2)
  end;
```

This time there is no syntax error, and even the correct results are produced. Our objection is that the Writeln statement is repeated in both the **then** clause and the **else** clause. A good programming rule of thumb is: **If something is repeated in the then clause *and* the else clause of an if statement, it doesn't belong inside the if.** In our case, the Writeln belongs after the **if**.

Here is another poor method on the same example. Can you spot the problem?

```
if Hours <= 40.0 then
  Pay := Rate * Hours;
if Hours > 40.0 then
  Pay := (Rate * 40.0) + 1.5 * Rate * (Hours - 40.0);
Writeln('The pay is $', Pay:6:2);
```

Once again the sytem finds nothing wrong with this segment, and it produces correct results. How picky can we get? Well, this time we object because of the use of two **if** statements where only one is needed. Here the computer must check to see if Hours is less than or equal to 40.0, then turn around microseconds later and check to see if Hours is greater than 40.0. The point is that Hours either is or it isn't, but we shouldn't make the computer check it twice. An **if...then...else** is far more appropriate in this case.

An **if...then...else** is a natural two-way decision maker. How would we make a three-way decision? No, there is no 'If...Then...Else...Otherwise' statement to learn. We simply use two **if...then...else** statements nested inside one another. Figure 5.5 shows a flow diagram for this situation.

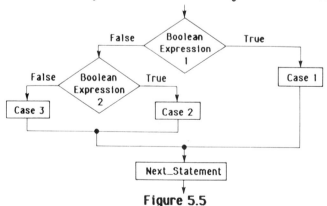

Figure 5.5

For example, suppose that Age is an integer variable and that we would like to print CHILD if age is less than 13, ADULT if age is greater than 19, and TEENAGER otherwise. The following segment accomplishes this (The line numbers are for the discussion that follows.):

```
1.  if Age < 13 then
2.     Writeln('CHILD')
3.  else if Age > 19 then
4.     Writeln('ADULT')
5.  else
6.     Writeln('TEENAGER');
7.  Writeln('DONE');
```

Lines 1--6 are all one statement! It is an **if...then...else** that just happens to have an **if...then...else** in its **else** clause. Of course, if Age has the value 7, then the Boolean expression in line 1 is True and the output is the two lines CHILD and DONE. That is, since the **then** clause was taken, the **else** clause (lines 3-6) is skipped and execution continues with the statement following line 6. If Age has the value 98, then the condition on line 1 is False and so the flow of control skips to the **else** clause, which begins on line 3. Here, another Boolean expression is found and this one evaluates to True. Hence, ADULT and DONE are output. To follow the flow of control, note that since we have executed the **then** clause of the **if** beginning at line 3, we have finished that **if**. Moreover, that completes the **else** clause of the outer **if** and, hence, control again passes to the statement following line 6. Finally, if Age is 17, then both the Boolean expressions are False and so control passes in each case to the **else** clause and TEENAGER and DONE is the output. Therefore, for every value of Age, exactly one of the three clauses is executed and control then passes in each case to the writing of the "DONE" message.

When **if**'s are used in this way they are said to be nested. That is, the second **if** is nested inside the first **if**. Remember, one **if...then...else** gives a two-way decision procedure. Two nested **if...then...else** statements give a three-way decision procedure. Likewise, 17 nested **if**'s will provide an 18-way decision procedure, but later we will learn a better way to handle large numbers of cases.

The next example shows that compound statements are quite possible with nested **if**'s. In addition to writing CHILD, ADULT, or TEENAGER, let us suppose that we also want to increment the appropriate variable Num_Kids, Num_Adults, or Num_Teens. That is, if Num_Kids, Num_Adults, and Num_Teens have the values 23, 9, and 56 respectively, and Age has the value 13, then we want our segment to output TEENAGER and to also count the teenager by incrementing Num_Teens to 57. Variables like Num_Teens, which *count* something, are called **counters**. Incrementing a counter is a very common operation in computer programs. Be sure you understand how this works. The structure of this segment is just like the previous one, except each clause is now compound:

```
if Age < 13 then        (Kid Case)
begin
  Writeln('CHILD');
  Num_Kids := Num_Kids + 1
end
else if Age > 19 then        (Adult Case)
begin
  Writeln('ADULT');
  Num_Adults := Num_Adults + 1
end
else                    (Beware Of Teenager)
begin
  Writeln('TEENAGER');
  Num_Teens := Num_Teens + 1
end;
```

The reader should trace the above segment for at least three carefully chosen values of Age.

Sometimes beginners fall so in love with nested If's that they get a bit carried away. See if you can spot any excesses in the following segment that assumes that Score has a value and uses this value to assign and print a letter Grade (Grade is a **string** and Score is an integer.):

```
1.  if Score >= 90 then
2.    begin
3.      Grade := 'A';
4.      Writeln(Grade)
5.    end
6.  else if (Score < 90) and (Score >= 80) then
7.    begin
8.      Grade := 'B';
9.      Writeln(Grade)
10.   end
```

```
11.  else if (Score < 80) and (Score >= 70) then
12.    begin
13.      Grade := 'C';
14.      Writeln(Grade)
15.    end
16.  else if (Score < 70) and (Score >= 60) then
17.    begin
18.      Grade := 'D';
19.      Writeln(Grade)
20.    end
21   else if Score < 60 then
22.    begin
23.      Grade := 'F';
24.      Writeln(Grade)
25.    end;
```

There are many ways to improve this solution. First of all, each clause contains a Writeln and, hence, the Writeln should be brought out of the **if**. The beginner is often so intent on printing the 'A', 'B', 'C', 'D', or 'F' that the "commonality" of the Writeln is often overlooked. More importantly, the Boolean expressions are far more complex than they need to be. We, as programmers, are doing unnecessary work and we are making the computer do unnecessary work as well. For example, the only way to get to line 6 or beyond is to fail the test at line 1. That is, the flow of control does not come to any line after line 6 unless Score is less than 90. Hence, it is totally unnecessary to check if Score is less than 90 at line 6. Likewise, the only way to get to the test at line 11 is to fail the tests at lines 1 and 6. Thus, if flow reaches line 11, we already know that Score is less than 80. Hence, the above can be greatly simplified to:

```
 1.  if Score >= 90 then
 2.    Grade := 'A'
 3.  else if Score >= 80 then
 4.    Grade := 'B'
 5.  else if Score >= 70 then
 6.    Grade := 'C'
 7.  else if Score >= 60 then
 8.    Grade := 'D'
 9.  else
10.    Grade := 'F';
11. Writeln(Grade);
```

Note that the condition at line 21 in the original version is totally unnecessary. That is, in the new version the only way to get to line 10 is to enter the **else** clause at each opportunity by failing the tests at lines 1, 3, 5, and 7. That is, we only reach line 10 if Score is less than 60.

Sometimes compound Boolean expressions can avoid the need for complex nested **if**'s. For example, suppose we need to count all male, senior, computer science majors at Abnormal State University. If we assume that Sex, Class, and Major are string variables with the appropriate values, then the following set of **if**'s does the trick:

```
if Sex = 'Male' then
  if Class = 'Senior' then
    if Major = 'CS' then
      Count := Count + 1;
```

However, the following single **if** statement is certainly clearer:

```
if (Sex = 'Male') and (Class = 'Senior') and (Major = 'CS') then
  Count := Count + 1;
```

The moral of this example is that some thought is required in writing clear programs. Even in a limited language like Pascal, there is usually more than one way to express your intentions. Strive for clarity!

As a final example of nesting, let us consider the following simple problem. We would like to provide an appropriate message for students with "exceptional" performance on an examination. A student who scored over 90 on the exam should be given an encouraging message. Also a student who scored less than 50 on the exam should be given a warning. Those who scored between 50 and 90 do not receive any message. See if you can figure out why the following segment does *not* work:

```
if Score > 50 then
  if Score > 90 then
    Writeln('Way to go!! Keep it up.')
  else
    Writeln('Have you considered another major???');
```

The problem is that we have two **if** statements fighting for one **else**. That is, in this case, we have a simple **if...then...** nested in an **if...then...else**. Unfortunately, even though we aligned the **else** with the outer **if**, Pascal always attaches a loose **else** to the nearest **if**. Here is another case where Macintosh Pascal helps us find our errors. Once again it formats the program to its understanding and shows us:

```
if Score > 50 then
 if Score > 90 then
  Writeln('Way to go!!! Keep it up.')
 else
  Writeln('Have you considered another major???');
```

This is certainly not equivalent to what we had intended, for even Neal Lee Perfect, who has a Score of 90, gets our nasty message, while Noe Hope, with a score of 4, escapes our wrath! How can we correct the problem? One method is to rewrite the Boolean expressions so that an **if...then...else** inside an **if...then** is what we want. We leave that solution to the reader because it dodges the main problem, which is to nest a simple **if...then** inside an **if...then...else**. Since an **else** is always attached to the nearest **if**, we provide a "do nothing else" for the inner **if**. The proper terminology for the "do nothing else" is the **null else**:

```
if Score > 50 then
 if Score > 90 then
  Writeln('Way to go!!!  Keep it up.')
 else  (do nothing)
else
  Writeln('Have you considered another major???');
```

What we have actually done is change the inner **if** to an **if...then...else**, so that the nesting is as we expect. Remember that if you are nesting **if**'s and some of them are **if...then...else** statements, then you would be wise to make them all **if...then...else** statements by providing null **else** clauses as needed.

The Repeat...Until

We now begin our discussion of control structures that allow for the repetition of groups of statements. The **if** allows us to choose between two courses of action while the repetitive statements allow our programs to "loop" back repeatedly through a given set of statements. For example, a payroll program loops through the employees creating the individual paychecks. It would really not be worth the effort if we had to write a separate program for each employee! The use of the conditional **if** allows us to plan for all contingencies and then the loop structure allows one program to process all the employees. This allows a program of 10 lines, if it loops 100 times, to be the equivalent of a 1000-line program. We begin to see the power and convenience for the programmer of repetitive control structures.

It will be common for us to want to repeat some group of statements until some property becomes true. For example, for the payroll problem above, we want to repeat the process of computing and printing checks until there are no more employees to be processed. Because this is often a useful way to view a problem, Pascal provides a 'Repeat...Until' statement. Its syntax is:

repeat
   Statement;
   Statement;
   . . .
   . . .
   . . .
   Statement
until Boolean expression;

The **repeat...until** is one statement. Those statements caught between the **repeat** and the **until** are called the body of the **repeat ...until**. Notice that no semicolon is needed after the last statement in the body. Of course, there is a semicolon after the Boolean expression if another statement follows the **repeat...until**. When execution reaches the **repeat**, the statements in the body are executed once, and then the Boolean expression is evaluated. If it is False, then the body is executed again. After each execution of the body, the Boolean expression is evaluated. If it is ever found to be True, then the flow of control passes to the statement following the **repeat...until**.

It is possible to write an infinite loop, that is, one that never terminates, but it is the responsibility of the programmer to make sure that there is some mechanism within the body of the loop for the Boolean expression to eventually become True, thus terminating the loop. Some examples help to make these points clear. Let us try to write a program that prints the integers from 1 to 20. That seems simple enough. Of course, we could use twenty separate Writeln's, but that would get pretty tedious if we wanted to modify the program to print the integers from 1 to 1000! Here is a basic outline of our approach using a **repeat...until**:

```
Initialize Num to 1
Repeat
    Output Num
    Increment Num by 1
Until Num = 20
```

You should trace the above outline to see that it does indeed produce a 1, then a 2, then a 3, etc. In fact, if you trace it very carefully you should be able to spot a small problem (that we will discuss later). Our outline is another example of what computer scientists call pseudo-code. The outline is not yet Pascal. Rather, it is very Englishlike and easy to read. Writing good pseudo-code is an art that you will need to practice, but the advantage of good pseudo-code is that it makes the writing of a Pascal program a much simpler task. With pseudo-code, one breaks a problem down into its constituent parts and repeats this process until the task is broken into manageable pieces. The use of pseudo-code is an important step in top-down, structured programming. We do not believe you should be forced to use a specific pseudo-code, and we will not attempt to create a new pseudo-code language for you to memorize. Rather, we illustrate throughout this text our pseudo-code for the example programs in the text. We think it is as worth your while to understand and practice writing pseudo-code outlines as it is to study the listings of our programs. Now back to the problem at hand. Listing 5.1 shows a Pascal program Count that implements our simple pseudo-code:

```
program Count;
(This amazing program is supposed to count from 1 to 20.)

var
   Num : Integer;

begin
   Num := 1;
   repeat
      Writeln(Num);
      Num := Num + 1
   until Num = 20
end.
```

Listing 5.1

The reader should compare the pseudo-code with the program to see how each statement in the pseudo-code was translated into Pascal. The advantage of the pseudo-code is that it is an intermediate step between raw English and the precise syntax needed in Pascal. If you haven't guessed what is wrong with the above program, load Count from the disk Sample (or type it in) and run it. What happened to that final value? Remember, it was supposed to print the integers from 1 to 20. The explanation is, of course, quite simple. Num is incremented at the *bottom* of the loop. After the incrementation, the expression 'Num = 20' is tested and the loop is repeated until the condition becomes True. Now, when Num is finally incremented to 20, control exits from the loop before the value of Num can be printed. We could "fix it up" by putting another 'Writeln(Num)' after the **repeat...until**, but it would be better to simply change the Boolean expression to read '**until** Num > 20'.

The moral of this story is that you should learn to check the special "boundary" values and make sure your loop repeats as you want it to. Later we shall see that there is, in fact, a better way to do a "counted loop" than the method we have used here.

As another simple but important example, let us write a program to add together the ten numbers 1, 2, 3, . . . , 10. The reason that this example is important is that it teaches us how the computer can sum a large group of numbers, and we shall use this fact over and over in the pages to come. Of course, the simplest way to add the integers from 1 to 10 is to use the following assignment statement:

Sum := 1 + 2 + 3 + 4 + 5 + 6 + 7 + 8 + 9 + 10;

However, that is not a very general solution and is certainly very tedious if we want to sum up all the integers from 1 to 1000. Therefore, we will devise a better, more general solution. Not surprisingly, we use a **repeat ...until**. But what is it that is going to be repeated? The answer is that we are going to loop ten times and on each execution of the loop add the "next" number to a **running sum**. At the end of the loop, the running sum should have accumulated the proper value. Trace the following pseudo-code carefully to see that Sum takes on the successive values 0, 1, 3, 6, 10, 15, . . ., 55.

Initialize Sum to 0.
Initialize Num to 1.

Repeat
    Add Num to Sum
    Increment Num to the next number
Until Num > 10
Output the results to a waiting world

The Pascal equivalent is called Add and is shown in listing 5.2.

```
program Add;
{This program adds the first ten integers. It introduces}
{the important notion of a "Running Summation".}

var
  Num : Integer;
  Sum : Integer;

begin
  Sum := 0;
  Num := 1;
  repeat
    Sum := Sum + Num;
    Num := Num + 1
  until Num > 10;
  writeln('The sum of the first ten integers is ', Sum : 3)
end.
```

Listing 5.2

Again notice how the pseudo-code has made the final step, the writing of an actual Pascal program, an easy task. Another point to be made about using a running sum is that one must always initialize the Sum to zero before beginning. Here is the way we look at it: Each time through the loop we drop another Num into the Sum bucket. At the end of the loop the bucket contains the Sum of all the Nums. But to get the correct answer we must make sure that we began with an empty bucket! That is the purpose and need for 'Sum := 0'.

Actually, Macintosh Pascal does initialize all variables to zero for you, but we think it is a poor programming practice to depend on the system to do your initializations. The system never re-initializes variables for you, so you should get in the habit of doing all initializations.

Sometimes students initialize every variable in sight. Consider the following nonsense example, which adds 5 and 7 to some number Z read in from the keyboard, and stores the answer in Sum:

```
X := 5;
Y := 7;
Z := 0;
Sum := 0;
Read(Z);
Sum := X + Y + Z;
```

Do you see any initializations that are unnecessary? Since Z is given a value in the 'Read', it is pointless to initialize Z to zero two lines before the 'Read.' The point is that Z does not need a value in order to obtain a value from the 'Read.' Hence, initializing Z is poor programming. Likewise, Sum does not participate in the final line, but only receives a value. Hence, Sum does not need to be initialized in this example. However, if the last line were 'Sum := Sum + X + Y + Z', then since Sum does participate in the addition, it must have an initial value. Finally, initializing a variable does not always mean setting it to zero. For example, in the program of listing 5.2, the variable Num is initialized to one.   The key to understanding when a variable needs to be initialized is to understand the notion of a variable (Chapter 3) and how that variable is used. **Any time a variable participates on the right hand side of an assignment or in the evaluation of any expression, it must already have been given a value**.

Loops are very important for what follows, so we consider the notion in more detail. A loop consists of four parts. There is an **initialization** portion that is needed before we enter the loop. Any variables that are referenced on the right hand side of assignments must have values even on the first loop execution. In the previous examples, this initialization is handled by the statements 'Num := 1' and 'Sum := 0.' The **body** of the loop is the group of statements that is repeated. In a **repeat...until** the body is caught between the **repeat** and the **until**. A loop also contains a **test**, or Boolean condition, that can be used to decide when to terminate the loop. In our two examples, the conditions have been 'Num > 20' and 'Num > 10' respectively. Finally, to avoid an infinite loop, there must be some means for the loop to finally terminate. This is called the **modification** portion of the loop. In our examples, the statement 'Num := Num + 1' guarantees that the loop eventually terminates. The modification statement is often put at the bottom of the body. In summary, the four parts of any loop are:

1. Initialization before the loop.
2. The body of the loop.
3. The test to end the loop.
4. Modification to avoid an infinite loop.

Look for these parts in our examples. We shall also see how they can be rearranged when we discuss further Pascal control structures.

Our next example needs the following mathematical fact: The series 1 + 1/2 + 1/3 + 1/4 + 1/5 + . . . eventually exceeds any given value. That is, if we add together enough terms of the above series, we eventually pass even 6.0. Our next program answers the burning question, "How many terms are needed to exceed 6.0?" This is a nice example for the **repeat . . . until**. This time we have no idea how many times we should repeat the loop. Indeed, that is our question. But we can provide the answer by counting terms until our sum exceeds 6.0. Here, then, is an outline:

```
Initialize Sum to 0
Initialize a counter, Count, to 0.
Initialize Term to 1.
Repeat
        Increment Count.
        Add the Term to the Sum.
        Compute the next Term.
Until the Sum exceeds 6.0
Output the value Count.
```

While the above pseudo-code could be implemented, we do not do so. Rather, we make some changes to it that make the program much easier to write. The point of this exercise is that time spent in planning a program is often time well spent. Do not dive into the writing of the program without having carefully considered the problem. Doing so only leads to a very complex program that is very difficult to get to run correctly. The observation that we would like to make about the current problem is that there is a very definite relationship between the value of Count, the counter of the terms, and Term, the current term. For example, the third term is 1/3, the eighth term is 1/8, etc. Hence, we do not need two different variables for Term and Count. Term, for example, can be obtained from Count. Here then is a second, simpler, and more specific pseudo-code from which the program Series can easily be written:

Initialize Sum and Count to 0.
Repeat
    Increment Count.
    Add the reciprocal of Count to Sum.
Until the Sum exceeds 6.0
Output the value of Count.

The reader should trace the above to see how Sum takes the successive values 1.0, 1.5, 1.83333, 2.08333, etc., as Count takes on the values 1, 2, 3, 4, etc. In listing 5.3, we have moved the 'Writeln' into the body of the loop. This does not change the result, of course, but gives us output to watch as the program runs.

```
program Series;
{ This program sums the series 1 + 1/2 + 1/3 + 1/4 + 1/5 + ... }
{ until the sum exceeds 6.0 and then announces how many terms}
{ were needed to exceed 6.0. }

var
  Sum : Real;
  Count : Integer;

begin
  Sum := 0.0;
  Count := 0;
  repeat
   Count := Count + 1;
   Sum := Sum + 1 / Count;
   Writeln('The sum after ', Count : 3, ' terms is ', Sum : 8 : 6)
  until Sum > 6.0
end.
```

Listing 5.3

The reader should make a guess as to how many terms are needed, then run Series to see how far off the guess was.

The While

Pascal provides another form of a repetitive control structure called the **while**. The **while** is contrasted with the **repeat...until** shortly.

There are many instances where either the **while** or the **repeat...until** can be used. It is often a matter of programming convenience where you choose whichever fits the given situation better. Actually, the **while** is slightly more general than the **repeat...until** and therefore most texts introduce the **while** first. We believe, however, that the **repeat...until** is simpler and easier to understand and, hence, we began with it. The order of their introduction is not important. Make sure that you understand the slight differences between them. Both are "tools" that are very important for your understanding of Pascal.

If, in a given situation, you would like to loop while such and such is True, then the **while** is the answer to your prayers. The format of the **while** is:

> **while** Boolean expression **do**
> Statement;

Fortunately, of course, the 'Statement' may be compound. When execution reaches the **while**, the Boolean expression is tested. If it is False, then the statement following the **do** is skipped and the flow of control passes to the next statement in your program. On the other hand, if the Boolean expression is True, then the statement following the **do** is executed once. Then the expression is tested again and the statement is repeatedly executed *while* the expression remains True. Hence, there must be some mechanism within the body of the loop for the Boolean expression to eventually become False and for the loop to terminate.

How do the **while** and **repeat...until** differ? There are several fundamental differences:

The **while** tests the Boolean expression at the top of the loop and the **repeat...until** tests the Boolean expression at the bottom of the loop. As a consequence, the **repeat...until** always executes the body of the loop at least once--even if the condition is initially True. The **while**, on the other hand, if the condition is initially False, will execute the body of the loop zero times and then continue with the next statement in your program. Fortunately, from the syntax of the **repeat...until** and the **while**, it is easy to remember which tests the Boolean expression where. Soon, we shall give an example of a situation where we might wish to execute some loop zero times. Hence, it is the **while** that is slightly more flexible than the **repeat...until**.

Another difference between these two statements is that the **while** loops while the expression is True and the **repeat...until** loops until the expression is True. Or if you like to view things perversely: The **while** loops until the expression becomes False and the **repeat...until** loops while the expression is False.

As our first example of a **while**, let's modify the amazing program that counts from 1 to 20 to a **while** loop. The program is shown in listing 5.4.

```
program Count_2;
(This amazing program counts from 1 to 20 using a WHILE.)

var
  Num : Integer;

begin
  Num := 1;
  while Num <= 20 do
   begin
     Writeln(Num);
     Num := Num + 1
   end  (While)
end.
```

Listing 5.4

Although Count_2 is a very simple program, some remarks should be made. Notice that whenever the body of the **while** is more than one statement, a **begin** and **end** pair is necessary to make the statement following the **do** a compound statement. Also note that, as always, all four parts of a loop are present. The initialization ('Num := 1') is done before the loop is entered. The test is, of course, whether Num is less than or equal to 20, and in the body of the loop is the modification ('Num := Num + 1) by which the loop eventually terminates.

Since the **while** and the simple **if** have similar formats,

while Boolean expression **do** statement

if Boolean expression **then** statement

let us compare and contrast them so that you clearly understand the difference. Both check the Boolean expression and skip the given statement if the expression is False. Likewise, both execute the given statement if the expression is True. However, the **if** executes the given statement *at most once* and then continues on to the next statement in your program. The **while**, on the other hand, continues to execute the given statement as long as the expression remains True. The **if** is used to choose between two courses of action; the **while** is used to create a loop.

Examples

Professor Pedantics likes to give quizzes, and therefore needs a program to compute averages for her students. Let us suppose that each of her students has taken three quizzes and that names and quiz scores of her students are stored on a text file Scores.   Each student has two lines in the text file. The first line consists of a name (30 characters), while the second line contains the three scores. Clearly, we want to loop, reading students' names and quiz scores, outputting averages as we go. How shall we terminate the loop? Probably the most natural suggestion would be to count Professor Pedantics' students and to loop that many times. But Professor Pedantics teaches at large, Abnormal State University and even she doesn't know how many students she has. She could count them, but that seems unnecessary with a computer around and, besides, humans are error-prone at such activities as counting.   Also, students, from our experience, are a pretty shifty lot. They add classes late; they drop like flies after the first exam. In short, you can never count on them anyway! Therefore, a better and more general solution to our problem is to make up a final, fictitious student whose sole purpose will be to signify the end of the data. This final value is often called a **trailer**, or **sentinel** value. It is chosen as some ridiculous value that could not possibly be in the real data. For example, if we were entering student ID numbers, a value of 0 or –1 would make a nice trailer value. Another term for a trailer value is a "Mickey Mouse" value. Hence, for our example we choose to end the loop when we encounter the name 'Mickey Mouse'.   Hence, the last line of the text file Scores is 'Mickey Mouse'. Stated in **while** language, we loop while we haven't found 'Mickey Mouse'. Here is our outline for Professor Pedantics:

```
Read the first Name
While the Name is not 'Mickey Mouse' do
      Read the three scores
      Total the three scores
      Average the three scores
      Output the Name and the Average
      Read the next name
```

Note that since this is pseudo-code, we have omitted the **begin**'s and **end**'s that are necessary in the final, Pascal version. Also note that, as always, we must be sure that the condition in the **while** makes sense the first time. Since this condition involves a comparison of Name with 'Mickey Mouse', we must make sure that Name has an initial value. Thus, the first input, which is implemented as a Readln (from a text file), is necessary before the **while**. Likewise, we know that there must be some mechanism for the condition to eventually become False. Hence, at the bottom of the body we modify the value of Name by obtaining the next name. Now, of course, the expression is tested again and if the name is a legitimate one, the body is executed again and Name again is updated. Eventually, at the bottom of the loop, Name becomes 'Mickey Mouse' and the loop terminates. Note also that the loop terminates without trying to process three scores for Mickey. The Pascal equivalent is shown in listing 5.5.

```
program Pedantics;
(This program averages 3 quizzes for a class of students.)
(The program reads the text file Scores, which has a trailer)
(name of "Mickey Mouse" to mark the end of the data.)
  var
    Name : string[30];
    Quiz1, Quiz2, Quiz3 : Integer;
    Average : Real;
  begin
   Close(Input);   (Redirect Input to come from the)
   Reset(Input, 'Scores');            (text file Scores.)
   Writeln('Professor Pedantics quiz averaging program.');
   Writeln;
   Readln(Name);
   while Name <> 'Mickey Mouse' do
     begin
       Readln(Quiz1, Quiz2, Quiz3);
       Average := (Quiz1 + Quiz2 + Quiz3) / 3.0;
       Writeln('The average for ', Name, ' is ', Average : 6 : 2);
       Readln(Name)
     end  (While)
  end.
```

Listing 5.5

In all of our examples using text files, we assume that the necessary text file has been copied to the Macintosh Pascal disk. (See the discussion at the end of Chapter 4.) Of course, if you have two drives, you can change the Reset to "Reset(Input, 'Sample:Scores');" and place the Sample disk in drive 2.

Several changes between the pseudo-code and the Pascal version of Pedantics are worthy of discussion. Note that in the program, the average was computed on one line, combining two lines from the pseudo-code. The pseudo-code is still the outline for the program, but it shouldn't be considered a strait jacket for the writing of the program. In the program we included a Writeln to announce the purpose of the progam. That is not really part of the solution, but it is a good programming practice. We also remark that if this program had used interactive input from the keyboard, we would also want to use a Writeln statement to remind the user of the trailer value needed to terminate the **while** loop.

The "End of File" Function

If you are interactively entering data from the keyboard, a trailer value is an effective way to control the processing loop. If you are reading data from a text file, there is another alternative supplied by the Pascal system. This is the built-in EOF or "End of File" function. EOF is a Boolean function that is only True when the system detects the end of the data file. Thus, unless the file is empty, EOF is initialized by a Reset command to False. When the last item is read from the file, EOF becomes true. Thus,

while not EOF(Input) **do**

is a natural construct to use with text files. Listing 5.6 shows Pedantics_2, which uses EOF to control the processing of the text file Scores2.

The only difference between Scores and Scores2 is that Scores2 does *not* contain any trailer value. Rather than quit when we find 'Mickey Mouse', we quit when the system sets EOF to True.

We would like to emphasize that EOF is particularly useful with disk files, but not of much use with interactive input from the keyboard. The reason for this is simple: With a file on disk, the system has the complete file, and, hence, can easily tell when the end of the file has been reached. On the other hand, with interactive input, the system is unable to read the mind of the user and is therefore unable to decide when all the data has been entered. Thus, in what follows, we shall use EOF with disk files and use trailer or sentinel values to terminate interactive input.

```
program Pedantics_2;
(This program averages 3 quizzes for a class of students.)
(The program reads the text file Scores2 and uses the )
(built-in function EOF to find the end of the data.)

var
  Name : string[30];
  Quiz1, Quiz2, Quiz3 : Integer;
  Average : Real;

begin
  Close(Input);    (Redirect Input to come from the)
  Reset(Input, 'Scores2');        (text file Scores2.)
  Writeln('Professor Pedantics quiz averaging program - Version 2.');
  Writeln;
  while not EOF do
    begin
      Readln(Name);
      Readln(Quiz1, Quiz2, Quiz3);
      Average := (Quiz1 + Quiz2 + Quiz3) / 3.0;
      Writeln('The average for ', Name, ' is ', Average : 6 : 2)
    end    (While)
end.
```

Listing 5.6

There is a subtle difference between listings 5.5 and 5.6 that is quite important. This difference is illustrated in figures 5.6 and 5.7. Consider figure 5.6 first. As we have said, the condition in the **while** must be initialized *before* the **while**. Hence, we must obtain the first item *before* the loop so that the test of the item with the sentinel value will make sense. If the item is not the sentinel, it is processed and the next item is obtained at the foot of the **while**. Eventually, after the last actual data value is processed, the sentinel is read and the flow of execution exits the **while**. Note that the sentinel value is not processed as an actual data value. Figure 5.6 illustrates the standard processing loop for a situation controlled by a sentinel value.

```
Read first item
While the item is not the sentinel do
Begin
    ...

    ...
    Process the item

    ...

    ...
    Read the next item
End
```

Figure 5.6 Processing Loop with Sentinel


```
While not EOF do
    Begin
        Read item

        ...

        ...
        Process item

        ...

        ...
    End
```

Figure 5.7 Processing Loop with EOF

On the other hand, figure 5.7 illustrates the standard processing loop for a situation controlled by EOF. Note that all the data values (including the first one) are read *inside* the loop, at the top of the **while**. The reason for this placement of the Reads (or Readlns) is clear if you understand how EOF works. EOF is initialized by the Reset statement and unless the file is empty, EOF is set to False. Hence, as always, we have ensured that the condition in the **while** makes sense when execution reaches the **while**. It is also important to note that the last data value is not "lost." When the last data item is read, EOF becomes True, but execution does not exit the **while** until the body of the **while** is completed. Thus, the last item is processed before the condition is tested again and before control exits the **while**.

The differences between figures 5.6 and 5.7 may seem slight, but they are not unimportant. Using the wrong processing method can lead to errors that are difficult to debug. Make sure you understand how to write a correct processing loop controlled by a sentinel and a correct processing loop controlled by EOF.

As another example of EOF, we present in listing 5.7 a very short but useful program called UTFR.

```
program UTFR;  {Universal Text File Reader}
{This program reads any text file, watching for EOF.}

var
  FileName : string;
  S : string;

begin
  Writeln('What is the name of the text file you wish to see?');
  Readln(FileName);
  Close(Input);
  Reset(Input, FileName);
  while not EOF do
    begin
      Readln(S);
      Writeln(S)
    end  {While}
end.
```

Listing 5.7

UTFR stands for "Universal Text File Reader." The program UTFR reads *any* text file. It works by prompting the user to enter the name of a file and then resetting Input as that file. It then simply reads and writes lines of the file until the end of the file is encountered. UTFR can be a useful program to see the "structure" of a given text file or to see the actual values in a text file. Remember that if you have two drives, you must include the volume name to access files on disk 2. For example, if the disk Sample is in drive 2, you would type "Sample:Scores4" to see the contents of the file Scores4 on the Sample disk.

One of the first things you learn about writing programs for people is that they are always thinking of changes to make to the programs. For example, Professor Pedantics would like to have class averages for each of the three quizzes. This seems like a reasonable request, so let's consider what modifications will be needed to the program. To compute an average for Quiz1, we simply need to total all the scores for Quiz1 and then divide by the number of students. Likewise for Quiz2 and Quiz3. Hence, our program needs three new variables, Total1, Total2, and Total3. Also, we need to have the program count the students, since Professor Pedantics refuses to do such work. Hence, we also add a variable Count to the program. Of course, all of our new variables, being running sums and counters, must be initialized to zeros. Listing 5.8 shows Pedantics_3, which also reads the text file Scores2.

Beginners often have trouble deciding which Writeln's go in the loop, which go before the loop, and which go after the loop. Obviously, those Writeln's that are to be repeated should go in the loop. Any headings that are to be printed only once at the beginning should be placed before the loop. Likewise, any summaries printed at the end should be placed after the loop. This seems simple enough, but for some reason, in the above example, beginners are inclined to include the class average calculations in the loop. Of course, class averages don't make much sense until after all the quizzes have been read in. The simple rule is this: How many times should a given statement be executed? If the answer is once, then the statement does not belong in a processing loop.

Finding Maxima and Minima

A frequent problem is to find the biggest or smallest value from among a set of values. For example, let us suppose we are to find the highest and lowest temperatures reported from among a group of cities. Think, for a moment, how the human processor would find the answer.

Figure 5.8

```
program Pedantics_3;
(This program computes student averages on three quizzes as well )
(as class averages on each quiz. It also reads the text file Scores2.)

  var
    Name : string[30];
    Quiz1, Quiz2, Quiz3 : Integer;
    Total1, Total2, Total3 : Integer;
    Count : Integer;
    Student_Ave : Real;

begin
  Close(Input);      (Redirect Input to come from the)
  Reset(Input, 'Scores2');        (text file Scores2.)
  Writeln('Professor Pedantics quiz averaging program - Version 3');
  Writeln;
  Total1 := 0;
  Total2 := 0;
  Total3 := 0;
  Count := 0;
  while not EOF do
   begin
    Count := Count + 1;
    Readln(Name);
    Readln(Quiz1, Quiz2, Quiz3);
    Student_Ave := (Quiz1 + Quiz2 + Quiz3) / 3.0;
    Writeln('The average for ', Name, ' is ', Student_Ave : 6 : 2);
    Total1 := Total1 + Quiz1;
    Total2 := Total2 + Quiz2;
    Total3 := Total3 + Quiz3
   end;  (While)
  Writeln;
  Writeln('The class contains ', Count : 3, ' students.');
  writeln;
  Writeln('The class average on quiz #1 was ', Total1 / Count : 6 : 2);
  Writeln('The class average on quiz #2 was ', Total2 / Count : 6 : 2);
  Writeln('The class average on quiz #3 was ', Total3 / Count : 6 : 2);
end.
```

Listing 5.8

To find the maximum, we can imagine the human in figure 5.8 scanning down through the data, remembering the largest number encountered so far. Likewise, for the minimum. If we give our human a little larger memory, he can find both the minimum and the maximum on one scan. Our program attempts to simulate this behavior. However, both Max and Min need to be initialized before the loop. One method (we shall see more general methods later) is to initialize Max and Min to ridiculous values so that any real temperature will be bigger than Max's initial value and smaller than Min's initial value. For example, letting Min start at Maxint, i.e., 32767, and Max at -Maxint, i.e., -32767, should do the trick. That is, since Max is getting bigger and bigger, we initialize Max to the smallest integer in the computer. Likewise, Min is getting smaller and smaller so it begins as the largest integer in the computer. Here is the outline:

```
Initialize Max to -Maxint
Initialize Min to Maxint
While there are more Cities do
        Obtain a City
        Obtain a Temp for the city
        Compare Temp and Max and change Max if necessary
        Compare Temp and Min and change Min if necessary
Output the Max and Min
```

The program corresponding to this pseudo code is shown in listing 5.9.

```
program Temperature;
{This program finds the highest and lowest temperature from}
{among a group of reporting cities. It reads the text file Temps}
{that is assumed to be on the Macintosh Pascal disk.}
{If you have two drives, see the text for an explanation of how}
{to read the text file from another disk.}

var
    Max : Integer;
    Min : Integer;
    Temp : Integer;
    City : string;
```

(Continued)

```
begin
  Close(Input);    {Redirect Input to come from the}
  Reset(Input, 'Temps');         {text file Temps.}
  Max := -Maxint;
  Min := Maxint;
  while not EOF do
   begin
     Readln(City);
     Readln(Temp);
     Writeln(City : 30, Temp);
     if Temp > Max then
       Max := Temp;
     if Temp < Min then
       Min := Temp
   end; {While}
  Writeln;
  Writeln('The maximum temperature reported was ', Max : 3);
  Writeln('The minimum temperature reported was ', Min : 3)
end.
```

Listing 5.9

Run Temperature from your disk, or enter it from the keyboard. Note that Temperature also needs the text file Temps. The program works, but something is clearly missing. See exercise 5.7 to fix it up.

Repeat vs. While

Our next example completes a promise made earlier in this chapter to give a situation in which a **while** loop is more appropriate than a **repeat...until** loop.

Suppose the **div** instruction is "broken" on your Macintosh. How could you live without it? Well, remember X **div** Y answers the burning question: How many Y's are there in X? A method (admittedly slow) of finding the answer is to use repeated subtraction. That is, 19 **div** 5 is 3 since 19-5=14, 14-5=9, and 9-5=4. That is, we subtracted 5 from 19 *three* times before we obtained a remainder less than 5. This seems like an ideal situation for a **repeat...until**. We simply subtract Y's from X and remember how many Y's we subtract, until we get a "remainder" less than Y. The program Division of listing 5.10 implements this alogrithm to compute X **div** Y. However, the program contains a subtle logical error. Can you spot it?

```
program Division;
(This program illustrates that a "Repeat ... Until" is not)
(always as appropriate as a "While". The program does)
(division by repeated subtraction, but has a small bug in it.)

var
    Divisor, Dividend, Quotient, Temp : Integer;

begin
    Writeln('I will do division problems by repeated subtraction.');
    Write('Please enter the Divisor: ');
    Readln(Divisor);
    Write('Please enter the Dividend: ');
    Readln(Dividend);
    Temp := Dividend;
    Quotient := 0;
    repeat
        Temp := Temp - Divisor;
        Quotient := Quotient + 1
    until Temp < Divisor;
    Writeln;
    Writeln(Dividend : 1, ' Div ', Divisor : 1, ' is ', Quotient : 1)
end.
```

Listing 5.10

Consider some typical output from various runs of the program Division:

```
19 Div  5 is 3
 4 Div  9 is 1
10 Div  7 is 1
 3 Div 11 is 1
```

Wait a minute! 4 **div** 9 is 0, not 1. Likewise, 3 **div** 11 is 0. The program produces correct output for X **div** Y if X ≥ Y, but it produces the answer 1, not 0, if X < Y. The reason for this, of course, is that the body of any **repeat...until** is executed at least once even if the condition (in this case, Temp < Divisor) is already true. What is needed is a **while** loop that executes *zero* times if the dividend is less than the divisor. The details are left to the reader as an exercise.

Nested Loops

Since the statements in the body of a loop can be any legal Pascal statements, it is possible for one loop to be nested within another one. That is, a **while** can be inside another **while** or inside a **repeat...until**. As an example of the complexities involved in nested loops, try to determine the output of the program Nested shown in listing 5.11:

```
program Nested;
(This program illustrates nested loops.)
(Determine the output of this program.)

var
   Outer, Inner : Integer;

begin
   Writeln('Output from program "Nested".');
   Writeln;
   Outer := 1;
   while Outer <= 20 do
    begin
      Writeln('Multiples of ', Outer : 2);
      Inner := 1;
      while Inner <= 10 do
       begin
         write(Outer * Inner : 4);
         Inner := Inner + 1
       end; (inner While)
      Writeln;
      Outer := Outer + 1
    end; (outer While)
   Writeln('That''s all folks!')
end.
```

Listing 5.11

In anticipating the output of this program, realize that the first and last Writeln's are outside of all loops and, hence, execute exactly once providing a "header" and "footer" to our output. On the other hand, the "Multiples of" statement is in the outer loop, which clearly executes 20 times. This, of course, gives us 20 slightly different lines of output. The

'Write(Outer * Inner : 4)' is caught inside both loops. It clearly executes
10 times (Inner runs from 1 to 10) for each value of Outer. Hence, this
inner Write executes 200 times. However, since it is a Write and not a
Writeln, we only get 20 lines of output. Run the program Nested to see the
output as it is produced. It is sometimes difficult for beginners to decide
which statements go inside both loops, which outside both loops, and
which in the outer but not in the inner loop. Considering how many times
the statement should execute usually solves this problem. If the answer
is one, then the statement belongs outside all loops. If the answer is 20
times or 200 times, then the placement of the statement should be clear.

```
program Nested_2;
{This program illustrates nested loops. It is a modification}
{ of "Nested". Determine the output of this program.}

var
  Inner, Outer : Integer;

begin
  Writeln('Output from program "Nested_2".');
  Writeln;
  Outer := 1;
  while Outer <= 10 do
   begin
    Writeln('Multiples of ', Outer);
    Inner := 1;
    while Inner <= 20 do
     begin
       write(Outer * Inner : 4);
       Inner := Inner + 1
     end; {inner While}
    Writeln;
    Outer := Outer + 1
   end; {outer While}
  Writeln('That''s all folks!')
end.
```

Listing 5.12

The value of the index in the inner loop changes most quickly. Hence, the successive values of Outer and Inner in the program of figure 5.11 are 1,1, 1,2, 1,3, 1,4, . . . , 1,10, 2,1, 2,2, 2,3, . . . , 2,10, 3,1, 3,2, . . . , 20,10. To see that the order of the inside and outside loops is critical, consider Nested_2 as in listing 5.12. Nested_2 is like Nested except that the loop from 1 to 10 is now on the outside. Predict the output from Nested_2 and run it to see if you were correct.

As a more useful example of nested loops, let's consider another program for Professor Pedantics. Because different students have taken different numbers of quizzes, she would like a program that would read a student's name, the number of quizzes that student has taken, and then the actual quiz scores for that student. The program should properly compute the average for each student. For example, the data might look like this:

```
Otto Mobile
4 87 45 77 86
Dyna Sore
3 97 95 76
Neal Lee Perfect
5 100 99 100 100 99
Noe Hope
2 43 7
. . .
```

Thus, Otto has taken 4 quizzes with the scores indicated, Dyna only 3 quizzes, and so on. Obviously, we loop on the students and since different students have taken different numbers of exams, we need an inner summing loop for each student. Here is our outline:

```
While there are more names do
      Obtain the Name
      Obtain the Number of Quizzes taken by this student
      Initialize Sum to zero
      Initialize a counter, Count, to zero.
      While Count < Number of Quizzes do
            Obtain the next score
            Add the Score to Sum
            Increment the counter
      Move to the next line of the file
      Compute the average
      Output the average for the given student
```

Notice how the indentation makes the extent of each loop clear. Once again, the translation into Pascal is very straightforward. Run Pedantics_4, which is shown in listing 5.13.

```pascal
program Pedantics_4;
{This program computes averages for students, and allows for }
{different students to have taken different numbers of quizzes.}
{It reads the text file Scores4.}

var
  Name : string[30];
  Num_Quiz : Integer;
  Score : Integer;
  Sum : Integer;
  Ave : Real;
  Count : Integer;

begin
  Close(Input);       {Redirect Input to come from the}
  Reset(Input, 'Scores4');          {text file Scores4}
  Writeln('Professor Pedantics program - version 4.');
  Writeln;
  while not EOF do
   begin
    Sum := 0;
    Readln(Name);
    Read(Num_Quiz);
    Count := 0;
    while Count < Num_Quiz do
     begin
       Read(Score);
       Sum := Sum + Score;
       Count := Count + 1;
     end; {Inner While}
    Readln; {Advance to next line of the text file.}
    Ave := Sum / Num_Quiz;
    Writeln('The average for ', Name, ' is ', Ave : 6 : 2)
   end {Outer While}
end.
```

Listing 5.13

This time, Pedantics_4 reads the scores from the text file Scores4. The purpose of the "Readln;" after the inner **while** is to advance the file to the next line (if there is one), since the inner **while** only contains Read statements (and not Readln statements). That is, after the first execution of the inner **while**, the file has been processed up to the end of the second line:

    Otto Mobile
    4 87 45 77 86↟

So that the next execution of "Readln(Name)" finds Dyna's name (and not the End-of-Line), the file pointer needs to be positioned at the start of the third line:

    Otto Mobile
    4 87 45 77 86
   ↟Dyna Sore

The "Readln;" accomplishes this for us.

An example that illustrates many of the topics covered up to this point is a program that determines prime numbers. This example requires no higher mathematics, only arithmetic. A prime number, recall, is a positive integer larger than 1 whose only divisors are 1 and itself. For example, 17 is prime, but 15 is not since 3*5 = 15. Let us write a program to find all primes between 1000 and 1500. Obviously, we have found our outer loop. However, since there are no even primes between 1000 and 1500, we need only consider the odd numbers between 1001 and 1499. Hence, we may initialize Number to 1001 and increment it by 2 each time. Here is a preliminary outline of the program:

    Initialize Number to 1001
    Repeat
        Determine whether Number is prime and print it if so
        Increment Number by 2
    Until Number > 1500

What is involved in determining if a given Number is Prime? We must try all possible divisors. Another loop! But where does this inner loop begin and end? Since Number is odd, it only has odd divisors (Why?). Hence, we may begin our testing with the possible Factor 3, and we increment Factor by 2 each time also. What is the largest factor we need to try? If a number has a factor, then it has a co-factor too. For example, 2 and 12 are co-factors of 24 since 2*12=24. Likewise, 6 and 9 are co-factors of 54. Notice that 7 is its own co-factor with respect to 49. We claim that if a Number has a Factor, then it has a Factor less than or equal to its own square root. For if both co-factors are bigger than the square root, then the product is bigger than the given number. Hence, to determine if a given odd Number is prime, we need only try odd divisors between 3 and the square root of the Number. For example, to decide if 391 is prime we need only try the factors 3, 5, 7, 9, 11, 13, 15, 17, and 19 since $\sqrt{391}$ = 19.7737. In this case we see that 391 is not prime since 391 = 17*23.

Of course, as we try the factors, if we find one that divides evenly into the given Number, we may reject that Number and continue with the next. However, just because 3 doesn't divide evenly into the Number, we are not permitted to declare the Number to be prime. We can only safely declare the number to be prime if no factor at all is found for it. Here is our expanded outline:

```
Initialize Number to 1001
Repeat
     Initialize Prime to True (Give every Number a chance)
     Initialize Factor to 3
     Initialize Limit to √Number
     While (Factor <= Limit) and Prime do
             If Factor divides Number evenly then
                     Set Prime to False
             Else
                     Increment Factor by 2
     If still Prime then
             Output the Number as a prime
     Increment Number by 2
Until Number > 1500
```

Several points about the outline still need to be discussed. Notice that the inner **while** loops until either we find a Factor or until the Factor exceeds the limit. Since there are two ways to exit from the **while**, an **if** is needed after the **while** to determine how the **while** ended. If it ended because all Factors were tried and none were found that would divide the Number, then the Number is granted "primehood." Of course, using such operations as **mod** we can express in Pascal the question of whether

"Factor divides Number evenly." Namely, "Factor divides number evenly" just in case the remainder upon division of Number by Factor is zero. Since the **mod** function computes the remainder upon an integer division, we have that "Factor divides Number evenly" if Number **mod** Factor equals zero. The Pascal program is shown in listing 5.14.

```
program Prime;
(This program finds primes between 1000 and 1500)

var
   Number : Integer;
   Factor : Integer;
   Prime : Boolean;
   Limit : Integer;

begin
   Writeln('Here are the primes between 1000 and 1500');
   Writeln;
   Number := 1001;
   repeat
     Prime := True; (Give Number every chance.)
     Factor := 3;
     Limit := Trunc(Sqrt(Number));
     while (Factor <= Limit) and Prime do
       if Number mod Factor = 0 then
         Prime := False ( A factor has been found.)
       else
         Factor := Factor + 2; (Try next odd factor.)
     if Prime then     (Time to announce the "Primehood" of Number.)
       Writeln(Number);
     Number := Number + 2 (Increment to next odd Number.)
   until Number > 1500
end.
```

Listing 5.14

Notice that the Boolean expression 'Factor <= Limit' cannot be changed to 'Factor < Limit' because to prove that numbers like 49 are not prime, we must include $\sqrt{49}$ or 7 in our list of factors. Also, conserving on variables and writing 'Factor <= Sqrt(Number)' is not wise as this forces the system to recompute the square root each time it makes the comparison. Using the variable Limit, the system needs to take the square root of each

Number only once. See exercise 5.14 for further details on this matter, an efficiency question.

The For Statement

The final repetitive statement in Pascal is the **for**, which is useful if you know in advance how many times you would like a loop to be executed. The **for** is often referred to as a "definite" loop, as opposed to "indefinite" loops like the **while** and the **repeat...until**. The format of the **for** loop is:

> **for** Index_variable := Initial **to** Final **do**
>   Statement;

where, for now, the Index_Variable must be an integer variable and Initial and Final are integer variables, constants, or expressions. For example, a counted loop that is to execute 10 times can be generated by:

> **for** Count := 1 **to** 10 **do**
>   Statement;

where, of course, 'Statement' may be compound. Listing 5.15 shows a simple program, Table, that produces a table of the squares and cubes of the first 20 integers.

Notice that several of the parts of the loop are performed automatically by the **for**. For example, in the above program when execution reaches the **for**, Number is automatically initialized to the initial value 1. Also, before each execution of the body of the loop, the system tests to see if Number has exceeded the final value of 20. Moreover, after each execution of the body, the system automatically increments the index variable Number by 1. Hence, all four parts of a loop are present, but no longer is each the responsibility of the programmer. Notice that since the test is made before the loop is executed, it is possible for a loop to execute zero times. Thus, although fairly dumb, the statement

> **for** I := 5 **to** 1 **do**
>   Statement

is not an error. In this case, the statement following the **do** is not executed and control passes to the next statement in your program.

```
program Table;
(This program produces a table of the squares)
(and cubes of the integers from 1 to 20.)
  var
    Number : Integer;
    Square : Integer;
    Cube : Integer;
begin
  Writeln('Handy dandy table of squares and cubes.');
  Writeln;
  Writeln('Number' : 10, 'Square' : 10, 'Cube' : 10);
  Writeln;
  for Number := 1 to 20 do
    begin
      Square := Number * Number;
      Cube := Number * Square;
      Writeln(Number : 10, Square : 10, Cube : 10)
    end (For)
end.
```

Listing 5.15

Very often, the final value of the index is given as a variable. Thus, in the Professor Pedantics problem of the last section, we could easily replace the inner **while** with a **for** as we know that the current student has taken Num_Quiz quizzes:

```
. . .
for Count := 1 to Num_Quiz do
  begin
    Read(Score);
    Sum := Sum + Score
  end; (for)
```

As another example of the **for** statement, consider a program that prints a table of dollar to German Mark conversions with the user selecting the initial and final dollar values. Here is an outline:

```
Obtain starting dollar value, Start, and final dollar value, Stop.
Output a heading for the Table.
For Dollar from starting value to stopping value do
    Convert Dollar to German Marks
    Output Dollar and Mark values.
```

Of course, to convert dollars to DM (Deutsche Mark), we need to know the conversion rate. Let us assume that it is 2.7389, i.e., each Dollar is worth 2.7389 DM. The program, given in listing 5.16, is again a direct translation of the pseudo-code.

```
program Dollars_To_DM;
{This program creates a table of Dollar to DM conversions}
{where the user inputs the starting and ending values.}

  const
    Rate = 2.7389;

  var
    Dollar : Integer;
    DM : Real;
    Start : Integer;
    Stop : Integer;

begin
    Writeln('This program converts US Dollars to German DM.');
    Writeln;
    Writeln('Enter starting dollar value for the table.');
    Readln(Start);
    Writeln('Enter ending dollar value for the table.');
    Readln(Stop);
    Writeln;
    Writeln('Table of conversions');
    Writeln;
    Writeln('Dollar' : 10, 'DM' : 10);
    Writeln;
    for Dollar := Start to Stop do
      begin
        DM := Dollar * Rate;
        Writeln(Dollar : 10, DM : 10 : 2)
      end  {For}
end.
```

Listing 5.16

You should run Dollar_To_DM several times including once where you enter a smaller final value than initial value.

There is an alternate form of the **for** that is useful if you need to run a loop backwards. Its format is:

```
for Index_Variable := Initial downto Final do
Statement
```

This time the Index_Variable is initialized to the Initial value and the body is executed if the index variable is not *smaller* than the Final value. Also, after each execution of the body, the index variable is *decremented* by 1. Here is a segment that sings a famous college song:

```
for Verse := 100 downto 1 do
  begin
    Writeln(Verse, ' bottles of beer on the wall.');
    Writeln(Verse, 'bottles of beer on the wall.');
    Writeln('Take one down, pass it around');
    Writeln(Verse - 1, ' bottles of beer on the wall.');
    Writeln
  end;
```

The Case Statement

Pascal provides a **case** statement that is useful when you have to choose one of many possibilities. For example, to make a six-way decision, one can use five nested **if...then...else** statements, but a **case** statement is probably the easier way. For example, suppose we have given scores between 0 and 5 on a programming assignment and would like to make an appropriate comment to each student. Suppose for this segment that Name already has a **string** value and Score already has an Integer value between 0 and 5. The following segment prints the appropriate messages:

```
Write(Name, ', you are ');
case Score of
 5:
  Writeln('outstanding! !');
 4:
  Writeln('good.');
 3:
  Writeln('OK.');
```

```
2:
  Writeln('barely passing.');
1:
  Writeln('failing.');
0:
  Writeln('hopeless.')
end;  (End of case)
```

When execution reaches the **case**, the value of Score is matched with one of the labels and the Writeln corresponding to that label is executed. For example, if Name is 'Neal Lee Perfect' and Score is 4 then the output is

Neal Lee Perfect, you are good.

On the other hand, if the Name is 'Prokras Tonater' and the Score is 0, then the output is

Prokras Tonater, you are hopeless.

Notice how the Write (and not Writeln) is used to write the first part of the line. As with **if**'s, the Write should not be repeated in each case. If any of the cases are compound, then **begin**'s and **end**'s are necessary. The syntax of the simple **case** statement is

```
case Index of
  Value_1:
    Statement_1;
  Value_2:
    Statement_2;
    . . .
    . . .
  Value_n:
    Statement_n
end;
```

For the present, Index must be an integer variable and Value_1 to Value_n must be distinct integer *constants*, called the **case labels**. At execution, the value of the **case index**, Index, is compared with the labels and if a match is found, the corresponding statement is executed. Flow of control then proceeds to the statement following the **case** statement. Standard Pascal says that it is an error if the **case** index does not match any of the labels. Macintosh Pascal provides an **otherwise** clause for such situations. The format of this extended **case** is:

```
case Index of
  Value_1:
    Statement_1;
  Value_2:
    Statement_2;
  . . .

  . . .
  Value_n:
    Statement_n;
  otherwise
    Statement_(n+1)
end;
```

In this case, if none of the values is matched, then the statement following the **otherwise** is executed. Note that in Macintosh Pascal it is an error if none of the labels matches and no **otherwise** clause is present. While not included in the standard definition of Pascal, the **otherwise** clause is surely a convenient way to handle all the special cases.

The **case** statement, we see, is useful when one of many possibilities is to be chosen. The **case** is clearer than a long sequence of nested **if**'s. But note that like the **repeat...until** that could be replaced with a **while**, the **case** adds nothing but convenience to the language. In later chapters we shall see that the **case** statement can be quite handy. Also note that the **case** has an **end** but no **begin**. Sorry, there is no good reason for such inconsistency. That's just the way it is. Also notice that the labels should be distinct. Violation of this is an error in Standard Pascal, although Macintosh Pascal does not report such an error but simply executes the first case that is matched.

As another example, consider a program to compute a simple, progressive tax. A progressive tax is designed to take more from the wealthy and less, percentage-wise, from the poor. Let us suppose that our progressive tax is designed in $5000.00 blocks and is given by table 5.1. Our first problem is to reduce the situation to a small number of cases as we do not want to write a **case** with 25,000 different cases. As we can see from the table, there are only six "brackets" in our progressive tax structure. We can almost compute each person's tax bracket by using

Bracket := (Income **div** 5000) + 1

Tax Table

Income Range	Tax Rate
Up to $4999.99	3%
Up to $9999.99	8%
Up to $14999.99	15%
Up to $19999.99	24%
Up to $24999.99	35%
Over $24999.99	50%

Table 5.1

Check that if Income has the value 12,500, then Bracket is properly assigned the value 3. Unfortunately, Lotta Bucks, with an Income of $85,000, is assigned to a nonexistent bracket number 18. This is easily corrected with an **if** and the program is as shown in listing 5.17.

Finally, let us point out that a **case** may have multiple labels. As an example, suppose we grade a project on a 20-point basis and then decide to give letter grades as follows:

```
18-20   A
15-17   B
13-14   C
10-12   D
 0- 9   F
```

Since there are really only five outcomes, it doesn't seem that we should need 20 cases. The following segment illustrates the use of multiple labels on one statement as well as the **otherwise** clause. In this segment, we assume Mark and Name already have values:

```
case Mark of
  18,19,20 :
   Grade := 'A';
  15, 16 :
   Grade := 'B';
  13,14:
   Grade := 'C';
  10,11,12:
   Grade := 'D';
```

```
  otherwise
    Grade := 'F'
  end;
  Writeln(Name, ', your grade is: ', Grade)

program Taxes;
{This program computes taxes based upon a progressive}
{scale. See the Tax Tables in Table 5.1.}

  var
    Income : Integer;
    Tax : Real;
    Bracket : Integer;

begin
  Writeln('Please enter your income - without the "$" sign.');
  Writeln('To avoid overflow, keep your income below 32767');
  Readln(Income);
  Bracket := (Income div 5000) + 1;
  if Bracket > 6 then
    Bracket := 6;
  case Bracket of
    1 :
      Tax := Income * 0.03;
    2 :
      Tax := Income * 0.08;
    3 :
      Tax := Income * 0.15;
    4 :
      Tax := Income * 0.24;
    5 :
      Tax := Income * 0.35;
    6 :
      Tax := Income * 0.50
  end; {Case}
  Writeln('The tax on your income of $', Income : 5, ' is $', Tax : 8 : 2)
end.
```

Listing 5.17

Here, naturally, if Mark matches any of the labels of a statement, then that statement is executed, while if Mark matches none of the labels, then the **otherwise** clause is executed. Note that the **otherwise** has no colon after it. In this regard it is more like an **else** than another regular case label.

Exercises

5.1   Write a program that creates a table of Celsius to Fahrenheit temperature conversions from 20 degrees to 40 degrees Celsius.   Of course, the magic formula is

$F = 9/5*C + 32.$

5.2 Modify the program of exercise 5.1 so that the user may choose the starting and ending temperatures for the table.

5.3 Modify the program of exercise 5.2 so that the user may also choose the interval (in degrees Celsius) between entries of the table. Use the program to request a table from −40 degrees Celsius to 50 degrees Celsius in steps of 5 degrees Celsius.

5.4 A colony of 700 Wallalumps increases by 8% each year. Write a program to predict the growth of the colony for each of the next 25 years.

5.5 Write a program that plays the following word game:

Player 1 chooses a word and enters it into the computer as the secret word for the game. Note that "Writeln(Chr(12))" clears the screen so that Player 2 cannot see the word.

Player 2 enters words, trying to guess the secret word. Suppose the secret word is "PASCAL and the user guesses "FORTRAN".   Then the computer gives the hint:

My word comes after FORTRAN in the dictionary.

Likewise, if the user guesses "ZEBRA", the computer responds with

My word comes before ZEBRA in the dictionary.

Finally (we hope), Player 2 guesses the secret word and the game ends with the message

> You guessed my word in XX guesses.

where XX is, of course, replaced by the appropriate value. Hint: If Guess and SecretWord are string variables, then

> Guess < SecretWord

is True if the value of Guess is alphabetically before the value of SecretWord. Actually, the computer orders the letters from 'A' to 'Z' and then from 'a' to 'z'. Hence, 'A' < 'M' and 'M' < 'a' are both True. To avoid this confusion, play the above game with the Caps Lock key depressed.

5.6 A piece of paper is 0.005 inches thick. How thick would the paper be if we folded it in half 35 times? Note that each time we fold the paper over on itself, it becomes twice as thick.

5.7 Modify the program Temperature so that it prints the name of the city with the maximum temperature as well as the name of the city with the minimum temperature.

5.8 Programs Ex5.8a, Ex5.8b, and Ex5.8c are all stored on the disk of sample programs and are all "buggy" versions of program Temperature. Execute each of these versions and from the erroneous output determine the error in each program.

5.9 Is the variable Temp necessary in program Division? What happens if we just use Dividend in place of Temp?

5.10 In the text file Porridge, each line contains the temperature of a bowl of porridge. Write a program for Goldilocks that prints the temperature of each bowl of porridge, and "Too Hot", "Too Cold", or "Just Right". Print "Too Hot" if the temperature exceeds 140 degrees, "Too Cold" if the temperature is less than 90 degrees, and "Just Right" otherwise. At the end of the program, you should print a count of how many bowls of each kind were found.

5.11 FICA (Social Security) tax is withheld at the rate of 6.7% on the first $35,700 of your salary. If you work for two or more employers and each withholds 6.7% of your first $35,700, you may end up paying too much FICA tax. Write a program that inputs the number of employers and the salary from each, and then computes the overpayment, if any, of your FICA tax.

5.12 Write a program that tabulates the totals of the Abnormal State University Cow Chip Throwing Contest. The information concerning the contest is found on the text file Chips. There are four lines of information for each entrant in the contest. The first line contains the name of the contestant, the second line contains a sex designation, the third line contains a status (Student or Faculty), and the fourth line contains the length of the throw in feet. A sample entry might look like this:

Polly Tishun
Female
Student
203.75

Your program should read the Chips file and print out a table of all contestants, listing the name, sex, status, and throw. At the end of the table, you should announce, with suitable fanfare, the winners in each of four categories (e.g., Male-Faculty, Female-Student) and the overall winner of the contest.

5.13 Write a program to help the Lemon Motor Company decide whether to keep its V-16 economy car, the Belchfire, in production. Data for the car is available on the text file Lemons and consists of two lines of data for each dealer. For example, the first four lines of the file Lemons are:

Tricky Dicks
10 5 8 3 0 7 2
Ottos Autos
100 7 56 24 0 89 120 99 34

The first entry of the second line means that Tricky Dick is expected to sell 10 Belchfires per month. The second value on that line indicates that 5 months of data are availabe for Tricky. The remaining data indicates that he has, in fact, sold 20 cars (8 + 3 + 0 + 7 + 2) in the last 5 months. Likewise, Otto, a big city dealer, is expected to sell 100 Belchfires a month; 7 months of data are available for Otto; and he has sold 56 + 24 + 0 + 89 + 120 + 99 + 34 = 422 cars in the last 7 months.

Your program for LMC should read the text file Lemons and output the following for each dealer: Dealer's name, expected monthly sales, average monthly sales, and an appropriate comment. If the dealer's average is less than half of the expected average, then the dealer should be warned severely that his/her business (or family) is in danger. On the other hand, dealers who have sold more Lemons than expected should be heartily congratulated. Those who deserve neither censure nor praise should receive a noncommital comment. Arrange the above output in 4 columns with appropriate headings. Finally, output the average monthly sales, the average expected sales, and an appropriate recommendation to Lemon Motor Company based on the above guidelines to the individual dealers.

5.14 Run program Prime from your disk of sample programs and time its execution. Also run Ex5.14 from your disk of sample programs and time its execution. Compare the two programs. Notice that they produce the same output. Why is Ex5.14 so much slower?

5.15 (Ulam's Conjecture) Write a program to generate a sequence of numbers according to the following scheme:
Begin with any positive integer greater than 1. If the current term is odd, then the next term is obtained by tripling the current term and adding 1, but if the current term is even, then the next term is obtained by halving the current term. Repeat this process until you obtain a term equal to 1.
For example, suppose we begin with 7. Then the sequence of terms is:

7 22 11 34 17 52 26 13 40 20 10 5 16 8 4 2 1

Of course, your program should prompt the user for the starting term. Run your program with 7 as the input to verify your program. Also, use 97 for an interesting sequence.
The claim that you will always come down to 1 is known as Ulam's conjecture. It has never been proven, but it has already been verified by computer for all "small" numbers. In our system, however, overflow occurs quickly. For example, why won't the program work properly if you begin the sequence with 30001? In Chapter 8, we shall see that Macintosh Pascal has a "long integer" type that is needed if you wish to test Ulam's conjecture on larger integers.
Hint: Use **mod** with a divisor of 2 to test the current term to see if it is even or odd.

5.16 (Armstrong Numbers) The number 153 has the odd property that
$$1^3 + 5^3 + 3^3 = 1 + 125 + 27 = 153$$
Namely, 153 is equal to the sum of the cubes of its own digits. Are there other three digit numbers that have this property? Write a program that tests all three digit numbers and prints out those that have the above property. There are four such numbers and they are known as the Armstrong Numbers of order three.

Hint: If you want to break a three digit number into its separate digits, use **div** and **mod** tricks with divisors like 100 or 10.

5.17 (Perfect Numbers) A number is said to be perfect if it is the sum of its own divisors (excluding itself). For example, 6 is perfect since 1, 2, and 3 divide evenly into 6 and 1+ 2 + 3 = 6. Verify by hand that 28 is also perfect. Write a program to find the next perfect number.

Warning: This program takes several minutes, even on the computer. Make sure that your program will find 6 and 28 before turning it loose.

5.18 (Abundant Numbers) A number is abundant if it is less than the sum of its divisors (excluding itself). For example, 12 is abundant since 1, 2, 3, 4, and 6 are the divisors of 12 and their sum is 16. The terminology "abundant" comes from the fact that such a number has an abundance of divisors. Write a program to find all abundant numbers less than 500. Since 1 is a special case, you may begin your search at 2. After your program runs, what do you notice about all abundant numbers less than 500?

5.19 (Odd Abundant Numbers) Write a program to find the first odd abundant number. Try to make your program as efficient as possible and use the results of Exercise 5.18. Even so, this takes several minutes to execute.

5.20 (Mad Dog) A man is in the center of the square garden depicted in figure 5.9. A well-trained, but vicious, dog is standing on the wall at the southwest corner of the garden. The dog can run Pi (3.14159) times as fast as the man, but the dog is trained to stay on the wall and not enter the garden at all.

Show by hand calculation that the ratio of distances for dog and man to point N is less than Pi, and, hence, the dog would be the winner to that point. Show, by another hand calculation, that the ratio of distances to corner C is even less favorable for the man. Thus, if the man can escape, he can only do so between points N and C.

Write a program that outputs the ratio for each point at two meter intervals from N to C. At each point, print its distance from N, the ratio, and a message ("OUCH" or "SAFE") depending on the ratio at that point. Can the man escape unscathed from the dog?

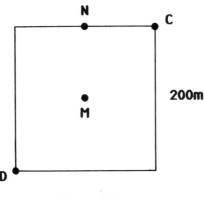

Figure 5.9

Chapter 6

Editing and Debugging

DEBUGGING – Removing a bug either by tinkering with the program or by amending the program specification so that the side effect of the bug is published as a desirable feature.
Devil's DP Dictionary

This chapter, like Chapter 2, is not about Pascal, but rather is about the Macintosh Pascal operating system. There are many elegant editing features of Macintosh Pascal, as well as useful, built-in debugging features to be revealed here. Thus, while you could skip this chapter, we believe you will find it most useful for your continued study of Macintosh Pascal. Only if you are perfect and never need to modify or debug your programs should you omit this chapter.

Do not try to memorize all the features of the system. This chapter demonstrates many features and the exercises help you practice them. Remember the kinds of things you can do with these editing and debugging tools, and then when you have need for them, refer back to this chapter.

The File Menu

Figure 6.1

Figure 6.1 shows the **File** menu. We briefly discuss each option.

New starts a new program window for you. The program is 'Untitled'. **New** is not available as a command if the program window is already open. Use **Close** (below) before **New**.

Open... presents a dialog box as shown in figure 6.2. The portion on the left is a partial catalog of the files available on your disk. By clicking the up and down arrows, you can scroll through the complete catalog.

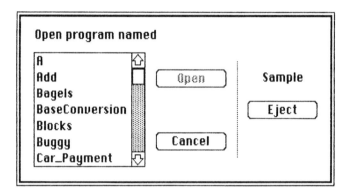

Figure 6.2

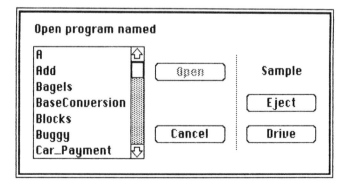

Figure 6.3

By clicking on a program and then clicking on the word **Open**, that program is loaded into the program window for you. Or by double clicking the program, you can select and open it. By clicking **Eject**, you eject the current disk. After inserting a new disk, the name and catalog of that disk are shown. With two disk drives, the dialog box appears as in figure 6.3. By clicking on **Drive**, you activate the other drive. Another click on **Drive** returns control to the original disk drive. As with **New**, **Open** is an available command only if the program window does not already contain a program. After a **Close**, **Open** is an available option.

Close puts away the current program in the program window. If your latest changes haven't been saved, then **Close** asks you if you wish to **Save** or **Discard** them before closing.

Save saves the current version of the program in the program window to the disk it was previously saved to. The manual says that if the program is 'Untitled,' then **Save** asks for its name. It is our experience that **Save** is not an available command until the program has been both named by **Save As...** and then subsequently modified. See the discussion below under **Save As....** for the differences between **Save** and **Save As....**

Save As... always asks for the name you would like to save your program as. If your program has been named already, this name shows in the dialog box. You may modify the name if you wish or leave it alone. See figure 6.4 and the discussion of **Save As...** in Chapter 2.

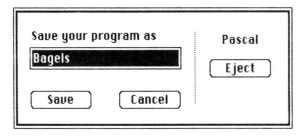

Figure 6.4

To actually save the program, you simply click in the **Save** box. **Eject** allows you to eject the disk and save the program on another disk. Again, if you have two drives, you may choose to save to the other drive by clicking **Drive**.

The differences between **Save** and **Save As...** are as follows: **Save As...** allows you to change the program's name or to change the disk. **Save** is quicker, but always saves under the same name to the same disk that the program was loaded from. **Save** is useful to make periodic saves of a program as you are working on it.

If neither **Save** nor **Save As...** is active in the **File** menu, it probably means that your program window is not the active window. Click anywhere in the program window and then **Save As...**, at least, should be an available option.

Revert allows you to return to the previously saved version of your program. Suppose you are editing a program and decide that you have really botched it and wish that you could return to the original version. **Revert** presents you with the dialog box shown in figure 6.5 and if you choose **Yes**, your program reverts to its previous form.

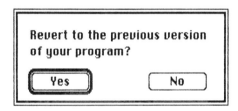

Figure 6.5

Warning: You cannot revert back past the last **Save**, so make sure that each **Save** you make is a step forward.

Page Setup allows you to choose from several different sizes of paper. For normal, American uses you should leave the settings at the standard sizes as shown in figure 6.6.

Paper:	⦿ US Letter	○ A4 Letter		OK
	○ US Legal	○ International Fanfold		
Orientation:	⦿ Tall	○ Tall Adjusted	○ Wide	Cancel

Figure 6.6

Print... begins the process of printing the program in the program window. You see the dialog box shown in figure 6.7.

Quality:	⊙ High	○ Standard	○ Draft	OK
Page Range:	⊙ All	○ From: [ ]	To: [ ]	
Copies:	[1]			
Paper Feed:	⊙ Continuous	○ Cut Sheet		Cancel

Figure 6.7

This permits you several choices, which you make by appropriate clicks. You choose from **High, Standard**, or **Draft** quality of print. The higher the quality, the slower the printing. You also choose a page range, if not **All** of the pages are to be printed. You decide the number of copies and tell the system whether the paper is **Continuous** feed (normal computer printout) or separate sheets of paper (**Cut Sheet**). If you are using separate sheets, then the system pauses after each page for you to insert the next page. The Tab key is used to move the flashing insertion pointer from option to option. Of course, you must also make sure that the printer is turned on and that it is ready. On an ImageWriter, the green select light must be on. Then click **OK** to start the printing.

    Quit closes the current program and exits the Macintosh system. If you have made changes to your program that have not been saved, you see the dialog box as shown in figure 6.8.

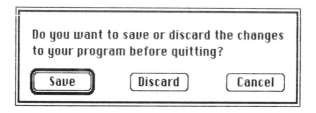

Do you want to save or discard the changes to your program before quitting?

[Save]   [Discard]   [Cancel]

Figure 6.8

The Edit Menu

    For reference purposes, the options under the **Edit** menu, shown in figure 6.9, are discussed together. Each is then illustrated in the example following the discussion of the options. Those who have used the

Macintosh for word processing or other applications are already familiar with these useful editing features.

Figure 6.9

For most of these options, some text must be selected or highlighted. Remember, as in Chapter 2, to select some text, drag the mouse over that text. A word can be selected by double clicking anywhere within the word.

Cut takes the currently selected text and moves it to the **Clipboard**, which is another window of the system. Only the most recently cut text is stored on the **Clipboard**.

Copy puts a copy of the currently selected text on the **Clipboard** without disturbing the currently selected text. Thus, **Cut** and **Copy** are very similar. The difference is that **Cut** removes the original and **Copy** does not.

Paste inserts the current contents of the **Clipboard** at the present position of the flashing insertion pointer (|). The contents of the **Clipboard** are left unchanged, so one item may be pasted repeatedly.

Select All is a shortcut whereby all text in the window becomes selected.

All of the **Edit** menu options are applicable to the **Instant** and **Observe** windows (discussed below) as well as the regular program window.

As an example, consider the program Edit shown in listing 6.1. Load Edit from your Sample diskette (or type it in now) and follow along with this example. Adjust the program and text windows so that they are larger and run the program to produce the output shown in figure 6.10.

```
program Edit;
begin
  Writeln('Unfortunately, this is the last sentence.');
  Writeln('This is the second sentence.');
  Writeln('This program prints three sentences.')
end.
```

Listing 6.1

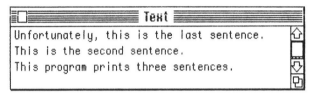

Figure 6.10

Clearly, the program runs without errors, but the output is in the wrong order. To readjust the lines, click in the program window and, by starting at the end of the first Writeln statement, select the first line and the previous carriage return by dragging the mouse up and slightly to the left as shown in figure 6.11.

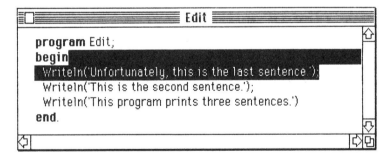

Figure 6.11

Now choose **Cut** from the **Edit** menu as shown in figure 6.12 and the selected text "disappears," leaving your screen as in figure 6.13. Move the mouse to the end of the last Writeln and click at that position to place the insertion cursor there. See figure 6.14.

Figure 6.12

```
┌─────────────────────────── Edit ───────────────────────────┐
│ ▤□                                                        ⇧ │
│ program Edit;                                                │
│ begin                                                        │
│   Writeln('This is the second sentence.');                   │
│   Writeln('This program prints three sentences.')            │
│ end.                                                       ⇩ │
│ ◁                                                       ⇦⇨ │
└─────────────────────────────────────────────────────────────┘
```

Figure 6.13

```
┌─────────────────────────── Edit ───────────────────────────┐
│ ▤□                                                        ⇧ │
│ program Edit;                                                │
│ begin                                                        │
│   Writeln('This is the second sentence.');                   │
│   Writeln('This program prints three sentences.')|           │
│ end.                                                       ⇩ │
│ ◁                                                       ⇦⇨ │
└─────────────────────────────────────────────────────────────┘
```

Figure 6.14

Since this is no longer the last Pascal statement in the program, we need to type a semicolon and then choose **Paste** from the **Edit** menu. The previously **Cut** line reappears at the end of the program as shown in figure 6.15.

The first two sentences are still out of order. We leave it to you to interchange them. You can **Cut** either sentence and then **Paste** it back into its proper place. When you finish, your program should appear as in figure 6.16.

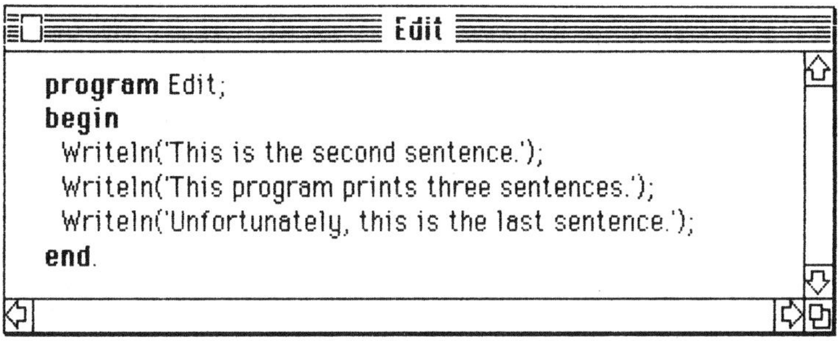

```
┌─────────────────────────────────────────────────┐
│▤□▤▤▤▤▤▤▤▤▤▤▤▤▤ Edit ▤▤▤▤▤▤▤▤▤▤▤▤▤▤│⇧│
├─────────────────────────────────────────────────┤
│  program Edit;                                  │ │
│  begin                                          │ │
│    Writeln('This is the second sentence.');     │ │
│    Writeln('This program prints three sentences.'); │
│    Writeln('Unfortunately, this is the last sentence.'); │
│  end.                                           │▽│
├─────────────────────────────────────────────────┤
│◁│                                            │⇨│⊡│
└─────────────────────────────────────────────────┘
```

Figure 6.15

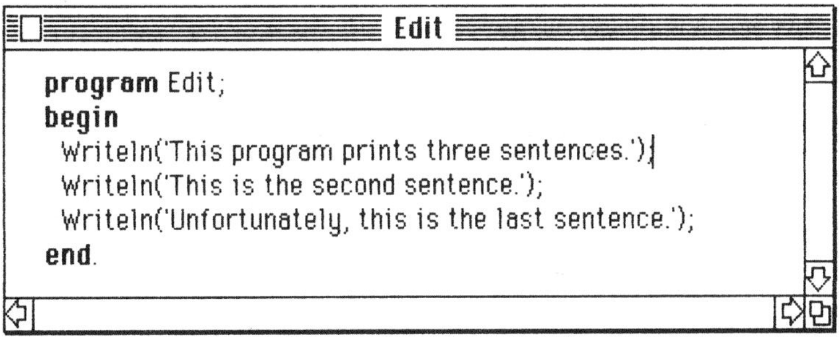

```
┌─────────────────────────────────────────────────┐
│▤□▤▤▤▤▤▤▤▤▤▤▤▤▤ Edit ▤▤▤▤▤▤▤▤▤▤▤▤▤▤│⇧│
├─────────────────────────────────────────────────┤
│  program Edit;                                  │ │
│  begin                                          │ │
│    Writeln('This program prints three sentences.')| │
│    Writeln('This is the second sentence.');     │ │
│    Writeln('Unfortunately, this is the last sentence.'); │
│  end.                                           │▽│
├─────────────────────────────────────────────────┤
│◁│                                            │⇨│⊡│
└─────────────────────────────────────────────────┘
```

Figure 6.16

Remember, if you mess it up completely, or would like to do this again for practice, use **Revert** from the **File** menu to restore your program to its original form.

To show how **Copy** can be useful, let's suppose that we want to double space the important output from this program To do so, we need to enter a "Writeln;" between the current lines of the program. Being basically lazy, we want to do as little typing as possible. Therefore, pick any of the Writeln statements in the program and select the word "Writeln" in that statement by double clicking it. Figure 6.17 shows the final "Writeln" selected.

Now choose **Copy** from the **Edit** menu. Nothing appears to happen, but a copy of the Writeln is placed on the **Clipboard**. (We shall learn how to view the Clipboard shortly.)

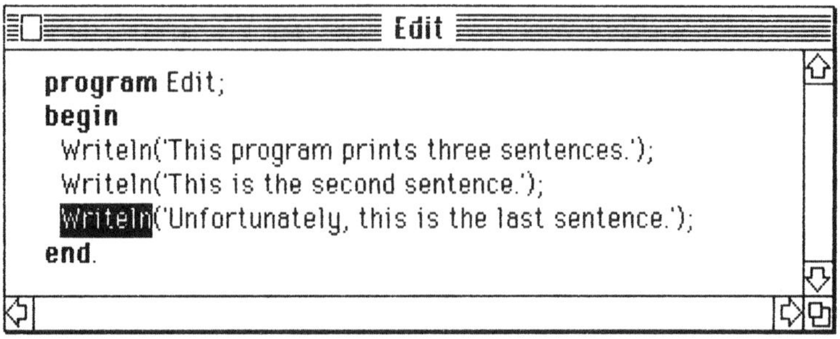

```
╔════════════════════ Edit ═══════════════════╗
║ program Edit;                                           ⇧
║ begin
║    Writeln('This program prints three sentences.');
║    Writeln('This is the second sentence.');
║    Writeln('Unfortunately, this is the last sentence.');
║ end.                                                    ⇩
╚══════════════════════════════════════════════╝
```

Figure 6.17

Move the mouse and place the insertion cursor after the first statement in
the program. Then choose **Paste** and your screen should appear as in
figure 6.18.

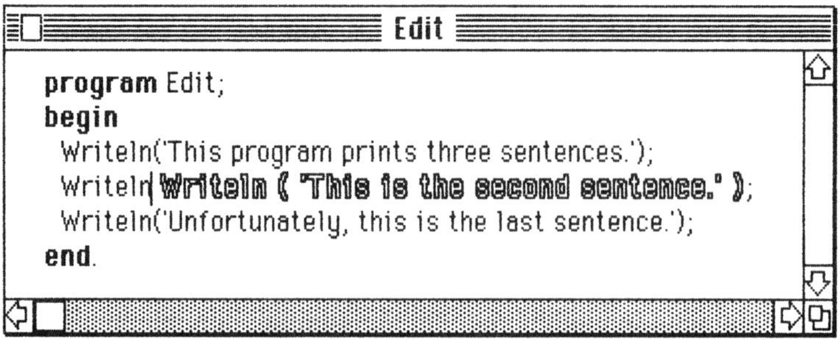

```
╔════════════════════ Edit ═══════════════════╗
║ program Edit;                                           ⇧
║ begin
║    Writeln('This program prints three sentences.');
║    Writeln|Writeln ( 'This is the second sentence.' );
║    Writeln('Unfortunately, this is the last sentence.');
║ end.                                                    ⇩
╚══════════════════════════════════════════════╝
```

Figure 6.18

The problem is that there is, of course, a missing semicolon after the
"Writeln." Since the insertion pointer is at that position, we simply type
the semicolon and the screen jumps to figure 6.19. Since the **Clipboard**
still contains "Writeln," we need only reposition the mouse behind the next
statement, choose **Paste** and then type the missing semicolon to make our
program appear as in figure 6.20.
        This example has been very simple, yet we hope it has shown you the
power of the **Edit** options. We have only cut and pasted lines, but whole
paragraphs may be cut and repasted by simply selecting a paragraph at a

time. The **Clipboard** preserves its contents between programs. Hence, you may even cut or copy text from one program and paste it in another.

```
program Edit;
begin
  Writeln('This program prints three sentences.');
  Writeln;
  Writeln('This is the second sentence.');
  Writeln('Unfortunately, this is the last sentence.');
end.
```

Figure 6.19

```
program Edit;
begin
  Writeln('This program prints three sentences.');
  Writeln;
  Writeln('This is the second sentence.');
  Writeln;
  Writeln('Unfortunately, this is the last sentence.');
end.
```

Figure 6.20

The Search Menu

Figure 6.21

The Search menu, figure 6.21, allows you to find and replace phrases in your program. We discuss the options and then provide an example for you to test yourself on. We discuss the options in a different order than the one shown on the menu, since **What to find** is the one with which you must always begin.

What to find, when chosen, displays the dialog box shown in figure 6.22.

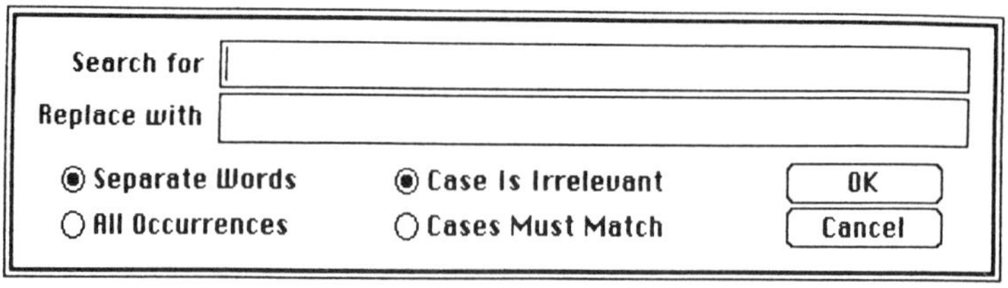

Figure 6.22

In the **Search for** box, you type, reasonably enough, the text that you would like to search for. In the **Replace with** box, you indicate what text (if any) you wish to have replace the sought-for text. Important: The Tab key, not the Return Key, advances you from one box to the other. The Return key is short for **OK**, which accepts your selections and returns you to the program. If you accidentally hit the Return key, them simply choose **What to find** again and start over. The **Cancel** box also returns you to the program window, but any selections you have made are lost. You have two other choices that you may make in the dialog box. The simplest is the **Case Is Irrelevant** and **Cases Must Match** choice. This specifies whether you want the string you are seeking to match *exactly*, with repsect to upper case/lower case, the string in the **Search for** box. For example, if the **Search for** string is "Target" and you choose **Case Is Irrelevant**, then "target", "TARGET", "Target", and even "tARGet" match. Of course, if you select **Cases Must Match** then only "Target" matches the given string.

Separate Words tells the system to look for the **Search for** string only as a *complete word* while **All Occurrences** looks for the **Search for** string anywhere it can find it. For example, a **Separate Words** search for "dog" in the sentence

To escape the big dogs, our dog went into his doghouse.

only finds "dog" once (at the seventh word). On the other hand, a search for **All Occurrences** of "dog" finds it three times in the above sentence. We cannot say which search method you should always use. Sometimes one is easier than the other. For example, if you wanted to change each instance of the string "I" to "We", you would be wise to use a **Separate Words** search. Otherwise, words like "Indeed" would be turned into "Wendeed". An **All Occurrences** search usually involves less typing, but can easily lead to unexpected changes. Remember, click **OK** to accept your choices in the **What to find** dialog box.

Find advances the insertion pointer from its current position to the next occurrence of the **Search for** string. Hence, remember to place the cursor at the beginning of the program if you wish to find the first occurrence of the string. Each **Find** advances to the next occurrence so that you can leaf through the program, stopping at each occurrence of the given string. The **Replace with** box (from the **What to find** dialog box) has nothing to do with a **Find**.

Replace replaces the currently selected text with the **Replace with** string. The **Search for** string has nothing to do with a **Replace**. **Find** and **Replace** can be used in tandem to find and then selectively replace text with other text.

Everywhere is the most powerful of the **Search** options. It begins at the top of the window and finds and replaces every occurrence of the **Search for** string with the **Replace with** string. Because **Everywhere** can wipe out a program, it asks for final permission before making the changes.

To illustrate these ideas, load or type the program Search into your Macintosh. The listing for Search is shown in listing 6.2. This program has two things wrong with it. "BASIC" is misspelled and also "Print" has accidentally been typed for "Writeln".

Of course, the easiest way to fix the spelling of "BASIC" is to drag the mouse over the "SA" and retype it as "AS". However, let us pretend that this is a very long program and that we know that "BASIC" is misspelled, but we don't know where the line containing the misspelling is since the program is so long.

```
program Search;
begin
Print('This program was written by a BSAIC programmer');
Print;
Print('who forgot that the output statement in Pascal');
Print;
Print('is the "Writeln" statement.');
Print;
Print('Use the "Search" options to fix the program.')
end.
```

Listing 6.2

We can use the **Search** options to do a find and replace for us. Choose **What to find** from the **Search** menu and type "BSAIC" as the **Search for** string. Hit the Tab key, then type "BASIC" as the **Replace with** string. Since we have entered whole words, we use a **Separate Words** search. Either case selection is fine: Our selections are given in figure 6.23.

```
┌─────────────────────────────────────────────────────────────────┐
│  Search for │BSAIC                                           │    │
│             └────────────────────────────────────────────────┘   │
│ Replace with│BASIC                                           │    │
│             └────────────────────────────────────────────────┘   │
│  ◉ Separate Words      ◉ Case Is Irrelevant      ┌──────────┐    │
│  ○ All Occurrences     ○ Cases Must Match         │    OK    │    │
│                                                   └──────────┘    │
│                                                   ┌──────────┐    │
│                                                   │  Cancel  │    │
│                                                   └──────────┘    │
└─────────────────────────────────────────────────────────────────┘
```

Figure 6.23

Click **OK** and watch nothing happen! All we have done is *define* how the find and replace will operate. We must now select those options to effect the change. Make sure that your cursor is near the beginning of the program and select **Find** from the **Search** menu. The word "BSAIC" should now be highlighted. Choose **Replace** from the **Search** menu and the spelling is corrected. Once again, **Find** and **Replace** may seem like more bother than they are worth, but as your programs grow in size you will find that these options become more useful.

Everywhere is certainly a useful option in this example. Keep it in mind when you decide to change a variable's name or make other such global changes. To begin we must again choose **What to find** and then enter "Print" and "Writeln" as the **Search for** and **Replace with** strings respectively. Once again, **Separate Words** and **Irrelevant Case** searches are fine. Don't forget that you need the Tab key between your test strings.

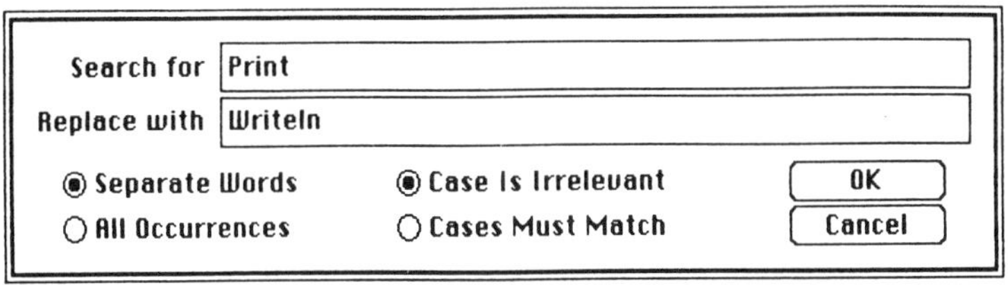

Figure 6.24

Click **OK** again to remove the dialog box. Then pull down the **Search** menu and choose the **Everywhere** option. Because you can make lots of changes that you may later regret, you are given one last chance to back out of the deal, as shown in figure 6.25.

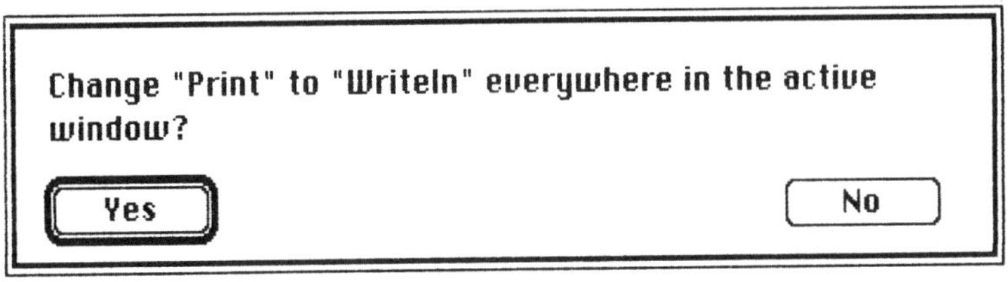

Figure 6.25

Since we want to continue, click **Yes** and watch all occurrences of "Print" become "Writeln".

As a final nonsense example, let's try to change all occurrences of the letter "e" in our program to the letter "z". Choose **What to find** and enter "e" and "z" as the **Search for** and **Replace with** strings. To see what happens, leave the other settings at **Separate Words** and **Case Is Irrelevant**, as in figure 6.26.

Click **OK**, choose **Everywhere,** and then click **Yes** to give permission for all the e's to be changed to z's. You should get the message shown in figure 6.27.

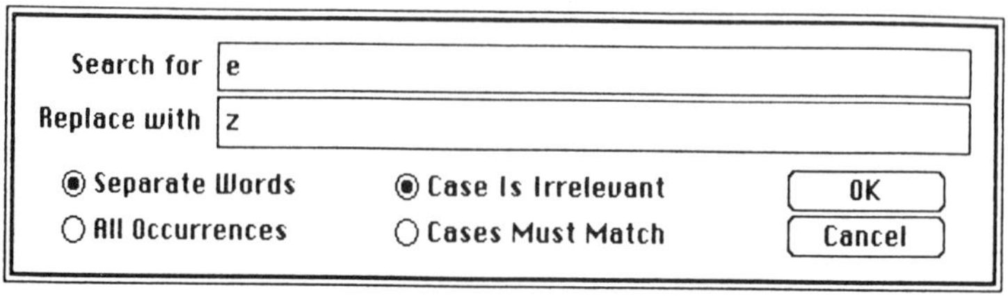

Figure 6.26

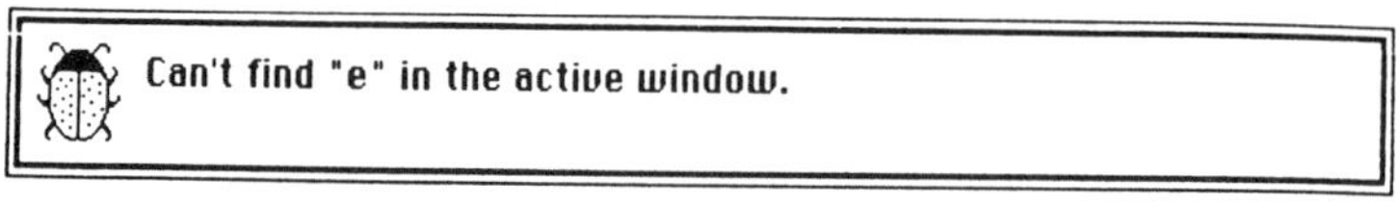

Figure 6.27

How can it be that the system can't find an "e" in our program? We can see about a dozen of them. The answer is that we asked for a search by **Separate Words,** and there are no *words* consisting of the single letter "e" in our program. Go back to **What to find** and select **All Occurrences.** This time your program should be converted to the gobbledygook shown in figure 6.28.

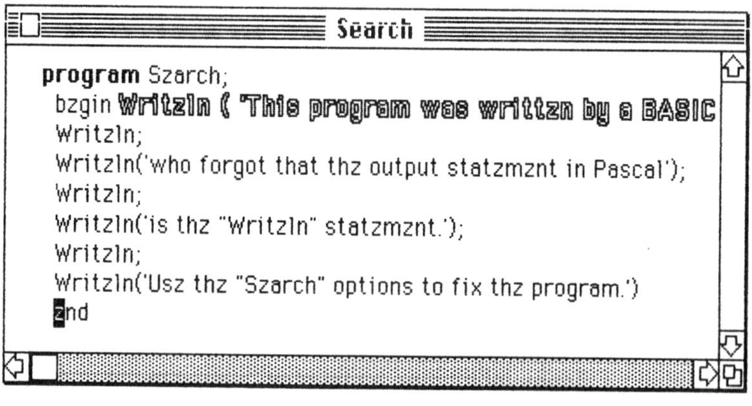

Figure 6.28

Fortunately, if you replace "z" with "e" everywhere, you restore your program to its previous form. Such "undoing" may not always work. It works in this example because the letter "z" does not occur in the original version.

Keep the **Search** options in mind as you start to write longer programs. Remember especially the power of **Everywhere**.

The Windows Menu

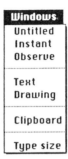

Figure 6.29

This menu, figure 6.29, allows the user to activate several different windows. The first is the program window, labelled **Untitled** above. Your screen may show the name of a specific program. Choosing this option makes the program window active and brings it to the top of the desk.

Instant is a window in which you can place Pascal commands and then have them executed instantly. The use of the **Instant** window will be illustrated after the **Run** options in the next section. Clicking **Instant** gives you a window as in figure 6.30. Use the close box to hide it again.

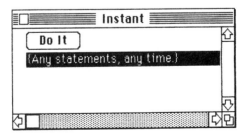

Figure 6.30

Observe is a window that allows you to watch the values of variables and expressions as the program executes. This window is extremely useful for debugging programs that run, but produce garbage. Its use is also illustrated in the next section. To see its appearance, choose **Observe** and you get the window shown in figure 6.31. Use the close box to hide it again.

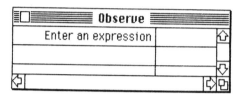

Figure 6.31

Text is the normal output window. Choosing **Text** simply makes the text window the active window of the system.

Drawing is the graphics window for the system. Its use is discussed in Chapter 12.

Clipboard is the window used by the **Edit** options **Cut**, **Copy**, and **Paste**. By activating the **Clipboard**, you can see its contents and see them change as the result of a **Cut** or **Copy**. Figure 6.32 shows our **Clipboard** still holding the "Writeln" from the editing of program Edit.

Figure 6.32

Type size is not really a window. It places a dialog box on the screen and allows the user to choose from three different sizes of text. We recommend the standard, medium-size type for most purposes.

The Run Menu

For reference purposes, the **Run** options, which are shown in figure 6.33, are all discussed briefly. Then these are illustrated along with the

Instant and **Observe** windows to show the user how a program may be debugged.

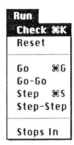

Figure 6.33

Check simply checks the program in the program window to see if its syntax is correct. **Go**, discussed below, does an automatic **Check**, so you do not need to explicitly use **Check**. This option is included for those occasions when you want to check but not run your program. For example, you may want to check the portion of a program that you are currently writing, but which is incomplete. Here, **Check** would be preferable to **Run**.

Reset reinitializes your program to its condition just prior to execution. The output window is cleared and the hand (if any) is removed from the program. See the discussion concerning **Go** below.

Go makes your program execute. If the program was halted in mid-execution, then **Go** resumes execution of your program from the point of interruption. Use **Reset** before **Go** if you wish to start a halted program over from the beginning. One halts a program, as we illustrate below, to investigate the program during execution.

Go-Go is much like **Go** except that it pauses briefly at "stop-signs" (explained below), updates the **Observe** window, and then continues execution. **Go-Go** is thus explicitly a debugging mode. It allows the program to execute, but also allows us to watch through the **Observe** window as the program executes.

Step permits execution of one line of your program at a time. Thus, **Step** is also a debugging tool. A hand points at the statement being executed so that you can see what the program is doing.

Step-Step is similar to **Step** except that the program only pauses after execution of each statement, updates the **Observe** window, then continues.

Stops In allows the user to set "stop signs" at various statements in a program. These stops permit the user to inspect the values of various variables before continuing execution. The setting of stop signs is described in the example program below. If **Stops In** has been chosen, then the menu reads **Stops Out**. Clicking **Stops Out** removes all stop signs from the program. Clicking a particular stop sign removes that stop sign.

The Pause Menu

Figure 6.34

The menu of figure 6.34 is only visible while your program is executing. Clicking **Pause** interrupts your program until the mouse button is released. Choosing **Halt** halts the execution of your program.

Fan Shortcuts

Many of the mouse actions can also be performed, if more convenient, from the keyboard. Each shortcut uses two keys, the so-called Fan key (⌘) and a regular key. For example, "Fan G" (hold down the Fan Key and push the G Key) is short for **Go** from the **Run** menu. For selections, such as **Go**, that are used very often, the Fan key shortcut can be worth remembering. Here is a table of Fan shortcuts for Macintosh Pascal:

Edit Shortcuts		**Search** Shortcuts		**Run** Shortcuts	
Cut	⌘X	**Find**	⌘F	**Check**	⌘K
Copy	⌘C	**Replace**	⌘R	**Go**	⌘G
Paste	⌘V	**Everywhere**	⌘E	**Step**	⌘S
Select All	⌘A	**What to find**	⌘W		

A Complete Debugging Example

Consider the program 'Debug' shown in listing 6.3.

```
program Debug; {WARNING: THIS PROGRAM IS BUGGY.}
{This program assumes that the text file QuizScores is}
{on the Macintosh Pascal disk.}

var
  Name : string;
  Score : Integer;
  Sum : Integer;
  Average : Real;
  Index : Integer;

begin
 Close(Input);
 Reset(Input, 'QuizScores');
 Writeln('This program is supposed to compute averages');
 Writeln('on four quizzes, but it has a bug in it.');
 Writeln;
 Sum := 0;
 while not Eof do
  begin
   Readln(Name);
   for Index := 1 to 4 do
    begin
     Read(Score);
     Sum := Sum + Score
    end; {For}
   Readln;
   Average := Sum / 4.0;
   Writeln('The average for ', Name, ' is ', Average : 6 : 2)
  end; {While }
end.
```

Listing 6.3

You should **Open** Debug from your Sample diskette and run it by choosing **Go** from the **Run** menu. Unless you have two drives, be sure that the text file QuizScores is also on the Macintosh Pascal disk. If you have to create your own text file, then use the format shown here:

```
Lowell
98 95 96 99
Bob
14 11 7 23
. . .
```

Notice that Debug is supposed to average four quiz scores for students. The output from this program begins as follows:

The average for Lowell is 97.00
The average for Bob is 110.75

The first line is reasonable, but that second line seems a bit odd. Bob's highest score is a lousy 23 and that stupid computer says his average is over 100! (Notice that you do not hear Bob complaining.) Observe as the program continues to run that the averages get bigger and bigger. Something is clearly wrong with the computer!

This is an example of a **logical error**. We apparently have managed to write a syntactically correct Pascal program. That is, the program runs without errors. Unfortunately, however, it doesn't produce the correct results to our problem. We have managed to write a "correct" program, but it's not the program that solves our problem. Remember that computers are just fast, accurate morons, and always check your output for reasonableness. Just because the computer says it's so doesn't make it so. A logical error indicates that our design of the program was faulty. Our algorithm has been implemented without syntax errors, but our algorithm doesn't solve the given problem. Apparently, the problem was more subtle than we thought and we missed some fine point. Too often the student thinks the objective is to get a program that runs and so anything is tried to remove pesky syntax errors. Finally the program runs, but produces garbage because the programmer has lost sight of the objective. This has happened often enough that programmers have an acronym for it: **GIGO--Garbage In, Garbage Out**, meaning that the quality of the output is no better than the quality of the input. You are responsible for the quality of the program, so always remember that your objective is a correct program that *solves* the given problem.

Logical errors are harder to find and fix than syntax errors. There are no error messages to direct us to the line(s) with the logical error(s).

Most systems leave the debugging of such errors entirely to the user. Fortunately, Macintosh Pascal provides a large set of tools that can help the programmer find and correct these kinds of errors. We suggest you follow along as we illustrate some of these tools on Debug.

Bring down the **Windows** menu and select **Observe**, giving us a window like the one in figure 6.35.

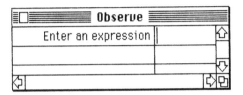

Figure 6.35

The purpose of the **Observe** window is to allow us to check the values of important expressions in our program as our program executes. For expressions we usually enter simple variables, but complex expressions are allowed. Our first problem is to decide what we would like to observe. Since the average is not correct, perhaps we should observe the variable Average. But that is not likely to get us anywhere as the program Debug itself displays Average each time through the **while** loop. Average is wrong, but to see why it is wrong we need to observe more deeply. Since Average is computed as Sum/4.0 and Sum is the sum of the scores, let's observe Sum and Score. To do so, click in the **Observe** window, if it is not already the active window, and type Sum (followed by the Return key) and Score. Your **Observe** window should now appear as in figure 6.36.

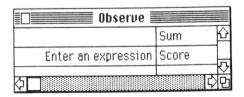

Figure 6.36

Now choose **Go** and begin the execution of your program. Click and hold **Pause** as the program runs. (You may have to hold **Pause** twice to get results.) The program will pause and the current contents of Sum and Score appear in the **Observe** window, much as in figure 6.37.

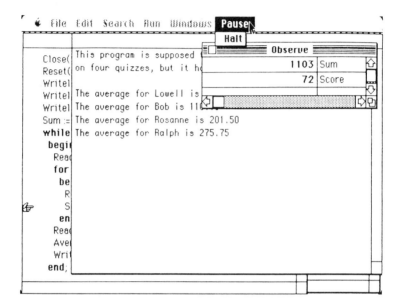

Figure 6.37

Note that there is also a hand that indicates the statement to be executed next. Release the button, then **Pause** the program several more times during its execution to see the values of Sum and Score updated. The **Observe** window only shows the values of variables during execution. At the end of the program the values of Sum and Score disappear and your **Observe** window appears as in figure 6.38.

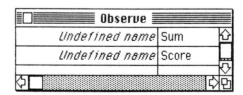

Figure 6.38

Besides **Pause**, you can also use **Halt** from the **Pause** menu during execution. Execution halts and the values of Sum and Score may be studied. When you select **Go**, execution continues. Run the program again using **Halt** to stop the execution several times while observing the changing values of Sum and Score.

Interrupting the execution of the program to observe values of key variables can be a very useful debugging tool, but it is difficult to know where the program will be interrupted. It would be more convenient if the system would pause at certain key statements so that we could make our observations. To perform this neat trick, pull down the **Run** menu and choose **Stops In**. The program window must be the *active* window before **Stops In** becomes a possible choice on the **Run** menu. Your program window should show a stop sign in the lower left hand corner.

```
Reset(Input, 'QuizScores');
Writeln('This program is supposed to compute averages');
Writeln('on four quizzes, but it has a bug in it.');
Writeln;
Sum := 0;
while not Eof do
  begin
    Readln(Name);
    for Index := 1 to 4 do
      begin
        Read(Score);
        Sum := Sum + Score
      end; {For}
    Readln;
    Average := Sum / 4.0;
    Writeln('The average for ', Name, ' is ', Average : 6 : 2)
  end; {While }
end.
```

Figure 6.39

Bring the mouse into this column and notice that it changes into a stop sign. Align the mouse with the **end** at the foot of the **while** loop and click the mouse. This leaves a stop sign at the **end** as shown in figure 6.40.

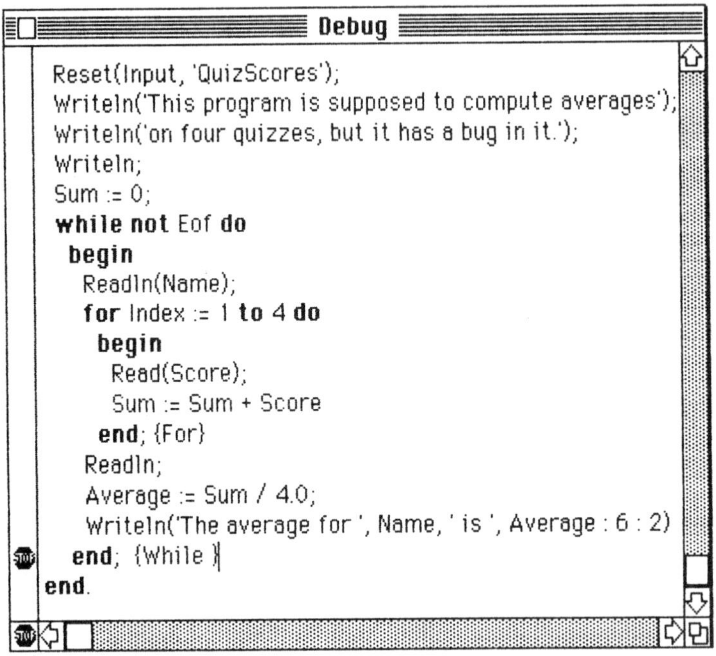

```
Debug
   Reset(Input, 'QuizScores');
   Writeln('This program is supposed to compute averages');
   Writeln('on four quizzes, but it has a bug in it.');
   Writeln;
   Sum := 0;
   while not Eof do
     begin
       Readln(Name);
       for Index := 1 to 4 do
         begin
           Read(Score);
           Sum := Sum + Score
         end; {For}
       Readln;
       Average := Sum / 4.0;
       Writeln('The average for ', Name, ' is ', Average : 6 : 2)
     end; {While }
   end.
```

Figure 6.40

Now, bring both the **Text** and **Observe** windows to the front of the desktop, arrange them so both can be seen, and execute the program by choosing **Go** from the **Run** menu. The program executes up to the stop sign, then halts and shows us Sum and Score as in figure 6.41. Also notice the hand to indicate that execution was interrupted at the stop sign. Continue the program by repeatedly choosing **Go**. Note that the program stops each time through the **while** at the stop sign.

A useful variant of **Go** is **Go-Go**. **Reset** the program and choose **Go-Go** from the **Run** menu. This time the program pauses briefly at the stop sign, updates the **Observe** window, and then continues. **Pause** may be used with **Go-Go** to suspend execution to allow you more time to observe either the program output or the values in the **Observe** window. Note that **Go-Go** is strictly a debugging tool. **Go-Go** is not even a possible choice from the **Run** menu unless **Stops In** has already been selected.

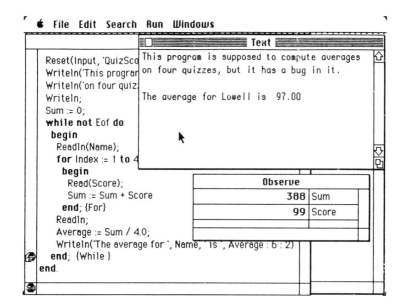

Figure 6.41

Step and **Step-Step** are also useful debugging tools. **Step** allows you to single-step through your program. That is, **Step** executes one line of your program and then halts. You may continue the execution with another **Step** (use the Fan-S shortcut!) or with **Go** or any other of the **Run** commands. **Step** can also be used to continue at the critical stage of a program that has been interrupted by a **Halt** or stop sign. Try stepping through the program Debug. You quickly see that **Step**, while a powerful debugging tool, must be used selectively. You do not want to **Step** through a long program a statement at a time.

Step-Step is much like **Go-Go** except that **Step-Step** pauses after each statement, updates the **Observe** window if necessary, and then automatically resumes execution of your program. Try **Step-Step** on the program Debug. Watch that hand go through the **for** loop four times and around and around through the **while** loop.

Our final debugging tool is the **Instant** window. Bring down the **Windows** menu and select **Instant** to see the window in figure 6.42.

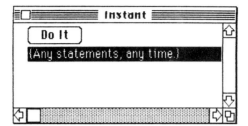

Figure 6.42

The purpose of the **Instant** window is to allow you, while a program is halted, to perform any statement at all. We can use the **Instant** window, for example, to view values that we didn't think to put in the **Observe** window. We can even use the **Instant** window to assign values to variables in our program. For example, if we feel that our program crashes whenever certain conditions arise, we can create those conditions in the **Instant** window and then test our hypothesis.

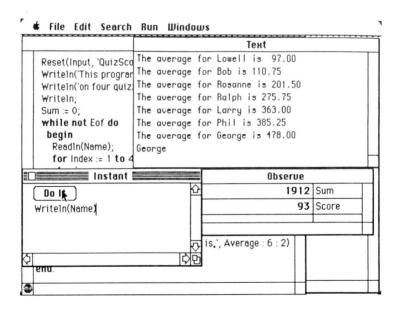

Figure 6.43

The Instant window can be very useful for discovering why a program is stuck in an infinite loop (see the exercises). To use the **Instant** window, we type our Pascal statement(s) in the window, then click **Do It**. Figure 6.43 shows the screen with the Instant window asking for a display of the variable Name. **Do It** has already been clicked, and "George" has been written in the **Text** window.

We have spent quite some time describing the debugging features of Macintosh Pascal. Since you are an error-prone human, you will probably find it worth your while to refer back to this section as you continue through the book. You can't really call yourself a programmer until you can debug your own programs. Learn to use Macintosh Pascal's tools to make this task as simple as possible.

Finally, what is wrong with the program Debug? We hope by now you have spotted the problem. If not, take another look at figure 6.43 How does George, even with four scores like 93, ever get a Sum like 1912? Or **Step-Step** through the program and watch Sum get bigger and bigger. The problem, of course, is that Sum is never reset to zero. Rather than being the sum of one person's four scores, Sum is accumulating the sum of all the scores. We leave the problem of finding the correct placement of the statement 'Sum := 0;' to the reader. We also point out that this is one instance in which we *must* do our own initialization of Sum, rather than rely on the system to do it for us.

This example makes one more point that we would like to emphasize about the process of debugging a program. To spot a problem, it helps to see that certain values are not what they should be. This means that it may be necessary to do some hand computations with which to compare the observed values. A very direct way to have debugged the above program would be:

> Since Bob's average is the first average that is wrong, observe Bob's four scores and add them up to obtain Sum. Immediately we see that Sum is wrong. We then see why Sum is wrong. If not, we start again and compare at each step Sum's expected value with Sum's actual value.

The Apple Menu

There is one other menu that is common to all Macintosh applications. This is the Apple menu. When you drag down the Apple, you will see the menu shown in figure 6.44.

Figure 6.44

Of the options listed, the **Alarm Clock** and the **Calculator** are probably the most useful. See your Macintosh manuals if you need more information about any of the selections.

Macintosh System Commands

This section lists, for quick reference, instructions for deleting, renaming, copying, and organizing disk files on the Macintosh. The menu items referred to here are available after you insert your Pascal disk into the Macintosh. Don't worry if your disk shows other files than those listed here.

Deleting Files
First, drag the file to be removed to the Trash can as in figure 6.45, which shows Junk on its way to the Trash. Place the arrow over the trash can to deposit Junk into the Trash. Second, you usually need to pull down the **Special** menu and select **Empty Trash** to actually delete the file from your disk.

Renaming Files
See the section on renaming files in Chapter 2.

Copying Files
To copy a single file from one disk to another, insert one of the disks. On one-drive systems, eject the disk and then insert the other disk. On a two-drive system, insert the other disk into drive 2. Arrange the two disk windows so that they share the screen as in figure 6.46. Now, drag the file from one disk window to the other. If you have only a one-drive system, you need to swap disks several times as requested by the system.

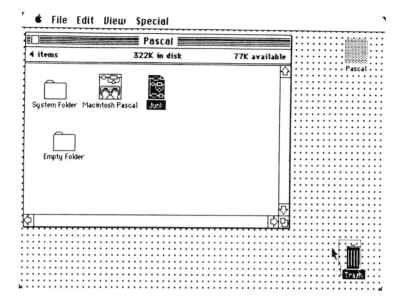

Figure 6.45

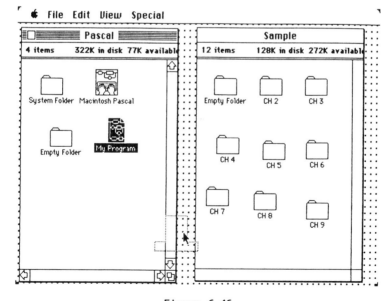

Figure 6.46

To copy more than one file at once, insert the disks as above. Drag the files to be copied to one corner of their window. Then select all the files to be copied by dragging a rectangle around them as in figure 6.47.

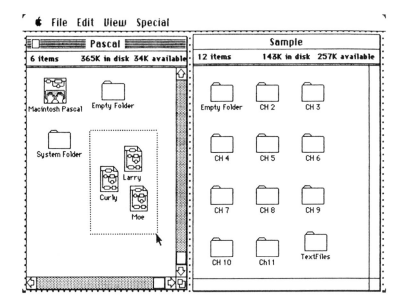

Figure 6.47

To form the rectangle, click the mouse above and to the left of the group of files and drag the mouse down and to the right. When all the files are caught in the rectangle, release the mouse button. Now, by dragging any of the files, all follow in tow. Figure 6.48 shows Larry, Curly, and Moe on their way to another disk.

To copy an entire disk, you can use the disk copy program on the Macintosh System Disk. However, you should be aware that certain files, such as Macintosh Pascal, are copy-protected and cannot be copied by any of the means described here.

Organizing Files in Folders

To keep your disk from getting too cluttered, we suggest you organize your programs from each chapter into a separate folder. To do this you

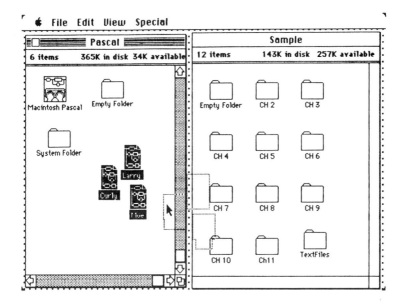

Figure 6.48

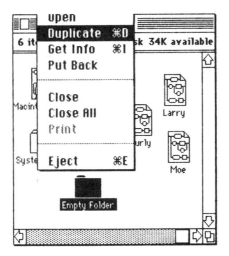

Figure 6.49

need to have an Empty Folder on your disk. If you do not already have one, then you may copy one, as explained above, from the System Disk.

The first thing to do is make a duplicate copy of the **Empty** Folder, so that the Empty Folder is available when needed again. To duplicate a document, select that document by clicking it, then choose Duplicate from the **File** menu as shown in figure 6.49. After a few seconds you have a copy of the document as shown in figure 6.50.

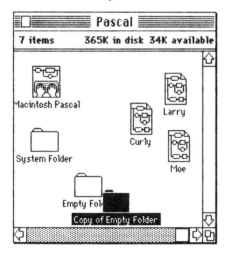

Figure 6.50

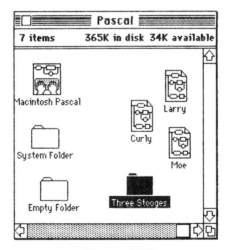

Figure 6.51

Hit the backspace key to delete the name "Copy of Empty Folder" and then type in your new name for the folder. You can even drag the folder to a more convenient location on the disk window if you wish. See figure 6.51.

Open the new folder by double-clicking it and then arrange its window to share the screen as shown in figure 6.52. Now drag, either one at a time or all together (by lassoing the group with a rectangle), the files that you would like to keep in the given folder. Figure 6.53 again shows Larry, Curly, and Moe on the move.

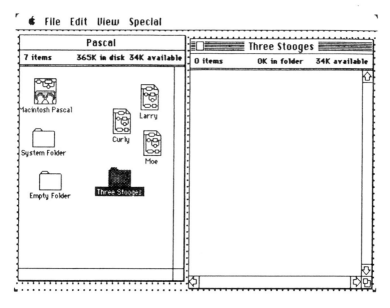

Figure 6.52

Note that this time the files are being *moved,* not just copied, into the folder. To tidy up the disk, close the folder (make it active if necessary). The secret to a well-organized disk is folder names that are descriptive. Folder1, Folder2, ... won't help you much when you are looking for Larry, Curly, or Moe.

Summary

This chapter has not presented any new Pascal constructs. But we hope it has convinced you that the Macintosh Pascal system contains a rich

assortment of debugging tools that make the human task of programming
as pleasant as possible. We don't wish you bad luck, but we expect you
will have many occasions to practice the debugging skills given here. We
repeat our admonition from the beginning of the chapter: Do not try to
memorize all the options of the system at once, but rather, return to the
chapter as needed.

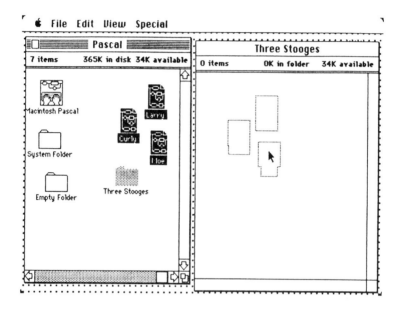

Figure 6.53

Exercises

6.1 Using the editing features described in this chapter, open the program
Sloppy (from the Sample diskette accompanying this book) and convert the
program into the program Neat. Listings of Sloppy and Neat are given in
Chapter 3.

6.2 The program BuggyGame, from the accompanying disk Sample, is a
very messed up program that is supposed to play the word game of
Exercise 5.5. Debug BuggyGame.

6.3 The program BuggyChip, from the disk Sample, is an incorrect version of the Cow Chip Throwing contest of Exercise 5.12. Debug BuggyChip.

6.4 The program Inf_Loop, from the disk Sample, is a program that is supposed to add up the first twenty integers. However, it gets caught in an infinite loop. Debug Inf_Loop.

Chapter 7

Functions and Procedures

> **TOP DOWN** – **A programming methodology whereby unwritten modules are linked together to produce the target program.**
> **Devil's DP Dictionary**

In this chapter, we are going to learn an extremely important concept that is indispensable for good programming--namely the notion of functions and procedures. This idea allows us to attack big problems by breaking them into smaller sub-problems. We then solve the small problems and put the solutions together to form a solution to our original problem. Such a strategy is referred to as a **divide and conquer** strategy or a **top-down** approach.

What this top-down approach encourages is **structured programming.** The idea of structured programming is that a computer program should be put together in an organized fashion so that the structure of the program models as closely as possible the solution path that the programmer used to solve the problem. Some languages by their very nature discourage structured programmming while others are well-suited for it. Pascal certainly falls into the latter category. And one of the language's features that encourages the programmer to take a structured approach is its function/procedure capability. There are some fundamental differences between functions and procedures, but the basic ideas are the same. Because they may be more familiar, we will discuss functions first.

Functions

Actually, we have already seen and used functions in Pascal. The functions that we have seen are called **built-in** functions because they come with the language. This should not be surprising--even the cheapest of calculators comes with some "function keys" like "square root" or "log."

Two of the functions that we saw in Chapter 3 were Round and Trunc. Recall that Round(X) rounded the real number X to the nearest integer while Trunc(X) chopped off the decimal part of the real number X. Each of these functions has a single **input**, which is a real number, and returns a single **output**, an integer. In general, we can think of a function as a "black box" that performs an operation for us. We do not have to understand how this black box works, only what it produces. We simply give the black box the input that it expects and it returns the output to us. In Pascal, functions can have a single input (like Trunc and Round) or they may have several inputs. All the computer really needs to know is how many inputs there are and what their types are. Regardless of how many inputs a function has, there is always a *single, simple* output. By this we mean that there is only one output and it must have a simple type—for now, Integer, Real, Boolean, Char, or **string**.

Table 7.1 contains the most commonly used built-in functions in Pascal. The reader is referred to Chapter 10 of the Macintosh Pascal Reference Manual for a complete listing of the standard functions.

Random Number Generation

In addition to the built-in functions of Standard Pascal, many versions of Pascal provide other functions for the programmer to use. We saw such an example in Chapter 4 where we used Xpwrl to raise a number to a power. The SANE library contains an extensive list of functions as described in the language reference manual. The Quickdraw Library, which is the graphics package for the Macintosh, also has several useful functions. The one we want to discuss here is a function for generating random numbers.

Computer simulation is an important applications area and in many simulations, the computer needs to exhibit random behavior. Examples of randomness include the tossing of a coin, the rolling of dice, and the presence of a genetic defect in an organism. Because the computer is a deterministic machine (meaning that it always does the same thing given the same instructions and the same circumstances), it might seem that a computer can't really exhibit random behavior. In fact, computers can't exhibit truly random behavior, but they can follow a "pseudo-random" pattern (meaning almost truly random), which in many applications is good enough. To generate a random number, the computer does some numeric computations on a starting number (called the random number "seed"). This input number in some sense needs to be random if random output is to be generated. How does the computer get this random input? There are various methods for doing this. In computers with a built-in clock, like the Macintosh, part of the seed may come from the precise time of day when we ask the computer to generate a random number for us. For now, we just accept the fact that Random is the name of a random number generator that has no input and returns as output a random integer between -32767 and 32767.

Name	Meaning	Input	Output
Abs(X)	Absolute Value	Integer or Real	Integer or Real
Arctan(X)	Arctangent of X (X in Radians)	Integer or Real Positive	Real Principal value
Cos(X)	Cosine of X (X in Radians)	Integer or Real	Real
Exp(X)	e^X e is base of natural logarithms	Integer or Real	Real
Ln(X)	Natural log of X	Integer or Real	Real
Round(X)	Rounds X to nearest integer	Real	Integer
Sin(X)	Sine of X (X in Radians)	Integer or Real	Real
Sqr(X)	Square of X	Integer or Real	Integer or Real
Sqrt(X)	Positive Square Root of X	Integer or Real Positive	Real Positive
Trunc(X)	Rounds to nearest integer between 0 and X	Real	Real

Table 7.1 Macintosh Pascal Built-In Functions

We are interested in generating random integers, but many times we don't want to generate such a large range of integers. For example, if we are simulating an experiment that involves rolling a die, we would like to generate random integers from 1 to 6. To do this, we can use Random with some of the other functions available. To generate random integers from 1 to 6, we can apply the **mod** operation to the integer generated by Random to get a remainder of 0, 1, 2, 3, 4, or 5. Then, if we add 1 to the result, we have a random integer from 1 to 6. Thus, the following expression assigns to Die an integer for a die-rolling experiment:

Die := Random **mod** 6 + 1

Consider some examples. First, we write a program that simulates the tossing of a coin 1000 times, counting the number of heads and the number of tails. All we need to do is generate 1000 random integers, where each integer is either 0 (for Tails) or 1 (for Heads). Thus, we use Random **mod** 2. This program, Coin, is found in listing 7.1. Run Coin several times and observe the random behavior.

```
program Coin;
{This program simulates 1000 tosses of a coin.}

var
  Toss : Integer;
  NumHeads, NumTails : Integer;
  Outcome : Integer;

begin
  Writeln('Please wait while I toss the coin 1000 times.');
  Writeln;
  NumHeads := 0;
  for Toss := 1 to 1000 do
    begin
      Outcome := Random mod 2;
      if Outcome = 1 then
        NumHeads := NumHeads + 1
    end; {For}
  NumTails := 1000 - NumHeads;
  Writeln('After 1000 tosses, the number of heads was ', NumHeads : 3);
  Writeln('and the number of tails was ', NumTails : 3)
end.
```

Listing 7.1

```
program Die;
(This program simulates 600 rolls of a fair die.)
 var
   Ones, Twos, Threes, Fours, Fives, Sixes : Integer;
   Roll, Outcome : Integer;
begin
 Ones := 0;
 Twos := 0;
 Threes := 0;
 Fours := 0;
 Fives := 0;
 Sixes := 0;
 Writeln('Please wait while I roll the die.');
 Writeln;
 for Roll := 1 to 600 do
  begin
   Outcome := Random mod 6 + 1;
   case Outcome of
    1 :
     Ones := Ones + 1;
    2 :
     Twos := Twos + 1;
    3 :
     Threes := Threes + 1;
    4 :
     Fours := Fours + 1;
    5 :
     Fives := Fives + 1;
    6 :
     Sixes := Sixes + 1
   end (Case)
  end; (For)
 Writeln('Summary of 600 rolls of a die');
 Writeln('Outcomes' : 12, 'Occurrences' : 14);
 Writeln(1 : 8, Ones : 12);
 Writeln(2 : 8, Twos : 12);
 Writeln(3 : 8, Threes : 12);
 Writeln(4 : 8, Fours : 12);
 Writeln(5 : 8, Fives : 12);
 Writeln(6 : 8, Sixes : 12)
end.
```

Listing 7.2

In our next example, we roll a fair die 600 times, printing the number of times each of the possible outcomes 1 through 6 occurs. In a random situation, each should occur about 100 times. You should run this program, shown in listing 7.2, several times to see how close the results are to what is expected.

To motivate a later chapter on arrays, notice that although this program is quite simple, it is somewhat bothersome and repetitive. Think how bothersome it would have been had we been rolling two dice instead of just one, or if we were performing an experiment that had 50 different outcomes. Remember that computers are supposed to make such repetition and drudgery easier to handle. This is exactly what arrays do for us in Chapter 9.

There are many other applications for random numbers. For example, many of the most popular arcade games have their main characters move in a random fashion so that the game does not play exactly the same every time. We mix randomness with graphics in Chapter 12.

Built-in functions are very useful because they allow us to do complex things, like taking a square root, by just using the name of the square root function. But the real power of functions in Pascal comes not from the built-in functions of the language, but from the programmer's ability to define any *new* function that is needed.

For example, we mentioned in Chapter 3 that in Standard Pascal there is no general exponentiation operator for raising numbers to powers. Although Macintosh Pascal provides several such functions in the SANE Library, let us pretend for a minute that there are no such functions. Suppose we had the need to raise numbers to the third power. Then we might find ourselves wishing that Pascal had a Cube function like it has a Sqr function. It doesn't, but we can write one if we want. If we name the function Cube, then whenever we need to raise X to the third power we just say Cube(X). Functions give us the unlimited capability to expand the vocabulary of the Pascal language.

As another example, suppose we were doing an arithmetic program and in several instances we needed to know if an integer were prime. Although the prime number program from Chapter 5 is not terribly difficult to write, we would soon tire of writing it every time we needed to test the primality of a number. But if we could write a function called Prime, which would have an integer input and a Boolean output (a "yes" or "no" answer to the prime question), then to test if an integer X were prime we could simply write

if Prime(X) **then** ....

This is really all there is to *using* functions. What we need to learn now is how to *define* them.

The Structure of Functions

The first thing that a function must have is a **heading**. This is analogous to the program heading but contains some additional information. The following information must be found in the heading:

The keyword **function**
The Name of the function
The Number and Types of input
The Type of the output

The heading is terminated by a semicolon. We present several sample headings.

The "test for prime" function has one Integer input, produces a Boolean result, and therefore has a heading such as:

function Prime(Candidate : Integer) : Boolean;

Suppose we wanted to write a function that compared three real values and returned the maximum value. Its heading could be:

function Max(Num_1, Num_2, Num_3 : Real) : Real;

Note that Max takes three Real inputs and produces a Real output.

Finally, so that we may see the syntax involved when we have inputs of different types, suppose we wanted to write a simple income tax function that uses as input a person's age, number of dependents, and taxable income, and returns as output a real number representing the amount of taxes to be paid. The following heading would suffice:

function Taxes(Age, Dependents : Integer;
                   Income : Real) : Real;

The items in parentheses are called the **parameters** of the function. Parameters have the syntax of variable declarations. There is no particular order in which the parameters have to be listed, but once they are listed, that order becomes important when we want to use the function.

The use of a function in a Pascal program is called an **invocation**, or a **call**, of the function. We call the function by using the function name and specifying the inputs to the function. These inputs are called **arguments**, and they may be variables, expressions, or constants. There must be exactly the same number of arguments as there are parameters. When the function is invoked, the first parameter receives its initial value from the first argument. Likewise, the second parameter receives its initial value from the second argument,..., and the last parameter receives its initial value from the last argument. So not only must we have the same number of each, the ordering of the parameters and the arguments must be "type compatible."

For example, the first invocation below is a legal invocation of Taxes, while the second invocation is illegal. The third invocation is legal, but is most likely incorrect because the arguments for Age and Dependents seem to be reversed.

```
Taxes(38,4,25420.79);      {OK}
Taxes(38.5,4,25420.79);    {Illegal}
Taxes(4,38,25420.79);      {Legal, but illogical}
```

The Body of a Function

Functions look like little Pascal programs except we use the keyword **function** in the heading instead of the word **program**. The body of the function, that is, the statements that carry out the function's task, whatever that may be, can contain any legal Pascal statements. There is, however, one fundamental difference. Since a function is supposed to compute a single, simple value (its output), when we are finished computing this value, we must **assign this value to the name of the function**. Often, beginning programmers forget this required step. Another common error is to try to use the name of the function within the body of the function for a use other than receiving the assignment of the final value. We now give some examples to illustrate these points. First, consider the simple, but complete, function for cubing an integer.

```
function Cube(Num : Integer) : Integer;
begin
  Cube := Num * Num * Num
end;
```

We make some remarks about the above function.

1. The function body is surrounded by **begin/end**, but with functions there is a semicolon and not a period after the **end** because function definitions are placed before the main program. The semicolon is needed because there are more statements after the function body.

2. Note that the body in this simple case is just a single assignment statement. The function name is used as the variable on the left hand side of the assignment operator and the parameter serves as a variable on the right hand side. Notice that neither of these "variable" names is declared. Parameters and function names are *not* declared explicitly by the programmer in a **var** section because they are implicitly declared by the function heading.

Listing 7.3 shows a complete program that uses the Cube function to print out a table of squares and cubes from 1 to 20.

```
program Squares_and_Cubes;
{This program creates a table of squares and cubes using the}
{built-in function, Square, and the user-defined function, Cube.}

var
 Entry : Integer;

function Cube (Num : Integer) : Integer;
begin
 Cube := Num * Num * Num
end; {Definition of function Cube}

begin { Body of main program Table}
 Writeln('Table of Squares and Cubes');
 Writeln('Number' : 10, 'Square' : 10, 'Cube' : 10);
 for Entry := 1 to 20 do
  Writeln(Entry : 8, Sqr(Entry) : 10, Cube(Entry) : 10)
end.
```

Listing 7.3

We point out to the reader that such a simple program does not require the use of functions and in fact is easier to write without functions by using the following Writeln statement:

Writeln(Entry, Entry * Entry, Entry * Entry * Entry);

However, we use such a simple example to point out how programs with functions work. The main program is called Squares_and_Cubes and of course consists of two major parts--a declaration part and a statement part. The declaration part informs the computer of the things that are used in the program--namely a list of all the variables and their types. Now we see that in the declaration part we may also define any functions that we intend to use. Thus, function definitions come after the **var** section and before the body of the main program. Of course, after we inform the computer about the function (with the function heading), we also explain how the function works (with the function body).

It is important for the reader to understand how the statements in the above program are executed, so we will give a detailed explanation. When the program Squares_and_Cubes is run, the first statement executed by the computer is "Writeln('Table of Squares and Cubes')," which prints the table heading. The reason for this is completely logical. That statement is the *first* statement in the program. The fact that the statement in the body of Cube appears first as we read the program does not make it the first statement in the program. It is the first (and only) statement in the Cube function and so it is the statement executed whenever we invoke the Cube function. It is important for beginning programmers to understand this flow of the execution.

So how is the table printed? After printing the two lines that serve as table headings, the computer begins to execute the **for** loop. When it comes to the Writeln statement inside the **for** loop, the value of Entry (which is 1 the first time through the loop) is printed. Next, the built-in function Sqr is invoked with Sqr(Entry). Thus, the square of Entry is computed and printed. Now, when the computer reaches the expression Cube(Entry), it realizes that Cube is the name of a function (that's why functions come before the program body), stops what it is doing (but remembers where it was), and goes off to find and execute the function as requested. Since Entry is the argument (the input to the function) and Num is the parameter by which we explained how the function is to be carried out, the value of Entry is given to Num. So Num is 1. Now the body of the function is executed. When the function is completed, the computer returns to where it was when it stopped to go to the function in the first place. But it carries back with it the value of the function (i.e., the function's output). This information is carried back through the function name and that is why we assign the output to the function name before we leave the function. When the computer returns to the point of the function invocation, it substitutes for the function call the output that it brought back. In this case, a 1 is brought back. The second time through the loop, a 2 is carried as input to the function and an 8 is brought back. The reader should trace through the entire program to see how the complete table is printed.

In the previous simple example, we were able to do all of our calculations in the function using only the parameter and the function name. There are occasions when these things are not enough. That is, we might need to use some other variables to store answers to intermediate calculations. In this case, we simply put a **var** section into our function just like the **var** section that appears in the main program. In this section we declare any variables that we might need to use in the function body. Such variables are called **local** variables. This terminology means that the variables are local to the function and have meaning only when the program is executing inside the function body. In fact, these variables do not even exist in the computer until we actually call the function. At that point, the computer allocates storage for the local variables. Then when the function ends, the variables no longer exist (until the function is called the next time).

The counterpart to a local variable is a **global** variable. These are the variables that are declared in the main program's **var** section. Such variables have meaning throughout the program and can be used anywhere in the progam. The reader may wonder why we need to declare variables in the function at all. Why not just declare everything at the main program level and not worry about local variables? The answer to this question is discussed in detail later when we cover procedures. For now, we simply state as another law of good programming practice the following advice:

In most cases, the use of global variables in functions should be avoided.

Using global variables inside functions can cause **side effects**, that is, changing the values of variables that exist outside the function. In very large programs, side effects can cause disastrous results and can be very difficult to detect. So the above law is saying that when you go into a function, you go there to compute an answer. Compute the answer, but leave everything else alone.

Now we start a series of examples that demonstrate the flexibility of functions. We have to use a **var** section in some of our functions and some of our programs use more than one function.

Recall the definition of the **factorial** function:

If N is a positive integer, then N! (read "N factorial") is equal to the product N*(N-1)*(N-2)* ...*3*2*1.

Examples:
    1! =   1
    2! =   2
    3! =   6
    4! = 24
    5! = 120

Let us write a function that computes the factorial of a given number. All we need to do is accumulate a product (similar to a running sum). We start our product at 1 and keep multiplying the product by successive integers until we have multiplied it by the number whose factorial we are trying to compute.

```
function Factorial(Number : Integer) : Integer;
var
 Product : Integer;
 Loop : Integer;
begin
 Product := 1;
 for Loop := 1 to Number do
  Product := Product * Loop;
 Factorial := Product
end;
```

Notice that we used a local variable Loop to count us through the loop. In a larger program, we wouldn't want to disturb the contents of some possibly important variable to get us through our factorial loop. So a local variable is appropriate. The careful reader might wonder why we use a second local variable Product, which seems to serve the same purpose as the function name Factorial. In other words, why not delete the last statement of the function and replace the loop body by

Factorial := Factorial * Loop;

The reason goes back to a remark we made earlier. Yes, it is true that we must always assign the function's result to the function's name. So in this instance, the function name is treated like a variable. But this is the *only* instance where the function name can be treated like a variable. If we consider a function name in an expression to be a function invocation, then the above statement makes it appear as if the Factorial function is trying to call itself. Such a thing is not only possible, but is in fact a very powerful and useful programming tool. However, we delay discussion of this topic until Chapter 15. Until then, whenever a function name is used in its body, it can *only appear on the left hand side of an assignment statement.* The above "revision" uses the name on the right hand side also. Thus, the use of the local variable Product is required.

Listing 7.4 contains a program that prints a table of factorials. We hope the reader begins to see the flexibility allowed by functions.

```
program FactTable;
(This program computes factorials, but overflows Integer values)

var
  Entry : Integer;

  function Factorial (Number : Integer) : Integer;
  var
    Product : Integer;
    Loop : Integer;
  begin
    Product := 1;
    for Loop := 1 to Number do
      Product := Product * Loop;
    Factorial := Product
  end;  (Definition of function Factorial)

begin  (Body of Main Program)
  Writeln('Factorial Table');
  Writeln('Number' : 10, 'Factorial' : 10);
  for Entry := 1 to 10 do
    Writeln(Entry : 4, Factorial(Entry) : 12)
end.
```

Listing 7.4

Of course, in this simple case, there is no requirement to use functions. But with a function, we can write a "generic" factorial loop that works for any size input. All we have to do is specify the input and the argument-parameter correspondence takes care of the rest. Observe how the argument, Entry, in giving its value to the parameter, Number, controls how many times the factorial loop is executed. So, in fact, we do get the proper factorial returned to the main program after each function invocation.

There is, however, one slight problem. Run the program FactTable. The factorial function grows so fast that we get an integer overflow when we try to compute 8!. Integer variables can only take on values in the range from -32767 to +32767. We can try to overcome this problem by using the "long integer" capability of Macintosh Pascal. These integers have a range between -2,147,483,647 and +2,147,483,647. So we should declare Product to be of type Longint and we must also indicate that the output of the function Factorial is also of type Longint. Make these changes and then run the program. Notice that the factorial function grows so rapidly, that with long integers, we still get overflow when computing 13!. We will discuss more about the other types available to us in the next chapter. But for the remainder of this chapter, we will employ the Longint type freely.

Combinations and Permutations

To continue the factorial example, we introduce another concept. In this application, it becomes convenient to have a value for 0! and the value that we need is 1. So, as is done in standard mathematics, we *define* 0!=1.

Suppose we have a group of N objects and that we have to select K of the objects. We might be interested in how many different ways we can make such a selection. In this first case, we aren't concerned with the order of the objects selected, only with which objects finally get selected. It turns out that the number of ways of making such a selection of K objects out of N, written C(N,K), is

$$\frac{N!}{(N-K)! * K!}$$

This expression is read as "N choose K." For example, suppose we have a group of 6 people and we want to form a team of 2 people to accomplish some project. Then there should be C(6,2) = 6!/(4!*2!) = 6*5/(2*1) = 15 different teams available. To see that this is really so, let us denote the people by the letters A, B, C, D, E, and F. A list of all possible teams is:

```
AB  BC  CD  DE  EF
AC  BD  CE  DF
AD  BE  CF
AE  BF
AF
```

```
program Combinations;
{This program computes C(N,K), the number of ways}
{of choosing K objects from N objects.}

   var
     N, K : Integer;
     NChooseK : LongInt;

   function Factorial (Number : Integer) : LongInt;
     var
       Product : LongInt;
       Loop : Integer;
   begin
     Product := 1;
     for Loop := 1 to Number do
       Product := Product * Loop;
     Factorial := Product
   end; {Definition of function Factorial}

begin {Body of main program Combinations}
   Writeln('This program calculates the number of committees of');
   Writeln('K people that can be formed from a group of N people.');
   Writeln('Please enter the value for N, the number of people.');
   Readln(N);
   Writeln('Please enter the value for K, the committee size.');
   Readln(K);

{Now calculate NChooseK, using the Factorial function.}
   NChooseK := Factorial(N) div (Factorial(K) * Factorial(N - K));
   Writeln('C(', N : 2, ',', K : 2, ') is ', NChooseK)  {Study this writeln to}
           {see where each printed item comes from!}
end.
```

Listing 7.5

Notice that team CD is, of course, the same as team DC (since we are not concerned with order, but only with the final makeup of the team). Listing 7.5 contains a Pascal program to compute an arbitrary value C(N,K) where N and K are entered from the keyboard. Again, to avoid overflow immediately, the Longint type is used. Note, however, that C(13,1) causes overflow. If we use a little ingenuity, we can compute higher values without causing overflow. This is explored in the exercises.

C(N,K) counts the number of **combinations** of N objects taken K at a time. Perhaps the reader has also heard the word **permutations** in the same context as combinations. Permutations are much like combinations except that when we select the K objects from our pool of N, we are concerned with the order of the selection. In other words, with combinations, we are only concerned with which K objects we select, whereas with permutations, a different order of selection constitutes a different permutation, even if the final K objects are the same. For example, suppose there is a club with 20 members and it has been decided that the club will be ruled by a committee of three people. If all three people on the committee are considered equal, then there are C(20,3) ways of forming different ruling committees. However, if the three people on the committee are designated as the club president, vice president, and secretary, then the same group of three people can form more than one committee, depending on which person holds which office. Thus, in this second situation, we need to count permutations. The notation for permutations is P(N,K) and this expression is equal to

$$\frac{N!}{(N-K)!}$$

Permutations and combinations often arise in the same application, so it would not be unusual to have a program with functions for calculating each of C(N,K) and P(N,K). Listing 7.6 contains a program that makes a table of each kind of number. Run the program and compare the two kinds of numbers. You might want to verify by hand some of the smaller values in the table. Note that P(10,10) = 3,628,800 while C(10,10) = 1. This contrast points out that the number of permutations grows much faster than the number of combinations. This should be no surprise, because once we make an unordered selection, there are many ways to give an order to the selection.

We conclude this section on functions with two remarks.

```pascal
program Combs_and_Perms;
(This program compares the number of combinations C(N,K), )
(with the number of permutations (P(N,K).)

  var
    N, K : Integer;

  function Factorial (Number : Integer) : LongInt;
    var
      Product : LongInt;
      Loop : Integer;
  begin
    Product := 1;
    for Loop := 1 to Number do
      Product := Product * Loop;
    Factorial := Product
  end; (Definition of function Factorial)

  function Combs (N, K : Integer) : LongInt;
  begin
    Combs := Factorial(N) div (Factorial(K) * Factorial(N - K))
  end; (Definition of function Combs)

  function Perms (N, K : Integer) : LongInt;
  begin
    Perms := Factorial(N) div Factorial(N - K)
  end; (Definition of function Perms)

begin (Body of main program Combs_and _Perms)
  Writeln('Table of Combinations and Permutations');
  Writeln('N' : 5, 'K' : 7, 'C(N,K)' : 14, 'P(N,K)' : 10);
  for N := 1 to 10 do
    for K := 0 to N do
      begin
        Write(N : 5, K : 7);
        Writeln(Combs(N, K) : 10, Perms(N, K) : 10)
      end; (For)
end.
```

Listing 7.6

1. Notice that we can use N and K as variables in the main program, as arguments when we call both functions, as well as parameters in *each* function. The arguments and parameters may be the same variables or they may be different. The computer keeps track of all the details involved. When we enter each function, a new (local) N and K are created and these are the variables referred to during execution of each function. The global N and K are not used during the execution of either function. While to the beginner this may seem like an opportunity for creating confusion, such a system allows different people to write different parts of one big program. If each person is writing a separate function, then the individuals do not need to worry that the names they choose for their parameters and local variables might conflict with someone else's choices. In the case of possible conflicts, the computer keeps track of everything for us. Such ideas are part of Pascal's Scope rules, which are described at the end of this chapter. After that discussion, it is suggested that you return to the program Combs_And_Perms and carefully trace through it by hand to see how the computer keeps track of the N's and K's.

2. The other point that we make at this time and that will be demonstrated in later examples, is that functions are indeed like Pascal programs in that they, themselves, can have other functions and procedures nested inside them.

Procedures

After our introduction to functions, the idea of a procedure should be easy to grasp. In fact, procedures and functions look much the same--each kind of structure has a heading and a body. A procedure is really just a generalization of a function. By that, we mean that functions are limited in what they can do, namely compute a single, simple value. But there are often times in a program where we might need to compute several values or no values--we might just need to print something. In these more general situations, we will use procedures.

We first consider some examples of when we might use procedures. Suppose we are writing a program that generates an extensive written report for a large company. The report would likely have several sections, for example, sales, inventory, taxes, personnel, etc. To make the report easier to read, it might be nice to print the report in such a way that the various sections are clearly separated from each other. An example is given in figure 7.1.

```
**************************************************
*                                                *
*                                                *
******************* Sales *********************
*                                                *
*                                                *
**************************************************
```

Month	Number of Units Sold
Jan	123
Feb	145
.	.
.	.
Dec	245

```
**************************************************
*                                                *
*                                                *
*********** Departmental Employees *************
*                                                *
*                                                *
**************************************************
```

Dept	Number
Sales	23
Shipping	12
Administration	8

Figure 7.1

If this were a very long report, there would be several instances where we would want the asterisks surrounding the section title and the line of dashes to separate the various sections. Note the the line is very easy to print. Simply perform a **for** loop the proper number of times, where the body of the loop consists of the printing of a dash. In the example above, the report is printed in a field width of size 50. So the following would draw the line:

```
for Dash := 1 to 50 do
  Write('-');
Writeln;
```

We would soon tire of writing this simple loop over and over in our program. Notice that we can't use a function here because drawing the dashed line does not involve the computation of anything. But we want the convenience of a function--that is, we want to be able to write the necessary instructions once, give this set of instructions a name, and then whenever we want to carry out these instructions, we invoke them by using the name. This is precisely what a procedure does. A procedure to draw the dashed line follows. We will explain in detail the various parts of a procedure later, but the reader should be able to follow this example because of its similarity to a function.

```
procedure Dashed;
var
  Dash: Integer;
begin
  for Dash := 1 to 50 do
    Write('-');
  Writeln
end;
```

We take this opportunity to point out some important differences between functions and procedures. The most obvious is the keyword **procedure** instead of the keyword **function**. Next notice that because a procedure doesn't return a value (which is what a function does), there is no output type listed at the end of the heading line. Despite these differences, there are similarities. Although the procedure above does not have any parameters (inputs), procedures may have parameters just like functions. Also notice that the procedure body is syntactically like a function body, with its own **var** section and its **begin/end** statement section. However, as to be expected, there is no assignment statement to assign a value to the procedure name. Again, this is because it is not the job of a procedure to compute one result.

Looking beyond appearances and investigating how procedures are used, we come to the most important difference between procedures and functions. It is this difference that probably gives beginning programmers the most trouble. Since functions compute a value, and in fact assign that value to the name of the function, function names are used anywhere in a Pascal program where the value could be used. In other words, **functions are invoked from within expressions**. For example, if Fun is a function with two integer inputs that returns an integer value, then Fun can occur anywhere that an integer value can occur. So statements like the following (in a main program that contains a definition of Fun) are legal:

        A := B **div** Fun(2,C);
        if Fun(A,B) < Fun(C,D) **then** ...

while the following statements would be illegal:

        Fun(3,C); (There is no legal Pascal statement that consists solely   )
                  (of an integer, so a statement containing only an evaluation)
                  (of Fun, which is just an integer, is likewise illegal.   )

        Fun(A,B) := 7; (This is illegal for the same reason "5 := 7;" is illegal.)
                  (The left hand side of an assignment statement must be)
                  (a variable. Fun(A,B) is an integer value.   )

        With procedures, the situation is completely different. Invoking a procedure is like asking the computer to carry out a sequence of statements (i.e., to do something without necessarily computing anything). To get the computer to carry out this sequence of statements, **the procedure name is used as a stand-alone statement**. So in the example above, any time we want a line of 50 dashes to be printed, we simply use the *complete* Pascal statement

        Dashed;

Like functions, procedures allow us to expand the vocabulary of Pascal in any way that we want. The procedure call can occur anywhere that a regular Pascal statement (assignment statement, output statement, etc.) can occur. So it makes sense to write

        if End_of_Section **then**
        Dashed
        else
        ... (Continue printing the report)

Procedures with Parameters

Because of its simplicity, let us continue with the example of the dashed line. As it is written now, we can only create a line of width 50. There might be occasions where we need more flexibility. The following procedure gives us this flexibility:

```
procedure Dashed_2 ( Width : Integer);
var
  Dash : Integer;
begin
 for Dash := 1 to Width do
  Write('-');
 Writeln
end;
```

This procedure has one integer parameter--Width. So to invoke this procedure correctly, we must call it with one argument, which must of course have an integer value. So if J is an integer variable with current value equal to 40, each of the following is a legal invocation of Dashed_2:

```
Dashed_2(25);  {Prints 25 dashes}
Dashed_2(J);    {Prints 40 dashes}
Dashed_2(2 * J - 10);  {Prints 70 dashes}
```

Let us make one more modification to the procedure, which uses the type Char (for character), discussed in Chapter 8. Suppose we wanted to print some character other than dashes. For example, in a bar graph, we might want to print dollar signs. Here is how to do this :

```
procedure Line(Width : Integer; Symbol : Char);
var
  Count : Integer;
begin
 for Count := 1 to Width do
  Write(Symbol);
 Writeln
end;
```

Then, to print 25 dollar signs we would write Line(25,'$') while Line(40,'!') prints 40 exclamation points.

It is important to understand how the procedure is executed. When the statement Line(25,'$') is encountered, the first thing the computer does is set up the argument/parameter correspondence. The arguments (the inputs to the procedure) are matched with their corresponding parameters in the procedure heading. There must, of course, be the same number of arguments as parameters, and their types must be compatible. So in the above example, since the first parameter is an integer and the second a single character, it is essential that the procedure be invoked with an integer first argument and a character second argument. When the procedure is entered, the system creates memory locations for the parameters and the parameters are then treated like variables. The *initial* value of each parameter is obtained from the value of the corresponding argument. So in the above example, Width is given the value 25 while Symbol is assigned the value '$'. At this point, the system also creates a memory location for each local variable declared in the procedure. After the procedure has completed, the storage locations for the parameters and the local variables are reclaimed by the system for possible use elsewhere. But that is of course no problem, because by that time we have successfully printed the 25 dollar signs. This local creation/destruction process is one of the features of Pascal that simplifies the writing of large, complex programs. We will discuss this in more detail at the end of this chapter.

Finally, can you tell why each of the following procedure calls is invalid?

```
Dashed(50);
Dashed_2(40,'+');
Line(80);
Line('*',40);
```

Variable Parameters in Procedures and Functions

The type of parameter used in the previous examples is called a **value** parameter. A value parameter gets its initial value from its corresponding argument, but while inside the procedure, it has its *own* memory location. Therefore, changes to the parameter, such as "X := X + 1" do *not* change the actual argument. There are, however, many occasions when we want the procedure to change the actual argument. We consider a very common example to motivate this discussion, that of swapping values.

The need to exchange the values of two variables comes up very often in programming applications. For example, one of the most common of all operations performed by a computer is that of sorting a list (of names, numbers, etc.). There are many ways to sort lists (we discuss sorting briefly in Chapter 9), but almost all sorts require the swapping of values. In general, let us see how this is done. Suppose X and Y are integer variables containing the current values 5 and 10 respectively. Many beginners attempt to swap the values with

```
X := Y;
Y := X
```

but it is easy to see that this does not work. X in fact takes on the value 10, but after execution of the first statement, the old value of X is lost, and so Y is assigned the new value of X, namely 10. So Y does not change values. What is needed is a third memory location, to temporarily remember X's old value, and a third assignment statement:

```
Temp := X;
X := Y;
Y := Temp
```

Now if a program is going to be swapping values repeatedly, it might be useful to have a procedure for swapping two values. Then we wouldn't have to keep repeating the same three assignment statements over and over. The program in listing 7.7 contains a swapping procedure, but it is *incorrect.* After we analyze the program, we will see why.

```
program Wrong;
{This program DOESN'T swap two values properly}
{because the parameters are not VARIABLE parameters.}

var
  First, Second : Integer;

procedure Swap (X, Y : Integer);
  var
    Temp : Integer;
  begin
    Temp := X;
    X := Y;
    Y := Temp
  end;  {Definition of defective procedure Swap}
```

(Continued)

begin
  First := 1;
  Second := 2;
  Writeln('Before the swap First and Second are:', First, Second);
  Swap(First, Second);
  Writeln('After the swap First and Second are:', First, Second)
end.

Listing 7.7

The output of this program is:

Before the swap, First and Second are: 1   2
After the swap, First and Second are :   1   2

So something has gone wrong.   Because we have used value
parameters, the exchange of values of the variables First and Second has
not taken place. This is because the corresponding parameters for these
values are given their own memory locations while the Swap procedure is
being executed. So when Swap is entered, the computer allocates storage
for X, Y, and the local variable Temp. Now X and Y are initialized to 1 and 2
respectively, the values of the corresponding arguments. And in fact, the
Swap procedure does indeed swap the values of X and Y. However, since X
and Y have their own storage locations separate from First and Second,
this exchange of values has no effect on First and Second, the variables
whose values we intended to swap.   What is needed is a **variable
parameter**.
    Variable parameters differ from value parameters in that they do not
get their own memory locations. Instead, a variable parameter *shares*
the memory location of its corresponding argument. Note that this implies
that the argument corresponding to a variable parameter *must* itself be a
variable (i.e., not an expression or a constant). In this case, changes that
the procedure makes to the parameters are reflected in the corresponding
arguments. So to effect the swap of First and Second, all that is required
is that we make X and Y variable parameters. This is accomplished by
using the abbreviation **var** before any parameter that we wish to be a
variable parameter. So the correct swap procedure follows:

  procedure Swap(**var** X, Y : Integer);
  var
    Temp : Integer;

```
begin
  Temp := X;
  X := Y;
  Y := X
end;
```

With this version of **procedure** Swap, the output of the program is:

Before the swap, First and Second are: 1   2
After the swap, First and Second are :   2   1

When we were discussing functions, we saw how declaring local variables was good practice because we avoided side effects. Now it seems that we are encouraging side effects through the use of variable parameters. In some sense this is true, because to write a swapping procedure, we do in fact want to change the environment outside the procedure. In general, variable parameters give us a way of communicating the effect of a computation to the outside world, so there are many times when we want side effects. But variable parameters give us *controlled* side effects in that the only values changed are those corresponding to arguments. As with functions, changing the value of a global variable is probably a risky thing to do. If you need to change the value of a variable in a procedure, make it an argument corresponding to a variable parameter. Functions can also have variable parameters, but we do not consider it good programming practice to use variable parameters with functions. Functions should compute a result and should have *no* side effects. Procedures may have side effects, but good programming practice dictates that these should be through variable parameters, not global variables.

Suppose all arguments to a procedure or function are variables and we don't need to change any of their values. Which type of parameter should we use? There is no simple answer, but the following advice should answer most situations for beginning programmers.

1. Value parameters should be used in most instances because they protect against accidental change of the arguments. Since value parameters have their own memory locations separate from their arguments, changes made to these parameters do not effect the argument values. So value parameters provide more safety than variable parameters.

2. If the arguments contain a large amount of data (see the chapter on arrays, for example), it may be preferable to use variable parameters. In this case, the system does not have to allocate a completely new set of memory locations and does not have to spend time copying (initializing) the argument values into the corresponding parameter locations. The sharing of memory locations between arguments and parameters makes the program more efficient in terms of both storage management and execution time.

Now we see how procedures really are generalizations of functions. Although we have indicated that functions compute and procedures do things, it turns out that one of the things that procedures can do is compute! But even when procedures do compute, they are not called from within expressions. They are still invoked as stand-alone statements. When we return from a procedure, we can then use the computed values in expressions just like any other value, and the values get returned through the procedure's arguments, not through the procedure name.

As an example, let us consider a procedure with one integer input, a year, that computes for us the day and month of Easter during that year. We use an integer variable for the day, but we introduce a new type, in a **type** section, for the possible months of Easter. Although this capability is not discussed until the next chapter, its use in this example is a natural one that should pose no problem to the understanding of the program.

We see already how this procedure is more powerful than a function because we are computing two things instead of just one. To see how the procedure is used in a program, suppose we wanted to print out a table of all Easters since 1940 to see if there is any kind of pattern. The program in listing 7.8 accomplishes this. This program uses an elementary, but strange, formula to compute Easter day for a given year. A similar algorithm was known to Karl Friedrich Gauss in the early 1800's.

Note that since the value of Yr does not change in the procedure, it is a value parameter. On the other hand, the job that the procedure is supposed to do for us, namely compute the day and month of Easter, requires that the parameters Da and Mo, corresponding to the arguments Day and Month, be variable parameters. While we are in the procedure, the calculations eventually assign values to Da and Mo, which are carried back to the main program and assigned to Day and Month in the main program.

You should carefully trace the execution of this program to gain a thorough understanding of the relationship between parameters and arguments and of the creation/destruction of the procedure's local variables.

```
program Easter_Sunday;
{This program computes the date of Easter in a given year.}
{The formula, used here without explanation, is valid}
{ in the range of years from 1900 to 2099.}

  type
    Months = (March, April);

  var
    Year, Day : Integer;
    Month : Months;

  procedure Easter (Yr : Integer;
            var Da : Integer;
            var Mo : Months);
{This procedure, given a Yr, computes the Da and Mo of Easter.}
    var
      A, B, C, D, E, F, G : Integer;  {We use one letter variables because}
                {these intermediate results do not represent anything.}
    begin
     A := Yr - 1900;
     B := A mod 19;
     C := (7 * B + 1) div 19;
     D := (11 * B + 4 - C) mod 29;
     E := A div 4;
     F := (A + E + 31 - D) mod 7;
     G := 25 - D - F;
     if G <= 0 then
       begin
        Mo := March;
        Day := 31 + G
       end
     else
       begin
        Mo := April;
        Da := G
       end
    end;  {Definition of (strange) procedure Easter}
```

(Continued)

```
begin
  Writeln('Easter Sundays from 1940 to 1990: ');
  Writeln;
  for Year := 1940 to 1990 do
  begin
    Easter(Year, Day, Month);
    Writeln(Month, Day : 3, ',', Year : 4)
  end  {For}
end.
```

Listing 7.8

Scope Rules in Pascal

We have seen how local variables are used in functions and procedures as "scratch paper" to remember details while the functions and procedures are executing. Some benefits of these local variables have already been mentioned--conservation of storage and protection against side effects. There is another very important benefit of local variables. Suppose you are a member of a team that is writing a very large programming project. In such situations, the project manager often breaks the project up into more manageable pieces and assigns the various pieces to members of the team. These pieces are written as separate functions/procedures, and then it is the project manager's job to combine them into one main program. Now, there might be some global variables that several different programmers need to use in their programs. In this case, there has to be some coordination among the team as to what these variables are. On the other hand, if you are coding your portion of the project and you need to write a **for** loop, it would be nice if you could write

```
for Index := 1 to 100 do
```

if you wanted, without having to worry about whether someone else is going to use the variable Index for some other purpose. Well, you can if you declare Index to be a local variable in your procedure/function. So local variables play an important role in making procedures truly independent from each other (if that is what is desired).

Of course, this poses a little bit of a problem. If you can safely use Index in your procedure, then anyone else should be able to use Index as well. So in a large program, it is not at all uncommon to have a variable declared and used several different times in several different ways in the same program. The question then is, "How does the computer know which variable goes with which memory location?" The answer is found in Pascal's **scope rules**.

A variable's scope is defined to be that part of the program where the variable is active. Pascal uses a scheme called **static scoping**, whereby the scope of a variable is determined by the textual structure of the program. By this, we mean that one only has to look at how the program is laid out on paper to decide how memory locations and variable names are associated. An alternate form of scoping, called dynamic scoping, which is used in languages like SNOBOL and APL, determines a variable's scope by the way the program executes.

As mentioned previously, procedures and functions can have other procedures and functions nested inside them. Eventually, everything is nested inside the main program. For this part of the discussion, we treat a main program just like another procedure, and we refer to programs, functions, and procedures as **blocks**. With this in mind, we explain the scope rules of Pascal.

1. If a variable X is declared in a block B, then X may be used in B and in all blocks nested inside of B.

2. When a variable X is used in a block B, where B is the innermost block surrounding this use of X, search the declaration part of B. If there is a declaration of X, then that is the X referred to in the statement using X. If there is no declaration of X, move *outward* one level of nesting, and search for a declaration of X. If one is found, that is the X referred to. If a declaration is not found, move out another level of nesting and search for a declaration. Repeat this process until the first declaration is found. If no declaration is ever found, then the original use of X in block B is illegal--it is an undeclared variable.

We illustrate the scope rules with three examples. We start with the simple program found in listing 7.9. The reader should carefully trace through the execution of the program Blocks and predict the output before looking at the output given below.

The output of the program Blocks is:

```
15      16
 1       2
15       2
```

```
program Blocks;

  var
    X, Y : Integer;

  procedure P1;
    var
      X : Integer;
    begin
    X := 1; ( This is P1's X)
    Y := 2;  (This is the main program's Y )
    Writeln(X, Y)
    end;  (Definition of procedure P1 )

  begin  (Body of Main program Blocks)
    X := 15;
    Y := 16;
    Writeln(X, Y);
    P1;
    Writeln(X, Y);  (Main program's X didn't change, but Y did.)
  end.
```

Listing 7.9

To understand where this output comes from, note that there are two Writeln statements in the main program and one Writeln statement in procedure P1. So the Writeln statements in the main program refer to the main program's X and Y. P1 has only a declaration of X, so the X referred to within P1 is P1's local X while the Y referred to in P1 is the global Y of the main program. So the global variables are set equal to 15 and 16 in the first two lines of the main program and are printed out in the third line of the program. P1 then sets its local X equal to 1 and the *global* Y equal to 2 and prints out these values. When we return from P1 to the main program, global X remains unchanged. However, Y reflects the value assigned to it from P1. Note that P1 has a side effect through the global variable Y. This is allowed, but we consider it poor programming practice. If P1 wants to change Y, a variable parameter should be included in P1's heading. Then the invocation of P1 would read P1(Y) and we are no longer so surprised that P1 changes Y.

The program Nest of listing 7.10 is a bit more complicated. This program contains one illegal statement.

```
program Nest;
 var
  X, Y : Integer;
 procedure P1;
  var
   V : Integer;
 begin
  V := 1;  (P1's V )
  Y := 2;  (Main program's Y )
  Writeln(V, Y)
 end;  (Definition of procedure P1 )
 procedure P2;
  var
   X : Integer;
  procedure P3;
   var
    Y : Integer;
  begin
   X := 5;(P2's X )
   Y := 6; (P3's Y )
   V := 7; (Illegal! P3 is nested inside P2 which is nested inside)
(the main program. None of these blocks has a declaration of V.)
   Writeln(X, Y)
  end;  (Definition of procedure P3 )
 begin  (Body of procedure P2 )
  X := 25;  (P2's X )
  Y := 35;  (Main program's Y )
  Writeln(X, Y);
  P3;
  Writeln(X, Y)
 end;  (Definition of procedure P2 )
begin  (Body of main program Nest)
 X := 100;
 Y := 200;
 Writeln(X, Y);
 P1;
 P2;
 Writeln(X, Y)
end.
```

Listing 7.10

```
program Scope;
(This program illustrates Pascal's scope rules)

   var
     A, B, C : Integer;

   procedure P1;
   begin
     A := 5;
     B := 6;
     Writeln(A, B)
   end; (Definition of procedure P1)

   procedure P2;
    var
      A : Integer;
   begin
     A := 10;
     P1;
     Writeln(A, B, C)
   end; (Definition of procedure P2 )

   procedure P3;
    var
      C : Integer;
    procedure P1;
     var
       B : Integer;
    begin
      B := 27
    end; (Definition of "other" procedure P1 )

   begin  (Body of procedure P3 )
     C := 5;
     P1;
     Writeln(A, B, C);
     P2
   end; (Definition of procedure P3 )
```

(Continued)

```
begin  (Body of main program Scope)
  A := 12;
  B := 13;
  C := 14;
  Writeln(A, B, C);
  P1;
  P2;
  P3
end.
```

Listing 7.11

Run the program Nest to see the error message. As usual, the error message is a little misleading. What the computer is trying to say is that "V is not defined in this section of the program." Remove the statement, run the program, and study the output, which is given in figure 7.2.

```
100    200
  1      2
 25     35
  5      6
  5     35
100     35
```

Figure 7.2

The third example, program Scope, is found in listing 7.11. This example shows that procedure and function names have a scope also and in fact follow the same scope rules that govern the use of variables. Try to predict the output of Scope, which is given in figure 7.3. You should be certain you understand where each item of output comes from.

```
12     13     14
 5      6
 5      6
10      6     14
 5      6      5
 5      6
10      6     14
```

Figure 7.3

BAGELS--An Extended Example

We conclude this chapter by demonstrating a game that one person plays against the computer. The name of the game is Bagels, a computerized version of the board game "Mastermind." In this game, the computer generates a random three-digit number, with all digits distinct and the first digit never zero. The player then tries to guess the number in as few guesses as possible. The player's guess must also be a three digit number with no repeated digits. The computer gives hints to the player about how close the guess is according to the following scheme:

One **Fermi** for each correct digit in its correct position
One **Pico** for each correct digit in an incorrect position
Bagels if no correct digits are guessed

For example, if the secret number were 482, then a guess of 127 would receive a **Pico**, a guess of 842 would receive a **Fermi Pico Pico**, and a guess of 375 would be rewarded with **Bagels**. Note that all **Fermi**'s, if any, are printed before any **Pico**'s. Also notice that we are not told which digit generates which hint!

We first outline a pseudo-code solution and then translate this solution into a Pascal program to play Bagels. Procedures are appropriate for two reasons:

1. There are several tasks to perform. Rather than trying to write a single **program** to handle all the tasks, let us break the program up into smaller, manageable pieces, tackling each piece as we go.

2. There are two different occasions when we need to do the same thing, namely break a three-digit number into its component digits and then make sure the first one is not zero and that all three digits are distinct. We must do this when the computer generates the secret number at the start of the game and we must also do this each time the player makes another guess. Rather than writing the statements to perform this analysis twice, functions and procedures allow us to write these statements once, give them a name, and then perform the analysis simply by calling the name. Here is a rough outline of the algorithm. Notice that we use the top-down approach where we worry about the big steps we need to take to solve the problem. We handle the details of each of these steps later.

The pseudo-code follows:

    Provide instructions to the player, if needed
    Repeat
        Repeat
            Have the computer generate a three digit number
            Break the generated number up into individual digits
            Check the legality of the generated number
        Until the generated number is valid
        Initialize the number of guesses to 0
        Repeat
            Repeat
                Accept a guess from the player
                Break the guess up into individual digits
                Check the legality of the guess
            Until the guess is valid
            Increment the guess counter
            If the game is over, summarize results
            Else analyze the guess and print the appropriate response
        Until the game is over
    Until the player quits

The Pascal equivalent of the above pseudo-code is given in listing 7.12.
Run this program and see how well you can do. If you're good (and a little
lucky), you should be able to guess the number in about a half dozen
guesses.

There is an important observation that we should make about the
Bagels program. Note that the procedure Analyze invokes the procedure
Give. This is a common occurrence in Pascal programs. The point to make
is that since Analyze makes use of Give, Analyze must *follow* Give. That
way, the system already "knows about" Give when Analyze invokes it.

program Bagels;
{This program plays the game of Bagels.}

var
    CompNum, Comp1, Comp2, Comp3 : Integer;
    Guess, Digit1, Digit2, Digit3 : Integer;
    NumGuesses : Integer;
    Over : Boolean;

(Continued)

```
procedure Instructions;
(This procedure gives the rules of the game.)
  var
    Response : Char;
  begin
    Writeln('Do you want the rules for the game of Bagels? (Y/N)');
    Readln(Response);
    if (Response = 'Y') or (Response = 'y') then
      begin
        Writeln(Chr(12));  (Clear Screen)
        Writeln('The computer will randomly generate a three digit');
        Writeln('number with all digits distinct and the first digit');
        Writeln('never zero. Your job is to guess the computer''s');
        Writeln('number in as few guesses as possible . Your guess ');
        Writeln('must also be a three digit number with no repeated');
        Writeln('digits.  The computer will give hints as follows:');
        Writeln;
        Writeln('One FERMI for each correct digit in the correct place.');
        Writeln('One PICO for each correct digit in an incorrect place.');
        Writeln('BAGELS if no correct digits are guessed.');
        Writeln;
        Writeln('Hit RETURN to continue.');
        Readln;
        Writeln;
        Writeln('For example, if the secret number is 482, then');
        Writeln('a guess of 127 receives a PICO,');
        Writeln('a guess of 842 receives a FERMI PICO PICO,');
        Writeln('and a guess of 375 receives a BAGELS.');
        Writeln;
        Writeln('Note that all FERMIs are given before any PICOs.');
        Writeln('Also notice that we are NOT told which digit');
        Writeln('generates which hint.')
      end (If)
  end; (Definition of procedure Instructions)

procedure Generate (var CompNum : Integer);
(This procedure generates a 3 digit number between 100 and 999.)
  begin
    CompNum := Random mod 900 + 100
  end; (Definition of procedure Generate)
```

(Continued)

```
procedure Break (Num : Integer;
          var Huns, Tens, Ones : Integer);
(This procedure splits the given Number into its three digits.)
begin
  Huns := Num div 100;
  Tens := (Num mod 100) div 10;
  Ones := Num mod 10
end; (Definition of procedure Break)

function Valid (Huns, Tens, Ones : Integer) : Boolean;
(This function determines if the digits are distinct)
(and if Huns is nonzero.)
begin
  if Huns = 0 then
    Valid := False
  else if (Huns = Tens) or (Huns = Ones) or (Tens = Ones) then
    Valid := False
  else
    Valid := True
end;  (Definition of function Valid)

procedure Obtain (var Guess : Integer);
(This procedure obtains the next guess from the player.)
begin
  Write('Please enter your guess: ');
  Readln(Guess)
end; (Definition of procedure Obtain.)

procedure Determine (var Over : Boolean;
          CompNum, Guess : Integer);
(This procedure decides if the game is over or not.)
begin
  Over := (CompNum = Guess)
end; (Definition of procedure Determine.)

procedure Summarize (NumGuesses : Integer);
begin
  Writeln('You finally got it.  It took', NumGuesses : 2, ' tries.')
end; (Definition of procedure Summarize.)
```

(Continued)

```
procedure Give (Message : string;
            var GaveHint : Boolean);
(This procedure actually gives the FERMIs and PICOs,)
(and sets the variable GaveHint to True.)
begin
  GaveHint := True;
  Write(Message, ' ')
end; (Definition of procedure Give)

procedure Analyze (X1, X2, X3, Y1, Y2, Y3 : Integer);
var
  GaveHint : Boolean;
begin
  GaveHint := False;
  if (X1 = Y1) then
    Give('FERMI', GaveHint);
  if (X2 = Y2) then
    Give('FERMI', GaveHint);
  if (X3 = Y3) then
    Give('FERMI', GaveHint);
  if (X1 = Y2) or (X1 = Y3) then
    Give('PICO', GaveHint);
  if (X2 = Y1) or (X2 = Y3) then
    Give('PICO', GaveHint);
  if (X3 = Y1) or (X3 = Y2) then
    Give('PICO', GaveHint);
  if not GaveHint then
    Write('BAGELS');
  Writeln
end; (Definition of procedure Analyze)

function PlayerQuits : Boolean;
(This function determines if the player wants to play again.)
var
  Response : Char;
begin
  Write('Do you want to play again? (Y/N) ');
  Readln(Response);
  PlayerQuits := (Response = 'N') or (Response = 'n')
end; (Definition of function PlayerQuits)
```

(Continued)

```
begin  (Body of main program Bagels)
 Instructions;
 repeat
  repeat
    Generate(CompNum);
    Break(CompNum, Comp1, Comp2, Comp3)
  until Valid(Comp1, Comp2, Comp3);
  NumGuesses := 0;
  repeat
   repeat
     Obtain(Guess);
     Break(Guess, Digit1, Digit2, Digit3);
   until Valid(Digit1, Digit2, Digit3);
   NumGuesses := NumGuesses + 1;
   Determine(Over, CompNum, Guess);
   if Over then
     Summarize(NumGuesses)
   else
     Analyze(Comp1, Comp2, Comp3, Digit1, Digit2, Digit3);
  until Over;
 until PlayerQuits
end.
```

Listing 7.12

Conclusion

We cannot overestimate the importance of this chapter in the development of programming skills. Most real world problems are too difficult to be attacked with a single program.   The top-down, divide-and-conquer strategy, which uses functions and procedures, provides an organized method for making difficult programs manageable. It is not unusual to see very large programs (more than 1000 lines) with a main program consisting of just a few dozen lines. These few lines are just procedure and function invocations.

The concepts of scope, local variables, global variables, dynamic storage allocation, arguments, and parameters are critical to the understanding of the programming process and are pertinent regardless of the language one is using.

Exercises

7.1 Write and save a program that prints out 10 pseudo-random numbers generated by the built-in function Random. Turn off the system and then load and run your program. Turn off the system a second time and load and run your program again. What do you notice about the output from your two runs?

7.2 The output from your two executions of the program of Exercise 7.1 should have been the same because the system initializes a global variable RandSeed to 1, and RandSeed determines the sequence of numbers generated by Random. This is unfortunate if you are using Random to play a game. Every time you turn on the computer, it starts to play the same old game. The easiest way to fix this is to use the built-in function TickCount. TickCount is a function, like Random, with no parameters. TickCount returns a long integer which represents the number of 60^{th}s of a second since the system was turned on. Hence, the statement

     RandSeed := TickCount

added at the beginning of your program has the effect of randomizing the generation of random numbers. That is, TickCount is used to determine the starting point for the random number sequence, and since TickCount changes so quickly, it is highly unlikely that two runs of a program containing this statement would produce the same results.

Add the above statement to your program of Exercise 7.1. Run the program from a "cold start" (a turned-off computer) a few times to verify that the output is indeed different. Note: You do not need to declare RandSeed or TickCount as they are both Macintosh Pascal system built-ins.

7.3 Write a function GenRandom(N) that generates a random integer between 1 and N. Make sure GenRandom uses RandSeed and TickCount (Exercise 7.2).

7.4 Write a program that uses GenRandom of Exercise 7.3 to simulate 50 rolls of two dice, a red die and a green die. The output should have 3 columns showing Red's value, Green's value, and the total value.

7.5 a. Why does the statement "Dice := GenRandom(12)" not properly simulate the rolling of two dice?

b. Why does the statement "Dice := GenRandom(11) + 1" not properly simulate the rolling of two dice?

7.6 (Burr vs. Hamilton) Mr. Hamilton and Mr. Burr are about to fight a duel. Hamilton hits his target, on the average, once in two tries, while Burr hits his target, on the average, once in three tries. Being a gentleman, Hamilton allows Burr to shoot first. The duel continues, with each taking turns, until someone is shot. Write a structured program with functions and procedures to simulate the duel 100 times. The output should announce how many times each person won, and the average length (in shots) of the duels. Of course, use random number generation to simulate the shots.

7.7 (Computer Roulette) Write a structured program that simulates the following perverse version of Russian Roulette. In a six-cylinder gun, place one silver bullet and two blanks. Three of the cylinders are left empty. Spin the cylinder and pull the trigger. If an empty chamber is beneath the firing pin, the gun goes "CLICK." If either a blank or the silver bullet is under the firing pin, then the gun goes "BANG." After a brief pause, you find out whether you are still alive and still playing, or whether the game is over. Hint: Use a "Readln;" to halt execution and allow the user to "pull the trigger" by typing the Return key. Simulate the pause after the BANG by giving the computer a big "do nothing" loop such as:

```
for Index := 1 to 2000 do
  ; (Nothing)
```

7.8 A dog has buried 3 bones randomly in his backyard, which is 50 feet by 50 feet. Naturally, he has forgotten where the bones are buried, so he randomly begins digging holes. His nose is so good (and his holes so big!) that he will find a bone if he digs within one foot of it. That is, suppose a bone is buried at point (x,y). The dog finds the bone if he digs at (x,y), (x-1,y), (x+1,y), (x,y-1), or (x,y+1). For simplicity, we assume x and y are integers. That is, the dog only digs at points with integer coordinates.

Write a program to randomly bury 3 bones and then randomly dig holes until a bone is found. Have the program repeat the experiment 20 times so that the dog gets a feeling for the average number of holes needed to find a bone. Make sure the program is structured by using functions and procedures. Also notice that the dog is so dumb that he may dig the same hole more than once.

7.9 A man leaves a pub in a slightly tipsy state. His home is 8 blocks west of the pub, while the jail is 8 blocks east of the pub. The man is as likely to go east as west, and after each block he falls down. When he gets up, he goes east or west with equal probability. In his journey, if he passes the pub, he goes in for one last drink before continuing his journey. Write a structured program to simulate the man's walk, which ends when he reaches home or jail. The output should include the man's current position (3 blocks east, etc) and, at the end, the program should output the length (in blocks) the man walked and the total number of times he returned to the pub.

7.10 Write a procedure Time that converts a number N of seconds into hours, minutes, and seconds. For example, 3724 seconds is 1 hour, 2 minutes, and 4 seconds. Assume that N is a long integer.

7.11 Write a program that uses the built-in function TickCount (see Exercise 7.2) and the procedure Time of Exercise 7.10 to print a message of the form

You turned me on 2 hours, 14 minutes, and 6 seconds ago.

Remember that TickCount returns a long integer which represents the number of $60^{th}s$ of a second since the system was turned on. Convert this number to seconds before calling Time.

7.12 The four digit number 9801 has the odd property that $(98 + 01)^2 = 9801$. This problem presents an outline of a structured program to find all such four digit numbers.

   a. Write a procedure Split(N, L, R) that accepts a four digit number N and returns L and R, the left and right two-digit numbers formed from N.

   b. Write a function SqSum(X, Y) that returns the square of the sum of its inputs X and Y. Important: SqSum should compute $(X + Y)^2$ and not $X^2 + Y^2$. To avoid integer overflow, have SqSum return a long integer.

   c. Write a main program that uses Split and SqSum fo find all four-digit numbers with the given property. Warning: Expect this program to be pretty slow. If you wonder about the status of your program, use the **Pause** option and the **Instant** window.

7.13 Perhaps you noticed a certain symmetry to the output of program Combinations. For example, C(6,1) = 6, C(6,2) = 15, C(6,3) = 20, C(6,4) = 15, C(6,5) = 6. That is, C(N,K) = C(N,N-K). This is easy to prove from the formula for C(N,K), but it is also obvious from the fact that for every committee of K people you choose, there is a corresponding committee of N-K people not chosen. Hence, if asked to compute C(N,K), we may compute C(N,N-K) if we wish. Thus we may suppose that K ≥ N **div** 2.

Notice that much cancellation is possible in the formula for C(N,K):

$$C(N,K) = \frac{N!}{K! * (N-K)!} = \frac{N* \ldots *(K+1)}{(N-K)!}$$

The last expression will not cause long integer overflow as easily as the first, especially if you alternate divisions and multiplications. Use these ideas to write a better version of the program Combinations.

7.14 Write a function SumDivs(N) that adds the proper divisors of its input N. That is, SumDivs(15) should be 9, since 1, 3, and 5 are the only positive integers less than 15 that divide evenly into 15.

7.15 (Perfect Revisited, see Exercise 5.17) Write a program that uses SumDivs to find all perfect numbers between 2 and 500.

7.16 (Abundant Revisited, see Exercise 5.18) Modify the program of Exercise 7.15 so that it finds all abundant numbers between 2 and 500.

7.17 (Primes Revisited, see Listing 5.14) Even though it is not very efficient, modify the program of Exercise 7.15 and use the function SumDivs to find all primes between 2 and 500.

7.18 Two integers M and N are said to be **amicable** if each is the sum of the divisors of the other. Use SumDivs to write a program that finds the first pair of amicable numbers.

Historical note: This pair was known to Pythagoras 2500 years before computers were invented and had great mystical significance even into the middle ages, where it was "used" in witchcraft and astrology. In 1636 Pierre de Fermat found the next amicable pair, 17,296 and 18,416. You can use SumDivs to verify that this is not a misprint. Computers have aided in the search for amicable numbers, and now more than 600 pairs are known.

7.19 In 1956 Easter fell on April Fools' Day (April 1). When will this happen again?

7.20 The latest that Easter can occur is April 25. When did this last happen? When will this next happen?

A Note Concerning the Disk of Sample

Programs Accompanying this Book

Because of limitations of the original Macintosh operating system, only about 100 files could be stored on any one disk. Since we have more than 100 text files and sample programs in this book, it was necessary to compact the programs for Chapters 8-16. Information on this compact-ification can be found by running the program RUN ME FIRST on the disk.

As this book goes to press, a new version of the operating system has been promised. As soon as it is available, a new version of the Sample disk will be made available. Again, run the program RUN ME FIRST to see which version of the disk you have.

Chapter 8

The Pascal Type System, User-Defined Types and Precision

> **BOTTOM UP** - A programming methodology in which the finer details are coded before any study of the overall needs of the system has been made.
>
> **Devil's DP Dictionary**

Earlier programming languages, like FORTRAN, are often called "action oriented" languages. This description stems from the fact that early applications were often numeric in nature. For example, many people think of programs that control rocket ships in outer space when they think of the uses of computers. Because these programs almost always dealt with numbers, the operations performed on these numbers were what was important. In fact, it was the nature of these early applications that earned the computer its name.

In more recent times, computers have developed into what might more appropriately be called information processors. Computers are used to simulate airplane flight and customer lines in a bank, to control processes on oil refineries and robots on assembly lines, and for storing massive amounts of data of varying types on people, places, and things. Thus, more modern languages, like Pascal, have become less action oriented and more "object oriented." Such languages have the capability of representing data in ways other than just numbers, and the goal of such languages is the capability to represent data objects in a way that more closely resembles the actual data items themselves.

Standard Pascal has four built-in types: Integer, Real, Char, and Boolean for representing numbers, whole and decimal, characters, and conditions that are either True or False. Since variables of the standard type Char can only hold values that are *one* character long, it is usually more convenient to use the Macintosh Pascal **string** type. In fact, we have used the Char type in only one of our previous examples. Because Char, and not **string**, is the standard Pascal type, we consider some examples of the Char type in this chapter. We also discuss briefly in Chapter 10 how one can survive with a version of Pascal that does not include a string package.

In addition, Macintosh Pascal has some additional types that are concerned with the precision of numeric data. These types will be discussed at the end of this chapter. Most older languages also have this same concept of different types. FORTRAN distinguishes between integers, real numbers, and characters, as do most versions of BASIC. Neither language has a corresponding Boolean type, although anyone who has programmed in either language should realize that a Boolean type is not required. In other languages, for example, a true condition could be represented as the number 1 and a false condition as the number 0. Since computer languages by their nature need to be as precise as possible, critics of such a representation would say that Boolean conditions are not numbers and should not be represented as numbers. It makes sense to divide one number by another or take a square root of a number, but corresponding operations on Boolean conditions make no sense at all and the language should prohibit such nonsense. While the reader may think that such criticism is unnecessarily picky, consider the following expressions in BASIC, where X = 7, Y = 5, and Z = 2:

```
IF X < Y < Z THEN ...
IF X > Y > Z THEN ...
```

Such expressions are usually written by beginning programmers and are intended to test the compound Boolean conditions

```
IF (X < Y) AND (Y < Z) THEN...
IF (X > Y) AND (Y > Z) THEN...
```

This second version is the correct way to write the compound test, i.e., compound conditions in BASIC are built as they are in Pascal, by separating simple conditions with the words AND and OR. However, many implementations of BASIC allow the syntactically incorrect versions, and even worse, assign the *wrong* truth value to them! The problem stems from the fact that Boolean conditions are actually treated as numbers. Thus, X < Y < Z is evaluated from left to right as follows: A test is made to see if 7 < 5. It isn't, of course, and so this part of the expression is replaced by the BASIC equivalent of False, which is 0. So now the computer tests to see if 0 < Z. But 0 < 2 is true, and so the entire expression is true. The reader should analyze the second expression and see why BASIC might evaluate that one incorrectly also. It is small wonder that beginners who have been led to believe that computers don't make mistakes find such occurrences to be very frustrating. This is also a frustrating problem for teachers who try to explain the correct way to form compound conditions, because the system seems to accept as syntactically correct almost any string of comparisons.

What would a Pascal translator do with an expression like X < Y < Z? It would also evaluate 7 < 5 as False. But then, when it tried to evaluate False < 2, it would generate a syntax error because one cannot compare two objects if they have different types. Thus, we see that one advantage of types is that the system can protect us from ourselves. In other words, languages with strict type rules tend to be more secure than languages with more permissive type mixing.

When we say that a variable (or a data object) has a particular type, we are actually specifying two properties of the data object:

1. The set of values that may be assigned to the object.
2. The set of operations that may be performed on the object.

For example, a variable of type Integer may take on any of the values from -32767 to +32767 and may have any of the standard numeric operations performed on it. Real variables of course take on a different set of values, from approximately 10^{-45} to 10^{38} in absolute value, and there are certain operations allowed on integers that are illegal for reals (**mod** and **div** for example). Boolean values may be operated on by **and**, **or**, and **not**, and may be assigned to and compared with other Boolean values. Character variables may be compared with other character values and assigned to other character variables.

We will discuss character manipulation in detail in a later chapter. The reason we do not include it here is because we normally use the special Macintosh Pascal String Package for most of our work with character information. The String Package is flexible and powerful, making character manipulation easy and convenient. As we mentioned earlier, strings were unfortunately omitted from Standard Pascal. This omission makes character manipulation tedious and difficult. But because the Char type is the standard Pascal type, it is worthwhile to consider some examples.

Example: Write a Pascal program that inputs a name from the keyboard in the form

 Last, First Middle

and prints the initials in the form

 F. M. L.

For example, the input

 Bear, Smokey The

should produce the output

 S. T. B.

  When dealing with the Standard Pascal Char type, we must remember that every value of that type is a *single* character. Thus, we must process the input character-by-character. Note that all we need to remember from each individual name is the initial letter. So we should scan these parts and save the initial. Then we print the initials, each followed by a period. Of course, we find our way through the name by looking for the blanks between the various parts of the name. We point out to the reader that character values are enclosed in single quotes. The program Initials is given in listing 8.1.

  Notice that the main part of Initials consists of 3 **repeat...until** loops. The first two read over letters until they find the blanks separating the names. The third loops until it finds the "End of Line." EOLN is a "cousin" of EOF that was introduced in Chapter 5. EOF is False unless the item you just read was the last item in the file. Similarly, EOLN is False unless the item you just read was the last item on the line. EOLN is, thus, very useful for controlling the reading of character input, either from a disk file or from interactive input. In general

 While not EOLN do
  Read a character
  Process a character

is the proper way to process a line of characters one character at a time. In Initials we used **repeat** loops instead of **while** loops, but that should be all right since we expect each name to consist of at least one letter.

```
program Initials;
(This program converts a name of the form)
("Bear, Smokey The" into its initials:   "S. T. B.")

  const
    Period = '.';
    Blank = ' ';

  var
    Letter, Last, First, Middle : Char;

begin
  Writeln('Enter your name in the form "Last, First Middle".');
  Read(Last);
  repeat  (Look for first blank.)
    Read(Letter)
  until Letter = Blank;
  Read(First);
  repeat  (Look for second blank.)
    Read(Letter)
  until Letter = Blank;
  Read(Middle);
  repeat  (Look for end of input line.)
    Read(Letter)
  until EOLN;
  Writeln;
  Write('The initials are: ');
  Write(First);
  Write(Period);
  Write(Blank);
  Write(Middle);
  Write(Period);
  Write(Blank);
  Write(Last);
  Write(Period)
end.
```

Listing 8.1

User-defined Types

Now we introduce the reader to a concept that first appeared in Pascal and has since been widely adopted in many recent programming languages. The topic is User-defined Types, and, as its name implies, this feature allows the programmer to "invent" types other than the standard data types (like Integer, Real, Char, and Boolean) to aid in solving problems. This feature in a language is very important for two reasons:

1. Computer programs are tools to help people solve problems. The more closely the program can reflect the real-world situation, the better the solution is likely to be.
2. Computer programs should be written with the human reader, not the computer, in mind. In general, the more readable a program is, the easier it is to understand, debug, and modify.

We start by giving a simple example that we have seen before. Let us input from the keyboard an hourly pay rate and seven hourly figures representing the number of hours worked on the days Monday through Sunday, and let us compute the amount of pay for the week. We assume that the pay rate is standard for Monday through Friday, with time-and-a-half for Saturday and double-time for Sunday. Listings 8.2, 8.3, and 8.4 show three versions of this program, with each successive version striving for more readability.

```
program Pay1;
{This program computes a weekly pay, given the hours worked each}
{day. Saturday gets time and a half, Sunday gets double time.}

var
    Rate, Hours, Pay : Real;
    Day : Integer;

begin
    Pay := 0;
    Write('Enter the pay rate per hour: ');
    Readln(Rate);
```

(Continued)

```
for Day := 1 to 5 do
  begin
    Write('Enter the hours for day', Day : 2, ': ');
    Readln(Hours);
    Pay := Pay + Hours * Rate
  end; (For)
Write('Enter the hours for day 6: ');
Readln(Hours);
Pay := Pay + Hours * Rate * 1.5;
Write('Enter the hours for day 7: ');
Readln(Hours);
Pay := Pay + Hours * Rate * 2;
Writeln;
Writeln('The total pay for the week is $', Pay : 5 : 2)
end.
```

Listing 8.2

```
program Pay2; (Slightly improved version)
(This program computes a weekly pay, given the hours worked each)
(day. Saturday gets time and a half, Sunday gets double time.)

  const
    Monday = 1;
    Friday = 5;

  var
    Rate, Hours, Pay : Real;
    Day : Integer;

begin
  Pay := 0;
  Write('Enter the pay rate per hour: ');
  Readln(Rate);
  for Day := Monday to Friday do
    begin
      Write('Enter the hours for day', Day : 2, ': ');
      Readln(Hours);
      Pay := Pay + Hours * Rate
    end; (For)
```

(Continued)

```
      Write('Enter the hours for day 6:  ');
      Readln(Hours);
      Pay := Pay + Hours * Rate * 1.5;
      Write('Enter the hours for day 7:  ');
      Readln(Hours);
      Pay := Pay + Hours * Rate * 2;
      Writeln;
      Writeln('The total pay for the week is $', Pay : 5 : 2)
   end.
```

Listing 8.3

```
program Pay3;  {Vastly improved version}
{This program computes a weekly pay, given the hours worked each}
{day.  Saturday gets time and a half, Sunday gets double time.}

type
   Days = (Monday, Tuesday, Wednesday, Thursday, Friday, Saturday, Sunday);

var
   Rate, Hours, Pay : Real;
   Day : Days;

begin
   Pay := 0;
   Write('Enter the pay rate per hour:  ');
   Readln(Rate);
   for Day := Monday to Sunday do
    begin
      Write('Enter the hours for ', Day, ':  ');
      Readln(Hours);
      case Day of
        Monday, Tuesday, Wednesday, Thursday, Friday :
         Pay := Pay + Hours * Rate;
        Saturday :
         Pay := Pay + Hours * Rate * 1.5;
        Sunday :
         Pay := Pay + Hours * Rate * 2
      end;  {Case}
    end;  {For}
```

(Continued)

```
    Writeln;
    Writeln('The total pay for the week is $', Pay : 5 : 2)
end.
```

Listing 8.4

The first and second versions are somewhat standard in that we use a loop controlled by an integer to get us through the weekdays. The second version makes some attempt at improving readability by using constants for Monday and Friday. In the third version, we see something truly different. Before the body of the program, up in the **const/var** section of the program, we now see a **type** section. It is in this section that we can define new types. Before we discuss these new types, let us review the purposes of types.

When we declare a variable to be of type Integer, we have implicitly accomplished two things:

1. We have specified the *values* that the variable is allowed to take, i.e., 5 and -234 are legal values while 2.7 and True and 'X' are illegal values.

2. We have specified the *operations* that may be performed on the variable, e.g., assignment or addition.

So, in general, types define allowable values and operations. Also, types provide some security--again the system tries to protect us from ourselves. If we try to assign a real value to an integer variable, or to divide one character value by another, the system alerts us that we are trying to do something illegal.

In the third version of the payroll program above, a new type, Days, is defined. This type exists throughout the program and as with other types, we can declare any variables we wish to be of this new type. Such a type is called an **ordinal** type, or an **enumerated** type, because we list (or enumerate) its possible values when we define the type. Thus, variables of type Days may take on any one of the values Monday, Tuesday, Wednesday, . . . , Sunday, but no other values. These are the so-called **constant** values of the type Days, just like True and False are the constant values of the Boolean type, and integers like 1, 2, and 3 are constant values of type Integer. We emphasize this point because many beginners confuse a constant value like Monday with the *string* constant 'Monday'. In other words, the assignment statement Day := 'Monday' is illegal because the types are not compatible. Also, if St is a **string** variable, the statement St := Monday is also illegal because Monday is not a **string**.

In this chapter, we only define ordinal types. In later chapters we see how to use records and arrays to form more complex, structured types. The adjective "ordinal" is important. Essentially, an ordinal type has a *first* (or smallest) value, a *last* (or largest) value, and a well-defined ordering among the values so that each value has a unique successor (except the last) and a unique predecessor (except the first). The Standard Pascal built-in types of Integer, Boolean, and Char are all ordinal types. The type Real is not.   The **string** type, when provided, is also not considered an ordinal type.

The reason the Real type is not an ordinal type should be clear after considering the following question: What real number comes *immediately* after 1.0376? Is it 1.0377, or 1.03761, or 1.03760000000000001? In a general mathematical setting, there is in fact no next number! Suppose there were. If X represents 1.0376 and Y represents the very next real number after 1.0376, then it is easy to see that (X+Y)/2 is smaller than Y and bigger than X. In fact, (X+Y)/2 is just half way between X and Y.   The reason there is no next number is related to the density of the set of all real numbers. Now on a computer, we can only represent a finite number of real numbers, so why aren't the reals considered to be an ordinal type? One reason is there would be too much confusion programming on different machines. Suppose one computer stores real numbers to 10 decimal places of accuracy while a larger computer might store real numbers to 30 decimal places of accuracy.   Then the answer to "What comes after 1.0376?" has different answers on different machines.   Consequently, programs that try to treat the real numbers as an ordinal type could possibly give much different results as they are moved from machine to machine.

Why are ordinal types important? There are many places in Pascal where we *must* use an ordinal type. For example, the variable that controls a **case** statement (that is, the variable following the keyword **case**) must be of an ordinal type so we can list, or enumerate, the alternatives. Likewise, the control variable of a **for** loop must again be ordinal. This restriction makes perfectly good sense, because when we finish an iteration of the loop, we must execute the loop again with the *next* value, and we must terminate the loop after we have used the *last* value.

With the ordinal user-defined types that we are discussing, it is easy to see how we specify the values of the type. We list the values, *in order*, within parentheses when the type is being defined. The next thing that we must know are the operations allowed on these types. These are not specified by the programmer but are part of Standard Pascal. The most basic operations that are available with all types are **equality** and **assignment**. That is, we can always assign values to variables as long as the types involved are the same and we can always test two values of the same type for equality. For example, if Workday and Dayoff are both of type Days, then all of the following are legal:

```
Workday := Thursday;
Dayoff := Monday;
Dayoff := Workday;
if Dayoff = Workday then ...
if Dayoff <> Wednesday then ...
```

With ordinal types, there are some important features that are built-in. The ordering of a user-defined type is given when we list the values in the type definition. So in the program of listing 8.4, Monday is the smallest value and Sunday is the largest. Thus, we can compare ordinal values using the relational operators <, <=, >, and >=. It is this ordering that also allows us to write **for** loops with ordinal types as control variables.

Succ, Pred, Ord, and Chr

A common operation performed on the integers is that of incrementing a value, as in Index := Index + 1. With a type like Days, addition doesn't really make any sense. But getting to the next value does. For example, we may be keeping track of a company's records and the first thing we need to do each day is update the day of the week. So if we need to change the value of Day from Tuesday to Wednesday, we do it with the built-in function Succ (for successor), which applies to all ordinal types:

```
Day := Succ(Day);
```

To get to the previous value, Pascal employs the function Pred (for predecessor). Thus, if Day is Tuesday, then

```
Day := Pred(Day);
```

assigns Day the value Monday. Often we may want to know where in the list a particular value is. For this, Pascal uses the function Ord (for ordinal position). One bothersome detail is that Pascal starts counting with zero. So Ord(Monday) equals 0 and Ord(Thursday) equals 3.

We point out that it is illegal to attempt to apply the Succ function to the last value of an ordinal type or to attempt to apply the Pred function to the first value of an ordinal type. So to write a segment that updates the day of the week, we would need to employ some sort of test as follows:

```
if Day = Sunday then
  Day := Monday
else
  Day := Succ(Day)
```

Representation of Characters

The observant reader may notice that the functions Succ and Pred are inverses of each other. This means that each function "undoes" the effect of the other. Another way of looking at inverses is to notice that if we apply the functions in succession, we end up where we started. It might seem natural to expect an inverse function for Ord, that is, a function that takes a nonnegative integer as input and gives us the element of the ordinal list corresponding to the position denoted by the input. That is, since Ord associates Wednesday with 2, there should be a function that associates 2 with Wednesday. The problem with such a general inverse is that we may define several different types in a single program. Then how are we to know which type we are talking about? For example, if in a program, we have the following delarations

```
type
  Days = (Mon, Tue, Wed, Thu, Fri, Sat, Sun);
  Colors = (Red, Violet, Blue, Green, Yellow, Orange);
```

should the inverse function of Ord associate Wed with 2 or Blue with 2? Because of this problem, there is a special inverse of Ord, called Chr, but it applies to only one specific ordinal type, the character type Char. Chr associates with the integer N the Nth character in the computer's set of characters. Notice that this does not necessarily mean the Nth letter of the alphabet, because the character set contains all the possible characters that can be typed from the keyboard, including special characters, some of which are invisible on the screen but which nevertheless have meaning to the computer. This representation of the character set is known as the American Standard Code for Information Interchange, or ASCII (pronounced "askey") for short. It is one of the two most common representations of characters in computers. The other representation is the EBCDIC ("ebsidik") representation, which is found primarily in IBM systems. We assume an ASCII representation throughout this book, but we caution the reader that one should always check the particular representation that a machine uses and try to write general programs that are independent of the character representation. If this is not possible, then such programs should be carefully documented in case problems arise when executing these programs on different machines. The use of the Chr function is useful when we want to embed instructions into output statements. For example, Chr(9) has the same effect as the Tab key (since the Tab key is the ninth character in the ASCII character set) while Chr(12) is the "form feed" or "page eject"; i.e., it causes printing to begin on a new page. Even when a printer is not being used, Chr(12) can be used to "clear the screen."

Table 8.1 shows the ASCII values for standard characters of the Macintosh character set. Empty positions in the table correspond to unprintable control characters (like the form feed) or to special Macintosh characters not found on ordinary keyboards (like mathematical symbols or letters for foreign alphabets). In addition to the tab key, Chr(9), and the form feed, Chr(12), some other useful "invisible" characters are the vertical tab, Chr(11), the carriage return, Chr(13), which returns the carriage to the beginning of the line *without* advancing to a new line, and the line feed, Chr(10), which returns to the beginning of the line and also advances to a new line. A list of the complete character set for the Macintosh is found in the Macintosh Pascal Reference Manual. The ordinal value of each of the standard characters in the table below is determined by adding its row and column labels. For example, Ord('A') is 65.

	0	1	2	3	4	5	6	7	8	9	10	11	12	13	14	15
0																
16																
32		!	"	#	$	%	&	'	(	)	*	+	,	-	.	/
48	0	1	2	3	4	5	6	7	8	9	:	;	<	=	>	?
64	@	A	B	C	D	E	F	G	H	I	J	K	L	M	N	O
80	P	Q	R	S	T	U	V	W	X	Y	Z	[	\	]	^	_
96	`	a	b	c	d	e	f	g	h	i	j	k	l	m	n	o
112	p	q	r	s	t	u	v	w	x	y	z	{	|	}	~	

Table 8.1

We began the chapter by explaining that a good type system makes a language more secure by separating objects that are of differing types. But now the truth must come out. Because the computer really only stores zeros and ones in its memory (for the absence or presence of electrical current), *everything, regardless of its type, is represented internally in the computer as a number!* How, then, are we able to separate Boolean values from numeric values and numeric values from characters? The answer is that we don't have to worry about this problem--this is a problem for the writers of systems programs. As programmers, we are in general not concerned about the internal representation of data. The purpose of high-level languages (like Pascal) is to free the programmer from worrying about such details. If the systems writer does a good job of implementing a high-level language, we as programmers should be able to picture the data in our minds in any way that is convenient for us. However, there are occasional instances where we do need to know how data is represented. Most of these instances involve character data and require an understanding of the ASCII representation.

For example, the ASCII code for the upper case A is 65. Suppose Ch is a variable of type Char with current value 'A', and that Num is a variable of type Integer with current value 65. Then, if it were possible for us to look into the Macintosh's memory at the memory cells corresponding to Ch and to Num, we would not be able to tell any difference between the two. To reinforce the discussion of the previous paragraph, it is the "magic" of high-level languages that causes the computer to "convert" the 65 to the letter 'A' when we access Ch but leaves the 65 alone when we access Num. It is the translator writer's job to make sure the magic works and it is precisely this feature that makes high-level languages the powerful tool that they are to the "common" programmer. Programmers do not have to be experts on machine architecture and internal representation. Their minds can be freed from such details so that they can focus on the problems they are trying to solve.

But what if we actually wanted to do some numeric calculations with some characters? This is where a knowledge of the ASCII code comes in handy, as we see in the next two examples.

Example: Input from the keyboard 10 grades, each of the form A, B, C, D, or F, and calculate a grade point average, where an A is worth 4 points, a B is worth 3 points, ... , an F is worth 0 points.

Discussion: We need to add to a running sum the appropriate point value for each of the grades. One possibility would be to use a **case** statement or nested **if...then...else** statements to assign the correct value. We take a different approach in the program in listing 8.5 to illustrate the Ord function.

```
program GPA;
(This program averages ten letter grades and reports)
(the Grade Point Average for the given individual.)

var
  Grade : Char;
  Count, Value, Total : Integer;
  Ave : Real;

begin
  Total := 0;
  for Count := 1 to 10 do
  begin
    Write('Enter the next grade (A, B, C, D, or F) ');
    Readln(Grade);
    if Grade = 'F' then
      Value := 0
    else
      Value := Ord('A') + 4 - Ord(Grade);
    Total := Total + Value
  end; (For)
  Ave := Total / 10;
  Writeln('The GPA is ', Ave : 5 : 2, '.')
end.
```

Listing 8.5

Note that the statement involving the Ord function assigns the correct number to Value, a 4 for an 'A', a 3 for a 'B', etc.

Example: Base Conversion

To follow this example, the reader needs some understanding of number bases. Ordinary numbers are written in base 10. Base 10 numbers have two basic properties:

1. These numbers are formed using any of 10 different digits, 0 through 9.

2. Each of the digits represents a power of 10.

For example, 372 is $3*10^2 + 7*10 + 2*1 = 300 + 70 + 2$.

There is nothing special about 10 except for its standard use, and it is possible to write numbers in any base. So 243 (base 7) is equal to 129 (base 10) since 243 (base 7) is $2*7^2 + 4*7 + 3*1 = 98 + 28 + 3 = 129$ (base 10).

The reader may be wondering why bases other than 10 are ever used. It turns out that non-decimal bases are not used much outside of computer applications, but are extensively used in the computer field. We have mentioned several times that computers essentially store their information as strings of 0's and 1's. Since computers only have two "fingers," the most natural base for numeric operations in a computer is base 2, or the binary number system. The binary system is easy to understand since the only digits used are 0 and 1, and the only number fact one needs to learn is that $1+1 = 10$ (base 2). However, for humans, base 2 is cumbersome because it takes so many digits to express even moderately sized numbers. For example, the decimal number 183 is written in binary as 10110111 (the reader should check that this is correct). Note that $183 = 128 + 32 + 16 + 4 + 2 + 1$.

Because of the clumsiness of the binary system, many computer systems also use base 8 (octal), or base 16 (hexadecimal). We will give a program shortly that converts base 8 numbers into decimal numbers. But first, we briefly explain the hexadecimal notation. Since in base 16 we need 16 different digits with which to form numbers, after using 0 through 9, we still need six more symbols. The symbols that are used are the upper case letters A through F, where A stands for 10, ... , F stands for 15. So in base 16, the decimal number 183 is written as B7 (which is 11 * 16 + 7). The hexadecimal system is explored a bit further in the exercises.

Now we present an algorithm that reads in a number from the keyboard in octal and prints out its decimal equivalent. Note that if we read the input in as an integer, it is treated as a decimal number. Thus, we must read the input as a sequence of characters. Moreover, observe that we do not know how many characters we are reading (because we do not know how long the number is). While this may seem like a difficult problem at first glance, it becomes easy when one key observation is made:

> Each time we scan a new digit, the previous number
> is multiplied by the base and the new digit is added.

To illustrate this, consider the *decimal* number 372. Now pretend you can't see all of the number and that you must scan it a digit at a time from the left. So you start with zero, see the 3, and add it to your total. So after scanning the first digit, you think the number is 3. If there are, in fact, no more digits to be scanned, you are correct. However, when you scan the 7, multiply the old number (3) by 10 and add in the new digit. This gives you 37, and again you are correct if the number stops there. Finally, upon scanning the 2, multiply the previous number (37) by 10 and add in the 2, giving 372. We use the EOLN (End of Line) function to determine when we have read the last digit of the number. This method works for any base and is the idea behind the program in listing 8.6.

```
program BaseConversion;
{This program converts base 8 numbers into base 10.}

var
  Digit : Char;
  Decimal : Integer;

begin
  Decimal := 0;
  Write('Enter a number in OCTAL (base 8) notation: ');
  while not EOLN do
    begin
      Read(Digit);
      Decimal := 8 * Decimal + (Ord(Digit) - Ord('0'))
    end; {While}
  Writeln;
  Writeln('The decimal equivalent is ', Decimal)
end.
```

Listing 8.6

Although the ordinal value of a digit is not equal to the value of the digit itself, the digits do in fact occur consecutively in the ASCII character set. Thus, we "convert" a character digit to its numeric value by subtracting the ordinal value of zero from the ordinal value of the digit in question.

There are two major restrictions in *Standard Pascal* that apply to user-defined types. The reader should be aware of them:

1. Values of a user-defined type cannot be written using the Write (or Writeln) statement.
2. Values of a user-defined type cannot be read using the Read (or Readln) statement.

While these restrictions were placed on the Pascal language for implementation simplicity and efficiency, they are sometimes bothersome and confusing, particularly for the beginning programmer. Fortunately, the authors of Macintosh Pascal have removed these restrictions and the programmer is free to treat user-defined types just like the other simple types. However, this is an exception, so we feel it is worthwhile to present an example so the reader can see how someone using Standard Pascal can get around the normal restrictions.

Consider a program that calculates for an individual the weekly total and daily average of the number of hours of television viewing. Such a program might have a prompt like this:

Enter the number of hours of television watched on Monday:
Enter the number of hours of television watched on Tuesday:
.
.
Enter the number of hours of television watched on Sunday:

If the days of the week are a user-defined type, how do we get their values printed in the prompt message? The procedure WriteDay in the program of listing 8.7 does it for us. Again we point out that such a procedure is not required in Macintosh Pascal because of the flexibility given to the programmmer in regards to user-defined types.

Another restriction concerning user-defined types is that two different types may not contain the same constant value. So the following segment is illegal

type
    FlagColor = (Red, White, Blue);
    StopLightColor = (Red, Yellow, Green);

because the value of Red is a constant of two different types.

```
program TV;
(This program shows how standard Pascal "writes" user defined types.)
 type
   Days = (Mon, Tues, Wed, Thurs, Fri, Sat, Sun);
 var
   Day : Days;
   Total, Hours, Average : Real;
 procedure WriteDay (Day : Days);
 begin
  case Day of
   Mon :
     Write('Monday');
   Tues :
     Write('Tuesday');
   Wed :
     Write('Wednesday');
   Thurs :
     Write('Thursday');
   Fri :
     Write('Friday');
   Sat :
     Write('Saturday');
   Sun :
     Write('Sunday')
  end (Case)
 end; (Definition of procedure WriteDay))
begin (Body of main program TV.)
 Total := 0;
 for Day := Mon to Sun do
  begin
    Write('Enter the amount of TV watched on ');
    WriteDay(Day);
    Write(' : ');
    Readln(Hours);
    Total := Total + Hours
  end; (For)
 Average := Total / 7;
 Writeln('The total number of hours of TV viewing for the week');
 Writeln('is ', Total : 5 : 1, ' which is a daily average of ', Average : 4 : 2, ' hours.')
end.
```

Listing 8.7

Subranges

There are occasions when we need only use a portion of the values of an ordinal type. If the values that we need are consecutive values, we can define a **subrange** of an ordinal type. Subranges are defined by listing the first and last values of the subrange, separated by two periods. Subranges can be defined for any of the built-in ordinal types or for any user-defined types. The following examples show the syntax of subrange definitions:

type
```
ExamScore = 0..100;
LowerCase = 'a'..'z';
Days = (Mon, Tue, Wed, Thu, Fri, Sat, Sun);
Workdays = Mon..Fri;
Weekend = Sat..Sun;
```

The overall type from which the subrange is taken is referred to as the parent type. Subranges can be mixed freely with their parent type and with other subranges derived from the same parent type, but, of course, the values involved must lie within the allowable ranges. Subranges provide two benefits:

1. Again, the system can protect us from ourselves. Using the above type definition, suppose we declare a variable Grade to be of type ExamScore. Then, if we try to assign a value to Grade that is not in the range from 0 to 100, the system reports an error. However, if we just declare Grade to be of type Integer, such a mistake would go undetected.
2. Subranges, like user-defined types themselves, can make programs more readable. The declaration

```
Grade : ExamScore;
```

carries more meaning than the declaration

```
Grade : Integer;
```

We point out that subranges can be used in the **var** section of a Pascal program instead of the **type** section if desired. This is sometimes helpful if there is no real reason to have a separate type name for a subrange. For example, the following two alternatives are equivalent:

```
type
   ExamScore = 0 .. 100;
var
   Grade : ExamScore;
```

and

```
var
   Grade : 0 .. 100;
```

We caution the reader that type names are required for parameters of procedures and functions and so there may be occasions when it is necessary to define a type name. We point out some examples of this later in the book.

Special Macintosh Pascal Types

Macintosh Pascal has some additional built-in numeric types that give the Macintosh increased arithmetic capabilities. The simplest enhancement deals with integers. In addition to the standard Integer type, whose set of values ranges from -32767 to +32767, there is the "long integer" type Longint. With Longint, the set of values ranges from -2,147,483,647 to +2,147,483,647. These strange values come from the way integers are stored in the Macintosh. The upper range of the Integer type is $2^{15}-1$ while the upper range of the Longint type is $2^{31}-1$. Long integers require 32 bits of storage as opposed to 16 bits for regular integers, so programmers should use variables of type Integer unless the expanded range is needed. The Macintosh converts all integers to long integers to perform arithmetic, so in fact, in a computation in which the result is supposed to be of type Integer, Longinteger values can be mixed with regular Integer values as long as all numbers fall in the range from -32767 to +32767.

The situation with real numbers is not quite so simple. Computers are able to represent integers exactly and to perform exact integer arithmetic. Such is not the case with real numbers. Real numbers can only be approximated in a computer, and, therefore, real arithmetic is approximate as well. For most beginners, real arithmetic can be assumed to be meaningful, although it should be pointed out that correct calculations involving real arithmetic can, because of "roundoff" errors, lead to nonsensical results. Without going into detail about how the

Macintosh stores real numbers, we simply list the type names in table 8.2, giving their range of values and their precision.

Real Type	Range	Digits of Precision
Real	$1.5*10^{-45}$ to $3.4*10^{38}$	7-8
Double	$5.0*10^{-324}$ to $1.7*10^{308}$	15-16
Extended	$1.9*10^{-4951}$ to $1.1*10^{4932}$	19-20
Computational	$-9.2*10^{18}$ to $9.2*10^{18}$	Exact (integer)

Table 8.2

Remarks:

1. The **precision** is given in decimal digits and measures how many digits of accuracy are maintained. For example, if Pi is a Real variable with value 3.14159265358979264846, it would be stored in the Macintosh as 3.1415927. But as a Double variable it would be stored as 3.141592653589793. If we needed the extra accuracy, we would declare Pi as follows:

```
var
  Pi : Double;
```

2. The Real type is sufficient for most of our purposes. The computational type is a special purpose real type that provides exact arithmetic. If decimal numbers are desired, it is up to the programmer to keep track of where the decimal point belongs. Macintosh Pascal provides a special form of the Write (Writeln) statement to handle the insertion of the decimal point into a number of Computational type. The reader is referred to the Macintosh Pascal Reference Manual for the use of this special type.

We conclude this chapter with a simple example of the kind of problem that can occur with the approximations involved in real arithmetic. We ask the reader to run the program RealEquality of listing 8.8. If you were surprised by the result, just remember never to test real numbers for exact equality.

```
program RealEquality;
var
  X, Y : Real;
begin
  X := 5.24;
  Y := 3.76;
  if X + Y = 9.0 then
    Writeln('Eureka')
  else
    Writeln('Phooey.');
  Writeln(X + Y : 3 : 1)
end.
```

Listing 8.8

Instead, decide on a margin of error (like 5 decimal places for normal Real numbers). That is, if two numbers are equal to 5 decimal places, then they are considered the same. Then test as follows:

```
Margin := 0.000001   (Margin should be declared Double precision)
if abs(X-Y) < Margin then
  Writeln('Eureka!')
else
  Writeln('Phooey.')
```

Although such problems are not of serious concern to us as beginners, it is important to be aware of the problems that can occur when doing real arithmetic on a computer.

Exercises

8.1 Write a program that picks a card at random from a standard, 52-card bridge deck. Define a type Suit with values Clubs, Diamonds, Hearts, and Spades, and a type Rank with values Ace, Two, Three, ..., Jack, Queen, King. Then generate two random integers, the first in the range 1 to 4 and the second in the range 1 to 13. Use these numbers to print out the card that was selected. Use a **case** statement to assign the value of the Suit and use a loop to assign the appropriate rank. For example, if the Rank value is 7, then loop through the values of the type Rank until you get to the seventh one.

8.2 Roxy wants to write "Dear John" letters to her 5 steady boyfriends Arnold, Bubba, Clarence, Drew, and Egbert, whose nicknames are Hunk, Moose, Cat, Bull, and Hulk respectively. To make the letters as personal as possible, she will use the real names, the nicknames, and the cities (Montreal, Chicago, Boston, Paris, Carbondale) in which they met. Write a program that writes Roxy's 5 letters for her.

8.3 FEMALES (The Fair Employment to Men and Ladies Equally Society) needs a program to report on alleged salary discrimination at the Widget Works. A text file Employees contains, for each employee, a line with 3 items: Sex (Male or Female), Category (Blue or White), and Monthly Salary. For example, the line

Female White 617.18

means some female, white collar employee earns $617.18 per month.

Your program should output three comparisons: Total male average vs. total female average, male blue collar average vs. female blue collar average, and male white collar average vs. female white collar average. Also, in each case, if any average exceeds the other by more than 10%, issue a comment indicating possible salary discrimination based upon sex.

Note: The data in the file Employees is arranged to give an unexpected result. What is the irony or "paradox" of the results?

8.4 The text file Payroll contains weekly payroll data on employees of the Widget Works. There are two lines of information for each employee in the following format:

C6.5 7.5 4.5 5.0 8.0 4.0 3.0
John Smith

The significance of each item in the data lines is:
First item--A, B, C, or D is the category of the worker. The hourly pay for these categories is $14.75, $16.25, $17.02, and $18.43 respectively.
Next seven items--These are the numbers of hours worked each day from Monday to Sunday. On Monday through Friday, the regular hourly rate is paid, while on Saturday, the worker is paid time and a half, and on Sunday, the worker is paid double time.
Last item--Worker's name.

Write a program that figures the payroll for the Widget Works. Your program should print a table with two columns--the first column should contain the name of the employee and the second column the weekly pay. Incorporate the following features into your program:

1. Define a type Day and use a variable of that type to control the loop for computing the pay.

2. Use a **case** statement to determine the appropriate rate.

8.5 Write a program that reads in a number in hexadecimal and prints out its decimal equivalent. You should read in the number as a string of individual characters. To find the decimal equivalent of a particular hexadecimal digit, you need to consider only two basic cases--the hex digits 0--9, and the hex digits A--F.

8.6 Write a program that prints out a handy base conversion table of the numbers from 1 to 31 as shown below:

Base Conversion Table

Decimal	Binary	Octal	Hexadecimal
1	00001	01	01
2	00010	02	02
...	...	...	...
...	...	...	...
31	11111	37	1F

Write separate procedures Convert_to_Binary, Convert_to_Octal, and Convert_to_Hexadecimal. These procedures should write out the converted numbers character by character. For simplicity in aligning the columns of the table, print leading zeros as shown above. Note that we can convert 27 to Octal, for example, by computing 27 **div** 8 and 27 **mod** 8.

Chapter 9

Arrays

> MIDDLE OUT – A programming methodology allowing progress up or down as the mood of the team dictates. This approach allows an early, honest, and reassuring report that the programming project is "definitely about halfway."
>
> **Devil's DP Dictionary**

Introduction

Each of our variables has been capable of holding just one value. That is, Name, a **string** variable, can "remember" one name for us while Number, an integer, can "remember" one integer at a time. To each variable we have associated a memory cell in the computer and each cell is large enough to store one string, one integer, one real, etc. We now learn how to make the computer "remember" an entire list or table of values. For example, the tonnage of marshmallows produced in the United States in the years 1975 to 1984 is an example of an **array**. This information is shown in table 9.1.

Since this is not a history of marshmallow production in the United States, we will not go into detail on the reasons for the decline in U.S. production. Suffice it to say that beginning about 1980 the importation of foreign marshmallows began to have a serious effect on U.S. suppliers. This can be seen from table 9.2 showing the growing importance of marshmallow imports from the Grand Duchy of Fenwick.

In each of the tables the year is called the **index** to the table. It is called an index since if someone asks what the U.S. production in 1979 was, the answer can be found by looking in the row labelled 1979. Arrays, or tables, come in many sizes and shapes. Table 9.1 is an example of a one-dimensional array. That is, it is simply a list of 10 values, indexed by the years 1975 to 1984. Table 9.2, on the other hand, is an example of a two-dimensional array as each row contains more than one value.

Tonnage of U.S. Marshmallows

1975	44,573.5
1976	46,734.9
1977	46,934.6
1978	48,324.3
1979	48,056.2
1980	47,298.4
1981	45,238.4
1982	44,573.2
1983	42,745.1
1984	39,298.0

Table 9.1

	U.S. Tonnage	GDF Tonnage
1975	44,573.5	583.4
1976	46,734.9	692.5
1977	46,934.6	1,745.2
1978	48,324.3	2,482.4
1979	48,056.2	3,264.1
1980	47,298.4	6,392.5
1981	45,238.4	9,883.4
1982	44,573.2	12,389.0
1983	42,745.1	15,399.3
1984	39,298.0	19,343.2

Table 9.2

Pascal allows arrays with any number of dimensions, but we shall not consider the general case until later. For now the term "array" is synonymous with "one-dimensional array."

Suppose that we wish to use the Pascal variable US_Tonnage to denote the array of table 9.1. We have two problems: How do we declare our intention to store many values under the one name, and how do we access the individual values? Let us consider the declaration first.

Because integers, reals, strings, etc. all have different storage requirements, we must inform the system of the type of the components of the list. In our example, the tonnages are obviously real numbers. Hence, the **component type** is real. Of course, we must also inform the system of the possible indices to be used with the array. The component type must be carefully distinguished from the **index type**. In our example the indices are a subrange of integers (1975 to 1984) while the values being stored in the array are real. Here, finally, is the declaration for US_Tonnage:

var
   US_Tonnage : **array** [1975 .. 1984] **of** Real;

When the system sees this declaration it realizes that US_Tonnage is an array, not a simple variable, that the indices are integers in the given subrange, and that the values being kept in this array are all real. With this information the system can determine how many elements there are in the array (10 in this case) and can provide proper storage for the array.

To refer to a particular item in the array US_Tonnage, we simply supply the appropriate index between square brackets. This index is also called a **subscript**. Thus, US_Tonnage[1979] is the fifth value in the list. Note that US_Tonnage[1979] is a real value, and as such can be read, written, or assigned a value as in:

   US_Tonnage[1979] := 48056.2;

The real power of arrays comes in the next section when we learn how to manipulate arrays with *variable* indices. That is, if Year is an integer variable in the range 1975 to 1984, then US_Tonnage[Year] is a legal expression, and if the variable Year currently has the value 1983, then US_Tonnage[Year] names the ninth element of the array.

The general form of the declaration of a one-dimensional array is:

   variable : **array** [low index .. high index] **of** component_type;

where "component_type" can be any Pascal type, and "low index" and "high index" are the limits of permissible indices for the array. The type of the indices is given implicitly by these limits and may be any *ordinal* type such as Integer, Char, or a user-defined type. The index type may not be Real or **string**. Also, in Pascal, the limits of the indices must be *constants*, not variables with values supplied at execution time.

Consider the following declarations:

const
  Num_Students = 30;
type
  Months = (Jan,Feb,Mar,Apr,May,Jun,Jul,Aug,Sep,Oct,Nov,Dec);
  Children = (John, Kathryn, Sarah, Anne, Natalie);
  Grades = (A, B, C, D, F);

var
  Rainfall : **array** [Jan..Dec] **of** Real;
  Birth_Month : **array** [John..Natalie] **of** Months;
  Sem_Grade : **array** [1..Num_Students] **of** Grades;
  Fee_Status : **array** [1..Num_Students] **of** Boolean;
  Names : **array** [1..Num_Students] **of string**;
  Month : Months;
  Child : Children;
  ID : 1..Num_Students;

Rainfall is declared as an array of twelve reals since the rainfall each month is measured to the nearest hundredth of an inch. Rainfall [Month] is used to denote the amount of rain received during the given Month. To initialize that amount to zero, we would write:

Rainfall[Month] := 0.0;

Birth_Month has component type Months and index type Children. It has 5 elements and Birth_Month [Child] is, of course, used to denote the month of birth of the given Child. To assign John's month of birth, we write:

Birth_Month[John] := Oct;

Sem_Grade is an array of 30 Grades and to assign the student with identification number ID, in the range from 1 to 30, the grade of C we would use:

Sem_Grade[ID] := C;

Fee_Status is an array of Boolean values. That is, the component type is Boolean. The interpretation is that Fee_Status[ID] is True only if the student with identification number ID has paid all the appropriate fees. Assuming that Fee_Status and Names already have values, we could check for negligent students with:

> **if not** Fee_Status[ID] **then**
>   Writeln(Names[ID], ', you have not paid your fees.');

where Names [ID] is the name of the student with the given ID number. Of course, this **if** needs to be in a loop on ID numbers in order to check all students.

There is an apparently alternate form of the array declaration whereby the index type is given explicitly and the limits of the index are given implicitly. For example, Rainfall or Birth_Month could be declared by:

> **var**
>   Rainfall : **array** [Months] **of** Real;
>   Birth_Month : **array** [Children] **of** Months;

While this method is more consistent in that both the index and component types are named, it is often slightly less convenient than the previous method. That is, to declare Summer_Rain to be an array of 3 real numbers to keep track of summer rainfall, we could use:

> **var**
>   Summer_Rain : **array** [Jun..Aug] **of** Real;

whereas to declare Summer_Rain using the second method, we must first declare explicitly a subrange type:

> **type**
>   Summer_Time = Jun..Aug;
> **var**
>   Summer_Rain : **array** [Summer_Time] **of** Real;

The reader should realize that the two methods are equivalent and that the system obtains the same information from each. For purposes of clarity, we think the first method is usually preferable and will use it throughout this book.

The Need for Arrays

Consider the following two problems:

> Snidely Whiplash, sales manager at The Widget Works, has a one hundred member sales staff. The name and dollar amount of sales for each person is kept on a text file. Snidely wants a program to print the names of all salespersons who have sales of at least $5,000.00 worth of widgets.

> Snidely Whiplash, sales manager at the Widget Works, has a one hundred member sales staff. The name and dollar amount of sales for each person is kept on a text file. Snidely wants a program to print the names of all salespersons who have sales of at least the average sales of all salespersons.

Obviously, these two problems appear to be very similar. However, as we shall see, the second is considerably more complex than the first. In the first problem no arrays are needed. We read a name and a sales amount. If the amount is at least $5,000.00, we print the name. We simply loop 100 times making the above simple decision. Listing 9.1 contains such a program, called Snidely_1. Note that the data is available on the text file Widget_Sales, which is assumed to be on the Pascal disk and which actually has data for considerably less than 100 salespersons in it. For each salesperson, there are two lines in the file. The first line consists of a name (30 characters) while the second line contains a sales amount.

```
program Snidely_1;
(This program commends persons with sales of $5,000.00 or more.)

  const
    Sales_Quota = 5000.0;

  var
    Name : string[30];
    Sales : Real;
    Loop : Integer;
```

(Continued)

```
begin
  Close(Input);
  Reset(Input, 'Widget_Sales');
  Writeln('Snidely Whiplash Program 1 - No arrays!');
  Writeln;
  while not Eof do
   begin
    Readln(Name);
    Readln(Sales);
    if Sales >= Sales_Quota then
      Writeln(Name, ' has met Snidely''s sales quota.')
   end (While)
end.
```

Listing 9.1

We leave it to the reader to improve upon Snidely_1 so that it also prints a "get on the stick" message for those who have not met Snidely's quota, as well as counts of the total number of salespersons and the number reaching the quota.

To solve the second problem, why can't we simply change the condition of the **if** to

if Sales >= Average **then** ...

The answer, of course, is that the average of the sales amounts is not known until all sales figures have been seen. That is, suppose the first person's name is 'Belle Ringer' and that Belle's sales are $7,894.86. It is easy to see that Belle's sales exceed $5,000.00 but it is impossible to say whether Belle's sales exceed the average or not. We cannot compute the average until all the sales amounts are known. In this case we need the computer to remember all the sales figures. The basic difference between the above problems is that there is no interaction between the data for the different salespersons in the first case. We can decide whether to commend a given salesperson in the first case simply by looking at the data for that salesperson. There is no need to save each of the names and sales figures; arrays should not be used in the first case. In the second case, however, arrays provide the elegant solution. We simply read the names and sales amounts into two arrays, compute the average, then look through the sales array to see whose sales have exceeded the average.

```
program Snidely_2;
(This program commends persons with average sales or better.)

  var
    Names : array[1..100] of string[30];
    Sales : array[1..100] of Real;
    Loop : Integer;
    Sum : Real;
    Average : Real;
    Count : Integer;

begin
  Close(Input);
  Reset(Input, 'Widget_Sales');
  Writeln('Snidely Whiplash Program 2 - Uses arrays!');
  Writeln;
  Sum := 0.0;
  Count := 0;
  while not Eof do
   begin
     Count := Count + 1;
     Readln(Names[Count]);
     Readln(Sales[Count]);
     Sum := Sum + Sales[Count]
   end; (While)
  Average := Sum / Count;
  Writeln('The average sales figure was $', Average : 7 : 2);
  Writeln;
  Writeln('Snidely''s best salespersons include:');
  for Loop := 1 to Count do
   if Sales[Loop] >= Average then
     Writeln(Names[Loop])
end.
```

Listing 9.2

Consider the other alternatives: We could have the computer read the data twice: once for the computer to find the average and once to determine whose sales are above the average. But reading from the text file is slow--and there is no need for the computer to do so a second time, unless the text file is so large that it can't be read into arrays in memory.

Another alternative would be to use one hundred different name and sales variables: Name1, Name2, ... , Name100, Sales1, Sales2, ... , Sales100. But then we would need distinct reads and writes for the one hundred different salespersons. The program would be more bother than it would be worth!

The array solution is given in listing 9.2. An improved version of Snidely_2 is left for the exercises. Note that the program contains two loops, a **while** loop and a **for** loop. The first loop reads in the names and sales figures. Note that the expressions "Names[Count]" and "Sales[Count]" run through the arrays Names and Sales as Count increases from one. That is, when Count is 1, we read and store Names[1] and Sales[1]. Then Count becomes 2 and we read and store Names[2] and Sales[2], etc. Also notice that the first loop also sums the sales figures. Since this can be done as the sales amounts are read in, it should be done in the same loop as the reads. Furthermore, note that the calculation of the average comes after the first loop and before the second loop. Beginners often place the average calculation within the first loop. This is inefficient, as the system then computes a "running" average. All we need is one final average, so, the average calculation belongs outside all loops. Once we know the average it is a simple matter for the second **for** loop to output those salespersons with better-than-average sales. Note that since the values were stored during the first loop, they are now referenced-- *without rereading them*--in the second loop. The second loop is a **for** loop since we now know (after the first loop) how many salespersons Snidely has. It is also important to observe that the program does not need to be changed to handle a larger sales force.

Run Snidely_1 and Snidely_2 and study their listings until the small but important differences between these programs are clear to you.

Simple Operations on Arrays

This section presents many elementary array operations. The reader who takes the time to carefully understand the segments that follow will be well-prepared when it comes time to write programs. For each of the following segments, we assume the following declarations:

```
var
   List : array [1..50] of Integer;
   Index : 1..50;
```

Example 1: Assign the value 37 to the 17th element of List. The solution is straightforward:

List[17] := 37;

Example 2: Assign the value zero to each element of the array List. In this case we use a **for** loop:

```
for Index := 1 to 50 do
  List[Index] := 0;
```

Notice the power of the **for** loop. The same statement with 5000 in place of 50 would initialize a list of 5000 elements to all zeros.

Example 3: Assign 1 to List[1], 2 to List[2], ... , 50 to List[50]. Again a **for** loop provides the most elegant solution:

```
for Index := 1 to 50 do
  List[Index] := Index;
```

Example 4: Assign List[1], List[3], List[5], ... , List[49] the value 87. This time, since we want Index to take on only odd values (increment by two each time), we use a **repeat ... until**:

```
Index := 1;
repeat
  List[Index] := 87;
  Index := Index + 2
until Index > 50;
```

Example 5: Input 50 values, obtained from the user, into List. Again, a **for** loop is called for:

```
for Index := 1 to 50 do
  begin
    Write('Enter the next number: ');
    Readln(List[Index])
  end;
```

Example 6: Assuming that List already has values, compute the sum of the elements of List. Also assume that Sum is an Integer variable. This is another **for** loop with a "running" Sum:

```
Sum := 0;
for Index := 1 to 50 do
  Sum := Sum + List[Index];
Writeln('The sum of your numbers is ', Sum);
```

Example 7: Let the user decide how many numbers are to be in the List. (The maximum is 50, of course.) Let the user enter that many numbers and then compute the sum of the numbers.

This example is a generalization and combination of examples 5 and 6. It shows that we should not always use small, separate loops, but should try to combine activities where possible into one loop. For this example, we assume that Len_List is also a declared Integer variable:

```
repeat
  Writeln('How many numbers do you want in your list?');
  Readln(Len_List)
until (Len_List > 0) and (Len_List <= 50);
Sum := 0;
for Index := 1 to Len_List do
  begin
    Write('Enter the next number:  ');
    Readln(List[Index]);
    Sum := Sum + List[Index]
  end;
Writeln('The sum of your numbers is ', Sum);
```

Example 8: Assuming that List already has values and that the length of the list is Len_List, count the number of negative elements in the List.

This time we assume that Neg_Count is an Integer variable and use a simple if:

```
Neg_Count := 0;
for Index := 1 to Len_List do
  if List[Index] < 0 then
    Neg_Count := Neg_Count + 1;
Writeln(Neg_Count, ' negative elements were found.');
```

An Extended Example

Let us return to the Widget Works and consider how we might use an array Sales to keep track of the number of widgets sold by each individual salesperson. Since The Widget Works has nearly 100 salespersons, who are identified by the ID numbers 1, 2, 3, ..., 100, we declare Sales by

var
    Sales : **array** [1..100] **of** Integer;

Notice that the Widget Works may not have exactly 100 salespersons. We know there are at most 100, but salesperson 49 may have quit last week. Certain of the cells of the array Sales may not be used. The extra space provides for expansion by the Widget Works, and as long as the true number of employees is not drastically less than 100, we are not wasting much memory space. Suppose ID is an integer variable. If ID is the valid ID of a salesperson, then Sales[ID] eventually contains the number of widgets sold by that salesperson. We begin by initializing each entry of Sales to zero:

    for ID := 1 **to** 100 **do**
    Sales[ID] := 0;

Each time widgets are sold, the salesperson fills out a sales transaction containing the salesperson's ID and the Quantity of widgets sold. For example, the transaction '7 12' would signify that salesperson 7 has sold 12 more widgets. Suppose these transactions are saved (batched) for a two-week period and then entered into the computer to be analyzed. Since we do not want to count the number of transactions, we shall simply ask the person doing the data entry to enter a fictitious negative ID after all of the valid transactions have been entered. Since each salesperson is expected to turn in many transactions during the two-week period, Sales is really an array of "running sums." Hence, we see the need for initializing each entry to zero before beginning the processing of the transactions. Here is the segment that processes the transactions:

    Writeln('Enter the first ID');
    Readln(ID);
    while ID > 0 **do**
      begin
        Writeln('Enter the quantity of widgets sold.');
        Readln(Quantity);
        Sales[ID] := Sales[ID] + Quantity;
        Writeln('Enter the next ID. Enter -1 to terminate program.');
        Readln(ID)
      end; {**while**}

The key statement in the above segment is the assignment

  Sales[ID] := Sales[ID] + Quantity;

which, of course, adds the Quantity from the current transaction to the total of the salesperson whose ID is also on the transaction.

Snidely Whiplash, the sales manager, has asked for a program that determines the maximum quantity of widgets sold by anyone during the two-week period. We discussed finding a maximum in Chapter 5 and we can use the same method on arrays. Recall that we set Max to some ridiculous value and then looped through the actual values adjusting Max whenever a larger value was found. Since all the entries in Sales must be nonnegative, we can initialize Max to -1 if we wish. Here is a segment that determines Max:

  Max := -1; {Initialize Max to a ridiculous value.}
  for ID := 1 **to** 100 **do**
   if Sales[ID] > Max **then**   {New Max has been found.}
    Max := Sales[ID];
  Writeln('The greatest number of widgets sold by anyone was ', Max);

When dealing with arrays, there is an alternate, more general, method of finding a maximum. We can initialize Max to the first value in the array and then compare all the other elements as before. This method has the advantage that it finds the maximum in an array even if all the numbers are negative (which the above strategy does not do). Of course, in our example we know that the entries of Sales are nonnegative so either method works. But if we are dealing with an array of low temperatures in International Falls, Minnesota, in January, it would be dangerous to begin by initializing Max to -1. At the end Max might still be -1 and we would not know if that were correct or not. Here is the segment using this alternate method:

  Max := Sales[1];
  for ID := 2 **to** 100 **do**
   if Sales[ID] > Max **then**   {New Max has been found.}
    Max := Sales[ID];
  Writeln('The greatest amount of widgets sold by anyone ', Max);

The output from either of the above segments is:

The greatest amount of widgets sold by anyone was 963

where 963, say, is the maximum value in Sales. When you take this information to Snidely, he is, of course, not pleased. Even though it answers his original question, it isn't what he wants to know. "Who," he wants to know, "is the salesperson who has sold 963 widgets?"

Let's see if we can modify the program that finds the maximum so that it also finds the associated ID of the salesperson. This time, when we find a new Max, we shall also have to remember the associated ID. Here is the segment:

```
Max := Sales[1];
Winner_ID := 1;  (Initialize Max and Winner_ID to first person.)
for ID := 2 to 100 do
  if Sales[ID] > Max then     (New Max has been found.)
    begin
      Max := Sales[ID]; (Remember new Max)
      Winner_ID := ID (Remember new ID)
    end
Writeln('Salesperson #', Winner_ID,' has sold ', Max, ' widgets.');
```

This time the output is:

Salesperson #47 has sold 963 widgets.

Snidely still isn't happy. "Who is salesperson #47? Why can't computers speak English?"

The answer, of course, is that the computer can tell us the name of the winner of the sales contest *if* we give it the names of all the salespersons. From the personnel office we should be able to get the ID and name of each salesperson. Suppose they look like this:

```
...   ...
...   ...
34  Belle Ringer
39  Lotta Bull
22  Polly Tishun
...   ...
```

Notice that the ID numbers are not in order. Also notice that we cannot use a **for** loop as we are not sure of the exact number of salespersons on the current payroll. It's another great opportunity for a trailer loop, or an EOF if using a text file. Here is the segment, assuming that some data entry clerk interactively enters the names. We assume that Names has been declared by:

    Names : **array** [1..100] **of string**[30];

Limiting the string's length is absolutely necessary to avoid wasting immense amounts of memory. Declaring an **"array** [1..100] **of string"** sets aside space for 100 strings of 255 characters each!

```
Writeln('Enter the first ID');
Readln(ID);
while ID > 0 do
  begin
    Writeln('Enter the name for this person.');
    Readln(Names[ID]);
    Writeln('Enter the next ID. Enter -1 to terminate program.');
    Readln(ID)
  end;
```

Notice how the ID's are accepted in any order. If the data begins as above, then 'Belle Ringer' is the first name read in and is stored in the 34th cell of the Names array. Likewise, 'Lotta Bull' goes into the 39th cell, etc. When all of the names have been read in they are in the correct places in the Names array. Notice that if there is no salesperson #59, then Names[59] is undefined. That is not a problem unless we try to print out by order of ID number the names of the salespersons. If we ever wanted to do this we could, of course, initialize each entry of names to '', the **null string**. The null string contains no characters and should not be confused with the string that consists of a single blank. The null string is written using two single quotes, a beginning quote and an ending quote, with nothing in between. More will be said about the null string in Chapter 14. After reading in all the names we would know that those cells that are still equal to the null string correspond to ID numbers that are not currently being used.

   Names and Sales are examples of parallel arrays. That is, the information in Names[ID] is related to the information in Sales[ID]. In this case Names[ID] is the name of the person who has sold Sales[ID] widgets. This is illustrated in figure 9.1.

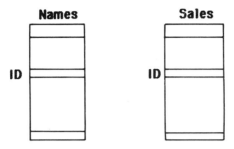

Figure 9.1

Now that the system knows the names of the salespersons, we can modify
the loop that determines the winner of the sales contest to finally provide
Snidely with the desired information:

```
Max := Sales[1];
Winner_ID := 1;  (Initialize Max and Winner_ID to first person.)
for ID := 2 to 100 do
  if Sales[ID] > Max then    (New Max has been found.)
    begin
      Max := Sales[ID];  (Remember new Max)
      Winner_ID := ID  (Remember new ID)
    end;
Writeln('The winner of the Widget Company sales contest is ...');
Writeln(Names[Winner_ID], ' who sold ', Max, ' widgets in the last ');
Writeln('two weeks. That"s incredible!');
```

   Snidely has one more request. He often needs to check up on a
particular salesperson. Of course, if he knew the salesperson's ID number,
then we could simply print out Sales[ID] to answer his question. But
Snidely can't be expected to learn nearly 100 ID numbers. Hence, we need
to write a segment that accepts a name of a salesperson and looks the
person up in the arrays. To be more precise, since the name is the only
information that we have, we shall need to look the person up in the Names
array and note the ID number. Then using that ID number we can find the
sales amount from the corresponding position in the parallel array Sales.
Since human input is involved, we shall also have to be careful to watch
for bad input. Due to a typing error or due to a recent dismissal, the name
may no longer be in the Names array. In such a case, all we can do is
report failure.

```
Writeln('Enter the name of the salesperson');
Readln(Target_Name);
ID := 1;
Found := False;
while (ID <= 100) and (not Found) do
 if Names[ID] = Target_Name then
  Found := True
 else
  ID := ID + 1;
 if Found then
  Writeln(Target_Name, ' has sold ', Sales[ID], ' widgets.')
 else
  Writeln('Sorry, ', Target_Name, ' is not in our records.');
```

Since there are two ways to exit from the **while** loop, either with the Target_Name found or with ID having exhausted the possibilities, we need an **if** after the loop to determine which condition caused the exit from the **while**.

The following **while** to search for the Target_Name seems simpler:

```
ID := 1;
while (ID <= 100) and (Names[ID] <> Target_Name) do
    ID := ID + 1;
```

However, this can lead to a subtle error. Suppose the Target_Name is not in the array of Names. Then ID eventually becomes 101 and we hope the **while** terminates. Certainly the condition

"ID <= 100"

is now False. Unfortunately, the moronic computer is not smart enough to realize that since the first part of the **and** is False, the whole condition must be False. It goes ahead and tries to evaluate the condition

"Names[ID] <> Target_Name"

But since ID is 101, "Names[ID]" is not a valid expression. In common language, our subscript is "out of bounds." Macintosh Pascal's language is a bit more stilted. Your program **abends** (abnormally ends), the hand points to the **while**, and you receive the error message:

The value of a variable or subexpression is out of range for its intended use.

Remember that the above message can mean "subscript out of bounds." Also keep in mind the **Instant** and **Observe** windows for help in interpreting error messages such as the above. By putting a stop sign on the statement that generates the error and by observing the variables involved in the statement, you can quickly determine which variable has run amuck.

Examples Using Arrays

Soggies, The Breakfast of Programmers

Each box of Soggies, the breakfast of programmers, has a prize in it. There are 10 different prizes in all and you would, of course, like to be the first programmer in your class to collect all 10 premiums. We assume that the 10 different prizes are randomly distributed in the boxes and also we assume that there are so many boxes of Soggies that the chances of getting any one prize always remains 1 in 10. That is, just because you already have 17 of the IBM punch card trinkets and none of the floppy disk lapel pins doesn't mean that either is more likely than the other in the next box of Soggies. The problem (finally!) is: How many boxes of Soggies, on the average, would you expect to buy to obtain all 10 prizes? That seems like a very vague question. You could, of course, obtain all 10 prizes in your first 10 boxes, but we've never seen it happen in many years of discussing this problem. You could, of course, still not have all 10 prizes after 1000 boxes of Soggies, but that is not likely either. Our question is this: If you repeated this experiment many times, what would the average of all your trials be? An experiment, of course, means buying boxes of Soggies until you have collected a full set of prizes. There are two obvious ways to solve this problem. The first is to run to your neighborhood grocery and begin ripping open (buy them first, please) boxes of Soggies. Before we begin to feel that our answer is at all reliable, we need to make many trials. This solution is messy and expensive. The second solution, of course, involves a computer simulation. That is, using Random, the random number generator from Chapter 7, we can easily instruct the computer to imagine that we are opening boxes of Soggies in order to note the prize within. We can put the simulation in a loop and quickly generate an average based upon many trials. We hope this simple simulation demonstrates the power and ease of computer simulations. As you shall see later in the exercises, simulations can also be a lot safer than the real thing.

Here is our outline for the Soggies problem:

Initialize Total_Boxes to zero and Trial to one.
Repeat
        Perform the experiment once. That is, remember Num_Boxes
            needed to collect all ten prizes.
        Increment Total_Boxes by Num_Boxes needed on this Trial.
        Increment Trial by one.
Until Trial = 20
Compute and print the average of the twenty Trials.

where, of course, "perform the experiment once" is a procedure that we shall have to refine further. We need some means of keeping track of which of the 10 prizes we already have. An array comes to mind. But an array of what? We could declare Prizes to be an array of Integer and then Prizes[7] would be 17 if we currently had 17 of prize 7. But we really don't need to know how many of each prize we have. We only need to know if we have or still need a prize. This suggests that Prizes could be an array of Boolean values, where Prizes[7] would be True if we have any of prize number 7. However, the most elegant way would be to define a new type consisting of "GotIt" and "NeedIt" and use an array of GotIt's and NeedIt's. The advantage of this method is that no one can fail to understand the meaning of the fact that Prizes[7] is GotIt. Although GotIt and NeedIt are eqivalent to the Boolean values True and False, it is possible to become confused about whether Prizes[7] being True means it is true that we have it or it is true that we need it. In order to make our program as clear as possible we shall use GotIt and NeedIt. Here is the outline of the procedure "Perform the experiment once":

Initialize Num_Boxes to zero.
Initialize the array Prizes to all NeedIt's.
Repeat
        Generate randomly a Premium number between 1 and 10.
        Set Prizes[Premium] to GotIt.
        Increment Num_Boxes by one.
Until no more premiums are needed.

Of the above statements, each except "no more premiums are needed" is easily expressed in Pascal. The latter can be expressed as a function that looks through the array Prizes and returns True only if some premium is still marked as NeedIt. Here is the pseudo-code for a function More_Needed:

Initialize More_Needed to False.
For each of the ten entries of Prizes
If any entry equals NeedIt Then
Set More_Needed to True.

Listing 9.3 shows the complete program Soggies. Please study it carefully. Make a "guesstimate" of the number of boxes that are needed on the average, and then run Soggies to see how it turns out.

```
program Soggies;
(This program simulates the purchase of boxes of Soggies)
(until all ten different premiums have been collected. It)
(performs the experiment twenty times and provides an)
(average of the twenty trials.)

const
  Trial_Limit = 20;

var
  Total_Boxes : Integer;
  Num_boxes : Integer;
  Trial : Integer;
  Average : Real;

procedure One_Experiment (var Num_Boxes : Integer);
  type
    Prize_Status = (NeedIt, GotIt);
    Prize_Array = array[1..10] of Prize_Status;
    Prize_Type = 1..10;
  var
    Index : Prize_Type;
    Premium : Prize_Type;
    Prizes : Prize_Array;
```

(Continued)

```pascal
function Generate_Premium : Prize_Type;
begin
  Generate_Premium := (Random mod 10) + 1
end; {Definition of function Generate_Premium}


function More_Needed (Prizes : Prize_Array) : Boolean;
  var
    Index : Prize_Type;
begin
  More_Needed := False;
  for Index := 1 to 10 do
    if Prizes[Index] = NeedIt then
      More_Needed := True
end; {Definition of function More_Needed}


begin  {Body of Procedure One_Experiment}
  Num_Boxes := 0;
  for Index := 1 to 10 do
    Prizes[Index] := NeedIt;
  repeat
    Premium := Generate_Premium;
    Prizes[Premium] := GotIt;
    Num_Boxes := Num_Boxes + 1
  until not More_Needed(Prizes)
end; {Definition of procedure One_Experiment}


begin  {Body of main program, Soggies}
  Trial := 1;
  Total_Boxes := 0;
  repeat
    One_Experiment(Num_Boxes);
    Total_Boxes := Total_Boxes + Num_Boxes;
    Writeln('Trial ', Trial : 2, ' took ', Num_Boxes : 2, ' boxes.');
    Trial := Trial + 1
  until Trial > Trial_Limit;
  Average := Total_Boxes / Trial_Limit;
  Writeln;
  Writeln('The average of all the trials was ', Average : 7 : 3)
end.
```

Listing 9.3

The way to read the above program is to begin with the body of the main program at the *end* of the listing. Notice that this calls a procedure One_Experiment(Num_Boxes) that performs the experiment once--and uses Num_Boxes of Soggies in so doing. Then look at the details of the definition of the procedure One_Experiment, beginning with its body. Note that this procedure uses two functions that are defined within it. Also, note that the **type** definitions are included in the procedure, but not in the main program. They could be moved out into the main program, but there is no reason to do so. We will investigate Soggies further in the exercises, where we suggest a more efficient way of answering the question of "More_Needed?".

The Twelve Days of Christmas

How many golden rings did the young lady receive from her true love in the song "The Twelve Days of Christmas"? Five is *not* the correct answer! She received 5 golden rings on several consecutive days, hence, she had a whole pile of golden rings after the twelfth day. In fact, how many gifts did she receive in total and how many of each of the 12 gifts did she receive? Since we are counting lots of things, you should smell an array. Let us suppose that Num_Gifts is an array of 12 integers. Note that on any given day the young lady receives gifts of all lower indices than the current day index. That is, on day 7 she receives 7 of gift 7, 6 of gift 6, 5 of gift 5, etc.

Here then is the outline of the program:

Initialize an array, Gift_Desc, to the twelve gifts.
Initialize an array, Num_Gifts to zeros.
For Day from 1 to 12
    For Gift from Day backwards to 1
        Increment Num_Gifts[Gift] by Gift
Sum the entries of the array Num_Gift.
Output the sum of each gift as well as the total of all gifts.

You should trace the above outline to see that on day one it gives one of gift one, on day two it gives two of gift two and one of gift one, etc. The program is shown in listing 9.4. Run Xmas to see how many gifts in all are involved in the song. We are deeply grateful to Fred Koch for granting us permission to use his lyrics to this traditional song.

```
program Xmas;
(This program sums the gifts of each type received)
(by the fair maiden in the song "The Twelve Days of Christmas".)
(Special lyrics by Fred Koch.)

    const
       Num_Days = 12;

    type
       Desc_Type = array[1..Num_Days] of string[25];
       Gift_Counts = array[1..Num_Days] of Integer;

    var
       Num_Gifts : Gift_Counts;
       Gift_Desc : Desc_Type;
       Day : 1..Num_Days;
       Gift : 1..Num_Days;
       Sum_Gifts : Integer;

    procedure Initialize (var Num_Gifts : Gift_Counts;
               var Gift_Desc : Desc_Type);
       var
          Day : 1..Num_Days;
    begin
       for Day := 1 to Num_Days do
          Num_Gifts[Day] := 0;
       Gift_Desc[1] := 'a pickle in a peach pie';
       Gift_Desc[2] := 'two talking turtles';
       Gift_Desc[3] := 'three French chefs';
       Gift_Desc[4] := 'four silly sisters';
       Gift_Desc[5] := 'five frozen frogs';
       Gift_Desc[6] := 'six ducks on diets';
       Gift_Desc[7] := 'seven Santas sleeping';
       Gift_Desc[8] := 'eight eggs escaping';
       Gift_Desc[9] := 'nine noisy neighbors';
       Gift_Desc[10] := 'ten tons of termites';
       Gift_Desc[11] := 'eleven lizards laughing';
       Gift_Desc[12] := 'twelve tubas tooting'
    end; (Definition of procedure Initialize.)
```

(Continued)

```
function Sum (Num_Gifts : Gift_Counts) : Integer;
 var
   Temp_Sum : Integer;
   Day : 1..Num_Days;
 begin
   Temp_Sum := 0;
   for Day := 1 to Num_Days do
     Temp_Sum := Temp_Sum + Num_Gifts[Day];
   Sum := Temp_Sum
 end; {Definition of function Sum}

 procedure Print_Results (Num_Gifts : Gift_Counts;
           Gift_Desc : Desc_Type;
           Sum_Gifts : Integer);
  var
    Day : 1..Num_Days;
 begin
   Writeln('Gift' : 10, 'Quantity Received' : 30);
   Writeln;
   for Day := 1 to Num_Days do
     Writeln(Gift_Desc[Day] : 25, Num_Gifts[Day] : 5);
   Writeln;
   Writeln('The total number of gifts received was ', Sum_Gifts : 3)
 end; {Definition of procedure Print_Results}

 begin {Body of Main Program, Xmas}
  Initialize(Num_Gifts, Gift_Desc);
  for Day := 1 to Num_days do
    for Gift := Day downto 1 do
      Num_Gifts[Gift] := Num_Gifts[Gift] + Gift;
  Sum_Gifts := Sum(Num_Gifts);
  Print_Results(Num_Gifts, Gift_Desc, Sum_Gifts)
 end.
```

Listing 9.4

Searching and Sorting Arrays

It has been said that computers spend more time "searching and sorting" than doing any other activity. Whether this is true or not, these applications are certainly two of the most important to learn. Searching

an array means, of course, that given an array and a target, we are to find
the location of the target in the array. The location is reported by giving
the index of the target. Even with this simple notion several problems can
arise. For example, what if the target is in the array several times? What
if the target is not in the array at all? We could, of course, ask that the
search return all indices in the first case, but since this is a beginning
text, we shall take the easy way out and assume that the search returns
any of the indices involved. If the target is not in the array, we shall
assume that the search returns this information by returning some absurd
value for the index. For example, if we are searching in an array whose
indices run from 1 to some upper limit, we could have our search return
the index of 0 to indicate an unsuccessful search. The simplest search,
which we have already used in the Widget problem earlier in the chapter,
is called a **linear search**. It begins at one end of the array and searches
each element in order until the target is found or until we reach the other
end of the array. Here is an outline of the linear search for a Target in a
List with indices from Lo to Hi. We assume that 0 is not a legal index and
return it if the target is not found:

```
Initialize Found to False.
Initialize Index to Lo.
While Index <= Hi and the Target hasn't been Found Do
    If List[Index] equals the Target Then
        Found := True
    Else
        Index := Index + 1
If Target is still not Found then
    Index := 0.
```

You should trace the above to see that if the target is in the array, then
Found is set to True. We exit the **while**, and Index "points" to the place in
the array occupied by the Target. On the other hand, if the Target is not in
the array, we eventually exit the **while** after Index finally exceeds Hi and
at that point we give Index the absurd value of 0. Of course, a program
that uses this search also must test the value of the Index returned and, if
it is zero, take appropriate action.

Writing the above as a Pascal function is extremely straightforward.
We assume that List is of type Some_List where Some_List is declared by:

type
    Some_List = **array** [Lo,Hi] **of** Component_Type;

and that Lo and Hi are some constants of type Index_Type and Component_Type is any type. We also assume that Absurd is a constant of the index type and that the function should return Absurd if the Target is not found in the List. The Pascal version of the function is found in listing 9.5.

```
function Linear1 (List : Some_List;    {NOT A COMPLETE PROGRAM}
              Target : Component_Type;
              Lo, Hi : Index_Type) : Index_Type;
var
  Found : Boolean;
  Index : Index_Type;
begin
  Found := False;
  Index := Lo;
  while (Index <= Hi) and not Found do
    if List[Index] = Target then
      Found := true
    else
      Index := Index + 1;
  if not Found then
    Linear1 := Absurd
  else
    Linear1 := Index
end;  {Definition of function Linear1}
```

Listing 9.5

Again the **while** in Linear1 has a compound condition and thus an **if** is needed after the **while** to decide whether the Target was Found or not. If you knew the Target was in the List you could simplify the program. This suggests the following trick: Guarantee that the Target is found by putting it in the List! In fact, if the Target is put in a special zero[th] cell of the array and the search proceeds down from the top, our function is made much simpler as in listing 9.6.

Here we have assumed that List was declared with lower subscript 0, although the actual elements of the List are stored from index 1 up to Hi. The zero[th] place in the List is for the Target. This means that the Target will be found. Hence, the **while** is very simple. Note that since we search backwards we return the index of the *last* Target in List. Of course, if the Target wasn't in the original List, then we find it at the zero[th] place (since that is where we put it), our **while** terminates, and Linear2 returns the absurd index 0.

```
function Linear2 (List : Some_List;  {NOT A COMPLETE PROGRAM}
          Target : Component_Type;
          Hi : Index_Type) : Index_Type;
{This version assumes that the array List has a zeroth cell}
{just for linear searches. It also assumes that the}
{search is between the subscripts of 1 and Hi.}

var
   Index : Index_Type;
begin
  List[0] := Target;  {Place Target in array.}
  Index := Hi;  {Search backwards from Hi}
  while List[Index] <> Target do
    Index := Index - 1;
  Linear2 := Index
end;  {Definition of function Linear2}
```

Listing 9.6

Binary Search

It is perhaps difficult to think of any other type of search to perform besides a linear search. What could we do that would be any better than starting at one end and looking through the array? Nothing, actually, unless the array is ordered. Consider the task of finding a book in the fiction section at the library. If the books were arranged by the colors of their jackets and all you know is the author's name, you would have no choice but to apply a linear search to the books in the fiction section. But if the books are arranged alphabetically by the authors' last names, you wouldn't start at one end of the fiction section and look at each book until you find the one you want! That is, you don't use a linear search at the library. Rather, you use your knowledge of the order of the alphabet to obtain useful information from a book even if it is not the book you want. For example, if the first book you see is by Asimov and the book you are looking for is by Ludlum, you know that you are not really warm yet and you can shift over several aisles. If, however, you find yourself among the Vonneguts, you know you've gone too far. In fact, your Ludlum book should be about halfway between the Asimov books and the Vonnegut books. This method may seem very clear to actually use in a library but difficult to give precisely to a computer. We shall, therefore, refine and define the algorithm.

Another example, perhaps, makes it clear that we use ordered searches in many instances in everyday life. Finding a telephone number for a given Chicagoan is not difficult if you have the proper spelling of the name. Imagine the opposite problem: Given a Chicago telephone number, find the name of the person who has that telephone number. Unless you have a "reverse directory" ordered by telephone number instead of name, you are forced to do a linear search through the directory.

Note that the array must be ordered before we can apply our fancy search method. If the items in the array are not ordered, then the only information we can get from a cell is that it is--or is not--the cell we are looking for. However, if the array is arranged in order, then each cell gives us information. If it does not contain our target, it at least tells us on which side of that cell to concentrate our search, allowing us to zero in on the target much more quickly.

Assume that List is an ordered array. For definiteness, assume that the elements of List are in increasing order. Note that the elements of List can be any ordinal type, such as Integer, Real, Char, or user-defined. Of course, only minor modifications are needed if the array is in decreasing order. In what follows, assume that we are looking for Target in List between the indices Lo and Hi. The **binary search** algorithm proceeds as follows: Start the search in the middle of the array List. That is, let Mid be the middle index between Lo and Hi. Then consider List[Mid]. Of course, if List[Mid] is our Target, then our search stops with success. However, if our Target is less than List[Mid] then it is clear that we should continue our search between the new limits, Lo and Mid-1. On the other hand, if Target exceeds List[Mid] then we should continue the search between the indices Mid+1 and Hi. The easiest way to continue the search between Lo and Mid-1 is to set Hi to Mid-1 and then repeat the entire process. Likewise, to continue between Mid+1 and Hi, we simply give Lo the new value Mid+1 and repeat the process. Let us illustrate this algorithm with an example.

Suppose we have a list consisting of the following numbers:

13 15 18 25 27 32 39 42 45 48 53 57 60 65 66

Assume that the Target is 48. Of course, we begin with Lo equal to 1 and Hi equal to 15. We set Mid equal to (Lo+Hi) **div** 2, or 8 in this case. Since List[8] is 42, which is smaller than our Target, we know that 48, if in the list at all, must be in the half between List[9] and List[15]. Hence, we set Lo to 9 and continue. The midpoint between 9 and 15 is 12, so we consider List[12] next. Since List[12] is 57 and therefore too large, the search has narrowed to between the indices 9 and 11 for Lo and Hi respectively. The Mid value is 10 and List[10] is the Target and the search ends with success.

Before we implement the binary search, consider how an unsuccessful search terminates. For example, suppose we search the above array for 26. We begin again with Lo equal to 1 and Hi equal to 15. The search begins at List[Mid] where Mid is 8. Since that value is too big, the search is narrowed to between the indices 1 and 7. The new Mid point is 4 and List[4] is too small, so the search continues between the indices 5 and 7. Since List[6] is too big, we continue between the indices 5 and 5. Aha! Since List[5] is not our Target, we must report a failure! Actually, there is no reason to consider the case where Lo equals Hi as a special case. First of all, we need to make one last check at that cell (List[5] in the above example) to see whether it is the Target or not. In our case the Mid value between 5 and 5 is, of course, 5. Hence, we compare Target and List[5]. Here List[5] is too large. That means that we should set Hi to Mid–1 and continue. Thus, Lo is 5 and Hi is now 4. The absurd condition that Lo is bigger than Hi is our signal that the Target is not in the array. What we have seen is that List[4] is too small and hence the Target, if in the List, must be at or beyond the 5th place in the List. Later we learn that List[5] is too large. Hence, the Target is at or before the 4th place. These two conditions together are contradictory. Hence, we may safely conclude that our Target is not in the List.

The Pascal function for the binary search is given in listing 9.7. It assumes the following **type** declaration:

type
    Some_List = **array** [Index_Type] **of** Component_Type;

where Index_Type is any subrange of the Integer type and Component_Type is any type. It also assumes that List is ordered in an ascending sequence and that you wish the search to proceed between the indices Lo and Hi. Further, we assume that Absurd is a constant of Index_Type and that its value is not in the range from Lo to Hi. Of course, the function returns the index of the Target if the Target is found and the ridiculous value Absurd otherwise.

```
function Binary_Search (List : Some_List;  (NOT A COMPLETE PROGRAM)
          Target : Component_Type;
          Lo, Hi : Index_Type) : Index_Type;
  var
   Mid : Index_Type;
   Found : Boolean;
begin
 Found := False;
  while (Lo <= Hi) and not Found do
   begin
    Mid := (Lo + Hi) div 2;
    if List[Mid] = Target then
     Found := True
    else if List[Mid] > Target then
     Hi := Mid - 1
    else
     Lo := Mid + 1
   end; (If and While)
  if Found then
   Binary_Search := Mid
  else
   Binary_Search := ABSURD
 end. (Definition of function Binary_Search)
```

Listing 9.7

It is worthwhile pointing out to the reader the difference in efficiency between the two kinds of searches. For example, if we are searching an array of size 1000, using a linear search it would take, on the average, 500 comparisons to find the target, while the binary search takes, in the *worst* case, only 10 comparisons. Doubling the size of the array *doubles* the number of comparisons needed with the linear search while the number of comparisons needed in the binary search only increases by 1! Thus, the difference becomes enormous as the array size gets large. For example, if the list is 1,000,000 elements long, the difference in the number of comparisons is 500,000 (on the average) for the linear search compared with 20 in the binary search. If the reader is surprised at this figure, think about how easy it is to find a book in a large library or a phone number in a large city telephone directory using an ordered search and how difficult these tasks would be if a linear search were used.

Sorting an Array

As we have seen, it is necessary that an array be in order before a binary search can be applied. Hence, sorting an array into order is obviously an important topic. Also, often before a list is output for human consumption, it is useful to sort the list into order.

Here we consider a simple, fairly efficient sort known as the **insertion sort**. Before we look at the implementation in Pascal, let's try to understand how insertion sort works. Insertion sort begins with the totally obvious idea that any list of one item is properly sorted. If we have a list of two items, then we simply decide whether the second item should be inserted before or after the first item. If we have a list of three items then we ignore the third item for a moment and insert the second in the correct spot relative to the first. Then we insert the third, either before the first, between the first and second, or after the second. In general then, if we have N items, we insert the second, third, ..., N^{th} items into their proper place with regard to those already present.

We illustrate the idea of the insertion sort with an example. Let us sort the list:

86 39 42 12 24 53

Note that here the items are integers. We could just as well sort reals or even strings since the system knows the alphabetical ordering of strings. Also, we are going to sort the list into ascending sequence. We could just as well sort the list into descending order. Moreover, the given list has no duplicates (no 39 twice, for example), but duplicates do not cause any problems to the insertion algorithm. We leave these cases to the reader as exercises.

Back to our sort. Since a one-element list is in order, we need only insert elements 2 through 6 into their proper places. The key to inserting an element is to ignore all elements with higher indices. That is, when inserting the Indexth element, we need only look at elements 1 to Index-1.

Index = 2, insert 39 with respect to the first element:

Before: 86|39 42 12 24 53   After: 39 86|42 12 24 53

Index = 3, insert 42 with respect to the first two elements:

Before: 39 86|42 12 24 53   After: 39 42 86|12 24 53

Index = 4, insert 12 with respect to the first three elements:

Before: 39 42 86 |12 24 53   After: 12 39 42 86|24 53

Index = 5, insert 24 with respect to the first four elements:

After: 12 39 42 86 |24 53   After: 12 24 39 42 86|53

Index = 6, insert 53 with respect to the first five elements:

Before: 12 24 39 42 86|53   After: 12 24 39 42 53 86|

Presto, the list is sorted. Notice that all numbers to the left of the veritcal bar are sorted, and on each pass the number to the immediate right of the bar is inserted into its proper place.

Now that we understand how insertion sort works, our concern becomes implementing it in a fairly efficient manner in Pascal. To be specific, let us suppose that the array is A and that there are N elements in A. Here, in general pseudo-code is the idea of the insertion sort:

For Index := 2 to N Do
    Find the Place where A[Index] should follow A[Place]
    Slide elements from A[Place+1] to A[Index-1] up one cell
    Insert A[Index] into A[Place+1].

Let's consider in more detail what is involved in finding the Place, sliding elements, and inserting a new element. In particular, consider the situation when the list is

A: 12 39 42 86 24 53

and Index = 5, i.e., it is time to insert 24 into the list. We see that 39, 42, and 86 must slide over to make room for 24, but how do we instruct the computer to do this? First, we know that whenever we swap elements around, we need a temporary storage location so we don't lose any values. Hence, let us first store 24 in Temp:

Temp: 24
A: 12 39 42 86 24 53

Now, cell A[5] is really not being used, so we can slide A[4] into A[5]:

    Temp: 24
    A: 12 39 42 86 86 53

Now, cell A[4] is free and we slide again:

    Temp: 24
    A: 12 39 42 42 86 53

And again:

    Temp: 24
    A: 12 39 39 42 86 53

Finally, A[1] is not larger than Temp, so the sliding stops and we insert Temp into A[2]:

    Temp: 24
    A: 12 24 39 42 86 53

Now the first five elements are sorted and the procedure continues by saving 53 in Temp, sliding 86 over and then inserting 53 into its proper place.

There is one problem with our algorithm. What if the element to be inserted is smaller than all the others? Obviously then, everybody should slide and the new element should be inserted into A[1]. However, we indicated above that the sliding should continue while the Temp element is smaller than the current element in the list. If we are not careful we get a "subscript out of bounds error." Namely, after we slide A[1] into A[2], our program is likely to check to see if the nonexistent element A[0] needs to slide.

One can handle this problem by special checks, but the most elegant method, since we need a temporary location anyway, is to declare zero to be a legal subscript for the array A and then use A[0] for Temp. Since we slide elements until we find one not smaller than A[0], A[0] itself, if necessary, stops the sliding! The procedure Insertion_Sort, given in listing 9.8, sorts the List A of length N into ascending order using this technique.

```
procedure Insertion_Sort (var A : List;   (NOT A COMPLETE PROGRAM)
          N : Integer);
(This procedure sorts the array A of N elements using insertion)
(sort. We assume A has a zeroth element. See text for details.)
  var
    Index, Spot : Integer;
begin
  for Index := 2 to N do
    begin
      A[0] := A[Index];   (Save A[Index] temporarily.)
      Spot := Index - 1;
      while A[Spot] > A[0] do (Slide bigger elements up.)
        begin
          A[Spot + 1] := A[Spot];
          Spot := Spot - 1
        end;  (While)
      A[Spot + 1] := A[0]  (Insert new element.)
    end  (For)
end;  (Definition of procedure Insertion_Sort)
```

Listing 9.8

Multi-Dimensional Arrays

The fact that you are reading this section labels you as a "survivor" of one-dimensional arrays. This section should seem natural to those who have learned the previous sections well (but may well push others "over the edge"). Actually the main subject of the remainder of this chapter is the care and feeding of two-dimensional arrays. Arrays in Pascal can come in any dimension, but two-dimensional arrays are very common and anyone who can handle them well understands the general principles and can implement 17-dimensional arrays without us.

A secret, well-kept from students, is that a two-dimensional array is nothing other than a "table" of information. For example, the table of marshmallow production in the United States and in the Grand Duchy of Fenwick (table 9.2) is an example of a two-dimensional array. It is two-dimensional since it has rows and columns. In this case each row is a one-dimensional array of two elements (don't count the index) representing marshmallow productions in a given year. In contrast, each column is a one-dimensional array of ten elements representing marshmallow productions over the 10 years in a given country. That is, the rows are indexed by years and the columns are indexed by countries. A particular entry in the table is determined if we fix a year and a country. For example, the marshmallow production in the Grand Duchy in 1980 is easily determined to be 6,392.5 tons.

We recommend that the reader view a one-dimensional array as a "list" of items, and likewise view a two-dimensional array as a "table" of items. The word array has frightened many a beginning student of programming. Realizing that an array is really not some strange object created by your professors to paralyze you is very important. Arrays, as we shall see throughout the remainder of this book, are critical to programming.

It may become difficult to picture, but if we add other products to our example, we obtain a three-dimensional array. That is, if we keep track of the production of marshmallows, bicycles, paper clips, and moustache wax over a period of several years in the U.S. and the G.D.F., then we have a table with three indices. To determine a specific entry we must give a product, a year, and a country. If we add a further complication, such as the color of the product, then we have a four-dimensional array. Again, Pascal has no limit to the number of dimensions that a given table may have. However, the reader should be aware that seemingly innocent tables can be giant memory hogs. For example, if the above table stores information for 20 products over a 10-year span for 15 countries, and lists 12 colors for each product, then that table occupies 36,000 cells in memory (Why?).

As with one-dimensional arrays, we have two major questions that we must answer. How does one declare and how does one use multi-dimensional arrays? The following declarations should seem natural:

type
    Countries = (US, GDF);
    Colors = (Red, Green, Orange, Yellow, Blue);
    Categories = (Student, Faculty, Alumnus, Guest);
    Students = (Amy, Bill, Carol, David, Edith, Fred);
    Grades = (A, B, C, D, F, INC, W, WP, WF);

var
    Marshmallows: **array** [1975..1984, US..GDF] **of** Real;
    Gradebook : **array** [Amy..Fred, 1..10] **of** Grades;
    Parking_Fees : **array** [1980..1985, Student..Guest, Red..Blue] **of** Real;
    Mult_Table : **array** [0..9, 0..9] **of** Integer;

Marshmallows is, as previously discussed, a table of 20 entries arranged into 10 rows and 2 columns. If Year and Country are variables of the obvious types, then Marshmallows[Year, Country] is a real number representing the tonnage of marshmallows produced in that Country in the given Year. Gradebook, on the other hand, is a table of sixty entries arranged in 6 rows and 10 columns. The rows of Gradebook are indexed by students' names and the columns are indexed by the subrange of integers from 1 to 10. Of course, Gradebook[Carol,7] is of type Grades and represents the grade Carol received from Professor Pedantics on project number 7. Parking_Fees is an example of a three-dimensional array. It is a table of the history of parking fees at Abnormal University for the years 1980 to 1985 for the various categories of users (students to guests) and for the various lots on campus, which are identified by colors. That is, if Year, Class, and Hue are variables of the proper types, then Parking_Fees[Year, Class, Hue] represents the fee needed to park in a lot of color Hue for a user of the given Class in the given Year. Mult_Table is a simple two-dimensional array--and we hope Mult_Table[R, C] stores the product of R and C, the row and column indices, each of which we assume is between 0 and 9.

There is an alternate form of the array declaration for multi-dimensional arrays that we now discuss. Since any type can be placed after the **of** in an array declaration, it is possible to define an array as follows:

Add_Table : **array** [0..9] **of array** [0..9] **of** Integer;

For most purposes this is fully equivalent to the array definition of Mult_Table given above. That is, Add_Table[R, C] is an integer, we hope the sum of R and C, the row and column indices.

Mult_Table must be used with zero or two indices. For example, if we assume that Div_Table is another variable declared in the *same* declaration as Mul_Table, then both of the following are valid:

Div_Table := Mul_Table; {This is an entire array operation. It is valid}
　　　　　　　　　　　 {only if both arrays are of the same type}
Mul_Table[7,6] := 42;　　 {This is an operation on a specific element}

On the other hand, Add_Table may be used with zero, one, or two indices. For example, if Sub_Table is another variable declared in the *same* declaration as Add_Table, then all of the following are valid:

```
Sub_Table := Add_Table;  (Entire array operation)
Add_Table[3] := Add_Table[7];  (This is a "row" operation.  The 7th row)
                                (of Add_Table is assigned to the 3rd    )
                                (row of Add_Table                       )
Add_Table[4,7] := 11;  ( Operation on a specific element)
```

That is, Add_Table[R] is itself an array of 10 integers, and can be assigned any value of that same type. In the above example, the 3rd row of the table is replaced by the contents of the 7th row. In summary, the two forms are very close. If one would like to do entire row operations, then the second form *must* be used. If there is no need in the given application for such operations, the first form is probably the preferable form to use. Also, since Add_Table[R] is an array, we may write Add_Table[R][C] to indicate the Cth item in the Rth row of Add_Table. This is an alternate form to the more common expression Add_Table[R,C].

Finally, we need to make a remark about when two variables in Pascal have the same type. Although this may seem obvious, it isn't. First, if a type has a name, then all variables of that type, or that are subranges of that type, are naturally considered to be of the same type. Prior to this chapter, this was always the situation. However, if we declare a variable

List : **array** [1..10] **of** Integer;

then List is said to be declared **anonymously**, that is, without a type *name*. In the anonymous case, variables are of the same type only if they are declared in the *same* variable declaration.
Consider the following examples:

var
   List_1 : **array** [1..10] **of** Integer;
   List_2 : **array** [1..10] **of** Integer;

In the above case, the statement List_1 := List_2 is illegal because the two variables are not of the same type. If we want them to be of the same type, we have two alternatives. The first one is to declare them together:

var
   List_1, List_2 : **array** [1..10] **of** Integer;

The second alternative involves making up a type name and using it in the variable declarations:

```
type
  Lists = array [1..10] of Integer;
var
  List_1 : Lists;
  List_2 : Lists;
```

In each of the previous two situations, List_1 := List_2 is now legal because both variables are of the same type.

This example points out a situation when the "invention" of a type name is desirable (or required). Although we can use the first alternative of declaring things together within any one block, we must use the second alternative if we are to set up argument/parameter correspondences with procedures and functions. This point is often a source of confusion (understandably) to beginners. Simply remember that to use arrays as arguments/parameters, the arrays must be declared with *named* types. They cannot be passed anonymously.

A two-dimensional array often has several parallel one-dimensional arrays associated with it. For example, suppose Marks is an array declared by:

```
Marks : array [1..30, 1..10] of Integer;
```

We assume that Marks is to be used to keep the scores of up to 30 students on up to 10 homework assignments. An obvious parallel array would be an array in which to keep the names of the students. Since strings are not compatible with integers, we must use different arrays for the names and for the marks. Thus, we could declare Names by

```
Names : array [1..30] of string[25];
```

The reader should reflect upon why we chose 1..30 and not 1..10 in the above example. Two other logical arrays to associate with Marks would be Student_Average and Homework_Average. Student_Average, of course, is designed to hold the average of each student, while Homework_Average is supposed to keep track of the class average on each homework. Hence, we declare these two arrays (very differently) as follows:

```
Student_Average : array [1..30] of Real;
Homework_Average : array [1..10] of Real;
```

We hope the picture of figure 9.2 helps to explain these parallel arrays. Simply for human understanding, those that deal with rows of Marks are drawn in a vertical format, while those that deal with the columns of Marks are drawn in a horizontal format.

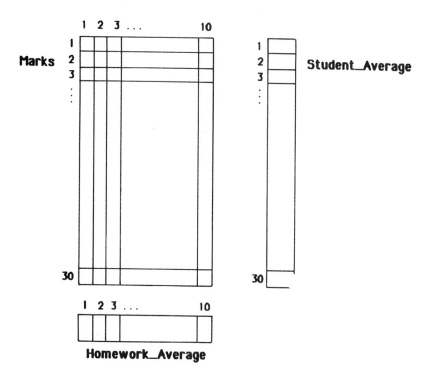

Figure 9.2

Simple Operations on Two-Dimensional Arrays

For each of the following segments we assume that the arrays Marks, Names, Student_Average, and Homework_Average have been declared as in the previous section. Further, we assume that the arrays Marks and Names already have values stored in them and that any index variables that we need have been so declared.

Example 1: Assign the score 0 to the element in the 3rd row and 2nd column.

Trivially, we write:

Marks[3,2] := 0;

Notice that this assignment means that we have given the 3rd student the mark of zero on the 2nd homework. This is radically different from

Marks[2,3] := 0;

so be very careful with the order of the indices!

Example 2: Assign the score of 100 to each element in the 17th row.

Here, obviously, someone has purchased "failure insurance." The point is that a row operation corresponds to an individual, while a column operation corresponds to a particular homework assignment. The solution uses a loop:

```
for Paper := 1 to 10 do
  Marks[17, Paper] := 100;
```

Example 3: Assign the score of 0 to each element in the 6th column.

This time, everyone got caught cheating on homework number 6. We obviously use a loop, but note that we loop 30 times, not 10, and also notice carefully the placement of the constant 6 in this example:

```
for Person := 1 to 30 do
  Marks[Person, 6] := 0;
```

Example 4: Count the number of zeros in the Rth row, where $1 \leq R \leq 30$.

This counts the number of homeworks "blown off" by the Rth student. The segment is very straightforward, assuming all the variables have been previously defined:

```
Blown_Off := 0;
for Paper := 1 to 10 do
  if Marks[R, Paper] =0 then
    Blown_Off := Blown_Off + 1;
```

Example 5: Count the number of 100's on the Hth homework assignment, where $1 \le H \le 10$. This is clearly a column operation. The details are left to the reader.

Example 6:   Count the number of 100's in the entire array Marks.

For this purpose assume that Num_Assignments is an integer (at most 10) that contains the number of assignments actually given and that Num_Students is also an integer (at most 30) that contains the actual number of students in the class.   That is, only Num_Students rows and Num_Assignments columns of the array Marks are in use.   There are two obvious ways to proceed:

```
Count := 0;
for Row := 1 to Num_Students do
 for Col := 1 to Num_Assignments do
  if Marks[Row, Col] = 100 then
   Count := Count + 1;
```

or

```
Count := 0;
for Col := 1 to Num_Assignments do
 for Row := 1 to Num_Students do
  if Marks[Row, Col] = 100 then
   Count := Count + 1;
```

The reader should trace the above to discover the slightly different paths taken to achieve the same final counts. For simplicity in the exposition, let us assume for a moment that Num_Students is 30 and Num_Assignments is 10. The first solution considers the elements of Marks in **row order**.   That is, it looks at Marks[1,1], Marks[1,2], Marks[1,3],..., Marks[1,10], then looks in the second row at Marks[2,1], Marks[2,2], Marks[2,3],..., Marks[2,10] and proceeds thusly through the rows of Marks. The second solution, on the other hand, has the column index on the outside and hence, it changes more slowly than the row index. The second method is therefore known as the **column order** solution. Trace enough of it to see that the elements considered are Marks[1,1], Marks[2,1], Marks[3,1],...,Marks[30,1], then the second column's Marks[1,2], Marks[2,2], Marks[3,2], ..., Marks[30,2], etc. In a situation where our object is simply to count the number of times that a particular value occurs in a given table, it obviously doesn't matter whether we proceed in a row or column order. But as we shall see in examples 7 and 8, sometimes one needs row order and sometimes one needs column order.

Example 7: Compute and store the entries of the array Student_Average.

For each student we add his/her scores and divide by Num_Assignments. Of course, we must repeat this operation Num_Students times, storing the results at each stage in the proper place in the array Student_Averages. Thus, since the outside loop is on people, the solution uses row order:

```
for Person := 1 to Num_Students do
  begin
    Sum := 0;
    for Paper := 1 to Num_Assignments do
      Sum := Sum + Marks[Person, Paper];
    Student_Average[Person] := Sum / Num_Assignments
  end;
```

Please observe very carefully the placement of the 'Sum := 0;' statement. Why must it go between the **for**'s instead of before both or inside both?

Example 8: Compute and store the entries of Homework_Average.

This time we must process the array by papers, not people. Hence, a column order is appropriate. We leave the details to the reader.

Example 9: Assuming that Who is a **string** variable containing the name of one of our students, find the score of Who on paper number 5. First, we must find Who in the parallel array of names, then remembering the index, look up Who's score in the table Marks. For this segment let us assume a linear search function, called Find, that accepts an array of names and a target string and returns the index of the target in the array (or zero if the search is unsuccessful). With this "black box" the segment is easy:

```
Place := Find(Names, Who);
if Place = 0 then
  Writeln('Sorry, ', Who, ' is not in the class.')
else
  Writeln(Who, ' has a score of ', Marks[Place, 5]);
```

An Extended Example

Previously we considered an extended example involving the Widget Works. The astute reader realizes, no doubt, that the example was fictitious and was devised just to give an example of one-dimensional arrays. The truth, of course, is that the Widget Works has a whole line of products, and, hence, needs a two-dimensional array to keep track of sales of individual products by individual salespersons. For simplicity, let us assume that the Widget Works has at most 100 salespersons and has 10 distinct products. We assume that each salesperson has an ID number between 1 and 100 and that each product has a product number between 1 and 10. Thus, we declare the array Amounts as follows:

Amounts : **array** [1..100, 1..10] **of** Integer;

We also assume a parallel one-dimensional array Names given by:

Names : **array** [1..100] **of string**[30];

Figure 9.3 illustrates the relationship between Amounts and Names.

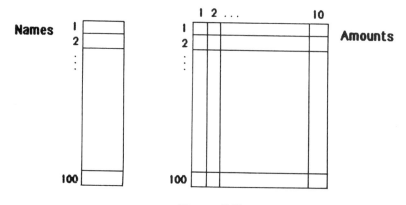

Figure 9.3

Other parallel arrays are explained as they are used. Here are some segments that solve simple problems posed by Snidely Whiplash, the Sales Manager. In each of these segments we assume that the arrays Amounts and Names already have values. We also assume that any indices needed have been declared.

Example 10: Snidely would like to see how salesperson number 15 is doing. Listing the sales by product for salesperson number 15 is a row operation on the array Amounts. Here is the segment:

```
Writeln('Sales by ', Names[15], ': ');
for Col := 1 to 10 do
   Writeln('Quantity of product # ', Col, ' was ', Amounts[15, Col]);
```

Example 11: Determine for Snidely the total number of product number 6 that has been sold by all salespersons. We need to scan down the 6th column of the array Amounts totalling the entries. Here is the segment:

```
Total_6 := 0;
for Row := 1 to 100 do
   Total_6 := Total_6 + Amounts[Row, 6];
Writeln('The company total for product #6 is ',Total_6);
```

In both of the above examples we have used the index names Row and Col to suggest the type of operation we are performing on the array Amounts. Alternately, it would be proper and acceptable to use index names that referred to the real situation. For example, in the first case an index such as Prod_Num would clearly indicate that we were looping on products. In the second example an index such as ID or Salesperson would clearly indicate that we were looping on people. Either way is all right and infinitely better than totally meaningless indices such as X and Y.

Example 12: Let Person_Totals be an array in which Person_Totals[ID] holds the total number of products sold by salesperson number ID. Since Person_Totals has an entry for each salesperson, it is declared by:

```
Person_Totals : array [1..100] of Integer;
```

To compute the entries of Person_Totals, we need to sum the entries of row 1, then sum the entries of row 2, etc. Here is the segment:

```
for ID := 1 to 100 do
begin
  Person_Totals[ID] := 0;
  for Prod_Num := 1 to 10 do
    Person_Totals[ID] := Person_Totals[ID] + Amounts[ID, Prod_Num]
end;
```

Example 13:   As an exercise for the reader, we leave the problem of writing a segment to compute and fill the array Prod_Totals so that Prod_Totals[Prod_Num] contains the total number of that product sold by all the salespersons. This is an extension of a previous segment that determined Total_6. Do not forget to declare Prod_Totals properly.

Example 14:   The array Person_Totals is not a very meaningful array. Since the Widget Works sells paper clips as well as tanks, it doesn't make much sense to simply total up the number of products sold by each individual. Total value of goods sold would be more meaningful to the Widget Works management. Thus, we need two more arrays, Price and Sales_Totals. Price contains the selling prices of the products and Sales_Totals is to contain the total dollar amount of sales by each salesperson. Hence, Price and Sales_Totals are declared by:

```
Price : array [1..10] of Real;
Sales_Totals : array [1..100] of Real;
```

In the following segment, we assume that Price already has values and use these to compute the entries of Sales_Totals:

```
for ID := 1 to 100 do
  begin
   Sales_Totals[ID] := 0.0;
   for Prod_Num := 1 to 10 do
    Sales_Total[ID] := Sales_Totals[ID] +
                   Amounts[ID, Prod_Num] * Price[Prod_Num]
  end;
```

Example 15:   Now let us consider how the array Amounts could obtain values in the first place. We assume that each salesperson, on completing a sale, fills out a sales transaction form. The information needed on that form is the salesperson's ID, the product number (Prod_Num) of the product, and the quantity (Qty) of the product sold. That is, the transaction '17 6 12' indicates that salesperson number 17 has sold 12 more of product number 6. We save (batch) the transactions for a two-week period, then enter them all into the computer. Thus, we expect (Snidely demands it) that there will be many transactions for each salesperson. Also, rather than count the number of transactions, we tell the data entry operator to enter a nonsensical zero ID when all the transactions have been entered. Thus, the array Amounts is really 1000 accumulators for running sums. For example, all the above transaction does is add 12 to the current value in the 17th row and 6th column of Amounts. Of course, before we process the transactions we should initialize every entry of the table to zero. That is left as an exercise for the reader. Here is the segment that processes the transactions:

```
Writeln('Enter the first ID');
Readln(ID);
while ID > 0 do
  begin
    Writeln('Enter product number and quantity');
    Readln(Prod_Num, Qty);
    Amounts[ID, Prod_Num] := Amounts[ID, Prod_Num] + Qty;
    Writeln('Enter the next ID. Enter 0 to terminate data entry.');
    Readln(ID)
  end;
```

The exercises at the end of this chapter indicate many other segments that you may write for Snidely.

We complete this chapter with one final example of parallel array processing. Let us suppose we have data on approximately 150 students who have taken the SAT exams. We would like to read in this data and store it in appropriate arrays. Since part of the information is numeric and part of the information is alphabetic (**string**), we need to use two arrays. One of the weaknesses of arrays is that they only may store information of one fixed type. When we have several types of data, we are forced to use several parallel arrays. Let us assume that each student has taken the verbal and the mathematics portions of the SAT examinations. Hence, for each student we store three scores, a verbal, a mathematics, and a composite score, which is the sum of the verbal and mathematics scores. Computers can add more quickly and accurately than people, so there is no reason for us to enter the composite score; the computer can compute it by itself. Thus, for each individual we have a name (30 characters) and two scores to enter. Thus, logically, the data might appear as follows:

```
Lowell Carmony
750 790
Robert Holliday
260 310
```

Jacque Strappe
130   40
Hi lque
800 740
. . .

Notice that the names are not separated from the scores. We cannot read in the 150 names followed by the 300 scores. We must read a name, then two scores for that person, and then repeat the process. Often, the data is prepared by someone other than the programmer and the programmer must adjust to the given data. The program of Listing 9.9 reads the data from the text file SAT_Scores and computes and prints the composite scores.

```
program SAT;
{This program reads SAT scores from the text file SAT_Scores.}

  type
    ScoreType = (Verb, Math, Comp);
  var
    Names : array[1..150] of string[25];
    SAT : array[1..150, Verb..Comp] of Integer;
    Person : 0..150;

begin
  Close(Input); {Redirect Input to be from the text file.}
  Reset(Input, 'SAT_Scores');
  Person := 0;
  Writeln('Name' : 25, 'Verbal' : 10, 'Math' : 10, 'Composite' : 15);
  Writeln;
  while not EOF do
    begin
      Person := Person + 1;
      Readln(Names[Person]);
      Readln(SAT[Person, Verb], SAT[Person, Math]);
      SAT[Person, Comp] := SAT[Person, Verb] + SAT[Person, Math];
      Write(Names[Person] : 25, SAT[Person, Verb] : 10);
      Writeln(SAT[Person, Math] : 10, SAT[Person, Comp] : 15);
    end {While}
end.
```

Listing 9.9

Summary

The concept of an array is indispensable for writing programs of any size or sophistication. It has been our experience that arrays are often the point in a begining programming course where many students begin to "lose it." One reason is that those students have never really understood the concepts of variables and memory locations, so when they try to use variable subscripts in a multi-dimensional array setting, there is nothing but confusion. We encourage the reader to tackle all the exercises in this chapter to ensure a thorough understanding of arrays. Many of these exercises also give practice using functions and procedures as part of a divide-and-conquer strategy.

Exercises

9.1 Modify Snidely_1 so that it prints a message to each salesperson. Salespersons with sales of less than $5000.00 should be warned that their jobs (health) are in jeopardy, while those who reach the sales quota should be commended. Also print out a count of those reaching the quota as well as a count of those failing to reach the quota. Note that the order of the output is *fixed* by the order of the salespersons in the text file Widget_Sales. You are *not* to use arrays in this problem.

9.2 Modify Snidely_2 so that it prints two lists. First, print a list of all the salespersons whose sales exceed the average sales, then print all salespersons who sales are less than average. Be sure to include a title for each list.

9.3 The function More_Needed in Soggies checks all ten premiums to see if any are needed. Obviously it could stop looping as soon as it finds one premium that is still needed. Write such a version of More_Needed and try it out in Soggies.

9.4 Try to eliminate the function More_Needed from Soggies by using a counter that is incremented by 1 each time a new premium is obtained.

9.5 Modify the program Xmas (Bah, Humbug!) so that it also computes the retail value of the gifts received. For this purpose, add an array Retail_Value, to the program. Allow the user to enter the retail value of each gift. Itemize the gifts, showing the number and total value of each, as well as the total number and the total dollar value of all the gifts.

9.6 The text file SAT_Scores contains names and two scores (verbal and math) for at most twenty students. The names and scores are on separate lines. Modify the program SAT of the text that reads the data into two arrays so that it also sorts the scores. The output should be three lists, in descending order by each type of score, giving the name and scores of each student. That is, rank the students by verbal, math, and composite scores. Caution: Be sure you keep the scores associated with the correct people.

9.7 (Selection Sort) Another simple sort is known as Selection Sort. It works as follows: On the first pass it finds the largest element in the array and swaps this element with the last element in the array. For example, if the array is

12 6 18 24 15 9 2 11

then on pass one it finds 24 in the fourth place and swaps 24 and 11, putting 24 at the end:

12 6 18 11 15 9 2 24

On the second pass it finds the largest element among the first N-1 elements (N is the number of elements in the array) and swaps it with the $(N-1)^{st}$ element. In our example, 18 is found and swapped with 2 to give

12 6 2 11 15 9 18 24

On successive passes the next biggest element is found and moved to the "back" of the array. After N-1 passes, the array is sorted.

Write a procedure Selection that implements this sort. Verify that it works by having it sort 25 randomly generated numbers into ascending order.

9.8 Write the segment for Example 5 on page 326.

9.9 Write the segment for Example 8 on page 327.

9.10 Write the segment for Example 13 on page 330.

9.11 Write a segment for Snidely that finds the winner of the sales contest. That is, find the person whose total value of sales is greatest.

9.12 Write a segment that ranks the salespersons for Snidely by their total values of goods sold.

9.13 Guess the number of jelly beans in the jar! Everyone enrolled in Pascal has entered the contest and the data is available in the text file Candy, which contains two lines for each person:

Debby Fulton
327 76

The first line contains the name and the second line contains the guesses for the total number of jelly beans in the jar and the number of yellow jelly beans in the jar. You may assume that there are at most 100 contestants. The grand prize winner is the person who guesses closest to, **but does not exceed**, the actual number of candies in the jar. Anyone who guesses within 25 of the **winning guess** is a runner-up and receives one jelly bean of each color. Anyone who guesses within 100 of the winning guess is a consolation prize winner and receives a jelly bean of his/her choice. The grand prize winner gets all the jelly beans except those awarded as runner-up and consolation prizes (and those eaten by the judges, Drs. Carmony and Holliday).

The actual number of jelly beans in the jar and the number of yellow jelly beans are given in the first line of the text file Candy. This is followed by pairs of lines giving names and guesses for each of the contestants.

Note the perverse rules of this game. For example, if there are 789 jelly beans in the jar and we have three contestants with guesses of 650, 790, and 551, then 650 is the grand-prize winning guess; there are no runners-up; and 551 gets a consolation prize while 790 gets nothing. On the other hand, if the three guesses are 750, 790, and 551, then 750 wins and 790 is a consolation prize winner.

Important: For this exercise you may assume that there are no ties for the Grand Prize. The next exercise asks you to handle ties using the yellow guess. Both exercises use the text file Candy. In this exercise read Candy only until you find the name 'George Pryjma'. If you stop without reading George's guesses, there will be no tie for the Grand Prize. Nevertheless, in this exercise you must be sure you properly ignore the data concerning yellow jelly beans.

9.14 Consider the above problem, but in case of a tie for the Grand Prize, the winner is the person whose yellow guess comes closest to, but does not exceed, the actual number of yellow jelly beans. In this exercise you should read Candy to the end of the file.

9.15 The table below contains the tonnage of Smurfberry wine consumed in the United States and in Smurf Village during the years 1976--1985. Write a program that interactively reads the data and prints two lists in the following format:

In the following years, the Americans drank more Smurfberry wine:
    1975
    1977
    . . .

In the following years, the Smurfs drank more Smurfberry wine:
    1976
    . . .

Smurfberry Wine Consumption

	United States	Smurf Village
1975	27,435	21,376
1976	23,358	25,212
1977	22,398	22,150
1978	19,327	24,386
1979	20,752	19,642
1980	23,882	26,321
1981	21,472	24,661
1982	24,752	25,371
1983	23,153	22,165
1984	21,252	21,853
1985	20,941	22,341

Table 9.3

9.16 The procedure Easter of Chapter 7 determines the day and month of Easter in a given year. The procedure is valid for the years 1900 to 2099. What date during the 20th and 21st centuries is the most common for Easter?

9.17 Each bottle of Debug, the headache relief medicine for programmers, contains a letter on the inside of the bottle cap. You win a free bottle of

Debug if you collect letters to spell

Out of every 100 bottles there are

    30 A's
    25 B's
    20 C's
    15 I's
    10 S's

Write a procedure that simulates the collecting of bottle caps until you win the prize. Write a program that runs your simulation twenty times and computes an average number of bottles purchased to win a free bottle.

9.18 Do exercise 9.17, except collect letters to spell

where the distribution of the letters in 100 bottles is

    10 A's
    10 C's
    20 L's
    25 P's
    35 S's

Why is this program more difficult than 9.18?

9.19 The Lake Forest College Running Club needs a program to sort out the winner in its Strawman Triathlon. The competition consists of a 1/4-mile swim, a 5-mile bicycle ride, and a 2-mile run. The data for each competitor is available on the text file Triathlon on the Sample diskette accompanying the book. There are two lines for each person. The first line is the name, of type **string**[30]. The second line contains a category (either the character 'S', 'F', or 'A' for Student, Faculty, or Administration respectively) followed by 3 real numbers representing, in hours, the swim time, bike time, and run time respectively.

Write a program that prints out the following:

The winner of the Swim Competition was ... with a time of ...
The winner of the Bicycle Competition was ... with a time of ...
The winner of the Running Competition was ... with a time of ...
The winner of the Overall Competition was ... with a time of ...

(Of course, the winner of each individual competition is the individual with the fastest time for that event, while the winner of the overall triathlon is the individual with the fastest combined time. You do not need to worry about ties.)

The above four statements should be followed by a table that prints all the entrants in increasing order of total time, e.g., the winner is listed first and the loser is listed last. Each line in the table should contain the participant's name and category, followed by the three individual times and the total combined time.

(Note: The category is not really used in this exercise. It is included for use with an exercise in Chapter 16.)

Chapter 10

Records

Introducing File Terminology

A **file** is an orderly arrangement of information. Usually the information is about some group of individuals or products. For example, the Social Security Administration maintains a large file with information on most Americans, while the Widget Works maintains inventory files both on raw materials and finished Widgets, as well as various personnel files. One should think of a file as a collective noun. That is, a file is the total collection of information .

When we open a file folder, we usually find many "forms," one for each person or product involved. These forms are called **records**. For example, there is almost certainly a record in the Social Security Administration's file for you. That record collects all the information that is kept about you, such as name, social security number, birthdate, address, as well as a list of contributions by you and your employers to your retirement account. Likewise, the Widget Works' inventory file contains a record for each product kept in the warehouse. That record contains the product number, the cost, the supplier, the quantity, etc. of the given product.

The individual data items that make up the record are called the **fields** of the record. In our examples above, the name, the address, the social security number, the supplier, the cost, etc. are all fields of their respective records. Files, records, and fields are easy to distinguish. The file is the complete collection of information while a record is the information about one individual product or thing. The file is the complete folder full of information. The records are the forms of which the file is composed. The fields are the individual data items. The record is composed of fields; the file is composed of records.

In this chapter we shall consider only **internal** files, which are files that reside completely in the memory of the computer. In the next chapter we shall take up the more interesting and valuable subject of **external** or **disk** files. Internal files allow us to introduce and study records without worrying about disk input and output. However, the limitations of internal files should be obvious: They must be small enough to fit in memory, and they are lost when the computer is turned off. Indeed, an internal file is simply an array of records.

As an example to develop in this chapter, let us consider creating a small internal file for a group of students, say those enrolled in a first Pascal class. We must first decide upon the fields that compose the record for each person. Let's say that we shall keep the name, class, identification number, grade point average, fee status (paid or unpaid), and sex of each member of the class. Since Pascal is a strongly typed language, we must also decide the type of each of these fields. Clearly, name should be a string, say, of maximum length 25. Let us also suppose that the indentification numbers have the form XXX-XX-XXXX and, thus, are strings of length 11. For the class we shall use the abbreviations FROSH, SOPH, JR, and SR and shall define an enumerated type for this purpose. Fee status can be chosen to be of type Boolean, while sex can be chosen to be of type Char. Hence, we see one fundamental difference between records and arrays--the types do not all need to be the same in a record. Indeed, our example is fairly typical in that records are often composed of many very different kinds of fields. There is another fundamental distinction between arrays and records that we should like the reader to consider. Both records and arrays are "sequences" of information. Records, however, are used to gather various non-homogeneous information about an individual while arrays are used to gather homogeneous information across a group of individuals. That is, an array of names or an array of grade point averages has one cell for each individual. Using arrays, the information is grouped by kind; using records, the information is grouped by the individual or object to whom the information refers.

A record type Student_Record, and an internal file, Students, are declared in Pascal as shown in listing 10.1.

```
type
  Class_Type = (Frosh, Soph, Jr, Sr);
  Student_Record = record
    Name : string[25];
    Class : Class_Type;
    ID : string[11];
    GPA : Real;
    Fee_Status : Boolean;
    Sex : Char
  end;

var
  Students : array[1..30] of Student_Record;
  One_Student : Student_Record;
```

Listing 10.1

The variable One_Student is a record variable. That is, it is an aggregate name for the six fields we have listed. In a moment we shall see how to access those individual fields. Students, on the other hand, is an internal file. Students is an array of 30 records. Students[17] is, of course, the record of the 17th student. Since Students[17] and One_Student are both of type Student_Record, they may be compared or assigned one to another as in

```
if One_Student = Students[17] then ...
```
or
```
Students[17] := One_Student;
```

That is, Pascal allows whole record operations. That should not be a surprise since statements like

```
X := Y
```

are legal whenever X and Y are objects of the same type.

The individual fields of a record are chosen by a mechanism known as **selection**. Selection simply adds the field name to the record name, separating them by a period. Thus, One_Student.Name is the name field of One_Student. Also, One_Student.Class, One_Student.ID, One_Student.GPA, One_Student.Fee_Status, and One_Student.Sex denote the other fields of

One_Student. Hence, the statements shown in listing 10.2 are all legal statements.

```
Writeln(One_Student.Name);
if One_Student.Fee_Status then  (Fees paid)
 if (One_Student.Class = Sr) and (One_Student.GPA >= 3.75) then
 Honor(One_Student)  (Invoke Honor procedure)
 else (Do Nothing)
else
 Send_Bill(One_Student);  (Invoke Send_Bill procedure)
```

Listing 10.2

Thus, a record is declared by using the **record** and **end** keywords and by placing the field names along with their types between the **record** and **end**.   Notice that there is no **begin** to match the **end**. In the example above, this record is declared and given a name in the type section. It is also possible to use anonymous record types. Thus, the declaration of Students in listing 10.1 is equivalent to the segment shown in listing 10.3.

```
var
 Students : array[1..30] of record
  Name : string[25];
  Class : Class_Type;
  ID : string[11];
  GPA : Real;
  Fee_Status : Boolean;
  Sex : Char
 end;
```

Listing 10.3

The first method, with the named type, is preferable on several grounds. First, it is less "intense," and hence, probably clearer. Secondly, and most importantly, once the record type Student_Record is defined, it may be used throughout the program.   Thus, variables such as One_Student can also be defined without repeating the record definition. Also, with the named record type, procedures and functions can be written, such as Honor and Send_Bill of listing 10.2, that accept arguments of type Student_Type. Hence, in the examples to follow, we shall always choose a name for our record type.

An Extended Example

Let us set up an employee file for a small hotel. We shall need a record for each employee and we shall suppose that the hotel has at most 50 employees. In this chapter, we shall keep the file in the computer's memory, so we will need an array of 50 records to hold the file. The format of each record is decided by the administration of the hotel. Let us suppose that they have agreed to store the ID number, name, address, department of the employee, birthdate, date of employment, marital status, and salary of the employee. Thus, each record consists of eight fields. For each of these fields we must determine an appropriate type.

The name is, of course, a **string**--or it could be three separate **strings** (first name, middle initial, and last name). In Chapter 14, we shall learn how to manipulate strings so that we can put together and take apart names and, thus, change from one form to the other. Here we shall assume that it has been decreed that we store three separate names. To keep the number of fields in the employee's record from increasing (and to make the example more interesting), we shall use a name field that is itself a record consisting of the three parts of the name. That is, we shall have a record, one of whose fields is itself a record. This nesting of records is very common in complex data structures. In fact, notice that the birthdate field and the date of employment field are clearly of the same type. Let us call this type Datetype. For Datetype we could use a string such as '1 Jan 1985', but it would be more convenient to think of a Datetype as the aggregate of three things: a day, a month, and a year. Hence, Datetype itself is implemented as a record with three fields.

Likewise, the address can be broken down into its components: street address, city, state, and zip. Hence, we shall make the address field of type Addresstype, which is itself a record with four fields. Marital status and department are simple, user-defined types. The possibilities for marital status are Single, Married, Separated, and Divorced while the possibilities for department are Administrative, Food Services, and Housekeeping. We shall declare the salary to be real. Actually, to ensure accuracy, the salary might better be declared to be of type Longinteger or Computational. We shall not be concerned here with such need for precision. Finally, let the ID number be a three-digit integer in the range 100 to 999. Listing 10.4, then, contains the complete declaration of the employee file.

Assuming that the array Employees has values stored in it and that Index is some integer in the range 1 to 50, then Employees[Index] is the complete record of the Index[th] employee of the hotel. As in the previous

```
type
  Months = (Jan, Feb, Mar, Apr, May, Jun, Jul, Aug, Sep, Oct, Nov, Dec);
  Days = 1..31;
  Years = 1860..2050;
  Departments = (Administrative, Housekeeping, Food_Services);
  Stats = (Single, Married, Divorced, Separated);
  InfoString = string[20];

  NameType = record
    First : InfoString;
    Middle : Char;
    Last : InfoString
  end;
  DateType = record
    Month : Months;
    Day : Days;
    Year : Years
  end;
  AddressType = record
    Street : InfoString;
    City : InfoString;
    State : InfoString;
    Zip : string[5]
  end;
  Employee_Record = record
    ID_Number : 100..999;
    Name : NameType;
    Address : AddressType;
    Birthdate : DateType;
    Employment_Date : DateType;
    Department : Departments;
    M_Status : Stats;
    Salary : Real
  end;

  EmployeeFile = array[1..50] of Employee_Record;

var
  Employees : EmployeeFile;
  One_Employee : Employee_Record;
  Index : 1..50;
```

Listing 10.4

example, Employees[Index].ID_Number is the ID_Number of this employee while Employees[Index].Birthdate is the birthdate of the given person. Since the birthdate is itself a record, we can obtain the month of birth with the expression

Employees[Index].Birthdate.Month

Likewise, since we can access the characters in a string as though the string were an array, the expression

Employees[Index].Name.Last[1]

picks off the first character in the Last field of the Name field of the Index[th] employee's record. In other words, it is the first initial of the last name of the Index[th] employee.

Suppose the hotel administration decides to host a birthday dinner during the birthmonth of all employees who have been employed for at least 10 years. That is, the June party is for all those employees with birthdays in June who have been with the hotel for 10 years or more. We are to write a program that prompts the user to enter the current month and year and then the program will search the records and print the names of all employees that should be honored that month. Here is our solution in outline:

Prompt user for desired Month.
Prompt user for the Current_Year.
Search the Employees file for those who have the given birthmonth and have been employed since Current_Year - 10.

We could, of course, assign the Current_Year a value in the program, but we expect this valuable program to have many years of useful life, so we let the user supply the Current_Year. Procedure Search is very straightforward. We simply search, using a linear search, the file of Employees and print the name fields whenever we find someone who satisfies the given conditions. To illustrate record notation, the program is shown in listing 10.5. Since you are going to interactively enter the data, Employee_Records have been abbreviated to contain just a single name (with a maximum length of 30 characters), date of birth, and date of employment.

This example shows that searching an array of records is really no different than searching an array of integers. Of course, if the array of

```
program Party;
(This program invites employees to this month's birthday party. )

  type
    Months = (Jan, Feb, Mar, Apr, May, Jun, Jul, Aug, Sep, Oct, Nov, Dec);
    Days = 1..31;
    Years = 1860..2050;

    DateType = record
       Month : Months;
       Day : Days;
       Year : Years
    end;  (Record)

    EmployeeRecord = record
       Name : string[30];
       EmploymentDate : DateType;
       BirthDate : DateType
    end;  (Record)

    EmployeeFile = array[1..10] of EmployeeRecord;

  var
    Birth_Month : Months;
    Current_Year : Years;
    Employees : EmployeeFile;

  procedure Enterdata (var Employees : EmployeeFile);
    var
      Index : Integer;
  begin
    Writeln('Next you must enter the data on the ten employees.');
    Writeln;
    for Index := 1 to 10 do
      begin
        Writeln('Enter the name of employee #', Index : 1);
        Readln(Employees[Index].Name);
        Writeln('Enter the birthdate in the form "Jun 8 1943"');
        Read(Employees[Index].Birthdate.Month);
        Read(Employees[Index].Birthdate.Day);
        Readln(Employees[Index].Birthdate.Year);
```
                              (Continued)

```
      Writeln('Enter the date of employment in the same form.');
      Read(Employees[Index].EmploymentDate.Month);
      Read(Employees[Index].EmploymentDate.Day);
      Readln(Employees[Index].EmploymentDate.Year);
      Writeln
    end; {For}
  end; {Definition of procedure EnterData}

procedure Search (Employees : EmployeeFile;
          Birth_month : Months;
          Current_Year : Years);

  var
    Index : Integer;

begin
  Writeln;
  Writeln('Employees invited to the ', Birth_Month, ' party.');
  Writeln;
  for Index := 1 to 10 do
    if (Employees[Index].EmploymentDate.Year <= Current_Year - 10) then
      if Employees[Index].BirthDate.Month = Birth_Month then
        Writeln(Employees[Index].Name)
  end; {Definition of procedure Search}

procedure Prompt (var Birth_Month : Months;
          var Current_Year : Years);
begin
  Writeln('Enter the birth month of the party.');
  Write('Give the 3 letter abbreviation, please: ');
  Readln(Birth_Month);
  Write('Enter the current year: ');
  Readln(Current_Year)
  end; {Definition of procedure Prompt}

begin
  Prompt(Birth_Month, Current_Year);
  EnterData(Employees);
  Search(Employees, Birth_Month, Current_Year)
end.
```

Listing 10.5

records is first sorted on some field, then it is possible to conduct a binary search of the records using that field. Since these are straightforward extensions of the binary search and insertion sort from the previous chapter, we leave these topics as exercises.

We also note, for the careful reader, that our Party program may not work quite the way intended by the hotel management. Very often, we find that the problem that we thought was so clear turns out in fact to be somewhat ambiguous. Take the case of the June 1985 party. Should an employee born in June 1943, who began employment in December 1975, be honored or not? The employee is in the 10th year of employment, but has not completed 10 years with the company yet. The procedure Party invites such employees. We leave it as an exercise to modify the program so that it doesn't invite anyone who has not yet *completed* 10 years of employment.

The with Statement

Even the simple procedure Search shows how awkward record variables can become because of the repetition of the record variable name. Fortunately, there is a construct, the **with**, that permits an abbreviation of some record names. The **with** is probably best illustrated with an example. Listing 10.6 gives an equivalent form for reading the birthdate in the procedure EnterData.

Writeln('Enter the birthdate in the from "Jun 8 1943" ');
with Employees[Index].Birthdate **do**
Readln(Month, Day, Year);

Listing 10.6

The format of the **with** statement is:

with record_variable **do**
Statement

where the statement may be compound if necessary. Any variable used in the body of the **with** first is considered to be a reference to a field in the record variable that follows the keyword **with**. Thus, we do not have to keep repeating the name of the record variable. Consider the following example:

```
with This_Record do
  begin
    X := X + 1;
    Y := Y + 1;
    Z := Z + 1
  end;
```

Suppose that there is a variable X declared in some block containing this statement and that X is also a field of This_Record. Then X, within the **with**, refers to the X field of This_Record, and not the variable X of the surrounding block. Suppose that there is no Y field of This_Record, but there is a Y variable in some block containing the **with** statement. Then the reference is really to that Y. Suppose that there is no variable Z declared and there is no Z field to This_Record. Then the reference to Z is an undeclared identifier error.

```
program Time_and_Date;
{This program displays the date and time from the built-in clock.}

  type
    DateTimeRec = record
      Year, Month, Day, Hour, Minute, Second, DayOfWeek : Integer
    end;

  var
    DateTime : DateTimeRec;

begin
  with DateTime do
  begin
    GetTime(DateTime);
    Writeln('Today''s date is: ', Month : 2, '/', Day : 2, '/', Year : 4);
    Writeln;
    Writeln('The current time is: ', Hour : 2, ':', Minute : 2, ':', Second : 2);
    Writeln;
    Writeln('and today is the ', DayOfWeek : 1, 'th day of the week.')
  end {With}
end.
```

Listing 10.7

Records are used extensively within Macintosh Pascal. For example, the built-in GetTime procedure returns a record consisting of 7 integers representing the Year, Month, Day, Hour, Minute, Second, and Day of the Week currently in the system clock. Again, these fields are all integers and their values are obvious except that Hours is measured from midnight, so 15 hours is 3 p.m., and the Day of the Week is in the range from 1 to 7, with 1 representing Sunday. Program Time_and_Date in listing 10.7 invokes GetTime for us.

Variant Fields

Sometimes we need different kinds of records for different kinds of situations. Suppose for example that we would like to store the name of the spouse, if any, of our employees. Obviously, there is a spouse only if the employee's marital status is Married or Separated. We could add a field to each record, and only use the spouse field for married employees, but Pascal has a more convenient and elegant way to solve the problem using **variant** records. Variant records permit some records to have an extra Spouse field. The syntax of the variant record is demonstrated in listing 10.8.

```
Employee_Record = record
    ID_Number : 100..999;
    Name : NameType
    Address : AddressType;
    Birthdate : DateType;
    EmploymentDate : DateType;
    Department : Departments;
    Salary : Real;
    case M_Status : Stats of
      Married, Separated : (
          SpouseName : NameType
      );
      Single, Divorced : (
      ) {Nothing}
    end; {record}
```

Listing 10.8

M_Status is called the **tag** field of the record. Note that M_Status is given a type in a **"case** like" construction that lists the variant fields. If

M_Status is Married or Separated, then that record has a SpouseName field. Listing 10.9 gives another nonsense example to illustrate the syntax and possibilities with variant records.

```
type
  Color = (Red, Blue, Green, Orange);
  Your_Record = record
    X : Real;
    Y : Integer;
    case Hue : Color of
      Red : (
        A : Integer;
        B : Boolean
      );
      Blue : (
        C : string
      );
      Green : (
        D, E, F : Real
      );
      Orange : (
      ) {Nothing}
    end; {record}

var
  Z : Your_Record;
```

Listing 10.9

Z has three fixed fields and from 0 to 3 variant fields. The fixed fields of Z are X, Y, and Hue. Of course, Z.X is real, Z.Y is an integer, and Z.Hue is a Color. The Hue field is also the tag field of Z. Note that the tag field must be an ordinal type, and it must occur after all the "regular" fields of the record. If Z.Hue is Red, then we may also speak of Z.A and Z.B, which are Integer and Boolean respectively. The situation is similar for the other values of Hue. Note that the variant declaration is much like the **case** statement. However, note that the tag variable has its type given and also note that there is no **end** for the **case**, only an **end** for the **record**. Furthermore, note the parentheses that are required to enclose the variant fields for each case.

Not surprisingly, a variant record is most often manipulated with a
case statement. For example, the segment of listing 10.10 prints the Y
field and the A, C, or D field of Z.

```
Write(Z.Y);
case Z.Hue of
 Red :
   Writeln(Z.A);
 Blue :
   Writeln(Z.C);
 Green :
   Writeln(Z.D);
 Orange :
   Writeln
end; {Case}
```

Listing 10.10

Avoiding Strings

Standard Pascal doesn't contain a **string** type and in this section we
demonstrate how one could live with a version of Pascal without strings.
Niklaus Wirth wanted his original Pascal to be small and simple.
Therefore, he chose to omit a built-in string type, leaving the creation of
this data type to the user. The type Char is, or course, a part of standard
Pascal, and, as we shall see, the string type can be based on the type Char.
Writing one's own string package is not very difficult now that you know
about arrays and records. However, for the beginning programmer, strings
are certainly a convenient data type and, hence, in this book we have
permitted from the beginning the use of Macintosh Pascal's **string** type.
Now we come clean and show you how you could function in a Pascal
without a built-in string.
   A string is very much like an array of characters. The problem with
defining a string to be an array of characters is that arrays in Pascal
always have to be of some fixed length. That is, if we view 'John' and
'Marsha' as arrays of characters, then 'John' is an array of four characters
and 'Marsha' is an array of six characters. Since Pascal is so highly typed,
arrays of four characters and arrays of six characters are considered to be
distinct types and hence not comparable. That is, in standard Pascal,
'John' < 'Marsha' is not True (or even False) but nonsense since 'John' and
'Marsha' are of differing types. The comparison is as silly as 3.14 < 'X',

which mixes reals and characters. Of course, it is possible to say that strings are arrays of 30 characters and pad 'John' with 26 blanks and 'Marsha' with 24 blanks, but typing

    if 'John   ' < 'Marsha   ' **then** ...

is pretty awkward.

The solution is to agree that a string is an array of characters that also has a length attribute. The array must be of fixed size, but the length attribute tells how many of the characters are currently being used. Thus, a string can be defined to be a record with two fields, Arr, a packed array of characters, and Len, an integer. We choose Arr to be a packed array to save memory (see the explanation below). Since Arr has to be declared of some fixed size, we choose a constant StringMax for this length. The value of StringMax is arbitrary, but 80 and 255 are common, reasonable choices:

```
const
   StringMax = 80;

type
   StringType = record
     Arr : packed array [1..StringMax] of Char;
     Len : 0..StringMax
   end;

var
   Name, Address : StringType;
```

The array Arr above is declared as a "**packed array**". This simply means that the system should store Arr as compactly as possible. For example, consider the declarations

```
A : array [1..100] of Char;
B : packed array [1..100] of Char;
```

Since a character can be stored in one byte (8 bits), the array B needs only 100 bytes of storage. The manner in which A is stored is system dependent. On many systems, A uses 4 bytes (32 bits) for *each* character, and hence, four times as much storage as B uses. If A and B are Boolean arrays, the difference can be even more dramatic since only one bit is needed to store a True or a False. A good rule of thumb is to use packed arrays with small ordinal types. The system automatically packs and unpacks for us, so we use packed arrays just like regular arrays.

Name.Arr[1] is the first initial of the name and Address.Len is the number of characters *actually* in the address. Notice that Len was declared to be in the subrange from zero to StringMax. If X is of StringType and X.Len is zero, then X is the **null** string. In Chapter 14, we shall see that the null string plays a roll similar to zero in arithmetic.

A string package is more than just a declaration of a StringType. The package should also contain useful functions and procedures for dealing with strings. In Chapter 14, we present the built-in **string** procedures and functions. The point is that this section is a "survival" course in how to function in Pascal without strings. It is also an interesting application of records and a review of functions and procedures.

Our first function, Length, returns the length of a string. If X is declared to be a StringType, then X.Len is the length of X. Why do we need a function for this? We don't absolutely need the function, but we might like to have it to help make our string package more natural. That is, the function Length hides the implementation and allows us to write Length(X) rather than X.Len. With the implementation "hidden", our programs are cleaner and a beginner, who has never even heard of records, could use our string package. Here is the simple function Length:

```
function Length(X : StringType) : Integer;

begin
  Length := X.Len
end; {Definition of function Length}
```

One disadvantage of our StringType is that we cannot write a string because we cannot write (directly) arrays and records. Therefore, we need a procedure WriteString that will output a string for us:

```
procedure WriteString(X : StringType);

  var
    Index : Integer;

begin
  for Index := 1 to Length(X) do
    Write(X.Arr[Index])
end; {Definition of procedure WriteString}
```

Notice that WriteString only writes Length(X) characters of X. Of course, WriteString is not as convenient to use as Macintosh Pascal's built-in **string** type that can be written with an ordinary Write statement. Using WriteString to output

Congratulations, John, you are the winner!

where 'John' is filled in with the value of Name uses the statements:

```
Write('Congratulations, ');
WriteString(Name);
Writeln(', you are the winner!');
```

As a more complex example, let us consider a **concatenation** function. Concatenation certainly sounds complex, but it is really one of the simplest ideas possible. The roots of the word mean to "chain together" and every preschool youngster practices concatenation by pushing alphabet blocks together to form words. For example, the concatenation of the two strings 'Macintosh' and 'Pascal' is 'MacintoshPascal'. That is, the concatenation of two strings is just the new string obtained by joining the two strings together. Figure 10.1 illustrates cartoonist Sandra Boynton's view of concatenation.

CONCATENATION

Figure 10.1

Concatenation takes two strings and produces a new string. Any procedure or function that defines a string must give that string a length as well as place values in the Arr field of the string. The length seems obvious: The length of the new string is the sum of the lengths of the old strings. But wait, what if both of the old strings are pretty long? The new string could be too long to fit into StringMax characters. We do the following: We store all the characters of the first string and as many as fit of the second string . If necessary, we also announce that the result was too large and truncation of the result has occurred. The function Concatenation is given in listing 10.11.

```
function Concatenation (X, Y : StringType) : StringType;

var
  Index : Integer;
  TempLen : Integer;

begin
{Determine the length of the result.}
  TempLen := X.Len + Y.Len;
  if TempLen > StringMax then
  begin
    Writeln('Concatenation overflow, result has been truncated.');
    TempLen := StringMax
  end; {If}
  Concatenation.Len := TempLen;

{Place the characters from X into the result.}
  for Index := 1 to X.Len do
    Concatenation.Arr[Index] := X.Arr[Index];

{Place as many characters from Y into the result as will fit.}
  for Index := X.Len + 1 to Concatenation.Len do
    Concatenation.Arr[Index] := Y.Arr[Index - X.Len]
end; {Definition of function Concatenation}
```

Listing 10.11

You should verify that the first section defines Concatenation.Len to be the smaller of StringMax and the sum of X.Len and Y.Len. The second section copies the characters of X into the first X.Len locations of the Arr field of

Concatenation. The third section copies characters up to the length of the concatenation from Y and places them after the characters from X. Note that the expression Index - X.Len runs up from 1 as Index runs up from X.Len + 1. Also note in section one that we did not write

```
Concatenation.Len := X.Len + Y.Len;
if Concatenation.Len > StringMax then ...
```

because the assignment may well generate an out of range error. That is, if X.Len + Y.Len is greater than StringMax, then it cannot, even temporarily, be assigned to the Len field of the result. If you wish to avoid the need for the temporary variable, then you should write:

```
if X.Len + Y.Len > StringMax then
  begin
    Writeln('Concatenation overflow, result has been truncated.');
    Concatenation.Len := StringMax
  end
else
  Concatenation.Len := X.Len + Y.Len;
```

With these examples, we leave other string handling functions and procedures such as ReadString, Left, Right, and Mid to the exercises.

Exercises

10.1 Write a ReadString(S) procedure. That is, since the standard Read/Readln statements cannot be used to read arrays or records, write a procedure that reads a line of characters (one at a time) into a variable of type StringType. Use EOLN to control the input.

10.2 Write a Left(S, N) function that returns a StringType consisting of the first N characters of S. For example, if S is a string with current value 'Programmer', then Left(S, 3) equals 'Pro'. Generate an error message if N > Length(S).

10.3 Write a function Mid(S, N, M) that returns a StringType consisting of the M characters of S starting at the Nth character of S. For example, if S has current value 'Programmer', then Left(S, 4, 4) equals 'gram'. Generate an error message if appropriate.

10.4 Modify the Party program so that employees in their 10th year of service are not honored unless they have actually completed 10 years of service.

10.5 Modify the Time_and_Date program so that it prints the date, time, and day in the form

> Today is June 4, 1985
> The current time is 3:35:22 p.m.
> Today is Tuesday.

10.6 Modify the Party program so that the employees are sorted and output in alphabetical order. Make the Name field into a record consisting of Last name and First name fields.

10.7 Modify the program of Exercise 10.6 to do a binary search (by Last name) for a given employee.

Chapter 11

Files

SEQUENTIAL FILE – A place where things can get lost in lexicographic order.
RANDOM ACCESS FILE – A place where things can get lost in any order.

Devil's DP Dictionary

In this chapter, we discuss both sequential and random access files. Because sequential files are included in Standard Pascal, we begin with them. A **sequential file**, as the name suggests, is simply a sequence of records. We view a sequential file as in figure 11.1.

Figure 11.1

Thus, a file is very much like an array. There are, however, some critically important differences. One difference is the manner in which elements are accessed. In an array you may access the elements in any order simply by giving the appropriate subscript. That is, you may first consider A[17], then A[45], and then go "backwards" to A[3]. In a sequential file, access always begins with the first element and proceeds element by element sequentially through the file. If you think of a book as a file of words, then you normally access a novel in sequential order from first to last (except when you jump ahead to the last page to find out who did it). The two forms of access are called "sequential" access and "random" access. The array is a random access data structure, and the sequential file is, of course, a sequential data structure.

Another major difference between files and arrays is the physical location of the information. An array is always in the volatile memory of the computer. A file is usually stored on some kind of disk. As a consequence, the information is not volatile, that is, is not lost, when the computer is turned off. Also, disk space is usually far larger than RAM memory in the computer. Hence, files can be far larger than arrays. Indeed, many files are so large that they do not fit into computer memory at one time. We simply access the file, a record at a time, and only the current record is actually in memory. A disadvantage of disk files is that the disk access time is much greater than memory access time. Hence, it is slower to read or write a record to a file than it is to read or write an element of an array.

In summary, sequential files are in many ways very limited, but their major advantages are that they can be very large and they can store information that is not lost when the current program is finished. Imagine how worthless a payroll program would be if after each pay period we had to type in all the data! With a file, we can store the name, address, number of dependents, total tax withheld, etc, on disk. Then each pay period we read the file sequentially from the beginning, compute and print the pay checks, and write the new information back to the disk to be used next time. Because of this ability to permanently store information, it is difficult to think of a business example where files are not important.

A file is declared much like an array. The actual syntax is:

var
  F : **file of** Some_Type;

where Some_Type is any non-file type. Some_Type is normally a record, but you may have a file of integers or even a file of Boolean values.

To continue our example from the previous chapter, if we wanted to keep a file on a group of students, we might well declare:

type
  Class_Type = (Frosh, Soph, Jr, Sr);
  Student_Record = **record**
    Name : **string**[30];
    Class : Class_Type;
    ID : **string**[11];
    GPA : Real;
    Fee_Status : Boolean;
    Sex : Char
  end;

(Continued)

Student_File = **file of** Student_Record;

var
  Students : Student_File;
  One_Student : Student_Record;

Here we have named the file type 'Student_File' so that variables of this type can easily be passed as parameters in functions and procedures. We could also have used the anonymous declaration

  Students : **file of** Student_Record;

but as mentioned in Chapter 10, named types are generally preferred over anonymous types.

Reset, Rewrite, and Close

Now that we have seen how to declare a file, the only thing left to do is to see how to manipulate files. Perhaps because files are so important in real applications, students think that files must be very difficult. Some older languages did make file handling a particularly tricky topic, but in Pascal, sequential files are very easy to use. We may either **read** from or **write** to a sequential file. In a read, we take information from the file and in a write, we place information into the file. With a sequential file, we may not mix reads and writes. Thus, to change one record in a sequential file, it is necessary to read from one version of the file and write to a new version of the file. All the records but one are written without change to the new file.

To create a sequential file, you use the Rewrite statement. This creates the file and prepares it for "write-only" access. Preparing a file for use is called **opening** the file. If the file already exists, then Rewrite *deletes* the old version of the file and begins a new version. The syntax of the Rewrite statement is:

  Rewrite(F, System_Name);

where F is the name of the file *in the program* and System_Name is the external, system name of the file *on the disk*. These two names can, but do not have to be, the same. Here are valid examples of Rewrite statements:

```
Rewrite(Students, 'Student_Data');
Rewrite(Students, 'Sample:Student_Data');
```

The first says that the file variable Students, which must have been declared in the program, is attached to a file on the Pascal disk that the system knows as Student_Data. If you have two disk drives, you can use the second Rewrite, which attaches Students to the file Student_Data on the diskette Sample in drive 2. After the Rewrite creates the file, you should see a Student_Data icon on your disk when you turn your Macintosh on or after you quit Pascal.

The System_Name can be given as a string variable, so that the user can select the name of the file at execution time.

```
Writeln('Enter the name of the file to be created.');
Readln(File_Name);
Rewrite(F, File_Name);
```

The above segment assumes that F has been declared in the **var** section as a file variable of some sort and that File_Name is a string variable. The segment creates a new file whose name is whatever name the user enters.

To write information into a file created by Rewrite, we use our friend 'Write'. The syntax is:

```
Write(F, Record_Name)
```

where F, of course, is the file variable and Record_Name is the record that you would like written to the file. Thus, we see that whole records are written at once. In our example from above, we would assign values to the fields of One_Student and then write all that information to the file Students with:

```
Write(Students, One_Student);
```

Notice that the above Write does not cause any output to occur on the screen, but rather writes the information contained in the record, One_Student, to the file 'Student_Data' associated via the Rewrite with the file Students. The general form of the Write statement has a file name after the opening parenthesis. If that file name is missing, the system assumes that you want to use the normal "output" file that sends information to your screen. But if a file name is present, the information is written to the given file. If X, Y, and Z are integer variables, then

Write(X, Y, Z);
and
Write(Output, X, Y, Z);

are equivalent and cause output to the screen, but the latter is not often used.

Note that we use Write, not Writeln, with general files. A sequential file is not composed of separate "lines," but rather is one long sequence of records. Hence, never use "Writeln" with general files (one exception to this, a text file, is discussed later).

We make one last remark about the 'Rewrite' statement. It can also be used in the form

Rewrite(F);

which creates an anonymous file. Such files are useful for "scratch" files that your program might need but that you do not wish to keep permanently. In this text we will not use anonymous files.

If a sequential file already exists, then you can prepare it for **read-only** access with the Reset statement. The format of the Reset is:

Reset(F, File_Name);

where F and File_Name are as above. It is an error if there is no file by the given File_Name or if the file is still open from a Reset or a Rewrite. There is an alternate form of the Reset given by

Reset(F)

It may only be used on a file that was previously opened, and it "rewinds" the file. That is, it resets the file as a read-only file and prepares the file to be read from the beginning. Reset(F) is useful if one part of your program creates a file with a Rewrite and then another part of that same program needs to read from the file.

As you may have guessed, we use the 'Read' verb with a file that has been Reset. The format of the Read is:

     Read(F, Record_Name)

which, of course, obtains the next record from the file F and places the
information into Record_Name. For example,

     Read(Student, One_Student);

obtains the next student's record and places the information in the fields
of One_Student. There should be no confusion between reading the file F
and reading the keyboard. If no file is given, then the system expects the
input to be from the keyboard. The name of the standard input file is
Input, so the following are equivalent:

     Read(X, Y, Z);
and
     Read(Input, X, Y, Z);

Notice that 'Read', not 'Readln', is used to input information from a general
file. This is because a general sequential file is not organized into lines,
but is just one long sequence of records.

     In summary, we use Rewrite to create (write) a sequential file and
Reset to access (read) an already existing sequential file. Remember that
you may not use both Read and Write at the same time on a sequential file.
Indeed, you may only use Read if the file has been Reset, and you may only
use Write if the file has been opened with a Rewrite.
     What is opened should eventually be closed and that is the purpose of
the Close statement, whose format is:

     Close(F)

Close breaks the association between F and any external file and marks
that external file as "closed". The system automatically closes any files
that we forget to close, but it is good programming practice to be
responsible for our own files. Hence, we should explicitly close files
when we no longer need them. Note that to keep the discussion concerning
redirecting input and output in Chapter 4 as simple as possible, we did not
close the files Input and Output in our examples.

     A few words on the placement of the Reset, Rewrite, and Close
statements may be in order. In a simple program, the Reset's and

Rewrite's are at the beginning of the program while the Close's are at the end. Almost certainly, we can say that none of these statements belong within a processing loop. If your Rewrite, for example, is in a processing loop, then you are continually deleting your file and beginning over. All you have at the end is the last record written to the file. In a more complex program, you may use Reset, Rewrite, and Close in the middle of the program, but these statements are almost certainly placed between processing loops. Any one file is opened and closed only a very small number of times in a program.

```pascal
program Create;
{This program creates a sequential file of five student records.}

type
  ShortString = string[30];
  Class_Type = (Frosh, Soph, Jr, Sr);
  Student_Record = record
    Name : ShortString;
    Class : Class_Type;
    ID : string[11];
    GPA : Real;
    Fee_Status : Boolean;
    Sex : Char
  end; {Record}

  Student_File = file of Student_Record;

var
  Students : Student_File;
  One_Student : Student_Record;
  File_Name : ShortString;

procedure Purpose;
begin
  Writeln('This program creates a sequential file of five');
  Writeln('student records, and names the file according to');
  Writeln('your wishes. Use program Fetch to recover the file.');
  Writeln
end; {Definition of procedure Purpose}
```

(Continued)

```
procedure ObtainFileName (var FileName : ShortString);
begin
  Writeln('Enter the name of the file you wish to create.');
  Readln(FileName)
end; {Definition of procedure ObtainFileName}

procedure ObtainData (var Students : Student_File);
  var
    Index : Integer;
    One_Student : Student_Record;

begin
  for Index := 1 to 5 do
   with One_Student do
    begin
      Writeln(Chr(12)); {Clear screen}
      Write('Enter name of next student: ');
      Readln(Name);
      Write('Enter class (Frosh, Soph, Jr, Sr): ');
      Readln(Class);
      Write('Enter ID  (XXX-XX-XXXX): ');
      Readln(ID);
      Writeln('Enter GPA for ', Name, ': ');
      Readln(GPA);
      Write('Enter Fee_Status (True for paid): ');
      Readln(Fee_Status);
      Write('Enter sex (M or F): ');
      Readln(Sex);
      Write(Students, One_Student) {Write record to file.}
    end {With and For}
end; {Definition of procedure ObtainData}

begin
  Purpose;
  ObtainFileName(File_Name);
  Rewrite(Students, File_Name);
  ObtainData(Students, One_Student);
  Close(Students)
end.
```

Listing 11.1

```
program Fetch;
{This program reads a sequential file of student records.}
 type
  ShortString = string[30];
  Class_Type = (Frosh, Soph, Jr, Sr);
  Student_Record = record
    Name : ShortString;
    Class : Class_Type;
    ID : string[11];
    GPA : Real;
    Fee_Status : Boolean;
    Sex : Char
   end; {Record}
  Student_File = file of Student_Record;
 var
  Students : Student_File;
  One_Student : Student_Record;
  File_Name : string[30];
 procedure ObtainFileName (var FileName : ShortString);
 begin
  Writeln('Enter the name of the file you wish to read.');
  Readln(FileName)
 end; {Definition of procedure ObtainFileName}
 procedure WriteData (var Students : Student_File;
            One_Student : Student_Record);
 begin
  while not EOF(Students) do
   with One_Student do
    begin
     Read(Students, One_Student);
     Writeln(Name);
     Write(Class : 6, ID : 12, GPA : 8 : 2);
     Writeln(Fee_Status : 6, Sex : 2);
     Writeln
    end {While and With}
 end; {Definition of procedure WriteData}
begin
 ObtainFileName(File_Name);
 Reset(Students, File_Name);
 WriteData(Students, One_Student);
 Close(Students)
end.
```

Listing 11.2

Listings 11.1 and 11.2 show two simple but important programs that the reader should consider carefully. The first creates a sequential file of 5 student records, and the second fetches those records. We choose only 5 records since you must enter the data, but the principle is the same for 500 or 5000 records. You should run Create and then Fetch to verify the programs. Note that as you quit the system, there is an icon for a new file on the disk. Remember that Fetch still works when you come back next week, as long as the file is not discarded.

Notice that in Fetch the processing loop of the WriteData procedure is controlled by an "end of file" condition. The expression EOF(Students) is, of course, False unless the last record has been read from the Students file. Thus, EOF(F) works just like our friend EOF, except that EOF(F) tells us whether file F is at the end or not. EOF is equivalent to EOF(Input), but as usual, the system infers Input if no file is mentioned. EOF(F) is a very useful way to control the processing of the reading of the file F, and the reader should expect to use it often.

File Applications, Merging, and Updating

We consider two traditional, important uses of sequential files. The first is the **merging** of two files into one new file. This is a frequent business problem, when for example, two mailing lists need to be combined into one new list. We assume that the two lists are ordered in some way, and the object of the merge is to form a new ordered list containing all the items from the two lists. The second problem deals with the **updating** of a file of accounts. This is a very standard billing problem, where we need to reflect both charges and payments made by the customer. Actually, the second problem is also a kind of merge. We are merging old balances with current transactions to yield new balances. In the true merge, we are merging files with the same structure to yield a new file of that same structure. In the update problem, the balances and transactions are different kinds of records, but the end result is still the merging of this information into new balance records. For this reason, we consider the merge problem in considerable detail and leave the update problem as an exercise.

Merging Files

To be specific, let us suppose that Adam Firstperson and Eve Applesnake have decided to get married. Being a modern couple, they both keep track of their friends with the computer. The problem is to merge the file Adam with the file Eve to produce a new file Adam_and_Eve. We suppose that both Adam and Eve are ordered alphabetically, and we suppose that no one is on both lists. The assumption that there are no duplicates is simply for convenience. In the problems, we let the reader extend the program to handle duplicates. We also make the unwarranted assumption that the two files Adam and Eve have the same structure. That is, they both contain the same kinds of records. Again, we leave it to the reader to consider what to do if this is not the case. For simplicity, let us assume that both files contain records with last name, first name, and telephone number.

Consider for a moment how you would merge two lists manually:

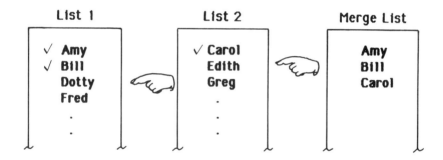

Figure 11.2

You look at the top item of each list and move the "winner" to the new list. Then consider the new top items and continue this process until one list is exhausted. At that point move all the remaining items to the new list. Here is the pseudo-code in Pascal:

```
Obtain the first record from each file
While neither file is at the end do
        Compare the current records of each file
        Write "winning" record to the new file
        Read the next record of the "winning" file
Transfer the nonempty file to the new file.
```

The corresponding Pascal program is shown in listing 11.3.

```
program Merge;
(This program merges the files 'Adam' and 'Eve' into 'Adam_and_Eve'.)
('Adam' and 'Eve' are assumed to be on the Pascal disk.)

  type
    FriendsRecord = record
      Last : string[15];
      First : string[15];
      Telephone : string[12]
    end;  (Record)

  var
    Adam, Eve, Friends : file of FriendsRecord;
    AdamsFriend, EvesFriend : FriendsRecord;
begin
  Reset(Adam, 'Adam');
  Reset(Eve, 'Eve');
  Rewrite(Friends, 'Adam_and_Eve');
  Read(Adam, AdamsFriend);
  Read(Eve, EvesFriend);
  while (AdamsFriend.Last <> 'END') and (EvesFriend.Last <> 'END') do
    if AdamsFriend.Last < EvesFriend.Last then
      begin
        Write(Friends, AdamsFriend);
        Read(Adam, AdamsFriend)
      end
    else
      begin
        Write(Friends, EvesFriend);
        Read(Eve, EvesFriend)
      end;  (If and While)
  while AdamsFriend.Last <> 'END' do
    begin
      Write(Friends, AdamsFriend);
      Read(Adam, AdamsFriend)
    end;
  while EvesFriend.Last <> 'END' do
    begin
      Write(Friends, EvesFriend);
      Read(Eve, EvesFriend)
    end;
```

(Continued)

```
        Write(Friends, EvesFriend);  {Write "END" to Adam_and_Eve file.}
        Writeln('Merge completed. Use "View_Friends" to see the results.');
        Close(Adam);
        Close(Eve);
        Close(Friends)
    end.
```

Listing 11.3

Notice how the **while** construct is perfect for this situation. We don't know which file will end first. The solution used here is to use two **while** statements after the main **while**, one of which executes zero times. The files Adam and Eve, as well as the program Merge, are on the disk accompanying this book so that you can try out the program. You may also want to use the program View_Friends so that you can see the contents of Adam, Eve, and Adam_and_Eve. To create your own lists to merge, use the program Make_Friends. Note that Make_Friends writes a sentinel "END" record to each file. This sentinel record is used to control the merging. Make_Friends and View_Friends are included on the disk, but are not listed here since they are easy modifications of Create and Fetch discussed earlier. A modification of View_Friends, called View_Friends2, is listed in the last section of this chapter. When using Make_Friends, be sure to enter the names in alphabetical order. (Why?)

Updating Files

The EZ COME--EZ GO credit card company keeps a master file on everyone who carries one of their credit cards. Each record in the file contains information about a customer, including name, address, employer, annual salary, years employed by present company, name of bank, account number at the bank, EZ COME--EZ GO account number, mother's maiden name, etc., etc. To keep it simple, we suppose in our example that only the name, the EZ COME--EZ GO account number, the current balance, and the credit limit are kept on each individual. The credit limit is, of course, the maximum amount that you are allowed to charge to your account. The problem is that people are always using their cards, running around charging things, and occasionally paying their bills. We must write a program to update the accounts for EZ COME--EZ GO.

Every time someone uses their credit card, a transaction slip is prepared. For simplicity we assume that there are only three kinds of transactions: payments, charges, and changes of credit limits. Of course, a more realistic example would also need to be able to handle changes of address, changes of name, interest charges, etc. Let us assume that the three transactions are coded by the letters P, C, and L. The transaction does not need to contain the complete credit history of the individual involved. The purpose of the transactions is to report that some action has taken place in a given account. Hence, all that is required on a transaction is an account number, a transaction code, and an amount. For example, these three transactions

        25385P9.98
        14676L750.00
        20032C49.98

mean that the person whose account number is 25385 has paid $9.98 on his/her bill, the person with account 14676 has had the credit limit on his/her account changed to $750.00, and someone has charged $49.98 to account 20032. It would be better to include the name of the customer on transactions as well and then not update an account unless both the name and the account number match. That way, a simple typing error, such as typing 25835 for 25385, could be caught by the program. In our simple case, we initially make the totally ridiculous assumption that the data is correct. Since EZ COME--EZ GO has millions of customers using its cards daily, you see how unwarranted this assumption is.

    At first glance this update problem does not appear to be a good one for a sequential file. An external file is needed simply because of the volume of data involved. There is no way that all of the millions of accounts can be read into an array. But with a sequential file, processing would appear to be very slow. For example, to process the above transactions we could proceed as follows: Hunt for account number 25385 and update that account. Then, reset the file and hunt for account number 14676, etc. Each time, we would need to reset the file and sequentially search from the beginning for one particular account. Sometimes we would get lucky, sometimes unlucky. On the average, we would need to look through half of the accounts just to update one. That is too slow.

    The solution lies through the observation that the update does not have to take place immediately upon receipt of the transaction. EZ COME--EZ GO bills its customers once a month, so it is only necessary to update accounts once a month. Hence, the transactions can be saved, or batched, and processed all at once instead of individually. The final ingredient to the solution is to require that the file of master accounts and the file of transactions be sorted by ascending account number. Thus,

If account 10012 is the first account, then all transactions for that account are at the front of the transaction file. After account 10012 is updated, processing can proceed to the second record of the file. Of course, it is possible that someone has not used his/her EZ COME--EZ GO credit card at all this month, and hence, some of the records do not need to be updated. Since EZ COME--EZ GO knows by experience that most of its customers use their credit cards very frequently, there are few records that do not require updating, and, hence, this is a very efficient algorithm to use on the update problem. With one pass over the file of master accounts and one pass over the file of transactions, we can create the updated file.

We leave the update problem to the exercises with the following cautions: Be aware that there are in general many transactions that "match" any one master account. A person is certainly allowed to use his/her credit card more than once a month. Each use of the card, as well as any payments made, create transactions. The point is that the newly updated record should not be written to the file until all transactions for that account have been processed. If we assume that Oldmaster and Transactions are the input files to your program, your program should create a new file called NewMaster. You need to create a new file Newmaster because you cannot both read and write to the sequential file Oldmaster simultaneously. Even if you could, it would be dangerous, for suppose your program "blows up" during execution. You may then have a mixed file with some updated accounts and some non-updated accounts. How do you proceed? It is better to preserve your input data, so that if the program dies you can try again. Of course, next month we rename Newmaster as Oldmaster and create a new Newmaster.

Text Files

A **text file** is a special file of characters that is organized into lines. The standard input and output files, Input and Output, are such files. Ever since Chapter 4 we have been redirecting Input to come from a text file. All of the file operations described previously apply to text files, and, in addition, other procedures and functions, such as Readln, Writeln, and EOLN apply to text files. Besides redirecting Input or Output to a text file, a text file F may be declared using the keyword **text** as follows:

var
  F : **text** ;

Macintosh Pascal allows the user to read or write integers, reals, **strings** , or enumerated types with text files. That is,

Read(F, X);

reads, depending on X's type, the next character, integer, real, ordinal type value, or string from the file associated with F. If X is a string variable, then all of the characters to the next "end-of-line" (or "end-of-file") marker are assigned to X. However, a **Read** of a **string** variable does *not* advance the file pointer beyond the current end-of-line marker, and thus subsequent reads to X assign X the null string. For this reason, one must always remember to use

Readln(F, X);

with a string variable as Readln reads to the end-of-line marker and advance the file pointer to the first character in the next line.

EOLN(F) is set to true if the last character read was the last character of the current line. Likewise, EOF(F) is true if the last character read was in fact the last character of the file. Actually, there is room for confusion in Pascal concerning what is the last character in a text file. We demonstrate the problem in a program TestEOF later in this section.

Write may be used with variables or expressions of character, integer, real, string, or ordinal types. In addition, the Writes may be formatted, exactly as with the standard output file Output. That is, you may give a width factor (and optionally with reals the number of places to the right of the decimal point) and your values are right justified in a field of that width. If the width you specify is too small, then the system "elbows" enough room so that your value can be printed.

To illustrate text files, consider a program that compares the two keyboards available on the Apple IIc. Many people have suggested alternate keyboards to the standard "QWERTY" keyboard. The QWERTY keyboard is so named by the placement of the first six keys on the upper row of letters on a standard typewriter or computer keyboard. The particular arrangement of letters in the QWERTY keyboard was chosen in the late nineteenth century. At that time, human typists could push the new typewriter technology to its limits and jam keys by typing too fast. Hence, the QWERTY keyboard was chosen partially to slow humans down. Today, of course, microcomputers can respond to keypresses in microseconds, so there is little danger of humans typing faster than machines can respond.

One of the many keyboards that has been proposed to supplant the QWERTY keyboard is the Dvorak keyboard, whose layout is as depicted in figure 11.3.

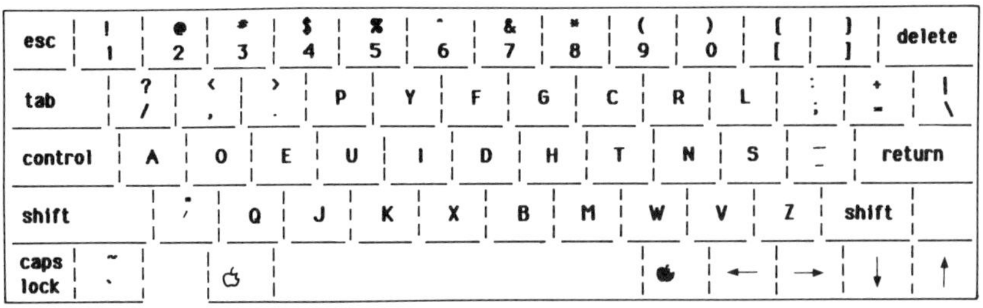

```
 esc  | ! | @ | # | $ | % | ^ | & | * | ( | ) | { | } | delete
      | 1 | 2 | 3 | 4 | 5 | 6 | 7 | 8 | 9 | 0 | [ | ] |

 tab  | ? | < | > | P | Y | F | G | C | R | L | : | + | |
      | / | , | . |   |   |   |   |   |   |   | ; | - | \

control | A | O | E | U | I | D | H | T | N | S | _ | return

 shift  | " | Q | J | K | X | B | M | W | V | Z | shift
        | ' |

 caps | ~ |     |      |          | ⌘ | ← | → | ↓ | ↑
 lock | ` |  ⌂  |      |          |
```

Figure 11.3

Just by flicking a switch on your Apple IIc you can choose between these two keyboards. The keycaps come arranged for the traditional QWERTY system, but you can rearrange them or obtain "dual" keycaps. Perhaps there will come a day when systems such as Dvorak's will be in widespread use. Certainly, the Apple IIc's switch is a good idea. If Dvorak's system can be demonstrated to be much better, perhaps new typists will learn this system while we old QWERTY typists die out. Let us consider a simple test of the two systems. We take a text file and read the file and count the number of times our fingers leave the home row, both for the QWERTY system and for the Dvorak system. Of course, the number of times we leave the home row is not the only factor that makes for a good keyboard, but it illustrates our point sufficiently. The program Keys that makes this comparison is shown in listing 11.4.

The text file Typing contains the text of the previous paragraph. The output of the program Keys is:

The Qwerty keyboard needed 1385 jumps.
The Dvorak keyboard needed 873 jumps.

You can also create your own text file if you wish. Be sure to use only upper case letters as these are all the program Keys looks for. Also note that in the program we have declared a file variable, F, of type text rather than redirect the Input file, as we did in Chapter 4.

```pascal
program Keys;
(This program compares the Dvorak and QWERTY keyboards.)
(It reads a text file, Typing, and counts how many times)
(your fingers would have to leave the home row in each case.)

  var
    F : Text;
    Dvorak_Hops : Integer;
    QWERTY_Hops : Integer;
    Ch : Char;

begin
  Reset(F, 'Typing');
  Dvorak_Hops := 0;
  QWERTY_Hops := 0;
  Writeln('Please wait while I process the text file');
  Writeln('Typing to see whether the QWERTY or Dvorak');
  Writeln('keyboard is best.');

  while not EOF(F) do
   begin
     Read(F, Ch);
     case Ch of
       'A', 'S', 'D', 'F', 'G', 'H', 'J', 'K', 'L', ';', '"' :
         ; (QWERTY home row - Do nothing.)
       otherwise
         QWERTY_Hops := QWERTY_Hops + 1
     end; (Case for QWERTY keyboard)
     case Ch of
       'A', 'O', 'E', 'U', 'I', 'D', 'H', 'T', 'N', 'S', '-' :
         ; (Dvorak home row - Do nothing.)
       otherwise
         Dvorak_Hops := Dvorak_Hops + 1
     end (Case for Dvorak keyboard)
   end; (While)

  Writeln('The QWERTY keyboard needed ', QWERTY_Hops : 3, ' jumps.');
  Writeln('The Dvorak keyboard needed ', Dvorak_Hops : 3, ' jumps.');
  Close(F)
end.
```

Listing 11.4

The text file EofFile contains precisely the 23 characters of the following sentence:

This file has 23 chars.

Yet, when read by the very simple program TestEOF of listing 11.5, the output is

There are 24 characters in the file.

This apparent discrepancy is due to the potentially misleading nature of the EOF indicator when a text file is read character by character. One would like the EOF indicator to become True when the last actual character is read. However, EOF does not become true until the "end of file" marker is read, and, incidentally, when this happens, a blank is assigned to the character variable Ch. The same kind of problem arises if you try to use Reads for numeric data in a text file. The best solution to the problem is to use Readlns with numeric data, and strings and Readlns with character data.

```
program TestEOF;
{This program illustrates a bug in version 1.0 of the software.}

var
  Ch : Char;
  Count : Integer;
  F : Text;

begin
  Reset(F, 'EofFile');
  Count := 0;
  while not EOF(F) do
   begin
     Read(F, Ch);
     Write(Ch);
     Count := Count + 1
   end;
  Writeln;
  Writeln('There were ', Count : 2, ' characters in the file.')
end.
```

Listing 11.5

Random Access Files

Standard Pascal does not support random access files, so the reader should be forewarned that programs using such files are probably not **portable** to other Pascals. Even other Pascals that support random access files do not use quite the same procedures as described here. Nonetheless, because of their power, random access files are useful tools in many situations.

Random access, again, simply means that we have the right to access the records of a file in any order. We may read record number 45 first, then backup to examine record number 2, then advance to record number 89. We are not limited, as with sequential files, to processing the records in their natural order. Nor are we limited to doing only reads or only writes to the file. We may read a record into memory, update that record, and then write the new record back to the file.

Random access files are very powerful and flexible. Fortunately, we now learn that manipulating random access files is really as easy as manipulating sequential files. There is only one "open" statement for random access files and it is:

   Open(F, System_Name);

If a file by the name System_Name already exists, then it is opened for read/write access. If there is no such file, then one is created by the open statement.

Obviously, there must be some mechanism for us to select the particular record that we wish to access. This we do through the 'Seek' procedure:

   Seek(F, N);

which advances (or retreats) the file associated with F so that the next read or write is to the Nth record of the file. N, of course, must be an integer constant, variable, or expression. Also, to make life as difficult as possible, records are numbered from zero. That is, the first record is record number zero. Hence, to get the "tenth" record in the file, you should seek the ninth record from the system. Also, if N is larger than the number of records in the file, then the file is advanced to the end, EOF(F) becomes true, but no error message is issued. This is so that you may append records to the end of a random access file, even without knowing how many records are in the file.

In summary, we Open random access files instead of using Reset or Rewrite, and then we precede every Read or Write with a Seek to the record we wish to access. In fact, Macintosh Pascal allows us to mix sequential and random access modes in that a file created sequentially with Rewrite can later be opened for random access with the Open statement.

Here is a segment that outlines how to update the Nth record of our file Students:

```
Open(Students, Students_Data);
 . . .
 . . .
Seek(Students, N);  {We assume N already has a proper value.}
Read(Students, One_Student);
 . . .
 . . .
{Update the record One_Student as needed.}
 . . .
 . . .
Seek(Students, N);
Write(Students, One_Student);  {Write the updated record back to the}
                               {file}
```

Note that both the Read and the Write are preceded by Seek's. Forgetting to precede each Read or Write with a seek is a common error, but you are less likely to make this error if you understand why the Seek's are necessary: After the Read obtains the Nth record, the file is automatically advanced to the $(N+1)^{st}$ record. If you forget to Seek back to the Nth record, your Write actually overwrites the $(N+1)^{st}$ record, wiping it out, and leaving your file with two versions of the Nth record. The reason that the system operates in such a perverse way is that it permits you to mix random and sequential access. If you Seek the Nth record and then do five consecutive Read's (without Seek's), you obtain records N, N+1, N+2, N+3, and N+4. Also, very often we create a random access file in sequential order. That is, we know the order of the file when we create it, so we create it with sequential Write's. But when we read the file or wish to update certain records of the file, we access the file randomly. Since the manipulation of random access files is so much like the manipulation of sequential files, we leave the remainder of this discussion to the exercises.

Get and Put

Pascal provides an alternate method of I/O (input and output) that we now discuss. Get and Put are more primitive routines than Read and Write and allow the reader to understand more clearly how I/O really operates.

Every time we declare a file F of SomeType, the system allocates a "buffer" or "window" in memory for the file F. We depict the file F and its buffer as in figure 11.4

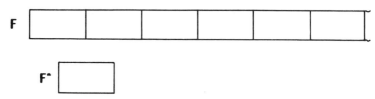

Figure 11.4

It is important to realize that the file F resides on a disk external to main memory, while the buffer is in main memory. The buffer has the same type as the record type of the file F. If we think of the buffer as containing the current record of the file, we see where the terminology "window to the file" comes from. All input from the file and all output to the file must go through the buffer. The system name for the buffer to the file is F^, which should be read as "the buffer to file F". The "buffer" character is typed by holding down the Shift key and pressing the 6 key.

A Get(F) simply transfers information from the next record of F to the buffer F^. Of course, it also advances the file so that the next Get obtains the next record. After a Get(F), *not* Get(F^), the fields of F^ have values (unless there was no record to get, in which case EOF(F) is set to True). A Put(F), *not* Put(F^), transfers the information in the buffer F^ out to the next record of the file F. Hence, before we execute a Put(F), we should place values in the fields of F^. As a word of caution, note that sequential files cannot mix Get's and Put's, just like they can't mix Reads and Writes. In fact, Put is used with files that you open with Rewrite and Get is used with files that are opened with Reset. Get and Put can both be used with files that are prepared for random access with Open.

It is very important to note *and remember* that a Reset *always* does an automatic Get. Hence, a Reset prepares the file F and brings the first record into the buffer F^. Students often forget that Reset includes the first Get and do their own Get. Then they wonder where the first record of their file went!

Before we demonstrate with a complete example the correct placement of Gets in a program, we indicate how Read and Write can be replaced with Gets and Puts. Let us suppose that F is a file of SomeType and that R is a record of SomeType. We know that Read(F,R) reads the next record of the file F into R. Since Reset did an automatic Get, the information is already in the buffer F^. Noting that F^ and R are both records of SomeType, we see that Read(F,R) is equivalent to:

```
R := F^; (Transfer buffer to R.        )
Get(F); (Prepare buffer for next Read.)
```

The order of these two statements is critical. The order is not what the beginner would expect, but the explanation is that the buffer is always one record "ahead" of the Read because of the original Get done by the Reset.

Likewise, Put can be used instead of Write(F,R). Write(F,R) writes the information in R out to the file F. Hence, Write(F,R) is equivalent to:

```
F^ := R; (Transfer information to the buffer.)
Put(F); (Put the information out to the file.)
```

The fact that Reset does the first Get also means that a control loop using Gets is structured differently than it would be with Reads. Figure 11.5 shows the differences:

```
(Using GETS)                     (Using READS)
Reset(F, 'Something');           Reset(F, 'Something');
While not EOF(F) do              While not EOF(F) do
begin                            begin
 ... (Process F^)                Read(F,R);
 Get(F)                           ... (Process R)
end;                             end;
```

Figure 11.5

Note that the Get is at the bottom of its loop and that the corresponding Read is at the top of its loop. The loop with the Get seems unusual since we use F^ before we do a Get. We leave the explanation for the reader.

The simple program View_Friends2, of listing 11.6, allows you to see the contents of any of the files Adam, Eve, or Friends used in the merge problem earlier in this chapter. Study the listing to see that the main while loop is controlled exactly as described above.

```pascal
program View_Friends2;
(This program views the files Adam, Eve, or Adam_and_Eve.)
(This program illustrates the use of Get instead of Read.)

  type
    FriendsRecord = record
      Last : string[15];
      First : string[15];
      Telephone : string[12]
      end;  (Record)

  var
    Generic : file of FriendsRecord;
    Ans : Char;

begin
  repeat
    Write('View Adam''s, Eve''s, or Friend''s file? (1/2/3) ');
    Readln(Ans);
    case Ans of
      '1' :
      Reset(Generic, 'Adam');
      '2' :
      Reset(Generic, 'Eve');
      '3' :
      Reset(Generic, 'Adam_and_Eve');
      otherwise
      writeln('Pay Attention!!')
    end;  (Case)
  until (Ans = '1') or (Ans = '2') or (Ans = '3');
  while not EOF(Generic) do
    begin
      Writeln(Generic^.First, ' ', Generic^.Last);
      Writeln(Generic^.Telephone);
      Writeln;
      Get(Generic)
    end;  (While)
  Close(Generic)
end.
```

Listing 11.6

Summary

Arrays, records, and files are the three most fundamental data structures in computer programming. Almost any sophisticated applications program uses at least one, if not all three, of these structures. Arrays of records and files of records are the most natural ways to structure most kinds of data, so it is crucial that the beginning programmer establish a strong understanding of each of these concepts. In fact, as programs become more complicated, the programmer soon learns that "understanding" the data is as important as writing the algorithms to process the data.

Exercises

11.1 The file Years, on the Sample disk accompanying this book, contains records with two fields, a name (25 characters) and an integer representing the number of years that person has been working at the Widget Works. For example, the record

Coffy Breaks
27

indicates that Coffy has been with the firm for 27 years. Snidely has decided to give year-end bonuses to those employees who have been with the company for at least 25 years. The bonus is to be $100 for every year beyond the 24th year of service. Thus, Coffy's bonus is $300. Write a program that reads Years and creates a file Bonus which contains the names of the employees earning a bonus, as well as the amount of that bonus. Also include a procedure to allow you to view Bonus and thereby verify that it is correct.

11.2 Write the update program described in the text for the EZ Come--EZ Go Company. The disk accompanying this book contains the files OldMaster and Transactions. Each record of OldMaster contains four fields: a name (25 characters), an account number (integer), the current balance (real), and the credit limit (real). As described in the text, each record of Transactions contains 3 fields: an account number (integer), a transaction code (1 character), and an amount (real). You may assume that both OldMaster and Transactions are in order by account number.

Your program should create NewMaster and Trouble. NewMaster contains the updated records for all customers. Trouble contains the record of any individual whose current balance exceeds his/her current credit limit. Include procedures so that you can view the contents of OldMaster and Transactions, as well as New Master and Trouble.

11.3 Use Make_Friends to create new versions of Adam and Eve. Include two or three individuals on both files. Modify Merge so that it handles these duplicates properly.

11.4 What could we do if the files Adam and Eve do not have exactly the same structure? Suppose the fields are similar, but not exactly the same. For example, maybe Adam keeps phone numbers as strings of 8 characters (555-1212) while Eve keeps phone numbers as strings of 12 characters (201-555-1212). Neither wants to recreate his/her file from scratch. How can they most easily merge the two different files?

11.5 Write a small inventory control program for the Widget Works. Since there are ten products, write a procedure that creates an 'Inventory' file of ten records containing:

   Description (25 characters)
   Part_No (1--10)
   Quantity_on_Hand (integer)
   Cost (real)

Write a procedure LookUp that uses the part number to find the corresponding record in the random access file 'Inventory'. Remember that part number 7 is stored in record 6 of the file. Allow the user to change the quantity on hand or the cost to reflect sales, receipt of goods, or price gouging.

11.6 Write a program UTFW, Universal Text File Writer, that reads strings and writes them to a file whose name is selected by the user. UTFW can serve as a substitute for MacWrite as a means to create text files. While UTFW lacks the power of MacWrite, it is convenient to use during a Pascal session because it is not necessary to exit the Pascal system to create text files for programs.

Chapter 12

Graphics and Sound

The graphics capabilities of the Macintosh are very extensive. Indeed, in reality, everything on the Macintosh is graphics. The icons that we manipulate with the mouse are a very fundamental part of the Macintosh's user-friendly operating system. This chapter introduces you to the most useful of the built-in graphics routines available in Macintosh Pascal. After you master the procedures and functions given here, you will find many more in Appendix C of the **Macintosh Pascal Reference Manual**.

Most of the graphics routines that we are going to describe are in the QuickDraw system library. Since the designers of Macintosh Pascal expected users to make heavy use of this library, it is automatically included when your program makes use of any of its routines. Thus, a **uses** statement is not necessary to use the Macintosh graphics package. We also point out that none of the statements described in this chapter is included in standard Pascal.

Coordinates

The Macintosh screen is 512 pixels wide by 342 pixels high. Each pixel can be white or black giving the Macintosh its incredible powers of resolution. To address a particular point on the screen we need to give its horizontal position (X coordinate) and its vertical position (Y coordinate). The upper left hand corner is the point (0,0), the upper right hand corner is (511,0), the lower right hand corner is (511,341), etc. Figure 12.1 illustrates these points as well as the points (100, 300) and (300, 100). Actually, due to the menu bar and the side bars, which are about 20 pixels wide, none of the corner points are available to the user. Remember that the horizontal coordinate is always given before the vertical coordinate.

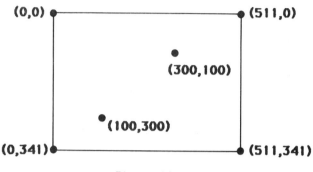

Figure 12.1

When you begin Macintosh Pascal, the system gives you the small drawing window shown in figure 12.2. We shall soon learn how to manipulate this window to make it any size and occupy any place on the screen, but for now let's accept it as it is and learn to draw in it. Each drawing window has local coordinates that simplify drawing in that window. Thus, (0,0) is the coordinate of the upper left hand corner of the drawing window, even though the window is in the lower right portion of the screen. The drawing window as set by the system is 200 pixels wide and 200 pixels high, so its coordinates range from (0,0) to (199,199). Again, (199,0) is the upper right corner; (0,199) is the lower left corner. As long as we keep our coordinates in these ranges we can use the system's predefined drawing window.

LineTo, Line, MoveTo, Move

These four built-in procedures are used to draw lines and to move on the screen without drawing. If we imagine a pen placed on the screen, then these procedures manipulate that pen.

The LineTo procedure

Format: LineTo(X,Y) where X and Y are integer values.
Effect: LineTo draws a line to the point(X,Y) from the current position of the pen. The new pen position becomes (X,Y).

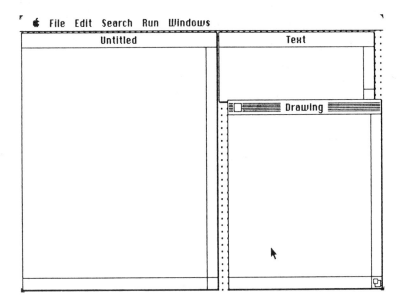

Figure 12.2

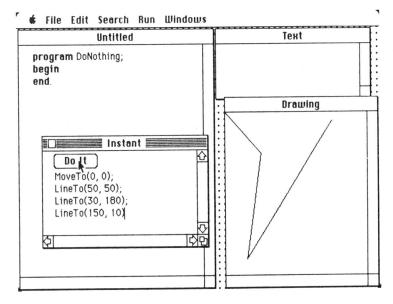

Figure 12.3

The **Line** procedure
Format: Line(dX, dY) where dX and dY are Integer values.
Effect: Line draws a line to the point that is dX units horizontally and dY units vertically from the current position of the pen. Remember that a positive dX moves the pen to the right and a positive dY moves the pen down. Actually, Line(dX, dY) calls LineTo(X+dX, Y+dY) where X and Y are the old pen coordinates. (X+dX, Y+dY) become the new pen coordinates.

The **MoveTo** procedure
Format: MoveTo(X,Y) where X and Y are Integer values.
Effect: MoveTo moves the pen to the point (X,Y), but no drawing is performed.

The **Move** procedure
Format: Move(dX, dY) where dX and dY are Integer values.
Effect: Moves the pen dX horizontally and dY vertically without performing any drawing.

You may try out these procedures in immediate mode as follows. Pull down the Instant Window and give commands through it as shown in figure 12.3. Note the DoNothing program in the Program Window. It is present because we have found that the Instant Window occasionally crashes the system if the Program Window is empty.

A Turtle Graphics Package

Some versions of Pascal come with the capability of manipulating an imaginary turtle on the screen. Many educators feel that "turtle graphics" is an ideal way to introduce children to computers and programming. Indeed, the language LOGO has gained much recognition as an introductory language for children because of its turtle graphics capabilities. Unfortunately, there are no built-in turtle graphics routines for the Macintosh, but in this section we present our own small turtle graphics package. Of necessity, some of the explanations in this section are fairly mathematical. We have included these discussions for the reader who wants to understand how the package operates. We stress, however, that the mathematically uninclined reader may skip the explanations and simply use the routines in the same manner that most people use the LOGO routines without understanding how they are actually implemented. Indeed, for reference purposes, we describe the routines together, then discuss their implementations.

A Macintosh Turtle Graphics Package

The routines described below are included (within programs that use them) on the disk that accompanies this book. Their listings are also given below. Remember that they are not system built-ins, so you must include them in your programs.

The Initialize procedure
Format: Initialize. (no parameters)
Effect: Initialize sets the global variables Angle (Integer), and X and Y (Real) that must be declared in your program. Angle is set to zero, which means the turtle is facing right. X and Y are each set to 100.0 and the turtle (pen) is moved to the point (100,100). This places the turtle in the center of the standard drawing window. If you change the size of the drawing window, as described below, then you will need to modify Initialize appropriately.

The Turn procedure
Format: Turn(Alpha) where Alpha is an Integer value.
Effect: Turn(Alpha) changes the turtle's heading by turning it Alpha degrees counterclockwise (a negative Alpha produces a clockwise turn). Thus, Turn(90) is a "left" turn from the turtle's viewpoint and Turn(-90) is a "right" turn. Turn produces no drawing, but the next Line, LineTo, or Forward draws in the turtle's new heading.

The Forward procedure
Format: Forward(Distance) where Distance is an Integer value.
Effect: Forward(Distance) moves the turtle forward Distance units in the direction of its current heading. Forward does not change the heading of the turtle, but Forward does draw a line as it moves.

The DegToRad function
Format: DegToRad(Degrees) where Degrees is an Integer value.
Result: DegToRad converts the angle given in degrees to an equivalent angle measured in radians. The casual user does not need to invoke the DegToRad function. It is needed by our graphics system to convert angles given by the user in degrees into angles in radian measure needed by the body of Forward.

The procedure Initialize is easy to write and is given in listing 12.1. Note that Initialize needs to be modified when we change the size of the drawing window. So, always be sure that you have the proper version of Initialize for your program. Also, remember to declare Angle (Integer), and X and Y (Real) in your main program as global variables that are used by the entire graphics package.

```
procedure Initialize;
begin
  Angle := 0;
  X := 100.0;
  Y := 100.0;
  MoveTo(Trunc(X), Trunc(Y))
end;
```

Listing 12.1

Procedure Turn is also very simple. Turn keeps track, using the global variable Angle, of the current heading of the turtle. We subtract Alpha from Angle rather than add Alpha to Angle because of the fact that "up" on the Macintosh coordinate system is "down" in a normal mathematical coordinate system. Turn also keeps the angle in the range from 0 to 359 degrees by using the mod function. Turn is given in listing 12.2:

```
procedure Turn(Alpha : Integer);
begin
  Angle := Angle - Alpha;
  Angle := Angle mod 360
end;
```

Listing 12.2

Function DegToRad, using the fact that Pi radians equals 180 degrees, converts an integer angle given in degrees to a real result in radians. The function is shown in listing 12.3. To use DegToRad you also need to declare Pi as a constant in your program with the value of 3.1415927.

```
function DegToRad (Degrees : Integer) : Real;
begin
  DegToRad := Degrees * Pi / 180
end;
```

Listing 12.3

The **Forward** procedure

Forward uses the Sin and Cos functions to compute the horizontal and vertical displacements involved in moving forward Distance units. Because Sin and Cos expect real, radian arguments, DegToRad is invoked by Forward. Forward then calls LineTo to actually draw the line. The geometry is given in figure 12.4 and the Pascal code in listing 12.4.

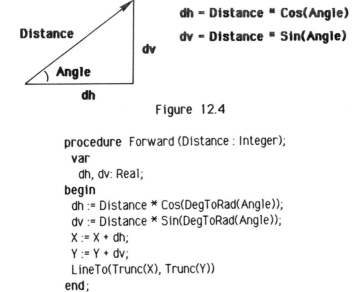

dh = Distance * Cos(Angle)

dv = Distance * Sin(Angle)

Figure 12.4

```
procedure Forward (Distance : Integer);
  var
    dh, dv: Real;
  begin
    dh := Distance * Cos(DegToRad(Angle));
    dv := Distance * Sin(DegToRad(Angle));
    X := X + dh;
    Y := Y + dv;
    LineTo(Trunc(X), Trunc(Y))
  end;
```

Listing 12.4

As an example of our turtle graphics package, consider a program that draws a hexagon, then turns 10 degrees and draws another hexagon, etc. The drawing of one hexagon is simple: We loop 6 times drawing an edge and turning 60 degrees. If we turn 10 degrees between hexagons, then we should repeat this process 36 times (360 degrees) to come back to where we started. Listing 12.5 shows the program RollingHex and figure 12.5 demonstrates its spectacular output.

Note that RollingHex declares the constant Pi as well as the global variables Angle, X, and Y, which are manipulated by the graphics package. The variables Side and Roll, on the other hand, are variables that RollingHex uses in its own body to control the two **for** loops.

```
program RollingHex;
(This program illustrates the use of our graphics )
(routines to draw and roll a hexagon            . )
 const
   Pi = 3.1415927;
 var
   Angle : Integer;
   X, Y : Real;
   Side, Roll : Integer;
(Graphics Package goes here.)
begin
 Initialize;
 for Roll := 1 to 36 do
  begin
   for Side := 1 to 6 do
    begin
     Forward(50);
     Turn(60)
    end;  (Inner For)
   Turn(10)
  end  (Outer For)
end.
```

Listing 12.5.

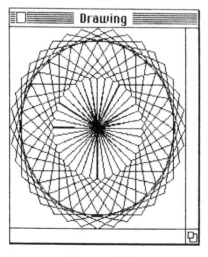

Figure 12.5

Manipulating Text and Drawing Windows

To really use the Drawing window we need to be able to make it the size we need and to move it about the screen. These manipulations are easy, but first we need the notion of a "rectangle."

In Macintosh Pascal, a rectangle is determined by four points, the coordinates of its left, top corner and the coordinates of its right, bottom corner. QuickDraw includes a predefined type Rect that is a record consisting of four integers. The four fields represent the left, top, right, and bottom coordinates of the rectangle. Hence, we may declare Window to be of type Rect by the declaration:

var
 Window : Rect;

Such a declaration is needed for some of the window manipulation routines that follow.

The **SetRect** procedure

Format: SetRect(Window, Left, Top, Right, Bottom) where Window is a variable of type Rect and Left, Top, Right, and Bottom are Integer values.

Effect: SetRect sets the four fields of Window to the four given values. Note the order of the points! A call to SetRect is often needed before a call to SetDrawingRect or SetTextRect as described below. Left, Top, Right, and Bottom should be relative to the global coordinates of the Macintosh screen (that is, (0,0) is the left, upper corner, (511, 341) is the right, lower corner, etc.) and they determine where the Window appears on the screen.

The **SetDrawingRect** procedure

Format: SetDrawingRect(Window) where window is a value of type Rect.

Effect: SetDrawingRect positions the Drawing window so that it occupies the rectangle whose coordinates are given in Window. Thus, SetDrawingRect is used to determine the location and size of the Drawing window. It does not make the Drawing window the active window (see ShowDrawing below). Also remember that the drawing window always uses a local coordinate system so that (0,0) is its upper, left corner, no matter where it is located on the screen.

The **SetTextRect** procedure
Format: SetTextRect(Window) where window is a value of type Rect.
Effect: SetTextRect determines the size and placement of the Text Window.

The **ShowDrawing** procedure
Format: ShowDrawing. (No parameters)
Effect: ShowDrawing makes the Drawing window the currently active window and brings the Drawing window to the top of the desk.

The **ShowText** procedure
Format: ShowText. (No parameters)
Effect: ShowText makes the Text window the currently active window and brings the Text window to the top of the desk. ShowText should be used before a prompt if there is any danger that the Text window is not visible.

How large can we make the Drawing Window? The top menu bar is 20 pixels wide and is not covered by the Drawing Window even if we use SetDrawingRect to place the Drawing Window in the area of the menu bar. Thus, if we set one corner of the Drawing Window at (0,0) then no point whose Y coordinate is less than 20 appears on the screen. Hence, (0, 20) is a good left, top coordinate for the Drawing Window. On the other hand, the side and bottom bars of the Drawing Window itself are 16 pixels wide. Again, any point whose coordinates place it in one of these bars will not be seen. However, as part of the Drawing Window, these side and bottom bars can be moved off the screen. Since the right, bottom corner of the screen is (511, 341) and the bars are 16 pixels wide, if we place the other corner of the Drawing Window at (527, 357) then the usable portion of the Drawing Window occupies the entire screen except for the menu bar. In terms of the local coordinates of such a Drawing Window, (0,0) is the left, top corner just below the menu bar while (511, 321) is the right, bottom corner. The coordinate of 511 comes from the fact that we are using the entire width of the screen while the 321 Y-cooordinate results from the fact that 20 pixels are "lost" at the top of the screen. Note, therefore, that in local coordinates (256, 161) is the approximate center of the screen.

To illustrate the use of these window manipulating procedures, consider the program Spiral of listing 12.6.

```
program Spiral;
{This program illustrates the use of our graphics    }
{routines to draw a spiral whose angle you determine. }

   const
    Pi = 3.1415927;

   var
    Angle : Integer;
    X, Y : Real;
    Distance, Alpha : Integer;
    WindowSize : Rect;

   procedure Initialize;
   begin
    Angle := 0;
    X := 256.0;
    Y := 161.0;
    Moveto(Trunc(X), Trunc(Y))
   end;

{Rest of Graphics Package goes here.}

begin
   Initialize;
   Distance := 1;
   ShowText;
   Write('Please enter angle for spiral: ');
   Readln(Alpha);
   ShowDrawing;
   SetRect(WindowSize, 0, 20, 527, 357);
   SetDrawingRect(WindowSize);
   repeat
    Forward(Distance);
    Distance := Distance + 1;
    Turn(Alpha)
   until Distance > 300
end.
```

Listing 12.6

Procedure Initialize has been included in the listing because it has changed. Spiral uses the whole screen as the Drawing window, so Initialize centers the turtle by moving it to the point (256, 161). Note that Spiral uses ShowText because it wants to prompt the user for some input. ShowText ensures that the text window is visible. Likewise, Spiral uses SetRect, SetDrawingRect, and ShowDrawing to make the Drawing window cover the entire screen. Finally, what is it that Spiral draws? The reader should trace the repeat...until loop in Spiral with an angle (Alpha) of 90 degrees to see where the name comes from. Run Spiral several times with differerent angles. Figure 12.6 shows the result with an angle of 89 degrees. Of course, the drawing fills the screen and the program window is no longer visible. You can recover the program window by pulling down the Windows menu and choosing "Spiral".

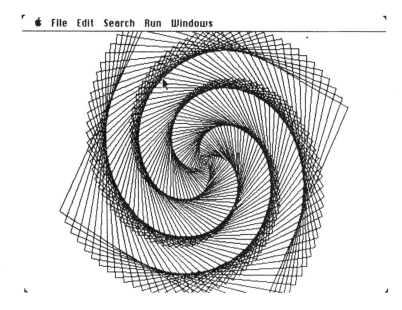

Figure 12.6

We mention in passing one procedure that may be of great interest to some readers. This is the SaveDrawing(Title) procedure with one parameter of type string. SaveDrawing saves the contents of your Drawing window to disk in a format that may be read by MacPaint, the Macintosh artists' program.

Text in the Drawing Window

Some systems make the placing of text within the graphics window an extremely difficult task. This is not so with Macintosh Pascal since QuickDraw includes several routines to make the work as simple as possible. We describe these now.

The **DrawString** procedure
Format: DrawString(Str) where Str is any string value.

Effect: DrawString writes the given string to the Drawing window. The string begins at the current pen location and the new pen location is at the end of the string. The appearance of the text, namely the size, font, and style, are determined by the procedures TextSize, TextFont, and TextFace.

The **TextSize** procedure
Format: TextSize(Size) where Size is an integer value.

Effect: TextSize changes the size of the text that is written by DrawString. For best results, Size should be one of the font sizes of the system (9, 10, 12, 14, 18, 24) or a multiple of one of these sizes.

The **TextFont** procedure
Format: TextFont(Font) where Font is an integer value.

Effect: TextFont sets the font that is used by DrawString. The only interesting fonts we have found correspond to Font values of zero to five. We leave it as an exercise for the reader to discover what these fonts look like.

The **TextFace** procedure
Format: TextFace(Face) where Face is a set of styles.

Effect: TextFace determines the style that DrawString uses when writing characters to the Drawing window. Sets are discussed in the next chapter, but it suffices here to say that the styles you want are placed between square brackets and given as the argument to TextFace. Thus,

TextFace([bold, underline]);

means that any string written with DrawString is both in boldface and underlined. The possible text styles are bold, italic, underline, shadow, outline, condense, and extend. The reader can experiment with these to see what each looks like.

The statement

TextFace([ ]);

will restore the style to plain text.

The program TextDrawing of listing 12.7 illustrates the ease of use of these tools. The resulting output is shown in figure 12.7. Note that TextDrawing sets the Drawing window so that a little portion of the program window is visible behind it.

```
program TextDrawing;
  var
    Window : Rect;
begin
  SetRect(Window, 70, 70, 500, 300);
  ShowDrawing;
  SetDrawingRect(Window);
  Moveto(10, 20);
  DrawString('This is all there is to it!');
  TextFont(5);
  TextFace([Bold, Shadow]);
  TextSize(24);
  MoveTo(20, 100);
  DrawString('Any child could do it.');
  TextFace([]); {Plain Text}
  TextFont(1); {Standard Font}
  TextSize(12); {Standard Size}
  MoveTo(30, 200);
  DrawString('Study the program to see how to get normal text back.')
end.
```

Listing 12.7

Rectangles and Ovals

Rectangles and ovals are two of the predefined shapes that can easily be drawn in Macintosh Pascal. A rectangle, as discussed earlier, is determined by four integers: The Left, Top coordinates and the Right, Bottom coordinates of the rectangle. Actually, a rectangle also uniquely determines an oval, namely the oval that is tangent to the midpoints of the

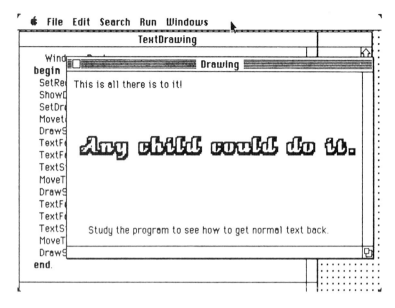

Figure 12.7

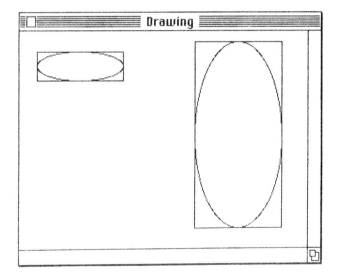

Figure 12.8

rectangle. For example, the rectangles of figure 12.8 determine the indicated ovals. Also note that if the rectangle is a square, then the oval is a circle. Since they are so similar we describe the routines for manipulating rectangles and ovals together.

The FrameRect and FrameOval procedures

Format: FrameRect(Box) or FrameOval(Oval) where Box and Oval are values of type Rect.

Effect: FrameRect and FrameOval draw the rectangle or oval determined by the argument. As always, the coordinates are interpreted to be in the local coordinates of the Drawing window.

The EraseRect and EraseOval procedures

Format: EraseRect(Box) or EraseOval(Oval) where Box and Oval are values of type Rect.

Effect: EraseRect and EraseOval erase the rectangle or oval determined by the argument.

The PaintRect and PaintOval procedures

Format: PaintRect(Box) or PaintOval(Oval) where Box and Oval are values of type Rect.

Effect: PaintRect and PaintOval draw, and then fill in, the rectangle or oval determined by the argument.

The sample program ModernArt illustrates the use of these procedures. ModernArt calls the random number function and then draws three rectangles and three ovals of random size at random positions on the screen. The program is shown in listing 12.8. One of the executions of ModernArt, showing great balance, bold imagination, and deep suffering, is shown in figure 12.9. Another illustration of these notions is shown in listing 12.9. The program given there, AnimatedBox, moves a box across the screen by repeatedly painting and erasing rectangles. Notice that SetRect is in the loop and that the size of the box is constantly growing. Since AnimatedBox involves animation, you have to run it for yourself.

Reading the Mouse

While not actually included in Macintosh's QuickDraw routines, we present two built-ins that can be used in conjunction with the graphics routines to produce some interesting results. These two routines "read" and report on the state of the mouse.

The **Button** function
Format: Button. (No Parameters)
Result: Button is a Boolean function that returns True only if the button on the mouse is currently being pressed.

The **GetMouse** procedure
Format: GetMouse(X,Y) where X and Y are Integer variables.
Result: GetMouse sets X and Y to the current coordinates of the mouse. X is, of course, the horizontal coordinate and Y is the vertical coordinate of the mouse's current location.

```
program ModernArt;
{This program uses Random to draw three rectangles and ovals.}

var
  Size, Box, Oval : Rect;
  Loop, Width, Length, Top, Left : Integer;

procedure SetSizes (var Width, Length, Top, Left : Integer);
begin
  Width := Random mod 150;
  Length := Random mod 200;
  Top := Random mod 200;
  Left := Random mod 300
end; {Definition of procedure SetSizes}

begin
  SetRect(Size, 0, 20, 527, 357);
  SetDrawingRect(Size);
  ShowDrawing;
  for Loop := 1 to 3 do
    begin
      SetSizes(Width, Length, Top, Left);
      SetRect(Box, Left, Top, Left + Length, Top + Width);
      FrameRect(Box);
      SetSizes(Width, Length, Top, Left);
      SetRect(Oval, Left, Top, Left + Length, Top + Width);
      FrameOval(Oval);
    end {For}
end.
```

Listing 12.8

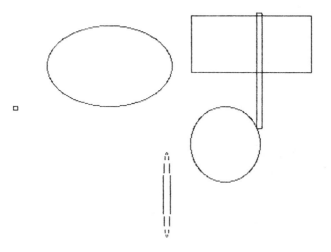

Figure 12.9

program AnimatedBox;
(This program moves a box across the screen.)

    var
      Box : Rect;
      Top, Left, Size : Integer;

begin
    SetRect(Box, 0, 20, 527, 357);
    SetDrawingRect(Box);
    ShowDrawing;
    Top := 0;
    Left := 0;
    for Size := 20 **to** 80 **do**
     begin
      SetRect(Box, Left, Top, Left + Size, Top + Size);
      PaintRect(Box);
      EraseRect(Box);
      Top := Top + 5;
      Left := Left + 5
     end
    end.

Listing 12.9

The program Sketch of listing 12.10 illustrates the use of Button and GetMouse, along with some of the graphics routines, to turn the Macintosh into a sketch pad.

```
program Sketch;
{This program uses the mouse to turn the Mac into a sketch pad.}

  var
    Size : Rect;
    X, Y : Integer;

  begin
    SetRect(Size, 0, 20, 527, 357);
    SetDrawingRect(Size);
    ShowDrawing;
    MoveTo(10, 20);
    DrawString('Stop');
    SetRect(Size, 0, 0, 50, 30);
    FrameRect(Size);
    Moveto(30, 320);
    DrawString('Hold button to draw.  Click in Stop box to stop.');
    repeat
      while not Button do {Wait for mouse click.}
        ; {Do Nothing}
      GetMouse(X, Y);
      MoveTo(X, Y);
      while Button do  {Draw until button released.}
        begin
          GetMouse(X, Y);
          LineTo(X, Y)
        end;
      GetMouse(X, Y)
    until (X < 50) and (Y < 30)
  end.
```

Listing 12.10

We want to draw whenever the mouse button is held down and not draw otherwise. Hence, we use two **while** statements inside a big **repeat until**. The first **while** does nothing until the button on the mouse is depressed. When the button is depressed, then the flow of control exits from the **while**. Hence, all the first **while** does is wait for the button to be pressed. The second **while** loops while the button is held down, uses GetMouse to find the mouse, and uses LineTo to draw a line to the mouse's current location. These two **while** statements then repeat unless the mouse is in the little stop box drawn at the top of the screen. The authors' artistic ability is demonstrated using program Sketch in figure 12.10

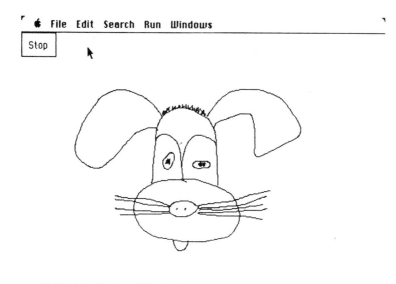

     Hold button to draw. Click in Stop box to stop.

Figure 12.10

Generating Sound

To go along with its dazzling graphics package, the Macintosh also has an extensive sound capability. There are three different sound synthesizers that we can use. These are:

1. The four-tone synthesizer, for making harmonic tones with up to "four voices" simultaneously.
2. The free-form synthesizer, for creating speech and complex music.
3. The single, square-wave synthesizer for producing simple tones.

All three synthesizers are accessed through built-in procedures. The first two synthesizers are quite complex to use and so we will not discuss them

In this book, but instead refer the reader to the **Macintosh Pascal Reference Manual**. However, we do mention that the concepts needed to work with these procedures are covered in this book (although the pointer type is not discussed until the last chapter) and so the reader who is willing to fight through the manual should be able to use the fancier synthesizers. We limit our discussion to the square-wave synthesizer.

To access the Macintosh's square wave synthesizer, all we need to do is invoke the built-in procedure Note to produce a single tone. A call to Note is of the following format:

Note(Frequency, Amplitude, Duration)

where Frequency is of type Integer (although the manual says Longint), and Amplitude and Duration are values in the subrange 0..255 of Integer. The value of Frequency determines the pitch of the tone, Amplitude controls the volume, and Duration controls the length of the tone. The smaller the value of Amplitude, the lower the volume is. Duration is measured in 60ths of a second. Table 12.1 shows some approximate frequencies to use to generate the various notes of a piano keyboard. We point out that the table can be easily extended to higher (lower) frequencies by multiplying (dividing) the last (first) table entry by 1.05946.

First Octave		Second Octave	
Note	Frequency	Note	Frequency
C	131	(Middle) C	262
C*	139	C*	277
D	147	D	294
D*	156	D*	311
E	165	E	330
F	175	F	349
F*	185	F*	370
G	196	G	392
G*	208	G*	415
A	220	A	440
A*	233	A*	466
B	247	B	494
		C	523

Table 12.1

The simplest way to use the table is to create a text file containing the frequencies of the notes we want to play. Then whenever we want to play some music, we can read the frequencies into an array in memory and access them directly. The text file Notes on the sample disk contains the frequencies that are listed in the table. The simple program Mary in listing 12.11 plays a primitive version of "Mary Had a Little Lamb." The program works by reading from a text file Numbers the sequence of notes that we want to play. That is, a 3 in Lamb means that we want to play the third note listed in table 12.1.

```
program Mary;
{This program plays "Mary Had A Little Lamb" by reading the   }
{26 numbers from the text file 'Lamb' that represent the       }
{frequencies of the notes for the song. The frequencies them- }
{selves are read from the text file Notes.                     }

  var
    Notes, Lamb : Text;
    Key : array[1..26] of Integer;
    Freq : array[1..25] of Integer;
    I : Integer;

begin
  Reset(Lamb, 'Lamb');
  Reset(Notes, 'Notes');
  for I := 1 to 25 do
    Read(Notes, Freq[I]);
  for I := 1 to 26 do
    Read(Lamb, Key[I]);

  for I := 1 to 26 do
    Note(Freq[Key[I]], 7, 30);   {This loop actually "plays" the song}
  { via the call to the built-in procedure Note. The 7 controls the}
  {volume and the 30 controls the duration.                        }

  Close(Lamb);
  Close(Notes)
end.
```

Listing 12.11

We counted the notes that we need to play the song--that is why there is a loop from 1 to 26. This is, of course, not very general and we will improve on our "playing ability" as we progress through this section of the chapter. Our rendition of "Mary" is not very good because all notes are played with the same duration. A simple-minded way of fixing this is to realize which notes need to be held longer (in "Mary" we should hold the 7th, 10th, and 13th notes twice as long as all the others) and then "fudge" the for loop by breaking it up into several smaller for loops. So we could change the body of the program of listing 12.11 to have the following structure:

```
for Tone := 1 to 6 do ....(Play first 6 notes)
(Play 7th note)
for Tone := 8 to 9 do....(Play notes 8 and 9)
(Play 10th note)
for Tone := 11 to 12 do....(Play notes 11 and 12)
(Play 13th note)
for Tone := 14 to 26 do...(Play the rest of the notes)
```

Again, this "band-aid" is far too clumsy to use in any sort of complex song so we develop a better way to play songs.

To hear how nice our general method sounds, run the program Composer and load and play the song Solf from the sample disk with this book.   This song, Solfeggietto, is a nice example for the square wave synthesizer because it is one of the few classical pieces that is played almost entirely with single notes. We will explain later how the program Composer was written.

Now we develop our song-playing capability. As a special bonus, we add a song-writing capability that allows us to compose our own works or allows us to "copy" songs from a piece of music. Thus, very little musical ability is required to "write" songs.

To get us in the proper mood, we use the graphics package to create our own piano keyboard. If you do not like our keyboard (for example, because it doesn't show enough keys), we urge you to make your own. Look ahead to figure 12.11 to see our keyboard. A few comments should prepare you for the program Piano of listing 12.12. The white keys are drawn with some vertical lines. To draw the black keys, we use a procedure that draws a black rectangle and nested loops (to get 2 black keys, then 3 black keys) to get them in the correct positions.

Now that we have our new piano, let's play it. How? With the mouse! We let the position of the mouse determine which key we want to press.

First, we read the frequencies corresponding to the white keys into an array White and the frequencies of the black keys into an array Black. Then, when we place our mouse on the fourth white key, for example, we call the Note procedure with a frequency of White[4]. We make two simplifying assumptions. Since the mouse position determines the notes that are played, we require the mouse to be on the lower part of the screen to play the white keys. That is, we can't play the white keys while up in the "black" area (even though we may actually be on a white key). This allows us to divide the screen essentially in half, so that the Y-coordinate of the mouse position can tell us immediately which *color* of key we are pressing. The X-coordinate determines *which* key. With the white keys, this is easy, since we can divide the screen (from left-to-right) into 15 equal pieces. We would like to do the same thing for the black keys. That is, since there are 10 black keys, if the mouse is in the third tenth from the left end of the screen, we would like to play the third black key. However, because of the lack of perfect symmetry among the black keys, such a simple-minded solution won't quite work. It will, however, if we insert three *invisible* black keys. These keys won't play any tones, but they cause the black keys to be uniformly distributed over the keyboard. The text file Scale contains the frequencies of the keyboard, much like the file Notes, except that the information in Scale is arranged in the order:

   15 white frequencies

   2 black frequencies
   very high frequency

   3 black frequencies
   very high frequency

   2 black frequencies
   very high frequency

   3 black frequencies

The very high frequencies are undetectable by human ears, so if we try to play one of our invisible black keys, we hear an "invisible" note. The program in listing 12.12 reads the frequency information from Scale, determines the key to be played based on the position of the mouse, and then actually calls the Note procedure when the mouse button is pressed.

```
program Piano;

const
  Amp = 7;
  Dur = 32;
  Width = 32;
  Depth = 180;

type
  List = array[1..15] of Integer;

var
  White, Black : List;
  X, Y, Tone : Integer;

procedure Instructions;
  var
    TextWindow : Rect;
begin
  SetRect(TextWindow, 16, 20, 500, 120);
  SetTextRect(TextWindow);
  ShowText;
  Writeln('Point mouse at key and press button.');
  Writeln('To play a white key, point at the lower half of the key.');
  Writeln;
  Writeln('Use HALT from the PAUSE menu to halt this program.')
end; {Definition of procedure Instructions}

procedure InitScreen;
  var
    R : Rect;
begin
  SetRect(R, 16, 20, 496, 320);
  SetDrawingRect(R);
  ShowDrawing
end; {Definition of procedure InitScreen}
```

(Continued)

```
procedure DrawWhiteKeys;
 var
   Key : Integer;
begin
 MoveTo(0, 125);
 for Key := 1 to 14 do
   begin
     Move(Width, 0);
     Line(0, Depth);
     Move(0, -Depth)
   end;
 LineTo(0, 125)
end;  (Definition of procedure DrawWhiteKeys)

procedure BlackKey (var Key : Integer);
 var
   Black : Rect;
   Lap : Integer;
begin
 Lap := Width div 4;
 Key := Key + 1;
 SetRect(Black, Key * Width - Lap, 125, Key * Width + Lap, 220);
 PaintRect(Black)
end;  (Definition of procedure BlackKey)

procedure DrawBlackKeys;
 var
   Key, Group, Pair, Triple : Integer;
begin
 Key := 0;
 for Group := 1 to 2 do
   begin
     for Pair := 1 to 2 do
       BlackKey(Key);
     Key := Key + 1;
     for Triple := 1 to 3 do
       BlackKey(Key);
     Key := Key + 1
   end
end;(Definition of procedure DrawBlackKeys)
```

(Continued)

```
procedure ReadTones;
 var
  Scale : Text;
  Index : Integer;
begin
 Reset(Scale, 'Scale');
 for Index := 1 to 15 do
  Read(Scale, White[Index]);
 for Index := 1 to 13 do
  Read(Scale, Black[Index]);
 Close(Scale)
end; {Definition of procedure ReadTones}

procedure PlayNote;
 var
  X, Y : Integer;
begin
 GetMouse(X, Y);  {Read Mouse}
 if Y > 220 then
  begin
   X := X div Width + 1;
   if X < 1 then
    X := 1;
   if X > 15 then
    X := 15;
   Note(White[X], Amp, Dur)
  end
 else
  begin
   X := (X + 8) div Width;
   if X < 1 then
    X := 1;
   if X > 13 then
    X := 13;
   Note(Black[X], Amp, Dur)
  end {IF}
end; {Definition of procedure PlayNote}
```

(Continued)

```
begin
  InitScreen;
  Instructions;
  ReadTones;
  DrawWhiteKeys;
  DrawBlackKeys;
  repeat
    while not Button do  (Wait for button.)
      ; (Nothing)
    GetMouse(X, Y);
    if Y > 125 then
      PlayNote
  until False
end.
```

Listing 12.12

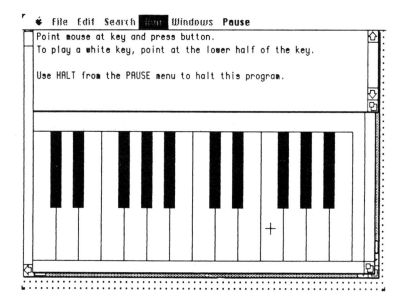

Figure 12.11

Now we add to our capabilities. Pointing to keys with the mouse and clicking the notes that we want to play might be amusing for a while, but is much too clumsy for playing anything other than short, slow songs. So let us use the mouse to indicate what sequence of notes we want to play, but instead of just playing them when we click the mouse, let us store the sequence of notes to a file on disk (with the name of the song!). When we have finished specifying the sequence of notes, we can "play the song" often and effortlessly by reading the file. So we modify the Piano program to obtain Composer. Composer gives us a menu of four options. We can play the keyboard as in Piano, and then select "Play" to hear our efforts played back to us. We may select "Save" to cause Composer to write our notes to a text file. The program asks us for the name of the song before creating a file. This is how Solf was written. "Load" requests the name of a previously stored song and places it into memory so that we can "Play" it. Finally, "Clear" erases the current song from memory so that we can start over. In addition to writing the frequencies of the notes to a file, Composer also allows us to specify a duration by clicking any of the notes drawn above the keyboard. The duration of each note pictured is half that of the note to its right. Thus, to write a song (or copy one from a piece of music), click a key and then click a note. The visible execution of Composer is shown in Figure 12.12

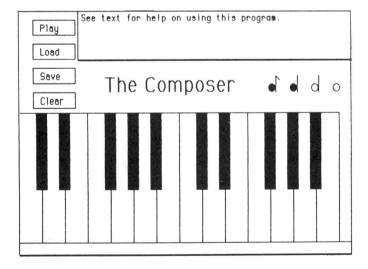

Figure 12.12

Because of the length of the program Composer, we will present it in pieces. Some of these pieces receive only short explanatory comments because of their similarity to the corresponding portions of Piano.

```pascal
program Composer;

   const
     Amp = 7;
     Eighth = 16;
     Fourth = 32;
     Half = 64;
     Whole = 128;
     Width = 32;
     Depth = 180;

   type
   List = array[1..15] of Integer;
   Music = array[1..200] of Integer;

   var
     White, Black : List;
     X, Y, Dur, NumNotes, Tone : Integer;
     Notes, Duration : Music;
     Song : string[20];
     F : Text;

   procedure InitScreen;
    var
      R : Rect;
   begin
     SetRect(R, 16, 20, 496, 320);
     SetDrawingRect(R);
     ShowDrawing;
     SetRect(R, 100, 20, 496, 80);
     SetTextRect(R);
     ShowText;
     Writeln('See text for help on using this program.')
   end;
```

(Continued)

```
procedure ReadTones;
 var
   Scale : Text;
   Index : Integer;
begin
 Reset(Scale, 'Scale');
 for Index := 1 to 15 do
   Read(Scale, White[Index]);
 for Index := 1 to 13 do
   Read(Scale, Black[Index]);
 Close(Scale)
end;

procedure PlayNote (var Tone : Integer);
 var
   X, Y : Integer;
begin
 GetMouse(X, Y);  {Read Mouse}
 if Y > 220 then
   begin
     X := X div Width + 1;
     if X < 1 then
      X := 1;
     if X > 15 then
      X := 15;
     Tone := White[X];
     Note(Tone, Amp, Dur);
   end
 else
   begin
     X := (X + 8) div Width;
     if X < 1 then
      X := 1;
     if X > 13 then
      X := 13;
     Tone := Black[X];
     Note(Tone, Amp, Dur)
   end  {IF}
end;
```

Listing 12.13

Listing 12.13 contains the declaration section of Composer and the procedures to set up the drawing screen, read the tones from the text file Scale, and actually play the notes using the Note procedure. These procedures are like the ones in Piano. Note that InitScreen also writes the "help message" to the text window.

The procedure DrawScreen of listing 12.14 contains the procedures for drawing the keyboard and the rest of the screen. DrawWhiteKeys, BlackKey, and DrawBlackKeys are as in Piano. DrawNotes draws the four notes above the keyboard, DrawChoices draws the menu boxes, and DrawName places "The Composer" above the keyboard.

```
procedure DrawScreen;
 procedure DrawWhiteKeys;
  var
    Key : Integer;
 begin
  MoveTo(0, 125);
  for Key := 1 to 14 do
   begin
    Move(Width, 0);
    Line(0, Depth);
    Move(0, -Depth)
   end;
  LineTo(1, 125)
 end;

 procedure BlackKey (var Key : Integer);
  var
    Black : Rect;
    Lap : Integer;
 begin
  Lap := Width div 4;
  Key := Key + 1;
  SetRect(Black, Key * Width - Lap, 125, Key * Width + Lap, 220);
  PaintRect(Black)
 end;
```

(Continued)

```
procedure DrawBlackKeys;
 var
   Key, Group, Pair, Triple : Integer;
begin
 Key := 0;
 for Group := 1 to 2 do
   begin
     for Pair := 1 to 2 do
       BlackKey(Key);
     Key := Key + 1;
     for Triple := 1 to 3 do
       BlackKey(Key);
     Key := Key + 1
   end
end;

procedure DrawNotes;
 var
   Note : Rect;
begin
 SetRect(Note, 350, 90, 360, 100);
 PaintOval(Note);
 MoveTo(360, 100);
 LineTo(360, 80);
 LineTo(365, 85);
 SetRect(Note, 380, 90, 390, 100);
 PaintOval(Note);
 MoveTo(390, 100);
 LineTo(390, 80);
 SetRect(Note, 410, 90, 420, 100);
 FrameOval(Note);
 MoveTo(420, 100);
 LineTo(420, 80);
 SetRect(Note, 440, 90, 450, 100);
 FrameOval(Note);
end;
```

(Continued)

```
procedure DrawChoices;
 var
  Box : Rect;
begin
 MoveTo(30, 25);
 DrawString('Play');
 SetRect(Box, 20, 10, 80, 30);
 FrameRect(Box);
 MoveTo(30, 55);
 DrawString('Load');
 SetRect(Box, 20, 40, 80, 60);
 FrameRect(Box);
 MoveTo(30, 85);
 DrawString('Save');
 SetRect(Box, 20, 70, 80, 90);
 FrameRect(Box);
 MoveTo(30, 115);
 DrawString('Clear');
 SetRect(Box, 20, 100, 80, 120);
 FrameRect(Box)
end;
procedure DrawName;
begin
 MoveTo(120, 100);
 TextFace([bold]);
 TextSize(24);
 DrawString('The Composer');
 TextFace([]);
 TextSize(12)
end;

begin {Body of DrawScreen}
 DrawName;
 DrawWhiteKeys;
 DrawBlackKeys;
 DrawNotes;
 DrawChoices
end;
```

Listing 12.14

The procedure Play is shown in listing 12.15. Play simply calls the built-in procedure Note. The frequency is determined by the key that was chosen with the mouse, while the duration is determined by which of the four notes drawn above the keyboard was chosen for that note.

```
procedure Play;
 var
   Index : Integer;
 begin
   for Index := 1 to NumNotes do
     Note(Notes[Index], Amp, Duration[Index])
 end;
```

Listing 12.15

The remaining procedures of Composer are given in listing 12.16. These procedures handle Composer's remaining menu options. Save writes information to a text file. The user is requested to enter a name of a song from the keyboard. This name is stored in the string variable Song, which is used in the Rewrite statement of Save.

Load reads information from a text file. As with Save, Load also asks for the name of a previously saved song. This name is, of course, used in the Reset statement.

DecideAction determines the position of the mouse on the screen and calls the appropriate menu procedure. Note that there is no Clear procedure. We simply set NumNotes equal to 0 in DecideAction if the mouse is clicked in the Clear box. The last **if...then** statement of Decide-Action also determines the duration of the note, again by monitoring the mouse position.

Finally, the main program is given in listing 12.17. Notice how simple it is. All the work is accomplished in the procedures. Because of this modularity, Composer is very easy to modify. We simply change the procedures that need changing and leave the rest of the program alone.

We make some final remarks about Composer. Because of memory limitations with a 128K Macintosh, Composer can only handle songs of 200 notes or less. In fact, after running Composer several times, you may receive an "insufficient memory" error. In this case, turn off your Macintosh and start all over. Finally, because of the memory limitations, our Composer program is as compact as we could make it. This explains the lack of comments within the routines themselves.

```pascal
procedure Save;
 var
  Index : Integer;
begin
 Writeln('Enter name of song (RETURN):');
 Readln(Song);
 Rewrite(F, Song);
 for Index := 1 to NumNotes do
  begin
   Write(F, Notes[Index]);
   Write(F, Duration[Index])
  end;
 Write(F, 0);
 Close(F)
end;
procedure Load;
 var
  Freq : Integer;
begin
 Writeln('Enter name of song (RETURN):');
 Readln(Song);
 Reset(F, Song);
 NumNotes := 0;
 Read(F, Freq);
 while Freq <> 0 do
  begin
   NumNotes := NumNotes + 1;
   Notes[NumNotes] := Freq;
   Read(F, Duration[NumNotes]);
   Read(F, Freq)
  end;
 Close(F)
end;

procedure DecideAction;
begin
 if Y > 125 then
  begin
   PlayNote(Tone);
```

(Continued)

```
            if NumNotes < 100 then
              begin
                NumNotes := NumNotes + 1;
                Notes[Numnotes] := Tone;
                Duration[NumNotes] := Dur
              end
          end
        else
          begin
            if (X >= 20) and (X <= 80) then
              begin
                y := y div 10;
                case Y of
                  1, 2 :
                    Play;
                  4, 5 :
                    Load;
                  7, 8 :
                    Save;
                  10, 11 :
                    NumNotes := 0;
                  otherwise (Nothing)
                end
              end;
            if (Y >= 90) and (Y <= 100) then
              begin
                X := X div 10;
                case X of
                  35 :
                    Dur := Eighth;
                  38 :
                    Dur := Fourth;
                  41 :
                    Dur := Half;
                  44 :
                    Dur := Whole;
                  otherwise (Nothing)
                end
              end
          end
    end;                    Listing 12.16
```

```
begin
  InitScreen;
  ReadTones;
  DrawScreen;
  Dur := Fourth;
  NumNotes := 0;
  repeat
    while not Button do {Wait for button.}
      ; {Nothing}
    GetMouse(X, Y);
    DecideAction
  until false
end.
```

Listing 12.17

We hope that this chapter has been an enjoyable one. The graphics on the Macintosh are striking and simple, and the sound capability is remarkable. Those readers who don't quite appreciate these capabilities should run one of the better commercially sold "arcade" games for the Macintosh or "listen" to the Macintosh recite the Gettysburg Address. We also hope the reader appreciates the power of *programming* the Macintosh. Although the graphics are stunning, if what you really wanted was a "turtle graphics" package to teach programming to small children, you essentially have three alternatives: Do without; buy another computer or a commercially produced turtle graphics package for the Macintosh (at a high cost, if one even exists); or program your own package, as we have outlined in this chapter. With a little bit of programming skill and a lot of creativity, you will be surprised at the remarkable things you can do. We suggest some projects for you to try in the exercises.

Exercises

12.1 Modify the simulation of exercise 7.9 so that we can see the man's progress from the bar to home or jail. Denote the man by a moving circle, and label the bar, home, and jail.

12.2 Write a program to simulate a typsy turtle that moves in random directions for random lengths (10-50 units).

12.3 Write a program that draws a gallows and a person at the gallows. Draw the person in six distinct procedures (head, body, 2 arms, 2 legs) so that in Chapter 14 we can make a Hangman game.

12.4 Write a program to allow two players to play Tic Tac Toe on the Macintosh. Just by clicking the mouse in the appropriate cell, an X or an O should appear.

12.5 Write a game of Pong with 3 walls (top and sides) and a moving paddle on the bottom of the screen. See figure 12.13.

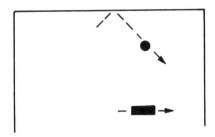

Figure 12.13

12.6 Write a program to simulate 600 rolls of two dice and display the results as a bar graph.

12.7 Dr. Noble Price of M.I.T. (Mouse Institute of Technology) has spent a lifetime studying the behavior of animals in mazes. His research indicates that mice are affected by the aroma of the cheese at the end of the maze.

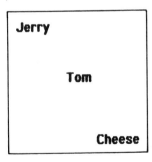

Figure 12.14

In fact, the mouse, Jerry, of figure 12.14 rolls a die and moves right if he obtains a 1 or 2 on the die. He moves down if he obtains a 3 or a 4, while a 5 causes him to move left and a 6 makes him move up. Thus, Jerry is biased toward the cheese and should move, in a staggering fashion, from the upper left to the cheese in the lower right portion of the diagram. Tom, the cat, is basically lazy and also hates cheese. Thus, Tom moves as Jerry except that Tom stays put if he rolls a 2 or a 4. Thus, Tom's behavior is to wander about his starting position, the center of the grid. Neither animal leaves the grid. If a move would take an animal off the grid, then the move is disallowed and the animal rolls the die again. Thus, for example, Jerry's first move must be either to the right or down. If he rolls a 5 or a 6, then he rolls again until he obtains a legal move.

Write a program to simulate and graphically display the animals on a 19-by-19 grid. Jerry starts in cell (1,1), Tom in (10,10), and the cheese in (19,19). Run the simulation until a winner is declared. Of course, Tom wins if he and Jerry ever occupy the same cell, while Jerry wins if he reaches the cheese without meeting Tom. Use an open oval to denote Jerry and a painted oval to denote Tom. Write a "C" in cell (19,19) to denote the cheese.

12.8 Add graphics to the Russian Roulette problem of exercise 7.7. In particular, show the gun, the CLICK or BANG, the bullet if any, and the happy or dead player.

12.9 Draw a helicopter that is controlled by moving the mouse. If you redraw the chopper at the new mouse coordinates, the chopper will jump all over the screen. Rather than that, use the current position of the mouse to determine how quickly the chopper moves. That is, determine the new location of the chopper with the statements

```
X := X + dX;
Y := Y + dY;
```

where the size and sign of dX and dY are determined by the mouse's position on the screen. For example, if the mouse is in the center of the screen, then dX and dY are zero. If the mouse is in the upper right corner, then dX and dY are +10, and so on. Draw a landing pad at the bottom of the screen. Can you land without crashing? (You crash if you miss the landing pad or if either dX or dY is larger than 3.)

Chapter 13

Sets

The final structured type available in Pascal is the **set** type. While nearly all modern structured languages have arrays and records, very few of them have a set capability. This is unfortunate because sets are easy to use and easy to understand.

The word "set" has many different meanings. In fact, the dictionary listing for "set" is typically one of the longest. In Pascal, a set is just a collection of objects. However, it is necessary in a programming language to place some restrictions on sets. That is, sets in Pascal are not quite as general as sets in mathematics. The major restrictions are:

1. The elements of a set must all be of the same ordinal type. This means that sets cannot contain real numbers, records, or arrays, nor can a set contain both integers and characters.

2. Sets must be finite. This makes sense because the computer is a finite machine. In fact, each Pascal implementation imposes an upper limit on the size of any set. Many implementations impose a fairly severe size limitation of 64, 128, or 256 elements in a set. The documentation for Version 1.0 of Macintosh Pascal is not completely clear as to the set size limitation. However, we have executed programs using sets with as many as 10,000 elements. Of course, too many large sets will cause

memory problems. We suggest defining subranges, particularly for sets of integers, and then using these subranges in set declarations. Specifically, do *not* use "Integer" as the type of a set element. Examples of set declarations are given after a discussion of the operations on sets.

Sets in Pascal are enclosed in square brackets. Although this is the same notation for array subscripts, we can always tell from the context of a statement what the square brackets mean. There are three basic operations performed on sets. These operations are binary operations because they take two sets as input and produce a third set as output. These operations are:

Union (denoted in Pascal by "+"): The union of two sets A and B consists of all the elements that belong to either A or B. With sets, we are only concerned with whether an element belongs to a set or not. There is no concept of belonging to a set "twice." So if an element belongs to both A and B, it appears in the union of A and B once. Thus, if A = [1,2,3] and B = [2,3,4], then A + B = [1,2,3,4].

Intersection (denoted in Pascal by "*"): The intersection of two sets A and B consists of the elements that belong to both A and B. So if A = [1,2,3] and B = [2,3,4], then A * B = [2,3]. Note that there is the possibility that two sets have no elements in common. For example, let C = [1,2] and D = [3,4]. Since the intersection of two sets results in a set, what set is C * D? This is the set that contains no elements, called the **empty set**. In Pascal, the empty set is denoted by "[ ]". So, C * D = [ ].

Difference (denoted in Pascal by "-"): The difference of two sets, written A - B, is the set that contains the elements of A that do not belong to B. In other words, to form A - B, simply remove from A any elements that also belong to B. So if A = [1,2,3,4,5] and B = [3,4,5,6,7], then A - B = [1,2].

In addition to the three binary operations on sets, Pascal also provides for some Boolean tests on sets. The first of these is the equality test between sets. That is, one may test whether two sets are equal or not. Two sets are equal if they contain exactly the same elements. We mention here that sets are "unordered" structures. That is, the order in which the elements of a set are listed is irrelevant. So, [1,2,3] = [3,1,2]. Additionally, there are two other Boolean tests that apply to sets. These are:

Subset (denoted in Pascal by "<="): This test involves two sets. A set A is a subset of a set B if every element of A is also an element of B. So if A = [1,2,3], B = [2,3,4], and C = [2,3,1,6], then "A <= B" is False while "A <= C" is True.

Membership (denoted in Pascal by "**in**"): This test involves an element and a set. The result of the test is True if the element belongs to the set, and False if the element is not a member of the set. For example, if A is a set of integers with current value [1,2,3] and if X and Y are integer variables with current values 2 and 5 respectively, then "X **in** A" is True, "Y **in** A" is False, and "(Y-X) **in** A" is True. This last example shows that the element in question does not have to be a variable, but can be any expression whose type is the same as the members of the set in question.

Remarks

There are two common sources of syntax errors among beginning Pascal programmers when working with sets. The first of these deals with confusion between the "**in**" and the "<=" relations. Remember that <= stands between two sets while **in** stands between an element and a set.

The second difficulty is in testing if an element X is *not* a member of a set A. Many beginners write an *incorrect* test like this:

if X **not in** A **then** ...

This is, of course, wrong because **not** is an operator that takes a single Boolean input (a value that is either True or False) and reverses it. In the above formulation, an attempt is made to apply the **not** operation to "**in** A", which is certainly not a Boolean value (since it isn't even a complete expression). What is needed is the membership test applied first, giving a True or False value, and then the **not** applied to this. But there is still a chance for error as many beginners then write a second *incorrect* version:

if not X **in** A **then** ...

The reason that this is still wrong is that the **not** operator has the highest precedence of all Pascal operators. This means that the **not** operator is always applied as soon as possible. So the system tries to perform "**not** X", which again is nonsense (unless X happens to be a Boolean type, which is usually not the case). So parentheses are necessary and the correct syntax is:

if not (X **in** A) **then**...

Set types/variables are defined/declared using the keywords **set** and **of**. We give several examples below, but first we point out that the subrange notation, ". .", introduced in Chapter 8 can also be used with sets. So the sets [1,4,5,6,7,9,10] and [1,4..7,9,10] are the same sets.

type
  Digits = **set of** '0'..'9';
  Uppercase = **set of** 'A'..'Z';
  Colors = (Red, Violet, Blue, Green, Yellow, Orange);

var
  Nums : Digits;
  Numbers : **set of** 0..9;
  Small : **set of** 1..5;
  Rainbow : **set of** Colors;
  Letters : Uppercase;

Some remarks are in order. We point out that Nums and Numbers are two sets with different types of objects. The elements of Nums are characters while the elements of Numbers are integers. It is important to realize that the variable declaration for Small is like any other variable declaration in its effect, that of simply naming a variable and telling what its type is. Small is *not* a set containing the integers from 1 to 5, as many beginners seem to think it is. Small is a set that is *permitted* to contain only the integers from 1 to 5, but the variable declaration does not assign any value to Small. This must be done with an assignment statement. So if the first statement in the body of the program were

  Small := [1,3,5];

then Small would in fact contain the odd integers from 1 to 5.

We mention again the difference between defining type names and then declaring variables using the type names (as is done with Letters above) and declaring variables anonymously, i.e., without using a type name (as is done with Numbers). The difference is that anonymous variables may not be used as the inputs to procedures and functions since arguments and parameters must have type names. So if we wanted Numbers to be the input to some function, we would need to define a type name, like

type
    Values = **set of** 0..9;

and then declare

var
    Numbers : Values;

Sets as Filters

A very common problem in programming is examining data to make sure it is of the proper form. An example from Chapter 8 involved reading in exam scores from the keyboard and computing a gradepoint average. Since typing errors are very likely, a thorough program needs to test each input to make sure it is a legal one, i.e., one of the characters 'A', 'B', 'C', 'D', or 'F'. In most languages, this test would be made as follows:

repeat
    Writeln('Enter the next exam score.');
    Readln(Score);
    if (Score < 'A') **or** (Score > 'F') **or** (Score = 'E') **then**
        Writeln('Illegal input. Try again.')
until (Score >= 'A') **and** (Score <= 'F') **and** (Score <> 'E');

However, in Pascal, such a "filtering out" of bad data is most naturally accomplished by using a set because all we are doing is making sure that the input belongs to a certain set of values. So with the variable declaration

var
    Valid_Grades : **set of** Char;

and the assignment statement

    Valid_Grades := ['A' .. 'D', 'F'];

the above loop can be written as

```
repeat
  Writeln('Enter the next Score.');
  Readln(Score);
  if not(Score in Valid_Grades) then
    Writeln('Illegal input. Try again.')
until Score in Valid_Grades;
```

As another example, suppose we wanted to read some text from a file and count the number of words. We assume that the text contains only letters, digits, blanks, and the following punctuation symbols: , ! . ? " ;

The program in listing 13.1 counts the words in the text file Typing. For simplicity we assume that the file begins with a word and ends with a single punctuation mark.

We now turn our attention to a different use of sets. In these next examples, sets are not used as filters, but are used as the natural data structure for solving the given problem. In each case, there is an alternate solution that does not employ sets--typically an array solution. However, it should be clear that the set solution is somehow "better." By this we mean that the set solution provides a clearer, less complicated algorithm for solving the problem than does the array solution. We repeat our earlier advice: "The sooner you start coding, the longer the job will take." In other words, the more time spent planning a solution, the better the solution will probably be. This does not mean just planning the algorithm, but also analyzing the best way to represent the data. Often, the proper choice of data structures can make a significant difference in the overall solution to a problem. This is an important lesson for programmers to learn. What we hope to illustrate with these examples is that using sets to solve these problems makes the programs much easier to write.

```
program WordCounter;
{This program counts the number of words in the text file Typing.}

var
  AlphaNumeric : set of Char;
  Separators : set of Char;
  Ch : Char;
  ScanningWord : Boolean;
  Count : Integer;
  Wordfile : Text;
```

(Continued)

```
begin
  Reset(Wordfile, 'Typing');
  AlphaNumeric := ['A'..'Z', 'a'..'z', '0'..'9'];
  Separators := [' ', '.', ',', '?', '!', ';'];
  Count := 1;
  ScanningWord := True;
  while not EOF(Wordfile) do
   begin
     Read(Wordfile, Ch);
     Write(Ch);
     if (Ch in Separators) and ScanningWord then
       ScanningWord := False;
     if (Ch in AlphaNumeric) and not ScanningWord then
       begin
         ScanningWord := True;
         Count := Count + 1
       end
   end; {While}
  Writeln;
  Writeln;
  Writeln('There were ', Count : 3, ' words in the text file Words.')
end.
```

Listing 13.1

Examples

Soggies, the Breakfast of Programmers

Every box of Soggies breakfast cereal contains one of 10 different prizes. If the prizes are distributed at random, on the average how many boxes of cereal must you purchase to acquire all 10 different prizes? We solved this problem in Chapter 9 using arrays. Again, we generate a random integer between 1 and 10 to simulate winning one of the 10 prizes. We stop when we have won all 10 prizes. Using sets, we start with the empty set (the set of prizes won so far), each time we win a prize, we add the number of that prize to the set (using set union), and we quit purchasing boxes of cereal when the set equals [1..10]. Note that sets are a natural structure for this problem because of the nature of set union. If we win a prize for the second or third or subsequent time, it does not hurt anything to "add" that prize number to the set again. The solution to the problem, which simulates 20 different people purchasing boxes of Soggies until each has obtained all 10 prizes, is given in listing 13.2. Try to predict the average before running the program.

```
program SetSoggies;
{This program uses sets to solve the Soggies problem.}

  const
    Experiment = 20;
  type
    Numbers = 1..10;
  var
    Prizes : set of Numbers;
    Premium : Numbers;
    Count, Trials, Total : Integer;
    Average : Real;

begin
  Total := 0;
  for Trials := 1 to Experiment do
    begin
      Prizes := [];  {Initialize Prizes to the Empty set.}
      Count := 0;
      repeat
        Premium := Random mod 10 + 1;
        Prizes := Prizes + [Premium];
        Count := Count + 1
      until Prizes = [1..10];
      Writeln('It took ', Count : 2, ' boxes to get them all.');
      Total := Total + Count
    end;  {For}
  Average := Total / Experiment;
  Writeln;
  Writeln('The average was ', Average : 5 : 2, ' boxes to get all 10 prizes.')
end.
```

Listing 13.2

The above solution is quite straightforward but there are some important comments to make. The variable Premium takes on random values between 1 and 10 representing the prize won. It is this value that needs to be added to the set of Prizes. This is accomplished using set union. Recall that set union is an operation applied to two *sets*. Therefore, the brackets around Premium are absolutely necessary. If Premium is a Number, then [Premium] is a set consisting of one Number. Beginners often write the syntactically *incorrect* statement

Prizes := Prizes + Premium

which generates a type incompatibility error. Also note that the use of the empty set as the initial value of the set of prizes is similar to the use of 0 to initialize "running" sums and counters.

The next example is one of our favorites. It demonstrates very clearly the importance of using the appropriate data structure. It is also complex enough that a divide-and-conquer approach using procedures and functions is helpful in solving the overall problem. Finally, the finished product is an entertaining and challenging number game for one player to play against the computer.

The Game of Taxman

This is a one-player number game designed by Diane Resek. The player chooses how many numbers (positive integers) are in the game, from 1 up to some upper limit. During the course of the game, the player and the computer each accumulate a total. The object of the game is for the player to accumulate a larger total than the computer, hereafter referred to as the Taxman.

The player's total accumulates simply by selecting one of the numbers left in the game. The Taxman then gets all the numbers left in the game that divide evenly into the player's chosen number. Once numbers are used (either by the player or the Taxman), they are removed from the game.

There is one major restriction on the numbers that the player may select. As in real life, the Taxman must always get something, so the player can never select a number unless at least one proper divisor of that number remains in the game. Once no numbers with divisors remain (at the end of the game), the Taxman gets all the numbers left and the game is over.

For example, suppose the game is played with the numbers 1, 2, 3, 4, 5, and 6. If the greedy player chooses 6, then the Taxman gets all the divisors of 6, namely 1, 2, and 3. But now the only numbers left in the game are 4 and 5. Neither has a divisor left in the game, so the Taxman gets those also and wins 15 to 6. However, if the player is a bit smarter and chooses 5 first, the player gets 5 and the Taxman gets 1. Now the numbers remaining are 2, 3, 4, and 6, and the smart player chooses the 4 (before the 6), giving the Taxman 2. Finally, the player chooses 6 and wins 15 to 6. When played with more than 50 numbers, the game can be quite challenging. Beginners are often surprised at the treasures they give the Taxman after a seemingly innocent choice.

An array solution to the Game of Taxman is certainly possible and is usually required in a language without sets. However, with arrays, there is a bothersome detail in the algorithm, namely testing if the game should be terminated, i.e., discovering when there are no numbers with divisors left in the game. Array solutions typically use a component of 1 to denote that a number is still left in the game and a 0 to denote that a number has been removed from the game. How, then, is the End_of_Game condition noted? The array must be scanned looking for a number left in the game, and then the divisors of that number must be examined to see if any of them is left. If none remains, then another number remaining in the game must be located and a similar test applied to its divisors. This looping and testing can become quite tedious, and the algorithms often become unnecessarily complicated.

However, when one considers utilizing sets, some new ideas spring forth. Although these ideas can be implemented in the array solution, it is interesting that the ideas seem to come to programmers who are thinking about sets in the first place. The point to be made here is that it is important to be thinking about solving the problem in its most natural setting and not about how to manipulate arrays.

Suppose the game consists of the numbers from 1 to N. Then the only integers that can ever qualify as divisors are 1 to N **div** 2, and, in fact, each of these numbers will be the divisor of some number in the game. Place these numbers in a set at the beginning of the program, and each time anyone gets a number, remove that number from this pool of possible divisors. When this set is empty, the game is over.

Another detail handled nicely with sets is determining whether a choice made by the player is illegal because it has no divisors left in the game. The set of divisors of the chosen number can be formed, and if the intersection of this set with the numbers remaining in the game is empty, the choice is illegal.

Since this problem is more complex than the Soggies problem, we present an outline of its solution in pseudo-code. This solution provides another example of structured, top-down programming where a sequence of small procedures is used to divide and conquer the original problem.

Observe how closely the pseudo-code resembles the main program in the Pascal solution. Here is the pseudo-code:

Set up the original list of numbers.
Repeat
    Repeat
        Display the scores and the list of numbers.
        Obtain a choice from the player.
        Form the divisors of that choice.
        If no divisors remain, threaten the player with an audit.
    Until the player makes a legal choice.
    Update the scores.
Until the player has no legal choices.
Give the rest of the numbers to the Taxman.
Determine the winner.

```
program Taxman;
{This program plays the game of Taxman, a number game}
{ designed by Diane Resek. See text for the rules}

  type
    Number_Set = set of 1..100;
  var
    Limit, Choice : Integer;
    Player_Score, Taxman_Score : Integer;
    Divisor_Pool, Number_Pool, Divisors : Number_Set;

  procedure Set_Up;
  {This procedure initializes the scores and the pool of numbers.}
  begin
    Taxman_Score := 0;
    Player_Score := 0;
    repeat
      Writeln('How many numbers do you want to play with?');
      Writeln('The maximum number allowed is 100.');
      Readln(Limit)
    until (Limit > 1) and (Limit <= 100);
    Number_Pool := [1..Limit];
    Divisor_Pool := [1..Limit div 2]
  end; {Definition of procedure Set_Up.}
```

(Continued)

```pascal
procedure Display_Scores;
{This procedure shows the scores and the remaining numbers.}
  var
    Index : Integer;
  begin
    Writeln;
    Writeln('Your score: ', Player_Score : 4);
    Writeln('Taxman    : ', Taxman_Score : 4);
    Writeln;
    for Index := 1 to Limit do
      if Index in Number_Pool then
        Write(Index : 4);
    Writeln
  end; {Definition of procedure Display_Scores.}


procedure Obtain (var Choice : Integer);
{This procedure loops until the player makes a legal choice.}

  begin
    repeat
      Writeln;
      Write('What is your choice? ');
      Readln(Choice);
      if not (Choice in Number_Pool) then
        Writeln('Try that again and I will have you audited!');
    until Choice in Number_Pool
  end; {Definition of procedure Obtain.}


procedure Form_Divisors (Choice : Integer;
            var Divisors : Number_Set);
{This procedure builds the set of divisors of the player's number.}

  var
    Index : Integer;
  begin
    Divisors := [];
    for Index := 1 to Choice div 2 do
      if (Choice mod Index = 0) and (Index in Divisor_Pool) then
        Divisors := Divisors + [Index]  {Set union with singleton set}
  end; {Definition of procedure Form_Divisors.}
```

(Continued)

```
function Sum (Nums : Number_Set) : Integer;
{This function sums the elements of the set Nums.}

   var
     Index : Integer;
     Total : Integer;
   begin
    Total := 0;
    for Index := 1 to Limit do
     if Index in Nums then
       Total := Total + Index;
     Sum := Total
   end;  {Definition of function Sum.}


procedure Update_Scores (Choice : Integer;
            var Divisors : Number_Set);
{This procedure adds the choice to the player's score and all of}
{its divisors that remain in the game to the Taxman's score.}

   var
     Index : Integer;

   begin
     Player_Score := Player_Score + Choice;
     Taxman_Score := Taxman_Score + Sum(Divisors);

{Now, remove Choice and its Divisors from the game}
     Divisor_Pool := Divisor_Pool - [Choice];
     Number_Pool := Number_Pool - [Choice];
     Divisor_Pool := Divisor_Pool - [Divisors];
     Number_Pool := Number_Pool - [Divisors];
     Writeln;
     Write('The Taxman gets: ');
     for Index := 1 to Choice div 2 do
      if Index in Divisors then
        Write(Index : 4);
     Writeln
   end;  {Definition of procedure Update_Scores.}
```

(Continued)

```
procedure Determine_Winner;
(This procedure decides who won and prints the final score.)

begin
  Writeln;
  Writeln;
  if Taxman_Score > Player_Score then
    Writeln('The Taxman won -- as usual.')
  else if Player_Score > Taxman_Score then
    Writeln('You won -- expect an audit soon.')
  else
    Writeln('The game ended in a tie.')
  end; (Definition of procedure Determine_Winner.)

begin (Body of Main program Taxman.)
  Set_Up; (Initialize the list of numbers.)
  repeat
    repeat
      Display_Scores;
      Obtain(Choice);
      Form_Divisors(Choice, Divisors);
      if Divisors = [] then
        Writeln('Don''t try to cheat the Taxman!')
    until Divisors <> [];
    Update_Scores(Choice, Divisors)
  until Divisor_Pool = [];
  Writeln;
  Writeln('No factors remain, the Taxman takes all.');
  Taxman_Score := Taxman_Score + Sum(Number_Pool);
  Number_Pool := [];
  Display_Scores;
  Determine_Winner
end.
```

Listing 13.3

The Pascal solution is given in listing 13.3. It should be read "bottom-up." That is, the reader should first read the main program at the bottom of the listing to see the overall strategy of the solution. Then, as each procedure or function is invoked, the details of that particular procedure or function can be examined. Run the program and see if you can beat the Taxman with 50 numbers in the game.

The last example of the chapter points out that although the elements of a set must be of some simple, ordinal type, the components of other structured types can in fact be sets. For example, we can declare arrays of sets or records with set components. Such a scheme can be very useful, particularly in applications related to Graph Theory. Graph Theory is an area of discrete mathematics that is becoming increasingly important. A **graph** is simply a set of points with some pairs of the points joined by edges. Graphs are very useful in representing various kinds of data. Examples include communications networks, transportation networks, relationships between pairs of people in a psychological study, and relationships between resources and users of a multi-user computer system.

The Hierarchical Company

The example we wish to consider is the following: The employee records of the Hierarchical Company contain an employee identification number and the identification number of the employee's immediate supervisor. The president of the company has employee number 1 and, of course, no supervisor. We present a program that reads in each employee's number, except for the president, followed by the number of the immediate supervisor of that employee. The program then prints out a summary listing all the subordinates of each employee.

For example, suppose the graph in figure 13.1 represents the supervisor/subordinate relationships between the company's employees.

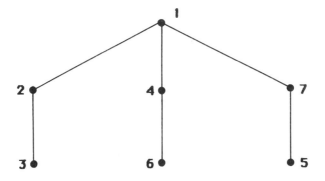

Figure 13.1

The input corresponding to the graph of figure 13.1 might be as follows:

```
5   7
7   1
2   1
6   4
3   2
4   1
```

The pertinent output in this case would be:

    The subordinates of Employee 1 are: 2 3 4 5 6 7
    The subordinates of Employee 2 are: 3
    The subordinates of Employee 3 are: None
    The subordinates of Employee 4 are: 6
    The subordinates of Employee 5 are: None
    The subordinates of Employee 6 are: None
    The subordinates of Employee 7 are: 5

Now suppose the relationships are given by the graph in figure 13.2.

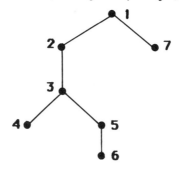

Figure 13.2

Then the input might look like this:

```
2   1
4   3
5   3
6   5
7   1
3   2
```

The pertinent output would be:

    The subordinates of Employee 1 are: 2 3 4 5 6 7
    The subordinates of Employee 2 are: 3 4 5 6
    The subordinates of Employee 3 are: 4 5 6
    The subordinates of Employee 4 are: None
    The subordinates of Employee 5 are: 6
    The subordinates of Employee 6 are: None
    The subordinates of Employee 7 are: None

To solve this problem, we use an array of sets. The array contains a component for each employee. Each of these components is a set that represents the subordinates of that employee. Whenever we read an employee's number, followed by the supervisor's number, we do the following:

1. Place the subordinate's number into the supervisor's set.
2. Add the subordinate's set into the supervisor's set.
3. Add the supervisor's set (since it has now possibly changed) into any set that contains the supervisor's number.

The solution shown in listing 13.4 obtains the structure of the company from the user at the keyboard, who enters Worker, Boss pairs for the graph in question. The user enters 0, 0 to terminate the input. Run the program and enter either of the graphs given in figures 13.1 and 13.2, or any other graph of your choosing. Note that the pairs may be entered in any order.

Summary

Although sets are rare among programming languages, they are an important part of the Pascal language. The filter example certainly makes a strong case for using sets to validate input. But not only are sets convenient to use, they are easy to understand. Beginning programmers tend to have more success (at least less trouble) understanding sets than understanding arrays or records. Sets also give the programmer more options for structuring data, and the more options available, the more natural the algorithm for solving a problem is likely to be. We invite those readers who are not convinced of this to write their own array version of Taxman and compare the readability of the array version with the set version.

```
program Hierarchy;
(This program lists the subordinates of each employee.)
 const
   Company_Size = 10;
 type
   Subordinates = set of 1..100;
 var
   Superiors : array[1..Company_Size] of Subordinates;
   Worker, Boss : Integer;
   Person, Individual : Integer;
begin
 for Person := 1 to Company_Size do
   Superiors[Person] := [];
 Writeln('For this program we assume a maximum of 10 employees');
 Writeln('numbered from 1 to 10.');
 Writeln('Please enter two numbers giving a worker and boss pair.');
 Readln(Worker, Boss);
 while Worker <> 0 do
   begin
     Superiors[Boss] := Superiors[Boss] + [Worker] + Superiors[Worker];
(Add the Worker and all of the Worker's subordinates to the Boss's set)
     for Person := 1 to Company_Size do
       if Boss in Superiors[Person] then
         Superiors[Person] := Superiors[Person] + Superiors[Boss];
(Add the Boss's set to the set of anyone superior to the Worker's Boss)
     Writeln('Please enter two numbers giving a worker and boss pair.');
     Writeln('Enter "0 0" to terminate the input.');
     Readln(Worker, Boss);
   end;
 for Person := 1 to Company_Size do
   begin
     Write('The subordinates of Employee ', Person : 2, ' are : ');
     if Superiors[Person] = [] then
       Write('None')
     else
       for Individual := 1 to Company_Size do
         if Individual in Superiors[Person] then
           Write(Individual : 3);
     Writeln
   end
end.
```

Listing 13.4

Exercises

13.1 Write a sets version of the program Keys (Chapter 11) that reads the text file Typing and compares the Qwerty and Dvorak keyboards.

13.2 Our program Hierarchy outputs information for ten employees even if there are only seven employees. Modify Hierarchy so that it reports the subordinates of an employee only if that employee's number was entered.

13.3 (Primes Revisited) If a whole number is not prime, then it must have a prime divisor less than or equal to its square root. Since Maxint is 32,767 and its square root is 181.01657, any odd integer represented in Macintosh Pascal must be either prime or divisible by some prime between 3 and the largest prime less than or equal to 181.

Write a procedure that generates the set of odd primes through 181. Notice that since the square root of 181 is 13.45362, you need only use the divisors 3,5,7,11, and 13 to generate the primes less than or equal to 181.

Write a function Prime that uses the set generated above to test for primehood any large odd integers entered by the user.

13.4 Write a program that reads a sentence from the keyboard and provides three lists:

1. All the letters included in the sentence.
2. All the letters excluded from the sentence.
3. All the letters included exactly once in the sentence.

Remember that 'A' and 'a' are distinct letters.

13.5 Everytime you visit Wendy's you get a piece of a WendyBurger puzzle. If you collect all five pieces to complete the puzzle you win a date with Clara Pell, the famous "Where's the Beef!?" lady. The probability of getting each piece is 0.5, 0.25, 0.10, 0.10, and 0.05 respectively. Write a program to run twenty trials that simulate the collecting of WendyBurger puzzle pieces. How many visits does it take on the average to win?

Chapter 14

String Manipulation

Computers probably spend more time dealing with non-numeric data than performing numeric calculations. Computers maintain lists of names, addresses, account numbers, and part numbers. Authors write books and articles using word processing programs and then store their works on magnetic disks. Thus, the programmer must have the ability to manipulate character information in a computer. The Macintosh has a powerful **string** package for manipulating characters. Before we investigate this, however, we will review the facilities available in Standard Pascal.

The fundamental built-in type in Pascal for handling characters is the Char type. Recall that variables of type Char consist of only one character. That is, character variables in Pascal are not used to store words, names, or addresses. We looked at a few simple examples in Chapter 8 that used the character type. The reader should recall that such simple tasks as changing a name from Last, First Middle to F. M. L. involved setting up **repeat...until** loops to process the information character by character.

Not every version of Pascal has a built-in string package, and there are certainly occasions where a program must process names or some other kind of data that is more than just a single character. In Standard Pascal, this processing is done using arrays of characters, as discussed in Chapter 10. For example, if we wanted to read the name 'Smokey The Bear' from the keyboard and store it into memory, we could do it as follows:

```
Index := 0;
while not EOLN do
  begin
   Index := Index + 1;
   Read(Name[Index])
  end;
```

Here we assume that Name is declared as a **packed array** [1..15] of Char. The difficulty of doing this is that the length of Name is a **static** attribute (or characteristic). The adjective static is a common one in computer science. It is usually used in contrast to **dynamic**. Static means unchanging while dynamic means varying. So we would be unable to store a name in Name that was longer than 15 characters. It is precisely this inflexibility that prompts most Pascal developers to include a string package.

Strings in Macintosh Pascal

As we know, strings are declared using the word **string**. When a string is declared, a **size** attribute, ranging from 1 to 255 and enclosed in brackets, can be given for the string. When there is no size given, the default value of 255 is assumed. An example of each kind of declaration is given below:

var
   Name : **string**;
   Address : **string**[30];

We point out that the *size* of a string is a static attribute indicating the maximum allowable length of any value of that string. However, the *length* of the string is in fact dynamic. So a string variable can store values of any length up to its maximum.

There is a special string value called the **null string**. This string has length 0 and is denoted by '' (two single quotes with nothing between them). Beginners sometimes confuse the null string with a blank. Although we can't see either one of them, they are different. A blank is just another character (entered by typing the space bar), and so treated as a string, has length 1. There are blanks between the words of this sentence (and we can see them). The null string, however, has no length at all. We could place 100 or 1000 null strings within the string 'Null' and when we printed the string out, it would still look like 'Null'. Believe it or not, the null string is very useful. It is often the initial value of strings, just like 0 is often the initial value for integer counters or "running" sums and the empty set is often the initial value for sets.

If one wants to think of strings as (packed) arrays of characters, Macintosh Pascal gives that flexibility. That is, if St is a string with current value 'Smokey The Bear', then St[4] is 'k', and the assignment statement

St[12] := 'P';

would change the value of St to 'Smokey The Pear'. If a reference is made to a component of a string that is undefined (in this case, for example, St[200]), this is an error.

Occasionally treating a string as an array of characters is useful, but for the most part the programmer is better off utilizing the built-in string functions and procedures of Macintosh Pascal. Before we present these, we describe the simple operations on strings that are available for most Pascal types.

First of all, assignments can be made freely among **string** types. Because of the dynamic property of string length, we do not have to worry about length compatibility. However, we do need to make sure that we do not violate any size restriction. For example, if St_1 is declared to have maximum size 2, then the assignment statement

St_1 := 'ABC';

is illegal, giving the error message:

A STRING value is too long for its intended use.

We can also test the standard relations between two strings, namely =, <>, <, <=, >, >=. The "less than" and "greater than" relations with strings are **lexicographic** (or alphabetic) relations. So, to say string A is less than string B means that A "comes before" B in the dictionary. Actually, since strings can contain any valid character, it is the ASCII code which really determines the lexicographic ordering. There are several points that need to be made concerning this ordering. The upper case letters precede the lower case letters, so 'Banana' is less than 'apple' (since 'B' < 'a'). The blank (or space) precedes all letters so 'Cat ' < 'Cats'. Finally, 'Cat' is not equal to 'Cat ' since they are of different lengths. In fact, 'Cat' < 'Cat ', and in general, an initial substring of a string is always less than the string itself.

Now we discuss several built-in string procedures and functions. We follow the descriptions of these with several examples.

The **Length** Function
   Format: Length(Str), where Str is any **string** value.
   Result: Returns the current length of Str.
   Example: If Str = 'Smokey The Bear', then Length(Str) is 15.

The **Position** Function

Format: Pos(Substr, Str), where both Substr and Str are any **string** values

Result: A search for an occurrence of the value of Substr within Str is made. The function returns the position of the first character of Substr within Str. If Substr is not found, the function returns zero.

Example: If Str = 'Smokey The Bear', Sub1 = 'The', and Sub2 = 'the', then Pos(Sub1, Str) is 8 and Pos(Sub2, Str) is 0. Also, Pos('e', Str) is 5 since that is the position of the first 'e' in Str.

The **Concatenation** Function

Format: Concat(Str1, Str2, Str3, . . ., StrN), where each parameter is a **string** value. According to the Macintosh Pascal Reference Manual, the number of parameters is limited to a "practical" number.

Result: The parameters are concatenated in the order listed.

Example: If Str1 = 'dog' and Str2 = 'house' then Concat(Str1, Str2) equals 'doghouse' while Concat(Str2, Str1) equals 'housedog'.

The **Copy** Function

Format: Copy(Source, Index, Count), where Source is a **string** value, Index and Count are Integer values.

Result: This function returns the **string** value that is Count characters long and begins at position Index of Source (i.e., at position Source[Index]).

Example: If Str = 'Example', Place = 3, and Len = 2, then Copy(Str, Place, Len) is 'am'. Note that if the Copy function attempts to access characters outside the range of the Source string, this is *not* considered an error. Only those characters within the range of Source are actually copied. So if Str is as above, then Copy(Str, 3, 9) is 'ample'.

The **Delete** Procedure

Format: Delete(Source, Index, Count) where Source is a **string** *variable*, Index and Count are Integer values.

Effect: The substring of Source of length Count beginning at position Index is deleted from Source. Note that the value of Source is actually changed by the Delete procedure. It is a variable parameter (which explains why it must be a **string** variable and not simply a **string** value).

Example: If Source = 'Through', then Delete(Source, 2, 2) causes the value of Source to be changed to 'Tough'. As with Copy, if characters are referenced outside the range of Source, there is no error, but only characters within the range are deleted.

The **Omit** Function

Format: Omit(Source, Index, Count) where Source is a **string** value, Index and Count are Integer values.

Result: Returns the substring of Source obtained by removing Count characters beginning at position Index. The value of Source remains unchanged.

Example: If Source = 'Through', then Omit(Source, 2, 2) is 'Tough'. Source is still equal to 'Through' after the evaluation of the function.

Although Delete and Omit appear similar, Delete is a procedure while Omit is a function. So Delete is used as a stand-alone statement to change the value of its source. Omit, however, is used within an expression and is replaced by its value (without altering the value of its source).

The **Insert** Procedure

Format: Insert(Source, Destination, Index), where Source is a **string** value, Destination is a string *variable*, and Index is an Integer value.

Effect: The **string** value given by Source is inserted into the **string** value of Destination beginning at position Index. Note that the value of Destination is changed by the Insert procedure. If Index is less than 1, Source is inserted on the left of Destination. If Index is greater than the length of Destination, the insertion is to the right of Destination.

Example: If Source = 're' and Destination = 'Bad', then Insert(Source, Destination, 2) changes the value of Destination to 'Bread' while Insert(Source, Destination, 3) changes the value of Destination to 'Bared'.

The **Include** Function

Format: Include(Source, Destination, Index) where Source and Destination are **string** values and Index is an Integer value.

Result: Returns the **string** obtained by inserting the value of Source into the value of Destination beginning at position Index. The value of destination is not changed.

Example: If Source = 're' and Destination = 'Bad', then Include(Source, Destination, 2) is 'Bread' and Include(Source, Destination, 3) is 'Bared'. In each case, the value of Destination remains equal to 'Bad'.

Examples

Now we use these procedures and functions to do some string processing. Some of the following examples have no apparent realistic applications, but are included just for practice.

Example 1: Suppose Word is a **string** variable. Write a segment to interchange the first and last letters of Word. That is, if Word = 'Something', the segment should change the value of Word to 'gomethinS'. While this may sound easy, the reader is encouraged to try to accomplish this before looking at the solution below. The solution should be a general one that works for any value of Word, and not just the value given.

This can actually be performed with one very "busy" statement, but for readability purposes, we write this as 4 statements:

```
First := Copy(Word, 1, 1);
Last := Copy(Word, Length(Word), 1);
Middle := Copy(Word, 2, Length(Word) - 2);
Word := Concat(Last, Middle, First);
```

It is worthwhile to explain the above process in detail. We are assigning a new value to Word, namely the concatenation of three strings--'g' + 'omethin' + 'S'. Clearly, the first statement above assigns the first letter of Word to First. Also, the second statement assigns the last letter of Word to Last. Notice that the use of the Length function within the Copy function is one way to make the solution a general one. Since we don't necessarily know how long the word is that we are dealing with, we use Length to find the end of the word for us. To obtain the middle part of the word, we, of course, start at position 2 and extract all of Word except for the first and last letters. Thus, we want all but 2 characters, or Length(Word) - 2 characters. A common mistake for beginners is to write Length(Word - 2). This is nonsense because Word - 2 is a meaningless expression. If the reader tests the above segment with several cases, it might be easy to be convinced that the solution is a completely general one. This demonstrates the danger of jumping to conclusions. There is, in fact, one case where the above segment does not perform as it should, namely when the length of Word is exactly one. What happens?

Example 2: Write a segment to change the form of Name (a **string** variable) from First Middle Last to Last, F. M..

We use the Pos function to find the blanks between names, the Copy function to extract the first and middle initials, and the Delete function to remove the first and middle names from Name. The solution is given in listing 14.1.

```
program Reverse_Name;

  const
    Period = '.';
    Comma = ',';
    Blank = ' ';

  var
    First, Middle : Char;
    Name : string[40];
    Place : Integer;

begin
  Writeln('Enter a name in the form:  First Middle Last');
  Readln(Name);
  First := Copy(Name, 1, 1);  {Find the first initial.}
  Place := Pos(Blank, Name);  {Find the first blank.}
  Middle := Copy(Name, Place + 1, 1); {Find the middle initial}
  Delete(Name, 1, Place); {Remove first name so we can search }
                          {for second blank}
  Place := Pos(Blank, Name); {Find second blank}
  Name := Copy(Name, Place + 1, Length(Name) - Place);
  {Name now equals Last name}
  Name := Concat(Name, Comma, Blank, First, Period, Blank, Middle, Period);
  Writeln('The reversed name is:  ', Name)
end.
```

Listing 14.1

Example 3: Enter a sentence of length less than 256 characters from the keyboard and count the number of occurrences of 'e'. For simplicity, we will not search for upper case E's, but we mention that in many text processing situations, care must be taken to handle both upper case and lower case letters.

This solution is shown in listing 14.2. Since the Pos function always searches from the beginning of the string, whenever we find an 'e', we chop off the first part of Sentence up through that 'e'. While this makes the searching more efficient, we are only able to do this because we don't need the value of Sentence.

```
program Ease;
  var
    Count : Integer;
    Place : Integer;
    Sentence : string;
begin
  Writeln('Enter a sentence.');
  ReadIn(Sentence);
  Count := 0;
  Place := Pos('e', Sentence);
  while Place <> 0 do
    begin
      Count := Count + 1;
      Delete(Sentence, 1, Place);
      Place := Pos('e', Sentence)
    end;
  Writeln('The number of e''s in the sentence is: ', Count);
end.
```

Listing 14.2

Example 4:   Remove all occurrences of the letter 'e' from a given sentence typed at the keyboard and print the sentence without the e's.

We present two strategies for removing e's. The first strategy treats the string as an array of characters. The second makes use of the string functions and procedures. In the first, we copy Sentence into another string variable called Alternate. We do this by concatenating letters of Sentence one at a time to Alternate. Of course, we copy everything but the letter 'e'. This program, EChop1, is given in listing 14.3.

The second program uses the Delete procedure to remove the occurrences of 'e' and doesn't require the additional storage of Alternate because the occurrences of 'e' are removed directly from Sentence. Notice that the value of Sentence is changed by EChop2, shown in listing 14.4.

One of the exercises at the end of the chapter is to test character strings to see if they are palindromes, which are words, phrases, or sentences that read the same forwards and backwards, like "Madam, I'm Adam". A good first step in that problem would be to follow the idea of this example and remove all blanks and punctuation marks to obtain "MadamImAdam".

```
program EChop1;

var
  Sentence, Alternate : string;
  Place : Integer;

begin
  Writeln('Please enter a sentence.');
  Readln(Sentence);
  Alternate := '';
  for Place := 1 to Length(Sentence) do
    if Sentence[Place] <> 'e' then
      Alternate := Concat(Alternate, Sentence[Place]);
  Writeln('The sentence without any e'' s is:');
  Writeln(Alternate)
end.
```

Listing 14.3

```
program EChop2;

var
  Sentence : string;
  Place : Integer;

begin
  Writeln('Please enter a sentence.');
  Readln(Sentence);
  Place := Pos('e', Sentence);
  while Place <> 0 do
    begin
      Delete(Sentence, Place, 1);
      Place := Pos('e', Sentence)
    end;
  Writeln('The sentence without any e''s is:');
  Writeln(Sentence)
end.
```

Listing 14.4

Example 5: Examine a piece of text and change all occurrences of 'cie' to 'cei'.

Before providing the solution, we discuss the application behind such a process. Many word processing programs can help find and correct spelling errors. Although most do so by looking words up in a "dictionary" stored on a disk, with certain rules it may be possible to actually program various error-detecting capabilities. This example is taking care of the rule:

"I before E except after C."

There are, of course, some exceptions to this rule (like "science" and its derivatives), but in many cases, the number of exceptions is small, and before a spelling change is made, the program could make sure it is not changing one of the exceptional cases. Natural languages are so complex compared to formal languages such as Pascal that we are a long way from having computerized proofreaders. For example, imagine trying to "teach" a computer how to recognize when to use "there" as opposed to "their." Will computers ever "understand" the intended meaning of everyday phrases such as

"This ticket good for one fare from **Chicago** to **Lake Forest** or **Vice Versa.**"

or will computers expect people to travel from **Chicago** to **Vice Versa**? Despite such difficulties, natural language understanding remains one of the most researched areas of **artificial intelligence**. The solution to the spelling checker is given in listing 14.5. The program reads a list of words (all entered on one line) from the keyboard. One of its executions is shown in figure 14.1.

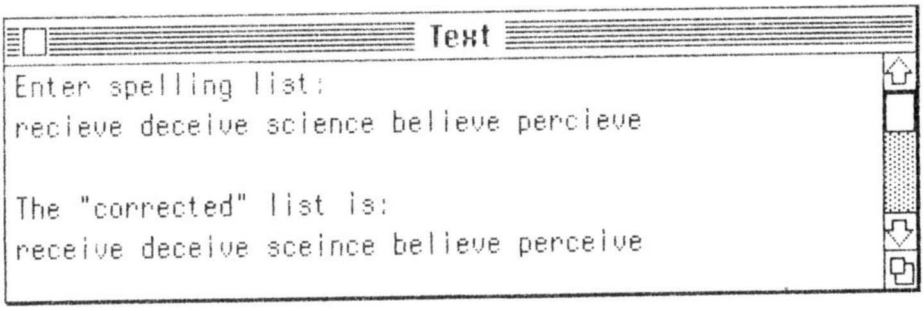

```
Enter spelling list:
recieve deceive science believe percieve


The "corrected" list is:
receive deceive sceince believe perceive
```

Figure 14.1

```
program Speller;

const
  Pattern = 'cie';

var
  Spelling : string;
  Place : Integer;
  List : Text;

begin
  Writeln('Enter spelling list:');
  Readln(Spelling);
  Writeln;
  Place := Pos(Pattern, Spelling);
  while Place <> 0 do
    begin
      Spelling[Place + 1] := 'e';
      Spelling[Place + 2] := 'i';
      Place := Pos(Pattern, Spelling)
    end;
  Writeln('The "corrected" list is:');
  Writeln(Spelling)
end.
```

Listing 14.5

Notice that in the above program we have used both the string capability and the array of characters representation. The reason for mixing here is one of efficiency. To find the pattern 'cie', it is easier to let the Pos function search as opposed to doing a character-by-character search. Such a character search would involve stopping at each 'c', checking the next letter to see if it is an 'i', and if so, checking to see if the next letter is an 'e'. However, once we have found such a pattern, it is more efficient to directly insert the two letters after the 'c' using the character components rather than employing the Delete/Insert procedures or the Concat/Copy functions. It is up to the programmer to choose those operations that are most efficient for the particular situation. In fact, we remark that using Pos as we have here is efficient in terms of the actual writing of the Pascal program but is less efficient in terms of execution. The reason Pos is not very efficient in this case is that it returns to the beginning of the string each time to resume its search for the pattern 'cie', and so is searching over text that has already been processed. Other string packages often provide a function similar to Pos, but with the capability of specifying a starting position other than the first position of a string. Such implementations tend to increase searching efficiency.

Summary

The beginner is often surprised at how often the need for character manipulation arises. It may seem that reversing strings is simply an exercise in using the string manipulation functions. But consider a business that keeps all of its customer records on disk. It is likely that these records are indexed by last names so that given records can be easily found. However, if the business wishes to pull the names from the disk to use in a letter, the names need to be in normal order. There are two options: Store the names twice, once as Last, First, and another time as First Last. This uses twice as much storage, and although computer storage is becoming less and less expensive, it still isn't free. The other alternative is to store the names only in the form Last, First, and make the software that processes the names and writes the letter manipulate the names into the form needed.

Systems programming is another area where manipulation of string information is crucial. A Pascal program is treated by the system translator as a string of characters. The translator's first job is to **parse** the program, that is, to break it up into its component parts, like keywords and operators, so that the program can be checked for syntax errors.

With so many different kinds of data being stored in computer systems, it is up to the programmer to find the way through the data, extracting the information needed for a given application. In many situations, the string manipulation functions, like Pos and Copy, provide the easiest way to find the desired information.

Exercises

14.1 Write a function that accepts a string and counts the number of Z's (both 'z' and 'Z') in the string.

14.2 Write a function Distinct that accepts a string and outputs True only if all the characters of the string are distinct. For example, Distinct('Macintosh') is True while Distinct('Pascal') is False since Pascal contains two a's. Notice that Distinct('Bob') is True.

14.3 As chief censor of Sikinia, it is your duty to implement the latest royal decree that states:

Henceforth, Red will be called White and White will be called Red.

Write a program that reads a sentence and outputs the "censored" version. Be careful that you do not keep changing the same word over and over.

14.4 Riteway ayay rogrampay hattay ranslatestay entencessay intoyay igPay atinLay. The rules for Pig Latin are:

If a word begins with a vowel (A, E, I, O, U), then "yay" is added to the end of the word. Thus, "Apple" becomes "Appleyay". On the other hand, if the word begins with a consonant, then that consonant is moved to the end and "ay" is added. Thus, "Macintosh" becomes "acintoshMay".

14.5 Write a program that translates Pig Latin back into English. Are there any problems with this translation? Can you think of a word or sentence that can't be translated back without ambiguity?

14.6 Write the function Place(Str, Pattern, Index), which is a smart version of Pos(Str, Pattern). Place returns the position of the first occurrence of the string Pattern in the target string Str starting its search at the index[th] place. For example, Place('Pascal', 'a', 3) returns 5, the location of the first 'a' beginning with the third character in 'Pascal'.

14.7 A palindrome is a phrase that reads the same backwards as forwards. For example

Able was I ere I saw Elba

is a palindrome. The notion of a palindrome can be extended to include phrases such as

Madam, I'm Adam

that, except for blanks and punctuation, read the same backwards as forwards. We include such phrases in our definition of a palindrome for this exercise.

Write a procedure Strip that removes all the blanks and punctuation from a string. Strip may assume that commas and hyphens are the only punctuation in the given string. Thus, Strip would turn 'Madam, Im Adam' into 'MadamImAdam'.

Write a procedure Flip that reverses a given String. Thus, Flip would turn 'Pascal' into 'lacsaP'.

Write a procedure LowerCase that converts all the letters of a given string to lower case. Thus, LowerCase would convert 'Pascal' into 'pascal'. Note that LowerCase leaves the blanks and punctuation, if any, alone. Hint: LowerCase should make use of the built-in functions Ord and Chr.

Write a program that finds the winner in a palindrome contest. The rather strange rules are:

1. If an entry is not a palindrome, it scores 0 points.
2. If an entry is a palindrome, it scores 1 point for each character, not counting blanks or punctuation. Thus, 'Madam, Im Adam' scores 11 points.
3. If an entry is a palindrome with respect to blanks and punctuation, then it scores a bonus of 30 points. Thus, 'Able was I ere I saw Elba' scores 19 + 30 = 49 points. Note that case changes are allowed in entries.

Here are the contestants and their entries. You may make a text file of them if you wish (two lines per entry) and add entries of your own. We include these to get you started.

Name	Entry
Eve Firstperson	Eve
Adam Firstperson	Madam, Im Adam
Abel Firstperson	Abel was I ere I saw Cain
Napolean Bonaparte	Able was I ere I saw Elba
Minnesota Fats	Doc, note, I dissent-a fast never prevents a fatness-I diet on cod
Theodore Roosevelt	A man, a plan, a canal, Panama
Marquis de Sade	Evil I did dwel-lewd did I live
Ralph Shively	Naomi-sex at noon taxes, I moan

Your program should output each person's score, whether the bonus was earned, and finally, the name of the winner followed by the winning entry.

14.8 Write a program that uses your graphics of exercise 12.3 to play a game of hangman. In the game of hangman the computer selects a secret word at random from a text file of words. The computer displays a star (*) for each letter in the word, thereby giving the player the length of the word. The player then tries to guess the word letter by letter. If the letter guessed is in the word, then the computer shows all instances of that letter in the given word. For example, if the secret word is "hangman" and the initial guess is "a", then the display changes from "*******' to "*a***a*". If the letter guessed is not in the word, then the computer draws the next piece of the player at the gallows. If the player guesses all the letters of the word before the computer completes the drawing then the player wins, otherwise the player hangs.

Chapter 15

Recursion

In Pascal it is possible for a procedure or function to invoke itself. This is known as recursion since the function or procedure "re-occurs" within itself. This chapter illustrates several instances in which recursion leads to elegant solutions of seemingly complex problems. We provide several examples so that you may begin to recognize situations where recursion is an appropriate instrument to apply.

To avoid an infinite sequence of calls, there must, of course, be some means whereby the given procedure or function stops invoking more instances of itself. Thus, for recursion to apply, both of the following must be true:

1. There must be at least one trivial case that ends the sequence of recursive calls.
2. There must be some way to put together solutions to "easy" instances to solve "hard" instances of the problem.

Let us consider an example to see how these principles apply. The factorial function was introduced in Chapter 7. For example, 5! is 5*4*3*2*1 or 120. In general, N! is N * (N-1) * (N-2) * ... * 3 * 2 * 1. This expression, written equivalently as N! = N * (N-1)!, is the approach needed if we wish to write a recursive factorial function. It says that the "hard" problem of finding N! can be solved by simply multiplying N and (N-1)!. Likewise, (N-1)! is simply the product of N-1 and (N-2)!. To prevent an infinite descent, we need a trivial, nonrecursive case that ends the process. Since 0! is defined to be 1, we use this case to end the recursion. For example, trace how the computer could use the above ideas to compute 3!. First, 3! = 3*2!, and 2! = 2*1!, and 1! = 1*0!. Since 0! is defined to be 1,

the computer traces backwards that 1! is also 1, 2! is 2, and thus, 3! is 6.
Listing 15.1 shows the recursive, Pascal version of Factorial:

```
function Factorial(N : Integer) : LongInt;
begin
  if N = 0 then
    Factorial := 1
  else
    Factorial := N * Factorial(N-1)
end;  {Recursive Definition of function Factorial}
```

Listing 15.1

Notice that the **then** clause contains the trivial case in which
Factorial is simply assigned a value. The **else** clause contains the general
case in which the factorial of N is computed using the factorial of N-1.
Also observe that unlike nonrecursive functions, recursive functions are
allowed to use the function name on the right-hand-side of an assignment
statement within the body of the function. As an exercise to aid in your
understanding of recursion, carefully trace the evaluation of Factorial(5).
If you see how Factorial(5) is evaluated, then you are well on your way to
understanding recursion.

Also note that Factorial returns a long integer, rather than a regular
integer, to help avoid overflow. Actually, 13! overflows even LongInts, so
LongInts postpone the overflow problem only a little bit. Furthermore,
note that recursion is not needed to compute the factorial function.
Indeed, in Chapter 7 we implemented Factorial as a simple, iterative
(looping) function. This illustrates a fact about recursion: Any problem
that can be solved with recursion can also be solved without recursion.
Why then should students "waste time" studying recursion? The answer,
illustrated in the examples that follow, is that in many instances the
recursive solution provides a short and elegant solution to what appears to
be a very complicated problem. Thus, recursion is simply a tool that can
make problem solving easier. The trick is to learn to recognize when
recursion applies. Let us consider several situations, some old, some new,
in which recursion can be used.

An excellent example of the power of recursion is provided by the
puzzle known as the Tower of Hanoi. Figure 15.1 illustrates the puzzle in
which one must move the tower of disks from peg 'A' to peg 'C' by only
moving one disk at a time. Also, one can never place a large disk on a

small disk. If you have never played with this puzzle, make some disks from paper and solve the puzzle with three or four disks before reading the next section.

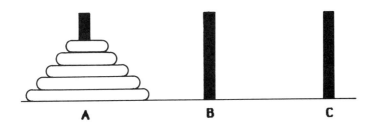

A   B   C

Figure 15.1 The Tower of Hanoi

We will write a procedure Towers(N, 'A', 'B', 'C') that will solve general Tower of Hanoi problems. That is, given a positive integer N, and three pegs labelled 'A', 'B', and 'C', the procedure should give us explicit move-by-move intructions for getting the N disks from peg 'A' to peg 'C' using peg 'B' as the auxiliary peg. For example, the output from Towers(2, 'A', 'B', 'C') should solve the two disk problem with the following instructions:

Move disk 1 from peg A to peg B.
Move disk 2 from peg A to peg C.
Move disk 1 from peg B to peg C.

Throughout this discussion, disk 1 is the smallest disk, disk 2 is the next smallest, etc.

It is far from obvious how to write the procedure Towers. Let us consider looking for a recursive solution. We need a trivial case of the puzzle to end the recursion. If there were going to be a Tower of Hanoi puzzle on your final exam, how many disks would you like to see on the first peg? Most of us would agree that the puzzle with only one disk is indeed trivial. Secondly, how can we use solutions to smaller puzzles to help us solve the N disk puzzle? Figure 15.2 shows how to patch solutions to easier puzzles together to solve "hard" puzzles. Namely, solve the N disk puzzle in three stages:

Move the N-1 top disks from peg A to peg B.
Move disk N from peg A to peg C.
Move the N-1 top disks from peg B to peg C.

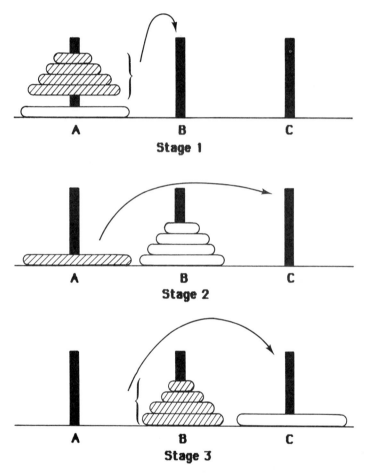

Figure 15.2 Recursive Solution

Moving the N-1 top disks is simply an instance of solving the N-1 disk problem. Thus, we have an algorithm, much as in the factorial problem, for solving N disk puzzles from N-1 disk puzzles. Listing 15.2 shows the Pascal for our pseudo-code:

```
procedure Towers (N : Integer;
        From, Aux, Dest : Char);
begin
 if N = 1 then
  Writeln('Move disk 1 from peg ', From, ' to peg ', Dest)
 else
  begin
   Towers(N - 1, From, Dest, Aux);
   Wr iteln('Move disk ', N : 1, ' from peg ', From, ' to peg ', Dest);
   Towers(N - 1, Aux, From, Dest)
  end {If}
end; {Recursive definition of procedure Towers}
```

Listing 15.2

You should work through the above procedure for N = 2 or N = 3 to see how it works. In particular, note how the From, Dest, and Aux pegs are used. That is, to move N disks from the From peg to the Dest peg, the Tower procedure first moves N-1 disks from the From peg to the Aux peg using the Dest peg as the auxiliary peg. Then it moves the Nth disk to the Dest peg and then moves the N-1 disks from the Aux peg to the Dest peg using the From peg as the auxiliary.

```
program Hanoi;
{This program recursively solves Tower of Hanoi puzzles.}

var
 N : Integer;
procedure Towers (N : Integer;
        From, Aux, Dest : Char);
begin
 if N = 1 then
  Writeln('Move disk 1 from peg ', From, ' to peg ', Dest)
 else
  begin
   Towers(N - 1, From, Dest, Aux);
   Writeln('Move disk ', N : 1, ' from peg ', From, ' to peg ', Dest);
   Towers(N - 1, Aux, From, Dest)
  end {If}
end; {Recursive definition of procedure Towers}
```

(Continued)

begin (Body of main program Hanoi)
   Writeln('Please enter the number of disks in the puzzle.');
   Readln(N);
   Towers(N, 'A', 'B', 'C')
end.

Listing 15.3

Listing 15.3 shows the complete program Hanoi that prompts the user to enter N, the number of disks, then invokes the recursive procedure Towers to print the explicit instructions for moving the N disks from peg 'A' to peg 'C'. If you are not impressed with the brevity and elegance of this solution, consider writing your own *non-recursive* solution. We think you will quickly learn to appreciate recursion.

In Chapter 14, we presented an exercise to test strings to see if they were palindromes. A palindrome, of course, is a phrase that reads the same backwards as forwards. Let us write a recursive function to test for palindromes. In general, we need only check the first and last letters of a string. If they are different the string cannot be a palindrome. If they are the same, then throw them away and repeat the process on the remaining string. Eventually, we must come down to a string of zero or one character. These are our trivial cases because any such string is a palindrome. Here, then, is our pseudo-code:

   If the length is zero or one, then it is a palindrome,
   else if the first and last characters don't match, then it isn't.
   Otherwise, throw away the first and last characters and repeat.

The resulting recursive function, Pals, is contained, along with a main program to show it off, in listing 15.4.

The next example is a counting problem. Suppose you would like to know how many strings of zeros and ones you can form of a certain length that do not contain two consecutive ones. For example, there are 3 such strings of length 2. They are 00, 01, and 10. Likewise, there are 5 of length 3. They are 000, 001, 010, 100, and 101. Can you find the 8 of length 4 and the 13 of length 5? (How about the 17,711 of length 20?). More importantly, do you see a pattern that will help you compute these numbers? Table 15.1 shows the values for lengths up to 5.

```
program RecursivePals;
(This program uses the recursive function)
(Pals to test given strings for "palindromeness")

var
  Sentence : string;

function Pals (S : string) : Boolean;
begin
  if (Length(S) = 0) or (Length(S) = 1) then
    Pals := True  (Trivial case of a palindrome.)
  else if S[1] <> S[Length(S)] then
    Pals := False  (Trivial case of a NON-palindrome.)
  else
    begin
(Delete the first and last characters and try again.)
      Delete(S, 1, 1);
      Delete(S, Length(S), 1);
      Pals := Pals(S)
    end  (If)
end;  (Recursive definition of function Pals)

begin
  Writeln('Please enter your candidate sentence:');
  Readln(Sentence);
  if Pals(Sentence) then
    Writeln('It is a palindrome.')
  else
    Writeln('Sorry, not a palindrome.')
end.
```

Listing 15.4

Length	Number of Strings
1	2
2	3
3	5
4	8
5	13

Table 15.1

We hope a pattern becomes clear. The next value is always the sum of the last two values. That is, in general, if Count(N) counts the number of such strings of length N, then Count(N) = Count(N-1) + Count(N-2). This is clearly a recursive relationship! Since the recursive expression involves two previous values, we need two trivial cases to get us started. We take Count(1) = 2 and Count(2) = 3 as the trivial cases and then use the recursive formula for any N ≥ 3.

Before we write the program, let's see if we can understand where the recursive relationship comes from. Consider constructing a string of length N that does not contain two consecutive ones. It either starts with a 0 or a 1. If it starts with a 1, then it must have a 0 next (why?) and then there are N-2 places left to consider. Any legal string of N-2 characters can occupy these spots. Hence, there are Count(N-2) legal strings of length N that begin with a 1. We leave it to the reader to argue that there are Count(N-1) legal strings of length N that begin with a 0. Thus, there are Count(N-1) + Count(N-2) legal strings of length N altogether, and the recursive relationship is established. If you are still confused, try to see how the 8 legal strings of length 4 come from the 5 strings of length 3 and the 3 of length 2.

Notice that we do not need two separate cases for the two trivial cases. Because of the simplicity of the situation, we have Count(N) = N + 1 for both N = 1 and N = 2. Finally, the simple program Zeros_and_Ones, which invokes the recursive procedure Count, is given in listing 15.5.

```
program Zeros_and_Ones;
{This program invokes the recursive function Count(N) to }
{count the number of strings of 0s and 1s of length N that}
{can be made that do not contain two 1s in a row.         }

var
  N : Integer;

function Count (N : Integer) : Integer;
begin
  if N < 3 then
    Count := N + 1
  else
    Count := Count(N - 1) + Count(N - 2)
end; {Recursive definition of function Count}
```

(Continued)

```
begin
  Writeln('N' : 5, 'Number of strings');
  for N := 1 to 20 do
    Writeln(N : 3, Count(N) : 10)
end.
```

Listing 15.5

Run the program Zeros_and_Ones and watch it slow down as N grows. Why does the program get so slow? Computers are supposed to be fast, but when the output reaches the upper teens, it gets much slower than we humans. For example, suppose the output is as follows:

...	...
14	987
15	1597
16	2584
17	4181
18	6765
19	10946

All the computer has to do to get the 20th term is to add 10,946 and 6,765. Why does it take so long? The answer is that even though the computer only has to add Count(19) and Count(18) to find Count(20), the computer didn't remember Count(19) or Count(18) and has to compute them both again. Of course, Count(19) involves Count(18) and Count(17), etc. And then, when it finally computes Count(19), it discovers that it needs Count(18) and starts all over on that calculation. Remember that computers are dumb and that recursion can be very inefficient! Recursion is not really appropriate for this situation and we leave the details of a more efficient, nonrecursive solution to this problem to the exercises.

Snowflakes and Flowsnakes

In 1904 Helge von Koch described an interesting geometrical shape that has come to be known as Koch's Snowflake. It is an ideal example for Macintosh Pascal as it combines graphics and recursion, and, hence, allows the beginner to "see" recursion at work. Koch's snowflake is constructed as follows: You begin with an equilateral triangle as in figure 15.3a. Then, on each side you place an equilateral triangle of one third the size of the original. This gives the design of figure 15.3b. Of course, one repeats this process on the new figure producing the designs of figure 15.3c and d.

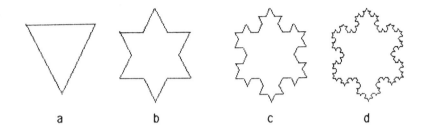

a   b   c   d

Figure 15.3

Koch's Snowflake is the figure you get if you repeat this process *forever!*
To avoid an infinite loop, we incorporate a level in our recursive procedure
and each time the procedure calls itself, the level is reduced by one. When
the level reaches zero, then the recursion stops. The procedure DrawSide
of Listing 15.6 presents the recursive Pascal version that draws one side
of Koch's snowflake. The reader should trace (with paper and pencil!) a
call to this procedure with a Level of 2 or so. Notice that DrawSide makes
use of our graphics package of Chapter 12.

```
procedure DrawSide (Length, Level : Integer);
begin
  if Level = 0 then
    Forward(Length)
  else
   begin
    Length := Length div 3;
    DrawSide(Length, Level - 1);
    Turn(60);
    DrawSide(Length, Level - 1);
    Turn(-120);
    DrawSide(Length, Level - 1);
    Turn(60);
    DrawSide(Length, Level - 1)
   end  {If}
end;
```

Listing 15.6

The program Snowflake, that calls DrawSides three times, is given in
listing15.7. Its execution with Level equal to 4, is given in figure 15.4.

```
program SnowFlake;
(This recursive program draws Koch's snowflake.)

const
  Pi = 3.1415927;

var
  Angle : Integer;
  X, Y : Real;
  Length, Level, Side : Integer;
  Size : Rect;

(Procedure DrawSide and Graphics Package goes here.)

begin (Body of main program Snowflake)
  SetRect(Size, 0, 20, 527, 357);
  SetDrawingRect(Size);
  ShowDrawing;
  Length := 243;  (3 to the 5th power!)
  Level := 4;
  Initialize;
  for Side := 1 to 3 do
    begin
      DrawSide(Length, Level);
      Turn(-120)
    end (For)
end.
```

Listing 15.7

It is clear why this design is called a snowflake. The reader who runs the program Snowflake also discovers why mathematicians call such designs "flowsnakes." We hope that carefully observing the execution of Snowflake will increase your understanding of how recursion actually works.

As another, different example, consider the recursive tree shown in figure 15.5. The tree has intentionally been constructed asymmetrically to make it look more like a real tree. We leave it to the reader to trace the program Tree, given in listing 15.8, to see how the recursion is performed. Many other interesting trees can be drawn by modifying the constants Size, LAngle, RAngle, and Level.

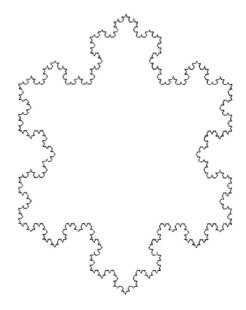

Figure 15.4

Figure 15.5

```
program Tree; (This recursive program draws a tree.)
 const
  Pi = 3.1415927;
  Size = 30;
  LAngle = 40;
  RAngle = 25;
  Level = 5;
 var
  Angle : Integer;
  X, Y : Real;
  Window : Rect;

(Graphics Package goes here.)

 procedure Backward (Distance : Integer);
 begin
  Turn(180);
  Forward(Distance);
  Turn(180)
 end;

 procedure DrawBranch (Size, Level : Integer);
 begin
  if Level = 0 then
   begin
    Forward(Size);
    Backward(Size)
   end
  else
   begin
    Forward(Size);
    Turn(LAngle);
    DrawBranch(Size, Level - 1);
    Turn(-LAngle);
    DrawBranch(Size, Level - 1);
    Turn(-RAngle);
    DrawBranch(Size, Level - 1);
    Turn(RAngle);
    Backward(Size)
   end
 end;                    (Continued)
```

```
begin  (Body of main program Tree)
   SetRect(Window, 0, 20, 527, 357);
   SetDrawingRect(Window);
   ShowDrawing;
   Initialize;
   Turn(90);
   Line(0, -3 * Size);  (Draw Trunk of tree)
   Y := Y - 3 * Size;
   DrawBranch(Size, Level)
end.
```

Listing 15.8

Exercises

15.1 Write a non-recursive version of the program Zeros_and_Ones from the text.

15.2 Modify the constants Size, LAngle, RAngle, or Level of the program Tree to produce some new varieties.

15.3 Write a recursive function Exponent(X, K) that computes X^K. Is this an appropriate use of recursion?

15.4 The greatest common divisor (gcd) of two positive integers X and Y is is defined to be the largest positive integer that divides evenly into both X and Y. For example, gcd(21,15) = 3, gcd(22,15) = 1, and gcd(30,15) = 15. The Euclidean algorithm is a standard way of finding the gcd of two integers. The Euclidean algorithm essentially says: Divide Y into X where Y is the second of the two numbers. (Usually Y is the smaller of the two numbers, but this is not necessary.) If Y divides evenly into X, then the gcd(X, Y) = Y. If Y does not divide evenly into X, take the remainder and divide it into Y. If that division is not even, divide the second remainder into the first remainder. Continue this process until a division operation has no remainder. The divisor for the "last" division is the gcd(X, Y).

The two statements on the following page give a nice recursive formulation for the Euclidean algorithm. Use these to write a recursive function to compute the gcd of two integers. Test your function on several pairs of integers by writing a main program that asks for two integers from the keyboard and computes their gcd.

gcd(X, Y) = Y if X **mod** Y = 0
gcd(X, Y) = gcd(Y, X **mod** Y) if X **mod** Y ≠ 0

15.4 Wallalumps breed according to the following strange rules: 1 and 2-year old Wallalumps produce 1 child each. 3-year old Wallalumps produce 2 children each. Older Wallalumps do not bear children. Assuming that you begin with 10 1-year old Wallalumps and 10 2-year old Wallalumps and that no Wallalumps die, write recursive and nonrecursive versions of a program to count the Wallalump population for each of the next 10 years.

Chapter 16

Pointers and Linked Lists

LINO - Last in, Never out.
Devil's DP Dictionary

The array is an example of a **static** data structure. It is called static because its size must be fixed when the program is written. For example, suppose you have an array of 100 elements, but suddenly you find that you need to store a 101st element in the array. It can't be done without halting the program, changing the declaration of the array, and running the program again. In this chapter, we are going to introduce linked lists as an example of a **dynamic** data structure. As we shall see, linked lists can grow to any arbitrary size (that fits into the RAM of the computer) and are not limited to some fixed, predeclared size.

In the general situation, you may need many arrays. Being static data structures, this probably leads to a poor utilization of memory. Figure 16.1 illustrates a frustrating problem that can occur with separate arrays.

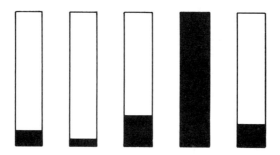

Figure 16.1

As illustrated, four of the arrays are nearly empty, and, hence, great amounts of memory are being wasted. But unfortunately, one of the arrays has overflowed, and the program abends (abnormally ends) because there is no more room in the indicated array. We call this poor memory management because we have simultaneously wasted memory in four of the arrays and yet have no available memory in the other array.

With linked lists, memory utilization is as depicted in figure 16.2. That is, each dynamic list uses just the amount of memory that it needs. Overflow only occurs when all available memory in the computer is in use.

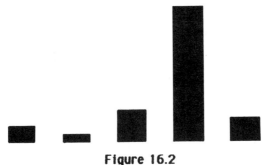

Figure 16.2

In the dynamic situation the system keeps track of memory utilization and gives and takes back memory from our linked lists. For now, let us suppose we have two "black boxes," New and Dispose, that magically fetch and dispose of memory for us. We shall have more to say about New and Dispose later.

The array is, of course, an ordered sequence of elements. Note that the elements of an array are even stored physically in order in RAM. We shall want our linked lists to be ordered sequences of elements, but we shall not insist that the elements of the linked list be stored physically in order. That is, we shall distinguish between the logical order and the actual physical order of the elements. As long as we can easily recover the logical order, it is not essential that the elements actually be kept in physical order. The mechanism that we use to recover the logical order is simple: Each element contains a "pointer" to the next logical element. Thus, a linked list is usually drawn as in figure 16.3.

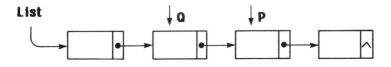

Figure 16.3

It is important to realize that the cells depicted above may be anywhere in memory. For example, the element that P points to is logically the element after the element that Q points to. However, the cell that P points to may come before, or even be on the "other side" of memory from, the cell that Q points to. As long as we have a pointer, List, to the first cell, we can use the pointers to quickly recover the logical order of the linked list.

The components of a linked list are called **nodes**. As shown in figure 16.3, we implement the nodes of a linked list as records with two fields. The first field is an information field and the second field is a link field to the next node in the list. The information field is determined by the given application. If much information is being stored, then the information field can itself be organized as a record. In the example that follows, let us suppose that the information field consists of just a name (30 characters) and an identification number (integer).

We first turn to the question of how the link field is implemented. This situation is so important that Pascal provides a "pointer type" just to implement such dynamic data structures. A pointer is declared as follows:

var
P : ^Integer;
X : Integer;

Notice the little ^ in the declaration. This means that P is not an integer, but a **pointer** to an integer. That is, P contains the address of a cell that can contain an integer. Contrast the difference between P and X as shown in figure 16.4.

Figure 16.4

Since P is a pointer (and not an integer), the assignment P := 6 is an illegal mixing of types and does *not* assign 6 to the integer that P points to. The correct statement is P^ := 6 and this is read as:

"The integer that P points to is assigned the value 6".

That is, the ˆ symbol is used in two distinct ways that the beginner must carefully distinguish:

The symbol ˆ is used on the **left** of type names in **var** and **type** sections to declare pointer variables.

The symbol ˆ is used on the **right** of pointer variables in the body of the program to reference the actual element that the pointer is pointing to.

The beauty (and confusion) of pointers is that we can use both the pointer (address) as well as the value (contents) of the cell being pointed to. That is, if P and Q are both pointers to the same type, then both of the following are valid:

Q := P;
Qˆ := Pˆ;

The first assigns P's value to Q so that Q now points to the same cell that P does. The second assigns the value pointed to by P to the cell that Q points to. Both operations are needed in what follows. The first moves pointers, the second moves information accessed through the pointers. For example, suppose that P initially points to an integer with current value 7 while Q initially points to an integer with current value 4. Then the effect of each of the above assignments is illustrated in figure 16.5.

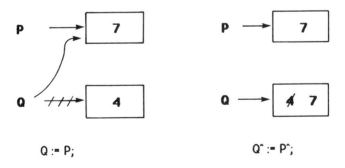

Q := P;   Qˆ := Pˆ;

Figure 16.5

Let's use pointers to declare a linked list. The complete declaration is given in listing 16.1:

```
type
  InfoField = record
    Name : string[30];
    ID_No : Integer
  end;
  ListPtr = ^Node;
  Node = record
    Info : InfoField;
    Link : ListPtr
  end;

var
  List : ListPtr;
  NewInfo : InfoField;
  Index : Integer;
```

Listing 16.1

Notice that the Node is a record with two fields as promised. The info field is very straightforward. The link field is of type ListPtr which is simply a pointer to another node. Note the "chicken and egg" problem with this declaration. That is, a Node references a ListPtr and a ListPtr references a Node. This is the one case in Pascal that something may be referenced before it is declared. That is, it is legal to declare a pointer to an object even before that object is itself declared. Also notice that we keep track of a linked list with just one pointer, List, to the first element of the list.

Operations on Linked Lists

Suppose that List has been declared as above as a ListPtr. Recall that declaring List does not give it any initial value. How should we initialize List? We shall suppose that every list has a special first element, called a **listhead**. The purpose of the listhead is twofold: It makes every list, even the empty list, "visible" and it makes many routines that follow easier to write. Figure 16.6 depicts two linked lists with listheads.

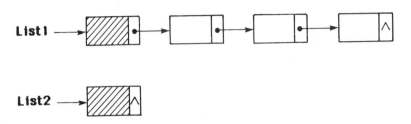

Figure 16.6

List1 in figure 16.6 contains 3 elements (in addition to the listhead). List2 is the empty list that contains no elements (other than the listhead). Notice that the last element of a list needs some special null pointer to indicate that there is no next element. In List2 we see that the pointer field of the listhead contains this special value. Again, because of this need, Pascal contains a special pointer constant **nil** for precisely this situation. The **nil** pointer is used to mark the end of a linked list. It is important that the last link be set to **nil**, for if some "old" pointer value is left in the last link field then we might mistakenly think that the list goes on beyond the last element, and we would likely end up accessing invalid data.

Thus, to initialize List, we need to get a new node (the listhead) and make List point to this node. We also need to put **nil** in the link field of this node. Note that we do not need to place any information in the information field of the listhead. Listing 16.2 shows the Initialize procedure in Pascal.

```
procedure Initialize (var List : ListPtr);
begin
  New(List);
  List^.Link := nil
end; {Definition of procedure Initialize}
```

Listing 16.2

The built-in procedure New is very useful. If P is a pointer to some type T, then New(P) causes the system to allocate a new cell of memory of type T, and to place the address of this cell in P. One should always draw pictures with linked lists to help visualize what is happening in the computer's memory. Figure 16.7 depicts the action of New(List).

Figure 16.7

Another simple procedure that is useful is one that prints the contents of a linked list. Clearly, the only way to print the contents of the nodes is to trace through the pointers going from node to node until we encounter the **nil** pointer. We must also skip the listhead and begin with the first node. Here is the pseudo-code for our plan:

> Set P to the link field of List (P points to first element).
> While P isn't **nil** do
> > Print the contents of the node P points to.
> > Advance P to the next node (P becomes link of P).

Listing 16.3 gives the Pascal equivalent of the above. The reader should draw a picture and carefully trace the code.

```
procedure PrintList (List : ListPtr);
var
  P : ListPtr;
begin
  P := List^.Link;
  while P <> nil do
    begin
      Writeln(P^.Info.Name : 30, P^.Info.ID_No : 10);
      P := P^.Link
    end
end; {Definition of procedure PrintList}
```

Listing 16.3

A routine to print a list is not of much value unless we also have routines that allow us to construct lists. As we shall see, inserting and deleting elements from lists is not difficult. Indeed, as figure 16.8 shows, to insert an element after the element Q points to only involves getting a new node, putting the new information into it, and then adjusting a couple of links:

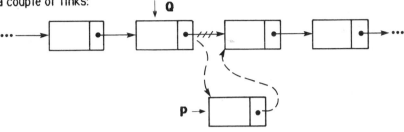

Figure 16.8

For ease in discussion in the remainder of the chapter, we shall use some "imprecise" but shorter teminology. Namely, we will refer to "node P" even though P is a pointer to a node and not a node itself. When we make such a reference, we are, of course, referring to the node pointed to by P. With this convention, we do not have to keep repeating phrases like "the node pointed to by P". With this in mind, we present the pseudo-code for the insertion operation that places a new node after the node Q:

Get a new node and let P point to it.
Place the new information in the info field of node P.
Set the link field of node P equal to the link field of node Q.
Set the link field of node Q equal to P.

The reader should verify that these instructions produce the drawing of figure 16.8. To test your understanding, you should also draw a picture and see what is wrong with the above pseudo-code if we reverse the order of the last two statements. When changing link fields, you should always be careful to consider the order in which you make your changes.

We include our insertion routine in a procedure Build that constructs an ordered linked list. That is, we shall choose to insert new elements into the list so that the list remains ordered. Notice that PrintList then prints the list in order! How do we find the correct place for a new element? We use two pointers P and Q, with Q following behind P. We want to find the place where Q's info is smaller than the new info and P's info is larger than the new info. Then, clearly, the new node belongs between P and Q, so we use the above routine to insert it after Q. What if the new info belongs at the end of the list? Then P eventually becomes **nil** and we insert after Q anyway. Hence, *since we are only interested in Q,* we can set P to **nil** as a signal that the proper place has been found.

Our build routine in pseudo-code is:

> Set Q to List.
> Set P to link of List. (Q will follow behind P)
> While P is not **nil** do
>> If P's info is bigger than the new info then
>>> Set P to **nil** (exit the loop with place found)
>> else (advance Q and P and keep looking)
>>> Set Q to P
>>> Set P to link of P
> Insert the new element after the node that Q points to.

Trace the above pseudo-code inserting "13" into the linked list shown in figure 16.9.

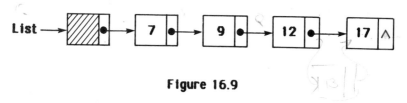

Figure 16.9

The Pascal equivalent of our pseudo-code is given in listing 16.4. It orders the nodes by the ID_No field of the information record. In our pseudo-code, we did not worry about such details. Of course, in the actual implementation we have to choose one of the fields as the "key" field on which all of the nodes are ordered. It is just a minor modification to order the nodes alphabetically by name.

Note that Build works even if the linked list is initially empty. In that case, Q points to the listhead and P is already **nil**, hence, the **while** executes zero times and the new element is inserted after the listhead. Thus, Build can be used, after Initialize, to construct an ordered, linked list.

We have gathered the procedures Initialize, Build, and PrintList into a main program, Linked_Lists, that uses these procedures to build an ordered, linked list of ten elements. The program is shown in listing 16.5. You should run the program with data of your own design.

```
procedure Build (List : ListPtr;
         NewInfo : InfoField);
var
  P, Q : ListPtr;
begin
  Q := List;   {Q will follow behind P.                    }
  P := List^.Link; {New element will go between Q and P.}
  while P <> nil do
   begin
    if P^.Info.ID_No >= NewInfo.ID_No then
      P := nil  {Exit loop}
    else
     begin
      Q := P;  {Move Q and P forward one link.}
      P := P^.Link
     end {If}
   end; {While}
{Get new node, put info into it, link it in after Q.}
  New(P);
  P^.Info := NewInfo;
  P^.Link := Q^.Link;
  Q^.Link := P
end; {Definition of procedure Build.}
```

Listing 16.4

```
program Linked_Lists;
{This program illustrates the use of linked lists.}

type
  InfoField = record
    Name : string[30];
    ID_No : Integer
  end;
  ListPtr = ^Node;
  Node = record
    Info : InfoField;
    Link : ListPtr
  end;
```

(Continued)

```
var
  List : ListPtr;
  NewInfo : InfoField;
  Index : Integer;

{Procedures INITIALIZE, PRINTLIST, and BUILD go here.}

begin {Body of main program, Linked_List.}
  Initialize(List);
  for Index := 1 to 10 do
    begin
      Writeln('Please enter name number ', Index : 1);
      Readln(NewInfo.Name);
      Writeln('Please enter the ID number for ', NewInfo.Name);
      Readln(NewInfo.ID_No);
      Build(List, NewInfo);
    end; {For}
  Writeln;
  Writeln('Here is your list in order by ID number:');
  PrintList(List)
end.
```

Listing 16.5

Deleting from a linked list is also easy. As shown in figure 16.10, we have only to adjust a pointer to delete the node that P points to. However, note that since the link field of the node before P must be changed, it is a good idea to have a pointer Q to the node that precedes P.

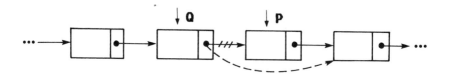

Figure 16.10

Also, what shall we do with the newly "freed" node P? It would be wasteful to simply abandon it. We should return it to the system for recycling. Since this is a common and important need with dynamic memory allocation, Macintosh Pascal provides a built-in recovery procedure, Dispose(P). We should think of Dispose(P) as the opposite of New(P). New(P) allocates a unit of memory from the system for our use while Dispose(P) returns that unit of memory to the system. We leave the details of the deletion routine to the exercises, but do not forget to invoke Dispose in your deletion routine.

Exercises

16.1 Write a function Count_Nodes that accepts a pointer to a list and returns a count of the number of nodes in the list. Do not count the listhead.

16.2 Write a procedure Delete(List, ID_Num) that deletes the node from the linked list List whose ID_No is the given ID_Num. If there is no such node, Delete prints a "Sorry, not found" message. Remember to invoke Dispose to actually free the given node.

16.3 Write a procedure Flip(List) that inverts the order of List. That is, the last element is now the first element, the next-to-last element is now the second element, etc.

16.4 (Compare with Exercise 9.19.) The Lake Forest College Running Club needs a program to sort out the winner in its Strawman Triathlon. The competition consists of a 1/4-mile swim, a 5-mile bicycle ride, and a 2-mile run. The data for each competitor is available on the text file Triathlon on the Sample diskette accompanying the book. There are two lines for each person. The first line is the name, of type **string**[30]. The second line contains a category (either the character 'S', 'F', or 'A' for Student, Faculty, or Administration respectively) followed by 3 real numbers representing, in hours, the swim time, bike time, and run time respectively.
    Using linked lists with pointers, identify the following individuals:
1. Overall Grand Champion (Best sum of times).
2. Grand Champion and runner-up in each category.
3. Overall best swimmer and runner-up.
4. Overall best biker and runner-up.
5. Overall best runner and runner-up.
6. Best Sport Award (Worst sum of times).

In case of a tie for a first prize, award duplicate prizes and no runners-up prizes in that competition. In case of ties only among the runners-up, award duplicate runners-up prizes.

Hint: Use several ordered, linked lists. Insert each person into the appropriate lists. Take advantage of modular programming--do **not** write an insertion routine for each list!

Warning: Remember, do not test real numbers for true equality.

Index

Entries followed by (Prog) are titles of programs in the text.

MACINTOSH PASCAL DISKETTE IS AVAILABLE

For your convenience, a diskette is available from the publisher to accompany this book. The diskette contains all sample programs from the book as well as text files for the sample programs and exercises. The diskette will operate on any Macintosh computer that utilizes Macintosh Pascal software, Version 1.0. To order the diskette, please return the order form below with check or credit card information.

"Macintosh" is a registered trademark of Apple Computer, Inc.

Ordering Information

Call (301) 251-9050 or write to Computer Science Press, Inc., 11 Taft Court, Rockville, Maryland 20850, to order our publications. Ask for our complete catalog of quality books at all levels from introductory to the advanced levels. Residents of Maryland should add 5% sales tax. Prices subject to change without notice.

	QUAN.	PRICE
MACINTOSH PASCAL	@$20.00_____	_____
DISKETTE	Sub Total	_____
ISBN 0-88175-088-3	Postage and Handling $2.00	_____
	Total	_____

☐Payment enclosed ☐Visa No. _____ ☐MasterCard No. _____

Signature_____ Expiration date_____

Name_____

Address_____

City_____ State_____ Zip _____

ALL ORDERS FROM INDIVIDUALS MUST BE PREPAID

☐ Add my name to your mailing list.   ☐Send me your current catalog.

Computer Science Press, Inc., 11 Taft Court, Rockville, MD 20850, USA, (301) 251-9050
